UNDERSTANDING

Mídple Earth

ESSAYS ON TOLKIEN'S MIDDLE-EARTH

Michael Martinez

UNDERSTANDING
MIDDLE EARTH

ESSAYS ON TOLKIEN'S MIDDLE-EARTH

Michael Martinez

VIVISPHERE
PUBLISHING

A division of NetPub Corporation
675 Dutchess Turnpike, Poughkeepsie, NY 12603
www.vivisphere.com   (800) 724-1100

Other books by Michael Martinez:

Visualizing Middle-earth
Parma Endorion: Essays on Middle-earth, 3rd Edition (eBook)
(edited by Matt Tinaglia)
Parma Endorion: Ensayos sobre la Tierra Media (eBook)
(translated by Leandro Pascual, edited by Matt Tinaglia)

Acknowledgements

Special thanks to Matt Tinaglia for his work in selecting, arranging, and formatting the essays used in this book. It would not have happened without your help.

Thanks to Bert Katz for many helpful technical comments with various essays.

Thanks to Rick House for your help and comments on the "History of the Last Alliance of Elves and Men."

Thanks to Steve Sears for saying "Just do it" and for putting a little Tolkien into Xena.

TABLE OF CONTENTS

TABLE OF CONTENTS
(CONTINUED)

Introduction:
Browsing the Compleat*
Middle-earth library

You have probably read *The Lord of the Rings* and *The Hobbit* so many times now that your books are dog-eared and you can recite all the rhymes, riddles, songs, and poems by heart. And yet, you wonder, where does all that other information about Middle-earth come from? How, for example, does someone like Michael Martinez know that the Eldar raise special corn to make their *lembas*, or that Cirdan was one of Thingol Greycloak's relatives? When you become that curious, you are ready to dive into the world of serious Tolkien research.

If you have read *The Silmarillion*, and your reaction was something along the lines of, "Wow! Is there any more like this?", then you should be able to handle the rest of the Tolkien library. You may, like many of us, have to take it in small doses, at least at first. Most of the books become long-winded, consumed with detailed analyses of how the various texts differed from one version to the next. In fact, for the first five years after Christopher Tolkien began publishing the twelve-volume *History of Middle-earth* series, I preferred curling up with a copy of *The Book of Lost Tales, Part One* if I had trouble sleeping. It cured my insomnia quickly.

There is just something about 100 pages of editorial commentary which sucks the wind from the sails of one's ship of literary adventure. Which is not to say that Christopher Tolkien's notes about his father's writing aren't interesting in their own right. But you pretty much have to be in the right frame of mind to be able to follow all the "and I wrote on page X of book Y that my father's manuscript D of version 2 was composed after he had sipped wine with his tea" references. Otherwise, you'll be as fast asleep as an Ent before that first Elf worked up the nerve to knock on wood.

*Look it up

There are several reasons for why anyone may want to look at the other Tolkien books. Like me, you probably want to read more cool stories. And there are indeed some cool stories to be found buried amid all the textual revision notes. But as Christopher hinted in *Unfinished Tales*, the stories become less and less complete after his father published *The Lord of the Rings*. Hence, the farther into the *History* you go, the less and less complete the stories you do find become, too. In fact, the story-to-commentary ratio degrades radically after *Unfinished Tales*, but there is a method to Christopher's meticulous annotation, and once you become familiar with the progression, the commentary becomes more helpful and less hindering.

When first starting out on their Middle-earth explorations, people frequently ask what books they should read and in what order, so that they can simply enjoy more adventures in Middle-earth. All too seldom (in my opinion) are they advised to read *The Adventures of Tom Bombadil*. The Tolkien library consists of works published both in Tolkien's lifetime and posthumously. *The Adventures of Tom Bombadil* was one of the books he published himself. So, in my humble opinion, if you want to read the Tolkien books the way he published them, the sequence should be:

1. *The Hobbit*, 3rd edition (1965) (Douglas Anderson's *The Annotated Hobbit* is recommended)
2. *The Lord of the Rings*, 2nd edition (1965) (the edited version with the Douglas Anderson "Note on the Text" is recommended)
3. *The Adventures of Tom Bombadil* (1962) (now included in *The Tolkien Reader*, 1966)
4. *The Silmarillion* (1977) (edited/compiled by Christopher Tolkien -- there is a 2nd edition which contains no textual alterations or additions)
5. *Unfinished Tales of Númenor and Middle-earth* (1980) (this is the first book with extensive commentary from Christopher)

Now, there are other books besides the *History of Middle-earth* books, and thorough Tolkien research occasionally requires dipping into those books. I'm speaking of *The Road Goes Ever On* (1967) and *The Letters of J.R.R. Tolkien* (1981), the latter being edited by Humphrey Carpenter. Carpenter also wrote the authoritative *J.R.R. Tolkien: A Biography* (1977), and some people recommend that as well, although its usefulness really depends on what sort of research you are doing.

In fact, if your goal is to study all the works of J.R.R. Tolkien, and not simply his Middle-earth-related books, there are many more books and essays to look for, such as *Farmer Giles of Ham*, which is sometimes published with *Smith of Wootton Major, Mr. Bliss, Roverandom*, et. al.

Tolkien research is not yet a fully developed science, but there are several recognizable sub-disciplines in the field. Academics are familiar with Tolkien literary criticism, which was launched almost immediately after the first publication of *The Lord of the Rings* in 1954-1955. Some Tolkien defenders continue to respond to critical works written in the 1950s even today. Linguists and Biblical scholars also study Tolkien's professional papers and translations in Anglo-Saxon and Biblical texts (he is credited for work done on *The Jerusalem Bible* [1945-55, 1956 -- the Book of Job represents Tolkien's largest contribution], although that does not appear in standard bibliographies. And students of literary theory may be quite familiar with Tolkien's "On Fairy-Stories" essay (based on a lecture he delivered as part of the Andrew Lange series in 1938).

But Middle-earth is the crown of Tolkien's writing achievements. He spent most of his life developing the mythology that we are loosely referring to by implication when we speak of Middle-earth. *The History of Middle-earth* strives to document most of J.R.R. Tolkien's work on that mythology, which in fact is a succession of mythologies, some of them quite unrelated to one another.

That is the most confusing aspect to the series, I think. Many people develop the mistaken idea that all of the stories are directly connected to Middle-earth, and they are not. In fact, none of the early material is part of the Middle-earth canon. There was no Middle-earth at the time, and Tolkien did not retrofit them into Middle-earth. He abandoned them, a fact Christopher makes clear in volume after volume. His father gave up on certain ideas and themes and moved on to new projects time and again through the years. But he kept reusing other ideas and themes.

The study of Middle-earth is therefore its own intricate and enveloping discipline. There is a great deal of material concerning Tolkien's Middle-earth -- both derived from Tolkien himself and from commentators -- that would require a lifetime to explore and absorb. Christopher documented the process by which his father advanced to the stage of creating Middle-earth, and he documented much but not all of the process of the creation itself. The twelve volumes of *The History of Middle-earth* easily offer enough material for a full year of study in any literary curriculum.

The languages of Middle-earth and their predecessors offer another area of study, and the Tolkien linguistic community is thriving, if not threatening to engulf all of his readership. Tolkien linguists have even gone so far as to propose extensions to some of his languages. Their work has evolved into true philological research as they attempt to reconstruct the processes by which Tolkien devised and added words to his various languages.

The study of Middle-earth's imaginary history is my personal favorite and specialty. In fact, Tolkien probably wrote more about the history and cultures of Middle-earth, including their philosophies and motivations, than about any other aspect of Middle-earth. Nearly every linguistic essay and note, if not all of them, offers insight into the peoples and events of Middle-earth. Tolkien firmly believed that words did not exist alone. A word possessed a history, and if you understood the history of the word you learned something about the history and character of the people who developed and used that word. The study of history and language were almost one and the same thing for Tolkien.

The construction of Middle-earth itself presents another opportunity for study. That is, Middle-earth can be documented cartographically and sociologically. The lay of the land, the changes in geography, the ethnic diversity and evolution of the various peoples, and the interaction between peoples and geography are all sufficiently explained by Tolkien that one could easily write a book on the subject (and the various atlases of Middle-earth do not do it justice).

Then there is the analysis of Tolkien's sources for Middle-earth. He felt the pursuit of sources and inspirations for stories was not a desirable practice, and yet he occasionally offered explanations of where he got his ideas from. Although this area shares considerable overlap with literary criticism, it is not as fully developed as it should be. The commentators focus too much on Tolkien's obvious connections to Anglo-Saxon literature and tradition and they virtually ignore his Biblical and Greco-Roman influences. Tolkien admitted to or implied influences from Babylon, Egypt, Finland, Wales, Ireland, and other regions. The Finnish and Welsh influences are given the most attention after Anglo-Saxon, and many commentators will concede some debt to Tolkien's love of the Gothic language in an "oh, by-the-way" fashion. Much work remains to be done in uncovering Tolkien's sources and influences, and sadly it may be another generation before we see a respectable attempt to document the non-Anglo-Saxon sources.

Literary criticism offers us insights into Tolkien's own motivations and priorities (or, at least, what the commentators believe are Tolkien motivations and priorities). But it also provides a rich discussion of the applicable symbology and relevance of Middle-earth in the framework of modern thought. Tolkien was quite the philosopher, and his writings reflect his long, deep thought on many issues, especially on the issues of dehumanization and man's relationship to God. Tolkien was not a frequent allegorist, but he borrowed from the allegorical tradition wherever he felt he might broaden the reach of a character to his audience by doing so. And he wrote some allegory himself, although he professed a "cordial dislike" for it. Allegory is thought-provoking and deep, and attempts to rationalize a (frequently) limited concept. But Tolkien wanted very much to entertain his readers, and not to burden them with the necessity of unraveling allegorical symbology.

Middle-earth's allegory is palpable but not pervasive. The reader can take it or leave it.

In order to study all these aspects of Middle-earth, one needs all the books I mentioned above, as well as one other: John Rateliff's as-yet unpublished *History of the Hobbit* (that is simply my euphemism for a book which, begun by the late Taum Santoski, has been called *Mr. Baggins* and other things less pleasant). The journal Vinyar Tengwar [http://www.elvish.org/VT/] (edited by the Elven Linguistic Fellowship of the Mythopoetic Society [http://www.mythsoc.org/]) also occasionally includes some of Tolkien's previously unpublished essays (the most notable of which have so far been "Osanwe-kenta" and "The Rivers and Beacon-hills of Gondor").

Extensions to Tolkien's Middle-earth -- of a credible nature, at least -- are still rare. That is, there are role-playing games, fan fiction, and extrapolative essays galore, but you won't really learn much from the bulk of these materials, if anything at all. Not if your goal is to learn about Tolkien's Middle-earth. The purist might stop with Tolkien, but I think there is value in studying extensions of Middle-earth. Tolkien wanted it to become a living tradition, on his foundations for which others would build new layers. Sadly, his desire seems to have been ignored or misunderstood by some of the purists, but I think the linguistic community has taken his dream to heart, and I applaud them for doing so.

In a small way, these essays are my contribution to the extension of Middle-earth. My extrapolations may be no better than the next person's, but the more extrapolating we do, the richer the fabric of Middle-earth becomes. Tolkien's objective was to offer a new tradition for literary development. That dream will die if we attempt to freeze it in place with just his own works. That well has run dry, and the baton has changed hands. In fact, the baton has changed hands twice.

In my introduction to *Visualizing Middle-earth*, I said that my own essays are tertiary works. One reviewer took mild exception to my definition, which is admittedly not a standard rule applied by academia to the study of literary works. However, Middle-earth is not a literary work any more than Greek or Norse mythologies are literary works. Middle-earth is a modern mythological and linguistic tradition, and it is encompassed by a family of modern traditions, all of which were created by J.R.R. Tolkien.

The study of these traditions must concede that there are multiple levels of authority. Any work published by J.R.R. Tolkien himself would be a primary source. The posthumous works offered by Christopher Tolkien, Humphrey Carpenter, and Douglas Anderson are secondary sources. And commentaries and analyses, including my own, are at best tertiary sources. At worst, they are quarnary sources. That is, any role-playing game, collectible card game, media adaptation, fan fiction, or other extension would provide a fourth level of authority. Such extensions should be received credibly though with restraint.

After all, two hundred years from now, there will almost certainly be books and libraries of books and journals which document and analyze the Middle-earth tradition. It has yet to be recognized as a phenomenon, but in reality the groundswell of popular extrapolation and extension has surpassed the levels of fad and phenomenon. Middle-earth will gradually be recognized less as the work of J.R.R. Tolkien and more as the product of a process Tolkien began. And it is important to understand and accept that this is, in fact, what Tolkien wanted, even if it does not happen in the way he anticipated or hoped for it.

Every literary tradition begins with one person. Someone, somewhere, wrote the first story about King Arthur. Somewhere in time, someone composed the first lay about Robin Hood. Homer composed "The Iliad" and "The Odyssey". Of course, all these people (like Tolkien and others after them) drew upon older sources. But they launched traditions which continue today. King Arthur, Robin Hood, and Troy remain vibrant and alive in our popular imagination, literature, and entertainment. There is no end in sight for these traditions, as well as others of equally ancient origin. Hence, we have no reason to doubt that Tolkien's tradition will succeed. It has already succeeded in a way that no other literary creation of the 20th century has succeeded.

So, if you're feeling brave and want to step out onto the road of Tolkien literary adventure, the good news is that you have a lot of material to explore, and many choices lie before you. There is a little something for everyone. And a lot of Middle-earth for everyone. The historical information is immense, and it provides insight into the way Tolkien envisioned a mythical storyscape, a world of continuously unfolding adventure.

Finally, since I've been asked this more than once, I'll conclude with a list of the primary and secondary sources, and some comments on each. Your mileage may vary. Don't obligate yourself to try to read every book. And keep in mind that one person's Silmaril is another person's Tree restored. We value these books in different ways. Two tertiary sources are also included in the list.

Primary texts

- *The Hobbit*
  For an introduction to Tolkien's sense of adventure and the basic setting of his northern world, *The Hobbit* works best. It's not very complex but is fun to read and very enjoyable. Although Tolkien eventually came to regret telling this story on a level intended for children, I think it serves to demonstrate the immense diversity in literary applicability that Middle-earth ultimately offers. Middle-earth began with *The Hobbit*, although Tolkien never intended to create Middle-earth, and had no idea of what the world of Bilbo Baggins would evolve into when he published this book. The 1st edition (1937) is notable for lying outside the Middle-earth canon. Tolkien suggested revisions for the book in 1947, and he received galleys for a 2nd edition in 1950 which forced him to alter some of the material in *The Lord of the Rings*. The 3rd edition of 1965 was produced in response to ACE Books' unauthorized reprint, and it introduced some minor changes to the Middle-earth canon.

- *The Lord of the Rings*

  People invariably identify Middle-earth with the world of *The Lord of the Rings*. This book is Tolkien's literary masterpiece, and it will stand on its own merits for centuries to come. But because of the numerous contradictions between the various primary and secondary sources, I have long maintained that *The Lord of the Rings* should be regarded as the most authoritative source of information on Middle-earth. Nonetheless, I find myself increasingly compelled to qualify that valuation. For example, when people ask about the Avari, I have to explain that there were no Avari when Tolkien first wrote *The Lord of the Rings*. There were West-elves (Eldar) and East-elves (Wood-elves). But today, most Tolkien readers are familiar with *The Silmarillion* and the concept of the Avari. It's impossible to reconcile *The Lord of the Rings* with Tolkien's clear intent to make the East-elves into at least a subset of Avari (who mingled with Nandor). The 2nd edition of 1965 was published with the 3rd edition of *The Hobbit*, and some significant changes were introduced into the canon with that edition.

- *The Adventures of Tom Bombadil*

  These poems offer the reader an opportunity to explore Middle-earth through the poetic traditions of its characters. There are some notes provided by Tolkien, but the bulk of the material is presented as genuine Hobbit-lore or folklore. Of course, in reality, the poems were written by Tolkien for other purposes. He created the collection to please his beloved aunt Jane Neave, who died only a few months after the book was published. Some aspects of the Middle-earth canon are derived only from this collection, and for that reason there are people who feel (inexplicably, in my opinion) they are not authoritative additions to the canon. You can still get this collection of poems and notes in *The Tolkien Reader*.

- *The Road Goes Ever On*

  Tolkien was approached by Donald Swann in the early 1960s with music Swann had composed for some of Tolkien's songs in *The Lord of the Rings*. Tolkien so appreciated the compositions that he endorsed them. Although the music itself offers little insight into Middle-earth, it represents the first sanctioned extension to Middle-earth, and Tolkien provided notes which established historical and linguistic elements not documented anywhere else. This was the last of the primary sources.

Secondary texts

- *The Silmarillion*

  Although an immense success when it was first published, and despite the fact that it has never gone out of print, *The Silmarillion* is a disappointment for too many reasons to list here. It is a superb narrative and represents a monumental effort by Christopher Tolkien to bring his father's most cherished collection of stories to print. Nonetheless, Christopher spent the years 1980 to 1996 explaining and apologizing for the many editorial decisions and alterations he made to the texts. On first read, this book stands out as extremely Biblical, and it is almost universally condemned for offering no more information on Hobbits. People really enjoyed the Hobbit stories. *The Silmarillion* thus demonstrates further that Middle-earth supports diversity in narrative form and theme.

- *The Letters of J.R.R. Tolkien*

  I still use this book on an almost daily basis. The Tolkien family and friends gave Carpenter unprecedented access to the author's private correspondence, which included many insights and explanations into the societies and history of Middle-earth. People who hungered for more Hobbit stories found some interesting and detailed trivia here about the Tooks, Bagginses, Smeagol's people, and Hobbits in general. Many, many questions are answered only in Tolkien's correspondence. However, the evolving nature of his work shows through clearly, and there are some lapses in memory and changes in mind as the years roll by.

- *Unfinished Tales of Númenor and Middle-earth*

  Just when people thought *The Silmarillion* was the final word in Middle-earth literature, Christopher Tolkien unleashed this bombshell. In fact, he mentioned an indeterminate amount of material yet remained to be published in the foreword to *The Silmarillion*, but *Unfinished Tales* opened up entire new vistas in Tolkien studies and revealed depths to Middle-earth never before imagined. It is unsatisfying in several respects, however, not the least being the fact that the stories and essays are indeed mostly incomplete. "Of Tuor and his Coming to Gondolin" promises to be a great story, and yet it ends with Tuor's arrival at the vale of Tumladen. "Aldarion and Erendis" is perhaps one of the greatest stories Tolkien wrote, because it does not focus on world-threatening events. It is simply a love story that is nonetheless interwoven with Middle-earth's histories. *Unfinished Tales* introduces the casual reader to the extensive resources Christopher's subsequent books provide without the overwhelming power of scholarly analysis and editorial interruption.

- *The Book of Lost Tales, Part One* (The History of Middle-earth, Volume I)

  I recommend this book for anyone who wants to see how Tolkien wrote stories when he was young. And you should also get Part Two at the same time you buy this book. If you give it as a gift, give both volumes. *The Book of Lost Tales* is completely useless, however, for any serious research into how *The Silmarillion* was composed. There is one story, "The Fall of Gondolin", which Christopher was forced to adapt to the published Silmarillion text, but you have to read his explanations in *The War of the Jewels* to understand what he did and why. *The Book of Lost Tales* should be enjoyed on its own merits. Sadly, too many people mistake it as a legitimate resource for the study of Middle-earth. It is invaluable in the study of J.R.R. Tolkien's literature, but not Middle-earth.

- *The Book of Lost Tales, Part Two* (The History of Middle-earth, Volume II)
  See my comments above.

- *The Lays of Beleriand* (The History of Middle-earth, Volume III)
  Although J.R.R. Tolkien attempted to write romantic prose fiction in epic form from circa 1916 to 1925, he abandoned the project. Instead, he turned to writing epic poetry, reusing two of the themes from *The Book of Lost Tales*. "Lay of the Children of Hurin" and "Lay of Leithian (Release from Bondage)" combine elements from several of the *Book of Lost Tales* stories, but Tolkien introduced radical changes in characterization, plot, and progression. The core "Silmarillion" mythology begins with these two lays, although when he composed the earliest versions there was no comprehensive vision for the mythology. "Lay of Leithian" is, in my opinion, the better composition and represents some of the most beautiful epic poetry ever written in the English language. It is a masterpiece which deserves far better recognition than the academic community has extended to it. I think future generations will enjoy it more than people have since this book was first published.

- *The Shaping of Middle-earth* (The History of Middle-earth, Volume IV)
  In the late 1920s and early 1930s J.R.R. Tolkien came to write down the first "Silmarillion" mythologies. Although very similar to the mythology of *The Book of Lost Tales*, these mythologies departed from the "mythology for England" concept. Tolkien began inventing an imaginary historical time and place in northwestern Europe where Elves and Men struggled against a powerful evil being. *The*

Shaping of Middle-earth documents how Tolkien continued to rely upon certain traditional elements from classical mythologies (such as the flat world, the existence of multiple gods, and the deeds of superhuman heroes). But it also reveals how he continued to refine and reinvent his "Silmarillion" mythology. And the sophistication of Tolkien's narrative structure and style improve visibly from text to text.

- *The Lost Road and Other Writings* (The History of Middle-earth, Volume V)

    This book introduces the last of Tolkien's pre-*Lord of the Rings* efforts to create a "Silmarillion" mythology. He almost succeeded. "The Quenta Silmarillion" is very close in form and style to the published book, but there are notable exceptions and differences. In some places, the texts are identical because Christopher was forced to go back to the 1937 material to complete the published book. Linguists who were tantalized by the early languages which appeared in *The Book of Lost Tales* finally received a gold mine of information in "The Lhammas", an essay about the historical evolution of the Elven languages, and "The Etymologies", a dictionary-like resource Tolkien compiled in the late 1930s. "The Etymologies" shows how Tolkien developed two early Elven languages, Qenya and Noldorin, which he used as the basis for Quenya and Sindarin (respectively). Some other dialects and proto-Elvish are also documented. There are differences between the languages of "The Etymologies" and *The Lord of the Rings*, so a one-to-one correlation is not possible. But "The Etymologies" has proven to be invaluable to the linguistic community. And many of the entries reveal fascinating glimpses into Elvish society, culture, and history.

- *The Return of the Shadow* (The History of Middle-earth, Volume VI)

    The Return of the Shadow begins the task of explaining how Tolkien began to consciously create the primary Middle-earth mythology. This book, the next two, and the first half of *Sauron Defeated* have been republished as *The History of The Lord of the Rings*. These books contain early drafts for the chapters of the book, and many notes and explanations by Christopher. Some very important historical and cultural information appears only in these books, although reconciling previously unpublished material with the primary sources is not an easy task. Anyone purchasing these four books for themselves or as a gift should be sure to also purchase *The Peoples of Middle-earth*.

- *The Treason of Isengard* (The History of Middle-earth, Volume VII)
  See comments under The Return of the Shadow.

- *The War of the Ring* (The History of Middle-earth, Volume VIII)
  See comments under The Return of the Shadow.

- *Sauron Defeated* (The History of Middle-earth, Volume IX)
  Concerning the first half of this book, see comments under *The Return of the Shadow*. *Sauron Defeated* is noteworthy, however, for including the two versions of the epilogue Tolkien wrote for *The Lord of the Rings*. Although he was persuaded to drop the epilogue from the book when he first published it, he came to regret that choice, and I believe it was indeed a mistake to drop this material from the primary canon. *Sauron Defeated* also includes material contemporary with Tolkien's final work on the *The Lord of the Rings* (not including pre-publication edits and work on the appendices), especially "The Drowning of Anadune", which was the source of the legend of Númenor. More linguistic information relevant to the study of Adunaic appears in this book.

- *Morgoth's Ring* (The History of Middle-earth, Volume X)
  Although Tolkien finished the primary narrative of *The Lord of the Rings* in 1948, he did not immediately turn to work on

the appendices. Instead, after a hiatus of 11 years, he returned to the "Silmarillion" mythology, and he began a comprehensive rewrite of the entire work. Through his decision to incorporate the world of the Silmarillion into Middle-earth, Tolkien committed himself to altering several fundamental aspects of the mythology. The most notable alteration was the final revocation of any notion that the Valar were gods in the ancient mythological tradition. Instead, because *The Lord of the Rings* was a Catholic work (that is, the story pays some reverence to Tolkien's Catholic belief in one supreme being), the Valar and their associates the Maiar became angelic beings created by God (Ilúvatar). The flat Earth myth remained largely intact, but Tolkien began foreshadowing events which occurred in or were documented in *The Lord of the Rings* and even *The Hobbit*. *Morgoth's Ring* covers the beginning of that process. But the book also includes some essays which Tolkien wrote as an offshoot of his extensive revisions to the Silmarillion mythology. And the final section, "Myths Transformed", collects essays and notes from the 1950s through the 1970s which reveal Tolkien's growing doubt about the feasibility of the original mythological concepts. He examines many troubling philosophical questions in both the essays and a story, "Athrbeth Finrod ah Andreth", which resembles some Greek plays in form and purpose.

- *The War of the Jewels* (The History of Middle-earth, Volume XI)

  Morgoth's Ring documents the history of the published *Silmarillion* only up to the point where the Noldor flee into exile. *The War of the Jewels* takes up the task of explaining how Christopher put the second half of the book together. Whereas he was able to rely extensively on his father's own narratives for the early part of the published book, the second half demanded increasing editorial compression, modification, and outright composition to maintain consistency (and there are still some problems). J.R.R. Tolkien simply never finished rewriting the "Silmarillion" mythology. Christopher's numerous admissions of changes and additions reveal that the published work is more a collaboration between father and son than anything else. *The War of the Jewels*, however, provides three valuable contributions to the study of Middle-earth proper: a chronology for the First Age; "The Wanderings of Hurin", which tells what really happened after Túrin killed himself; and "Quendi and Eldar", another etymological and linguistic work which blurred the distinctions between Tolkien's linguistic and historical interests. There remain some inconsistencies between "Quendi and Eldar" and other works from the same period, but it establishes some very clear foundations for the study of Elvish history and culture (and languages). The work also includes a short story about the first Elves, written in the form of a nursery tale, which thus demonstrates further the complexity and flexibility of the Middle-earth tradition.

- *The Peoples of Middle-earth* (The History of Middle-earth, Volume XII)

    For reasons not entirely clear to me, Christopher Tolkien elected not to publish the source materials for the appendices to *The Lord of the Rings* when he was working on *Sauron Defeated*. I wish he had done so, as this is very important material. Tolkien cut a great deal of information from the appendices in order to accommodate the publisher's production needs and schedule. There is a wealth of information which can be found in this book and nowhere else, and it is largely consistent with the text of *The Lord of the Rings*, far more so than most of the other material published in *The History of Middle-earth*. But this book wraps up Christopher's examination of his father's career with regard to developing Middle-earth (except for the *Hobbit*-related material, which had been delegated to Taum Santoski). Hence, other sections include the complete text for the two versions of *The New Shadow*, a sequel to *The Lord of the Rings* which Tolkien started and abandoned early on, "Of Dwarves and Men", an essay of which part was published in *Unfinished Tales*, "The Shibboleth of Fëanor", which is important for the study of linguistics and corrects errors and omissions Christopher introduced to the genealogy of the Finwëans in *The Silmarillion*, and several other essays which address some questions about the Elves. There is also a short story fragment called "Tal-Elmar" which is set in a Middle-earth like world, but is not really canonical.

Tertiary sources

- *J.R.R. Tolkien: A biography*
  Although the book reveals very little information about Middle-earth, it does provide a framework for the study of Tolkien's life and career. It also places oblique references to many acknowledged or attributed sources within a chronological context. Commentators often simply tell you, "Tolkien used X from Y" without explaining when he would have studied Y and what the appeal of X may have been. Humphrey Carpenter's book helps in that respect. Some of the more recent Tolkien biographies may do better, but this one is the least controversial.

- *J.R.R. Tolkien: Artist & Illustrator*
  There was an earlier book, *Pictures by J.R.R. Tolkien*, which this book was intended to replace. If you seriously want to know how Tolkien visually depicted events and characters in the Middle-earth stories (or their predecessors), you'll want to buy this book. More than a hundred paintings and illustrations are included, and the authors provide extensive commentary and analysis. The book helps to explain when, where, and why Tolkien made many of his decisions about Middle-earth. And it's just fun to look at, too.

Understanding *The History of Middle-earth*

Occasionally, someone will ask what new stories appear in the History of Middle-earth books. Although one could sit down and list all the chapter sections relatively easily, such a list would be misleading. In 1977, when Christopher Tolkien published *The Silmarillion*, he wrote in the Foreword: "There is indeed a wealth of unpublished writing by my father concerning the Three Ages, narrative, linguistic, historical, and philosophical, and I hope that it will prove possible to publish some of this at a later date."

A few years later, Christopher began to fulfill that hope by publishing *Unfinished Tales*, in which he organized the materials according to the ages they addressed. He justified the unusual presentation of unfinished stories and notes by saying, "the book will be found unrewarding by readers of The Lord of the Rings who, holding that the historical structure of Middle-earth is a means and not an end, the mode of the narrative and not its purpose, feel small desire of further exploration for its own sake,....for some, as for myself, there is a value greater than the mere uncovering of curious detail in learning that Vëantur the Númenorean brought his ship Entulessë, the 'Return', into the Grey Havens on the spring winds of the six hundredth year of the Second Age, that the tomb of Elendil the Tall was set by Isildur his son on the summit of the beacon-hill Halifirien, that the Black Rider whom the Hobbits saw in the foggy darkness on the far side of Bucklebury Ferry was Khamul, chief of the Ringwraiths of Dol Guldur -- or even that the childlessness of Tarannon twelfth King of Gondor (a fact recorded in an Appendix to *The Lord of the Rings*) was associated with the hitherto wholly mysterious cats of Queen Beruthiel."

Most people who have contacted me about my own published research share Christopher's sentiment. Obviously, I also enjoy studying the pseudo-history for itself. The construction of Middle-earth was an unprecedented event in modern literature. I don't believe anyone has successfully duplicated Tolkien's achievement since *The Lord of the Rings* was first published, although many writers have made the attempt. I have myself, as have tens if not hundreds of thousands of Tolkien's readers, written unpublished novels and history books documenting a world of my own imagination. In any comparison with Middle-earth, what I have composed for my own enjoyment seems little more than what Gandalf might call an "essay in the craft". There is just something about the history inside Middle-earth which draws the reader into the entire mythology.

But, for that reason, many people have been confused by and disappointed in the twelve volumes of *The History of Middle-earth*, the title of which is somewhat confusing (although it is, in fact, quite accurate). Many people, upon first seeing references to the History, assume that someone has collected all the facts and stories into a single, comprehensive and coherent narrative. How I wish that could be done! Perhaps one day it will happen. But Christopher could have more accurately entitled the series *The History of How J.R.R. Tolkien Devised The Middle-earth Mythology*. An academically acceptable title might have been, *Studies In Myth-making: How Tolkien Created Middle-earth*. But *The History of Middle-earth* is exciting. It sings. One knows, deep inside the heart, that as soon as a marketing person heard that title, it became stamped in Valinorean Law.

Nonetheless, we are left with twelve books which collectively are named *The History of Middle-earth*. Those books merely document the methods by which J.R.R. Tolkien (and Christopher after him) created the mythology represented by *The Hobbit, The Lord of the Rings, The Adventures of Tom Bombadil, The Road Goes Ever On, The Silmarillion*, and *Unfinished Tales*. The History series documents how J.R.R. Tolkien wrote story after story throughout his adult life, ultimately producing a nearly coherent vision of an artificial mythology. That vision does not, however, include everything recorded in the History books. In fact, the History books preserve earlier mythologies which resemble the Middle-earth mythology. Those mythologies are interesting in themselves, but they do not provide much insight into Middle-earth. The story of Tinwelint and how he swindled a group of evil Dwarves, for example, has no place in Middle-earth's history. But everyone who has read "The Tale of the Nauglafring" knows that Tinwelint evolved into Thingol Greycloak, just as Sauron eventually assumed the role (but did not evolve from the character) of Tevildo, Prince of Cats.

Did I say "these books merely document the methods by which" the Tolkien devised the mythology? That was misleading. These books achieve far more than that. Particularly in the later volumes, starting with *Morgoth's Ring*, Christopher began revealing aspects of the Middle-earth mythology which had previously not been referred to. He published substantial texts such as "Athrabeth Finrod ah Andreth", "The Wanderings of Hurin", and "Dwarves and Men" which vastly expanded our vision and understanding of the mythology's scope. New characters, new events, new lands and peoples were added to the canvas with masterful brush-strokes, mostly in the original contexts provided by J.R.R. Tolkien.

If you want to learn more about Middle-earth, you'll find a huge treasure of facts and details buried in the analyses of differences between versions of manuscripts and mythologies. While some people seek to discourage casual readers from reading these books (justifying such discouragement by pointing to the repetition of themes and immense editorial commentary), I think people who are genuinely curious about the details will benefit the most from reading these books. Literally hundreds of books and journals have been filled with essays and commentaries on Tolkien. Most of them seek to define some greater meaning for Tolkien's mythology, plugging it into a context derived from the study of "Beowulf" and Anglo-Saxon manuscripts (a context much smaller than that which Tolkien himself used).

In my opinion, if you really want to see where it all came from, and why Tolkien had the stories progress as they did, you first need to see what it all is. Few Tolkien commentators are knowledgeable enough about the facts and events in Tolkien's stories to explain much about them. The majority of commentaries I have read get some of the simplest details wrong. If one cannot accurately summarize the story, then how can one possibly explain the story's meaning, its relevance to its audience, or determine from whence the author drew his inspirations?

Literary analysis, whether it seeks the meaning of literature or to document its evolution, reflects a desire to appreciate the art of the author. But Tolkien is not merely an author. He is a mythologist. He is a master craftsman whose work transcends literature. At best, the reader can only hope to *read* Tolkien, because understanding him is the task of a lifetime of study. And if most of us must simply read Tolkien, then give us the freedom to read all of Tolkien, and not just those portions of his works which are popular or strictly written for entertainment.

If you ever asked yourself, "Why were the Elves so consumed with regret? What were they sorry for?", you can read my essays and I'll give you my opinion. Or you can read someone else's essays and they will give you their opinions. Or you can read the Tolkien books and form your own. In the end, which experience will be more satisfying for you? To truly understand Middle-earth, you need to focus on Middle-earth, not on someone's idea of where Tolkien got it from. Middle-earth is best appreciated for itself. That is why you should read all twelve volumes of the History, from start to finish. Like the rest of us, you'll have to do it more than once. And you'll change your opinions as the years pass. It's okay. Just look around you. You'll see that you are not alone on your journey through the Great Mythology. By the time you close The Peoples of Middle-earth, you'll understand how Middle-earth is more than what the experts have made of it.

About *Understanding Middle-earth*

As with my first book, *Visualizing Middle-earth*, most of the essays which follow were written for the Suite101 Web site, where I have been the contributing editor for the Tolkien and Middle-earth topic since late 1999. However, we did not simply transpose the essays from the Web site to this book. I have reviewed them and have updated many references, as well as revised some sections which were a little confusing or incomplete. It is best to regard these essays as second editions, or substantial revisions of the original texts, with one exception. The chapter "How the elves have changed" was written especially for this book, and it appears nowhere else.

These essays draw upon virtually all of the sources listed above. Various editions have been used, as I often grab the closest book when I am just looking up well-established facts. For the most part, page numbers are not provided in the citation references, and where it seemed to me that the reader should clearly understand I am summarizing material from a previously named source, I have provided only occasional mentions of sources. A formal notation system tends to be very distracting for the casual reader. The chapter on the Last Alliance of Elves and Men was originally written as a standalone article for the journal *Arda*. Regrettably, the planned volume was never published. I revised the article and broke it into three parts for the Suite101 Tolkien and Middle-earth topic. Nonetheless, "A History of the Last Alliance of Elves and Men" is written to a higher standard than the rest of the book. The incongruency is intentional, as my essays have often been complimented for their conversational tone. I did not wish to lose that style by seeking consistency or the approval of academics.

I am a populist commentator. I write for those people who merely seek the pleasure of discovering new regions of Tolkien's Middle-earth. Because so many of these essays address questions raised by Tolkien fandom through the years, they are necessarily speculative on many points. But if I state something in a very matter-of-fact way, I am drawing upon some comment (or lengthy tale) published in one of the Tolkien books. The facts of Middle-earth's history are scattered across many books. Often, they occur as nothing more than single footnotes (such as the fact that Easterlings related to the Folk of Bor lived in northern Eriador in the Second Age) appended to lengthy commentaries about unrelated matters. Noting every discrete source of the thousands of facts included in these essays would be tedious and burdensome for both writer and reader. My desire is to provide a historical analysis of the mythological events and peoples Tolkien wrote about. But a historian's task is not merely to collect and present all the available facts. A good historian provides opinion, perspective, context, and as many unanswered questions as possible. I have striven to frame my speculations appropriately, so that the reader sees clearly what I am saying for myself, as opposed to what I have summarized from the texts.

Understanding Middle-earth differs from *Visualizing Middle-earth* in one respect: the essays have been organized topically by Matt Tinaglia so the reader may appreciate a much fuller discussion of various aspects of the mythology than is possible through the Web site. We have, accordingly, tried to edit out some of the more frequent redundancies. Essays which were written months apart often recap similar points, which is convenient for casual readers who don't have time to scour 100+ articles to find earlier references to specific sources, characters, or events. But removing all the redundant passages would have forced me to rewrite many of the essays so thoroughly, this book would never have been realized. And, in a few places, some portions of the original essays have been omitted because they did not suit the style and purpose of this book. Where it seems necessary, I have included explanations of the omissions.

Finally, some of the essays have been combined because they were written as multi-part discussions on specific topics. Matt felt the reader would best enjoy these works with as little interruption as possible, and I agree.

SECTION I:
THE INHABITANTS
OF MIDDLE-EARTH

MICHAEL MARTINEZ

Chapter 1:
Do Elves dream of eclectic sleep?

J.R.R. Tolkien devoted a lot of time and thought to determining what it means to be an Elf. He described the Elves (*The Letters of J.R.R. Tolkien*, No. 144) as representing "Men with greatly enhanced aesthetic and creative faculties, greater beauty and longer life, and nobility -- the Elder Children, doomed to fade before the Followers (Men), and to live ultimately only by the thin line of their blood that was mingled with that of Men, among whom it was the only real claim to 'nobility'."

But what does all that mean? Tolkien mentioned as an aside that the Elves represent "beauty and grace of life and artefact" (Ibid., No.73). Much later, Tolkien wrote: "Elves and Men are represented as biologically akin in this 'history', because Elves are certain aspects of Men and their talents and desires" and "they have certain freedoms and powers we should like to have, and the beauty and peril and sorrow of the possession of these things is exhibited in them...." (Ibid., No. 153)

Sorrow and regret are commonly associated with the Elvish nature. The Elves acknowledge these feelings as easily as we acknowledge hope and desire. When Frodo meets with Gildor Inglorion in the Shire, Gildor says, "The Elves have their own labours and their own sorrows, and they are little concerned with the ways of hobbits, or of any other creatures upon earth." That is a very curious thing to say, for it contrasts deeply with the picture that others paint of the Elves, such as Gandalf and Treebeard.

Gandalf tells Frodo that some of Sauron's greatest foes remain in Rivendell, the Elven-wise, lords of the Eldar from beyond the Sea. When other Elves have fled from Middle-earth, and while some are still only lingering as Gildor's folk do, a few of the Eldar hold steadfast to the purpose of opposing Sauron.

And Treebeard tells Merry and Pippin that it was the Elves who first woke up the trees, and taught them to speak. The Elves were once curious about everything, and they wanted to know as much as they could about the world in which they themselves had awakened.

In an interview he made for a documentary of his father's life, Christopher Tolkien notes that the Elves are almost consumed with regret. By the time of the War of the Ring, the Elves no longer look forward. Rather, they look back. And in looking back, they bring about their own eclipse or twilight, or welcome it. For it is indeed their fate to fade, to vanish from the world and the light, leaving all that they had achieved to the merciless hands of Men.

But how do the Elves become so embroiled in regret? What is the difference between the Elven nature and the Mannish nature which leads the Elven races to dwell in sorrow?

On numerous occasions, Tolkien wrote or stressed that the Elves are immortal within the timeframe of Arda's existence, but that they are not eternal. It is their nature to exist as living beings for the duration of Time itself, as measured by "the life of Arda". And yet, Arda has not existed from the beginning of Time, and is not necessarily fated to exist until the end of Time. Arda may end and Ea, the rest of the universe, may continue. But Ëa is identified with Time and Space. So, if the Elves endure until Arda ends, does Arda end with Time, and Time with Arda, or does Time continue onward to some other end?

The Elves did not know the answer to this question. Nor could they perceive or foresee any ultimate fate for themselves beyond the inevitable conclusion of their existence. In a note attached to "Athrabeth Finrod ah Andreth" (the Debate of Finrod and Andreth), Tolkien stipulated that "Elvish 'immortality' is bounded within a part of Time (which [Finrod] would call the History of Arda), and is therefore strictly to be called rather 'serial longevity', the utmost limit of which is the length of the existence of Arda....A corollary of this is that the Elvish *fëa* is also limited to the Time of Arda, or at least held within it and unable to leave it, while it lasts."

In elucidating further upon this point, Tolkien said that "beyond the 'End of Arda' Elvish thought could not penetrate, and they were without any specific instruction....It seemed clear to them that their [bodies] must then end, and therefore any kind of re-incarnation would be impossible....All the Elves would then 'die' at the End of Arda. What this would mean they did not know. They said therefore that Men had a shadow behind them, but the Elves had a shadow before them."

Now, the shadow behind Men was the shadow of their Fall, whereas the shadow before Elves was the shadow of their End. Men, in the perception of the Elves, were granted release from life, from the bondage to the world which to the Elves became a great burden. It was confusing for the Elves to learn that Men should so want to remain in the world, whereas the Elves wanted to be assured they would continue after the world. It was rather like the crew of a sinking ship watching in amazement as passengers leaped from the lifeboats back aboard the larger vessel.

The Elvish longing for release was not necessarily a part of their natural state. By the time the Valar discovered the Elves living in Cuiviénen, they had already been harassed by Melkor and his servants. Some of the Elves had vanished, and since Mandos himself apparently knew nothing of their fate, they must have been completely entrapped by Melkor in Utumno or some other dread prison. The Elves thus lost the innocence with which they had awakened before they even met the Valar.

The loss of innocence was the first step on a long road toward sorrow, a road filled with grief and loss. But sorrow and grief were not the same thing for the Elves. Grief apparently passed, whereas sorrow did not. A grief might become extended and turn into sorrow, but the greater part of Elvendom seems simply to have grown into sorrow. Overcoming grief was something they did time and again.

For example, Tolkien explains in Letter 212 (actually a draft for a continuation of Letter 211 which was never sent) that "in the Elvish legends there is record of a strange case of an Elf (Miriel mother of

Fëanor) that tried to *die*, which had disastrous results, leading to the 'Fall' of the High-elves....Miriel wished to abandon being...."

Míriel's death was so unusual the Eldar had to devise a new word to describe it. They had experienced physical death before, whereby some members of their race had succumbed to grief or violence and their bodies died. But the Eldar learned in Aman that their spirits were intended to pass to the Halls of Mandos and, after a time of reflection in which they would be healed of their griefs, they could and should be re-admitted to the ranks of the living.

Miriel did not wish to live again. She wanted to be dead, truly dead, and to have nothing more to do with the world. Míriel's choice, or stubbornness, led to an important debate among the Valar, and to the establishment of a law which altered the natural course of Elven fate. The Valar were empowered by Ilúvatar to mandate the permanent death of an Elf within the life of Arda. That is, they could refuse to let an Elf live again.

Miriel refused to accept life, even though she was all but ordered to live again. The Valar therefore reluctantly consigned her to the Halls of Mandos until the end of the Time of Arda. Finwë, her husband, thus became free to seek another wife. But after Finwë was murdered by Melkor, his spirit communed with Míriel's spirit in Mandos (and that was apparently a rare occurrence). When Miriel learned of all that had befallen her people, she regretted her decision to stay dead, and appealed to the Valar. Finwë now agreed to remain dead, because he could not return to life and have two wives (a state which the Elves regarded as unnatural).

Míriel's decision was made at least in part as a result of regret. And though permitted to live again, she elected not to live among her people, the Elves, but instead was admitted to the service of one of the Valar. Miriel from that time forward documented the deeds of her people. Rather than doing new things and seeking new knowledge, she became engrossed in recording the events of her people's history. Miriel was therefore the first Elf (among the Eldar, at least) to succumb to regret, choosing to live again out of regret, and perhaps devoting her life to remembering that regret.

Some of the rebellious Noldor gave in to regret -- a healthy regret -- before going too far along the road to Exile. These Noldor, led by Finarfin, returned to their city of Tirion and were forgiven their part in the rebellion by the Valar. But the majority of the Noldor continued on their path with resolution, perhaps mostly because of Fëanor's determination.

In Middle-earth most of the Noldor tried to look forward despite the hopelessness of their war against Melkor. But Turgon, who was inspired to build the greatest city of all, seems to have become mired in regret. Gondolin was modeled after Tirion, and Turgon's people seldom went to war. Ulmo warned him that the time would come when Turgon would have to give up everything to save his people, but when that day came Turgon proved unwilling to make the sacrifice. Rather than lead his people safely out of Gondolin, Turgon trusted to the city's natural defenses. He wanted to preserve his way of life at the risk of losing his life.

After the fall of Gondolin, the Noldor squandered their last resources in the bitter conflicts over possession of the Silmaril which Beren and Lúthien had recovered from Melkor. The Sons of Fëanor, unable to recover the other jewels, destroyed first Doriath and then Arvernien in fruitless attempts to seize the gem. They no longer dreamed of avenging their father and grand-father's deaths, nor of recovering the Silmarils. Instead, they merely focused on what they felt was theirs by right, failing to realize they had lost that right through their misdeeds. Their minds were trapped in a past which could not be recovered.

After the First Age, the Noldor began anew. Gil-galad established a kingdom in what had been Ossiriand, and some of the Noldor migrated eastward to establish Eregion. But as the centuries rolled by, the Elves succumbed to worries about fading. The Noldor of Eregion decided to do something about the fading when Sauron (in disguise) offered them an opportunity to stop or delay the effects of Time.

Tolkien said of this second "Fall" that the "Elves wanted to have their cake and eat it". They wanted to remain in Middle-earth for the rest of Time, rather than sail over Sea to avoid a fate worse than death. Instead of crafting new beauty, the Elves turned their thoughts to preserving the old beauty of Middle-earth, and of healing its hurts. So they created the Rings of Power. But even after the Elves discovered Sauron's treachery, they could not bring themselves to destroy the Rings, which Sauron obviously intended to use against them.

The regret which Gildor alluded to undoubtedly began in the conflict between the Elves and Sauron in the Second Age. For they not only lost many Rings of Power, they lost most of the lands they were trying to hold on to. Elvish homes with all their mementos and special artifacts must have gone up in smoke across hundreds of miles. The Elves would have preserved nothing of their former world -- in which they were a superior caste, as Tolkien put it.

Regret should not have consumed the Elves merely for what they had lost, but also for what they had done. Betrayal and loss go hand in hand throughout Elvish history, and their betrayal of the natural order in the Second Age ensured that they would lose nearly everything. The Elves who survived the war -- especially those who did not know anything at all about the Rings of Power -- must surely have questioned what had brought on the conflict.

In the late Third Age, Frodo teased Gildor by repeating a popular saying among Hobbits concerning Elves: go not to the Elves for advice, for they will tell you both yes and no. And Gildor laughed, pointing out that "Elves seldom give out unguarded advice, for advice is a dangerous gift, even from the wise to the wise, and all courses may run ill." All the historic choices made by the Elves, perhaps even after grave deliberation by their wisest leaders, do seem to have led them down paths filled with grief and suffering. So, at the very least, in the Third Age the Elves appear to have become reluctant to give out advice.

In the Third Age, the Eldar concentrated on preserving their dominions, but they gave no thought to expanding their power and influence. As Men grew more numerous, the Elves withdrew into enclaves. In their seclusion, the Elves could only perfect their skills in poetry and music, celebrating the events of their past and the glories of their youth, and looking forward to their return to Valinor. The Elves were not so much looking forward as looking back. Their future became a reactionary movement across the Sea.

Whereas in the Second Age the Eldar had hoped to exercise their art upon all of Middle-earth -- or at least a great portion of it -- in the Third Age they elected to confine their art to small regions protected by the Three Rings of Power they still controlled. The Third Age Elves remembered all the great stories that the First and Second Age Elves had made. They made no new tales to preserve in future ages. Or, as Tolkien put it, they attempted nothing new.

The transition from making the past to remembering the past was undoubtedly a slow one. The Elves did not simply decide in a day that they would seek to accomplish no more. Rather, they must have gradually settled down to enjoy life and celebrate their achievements. But as the world grew dark and lonely, the Elves elected not to expand. For a brief time the Silvan Elves of Lothlórien became the most prominent champions of freedom in the West, but with the departure and subsequent death of Amroth their king, they withdrew into their forest and were seldom heard from again.

All choices made by the Elves were fraught with the gravest peril. Everything they did, everything they touched, was ultimately consumed by the consequences of their actions. They tried to avoid suffering the fate which had been set before them. Instead of destroying the Rings of Power, the Eldar used them in the Third Age. And when the One Ring was finally destroyed, all that the Eldar had achieved in the way of preserving and healing was undone. They could no longer think in terms of building up a future. They only wanted to preserve a past which was ideal for them.

The shadow the Eldar saw upon their horizon must therefore have loomed large over them all toward the end of the Third Age. Sauron's rise and return to Mordor were inevitably a result of the Elves' failure to resolve their conflicts in the past. Middle-earth's change in power and structure was just another mark against them. The candle could only burn down so far, and then there would be no more wick. Despite their best efforts to hold back change, they had really failed to prevent its onset. Change ensured that Middle-earth evolved around them; the world continued without the Elves. Time simply dragged the Elves back into the natural course of things once the Rings were out of the way.

And once the Rings of Power were gone, the Elves had no choice but to face their future, which to them seemed like no future. To a mortal Man, the uncertainty of immortality would be an opportunity to make new stories. But to an immortal Elf, the certainty of the end of that immortality meant there was less and less time to celebrate the great stories of the past. Crowding them out with new stories might only deprive the tales of their dutiful audience. Or, worse, living a new tale might bring on more grief and suffering, and so add to that burden of regret which grew heavier year by year.

It was all about choices: the choices they had made, the choices they had to make. The Elves were really burdened by the need to choose, and they wanted to choose both ways. For an Elf, Time in the Third Age was just a means of deferring the ultimate choice. Tolkien implies that many of them chose to remain in Middle-earth and fade, dwelling near the places they had loved in life, remembering only the events most dear to them.

Maybe in the end the only Elves to actually let go of the past were those who finally resolved to leave Middle-earth forever. It was a fate better than death, and one of their own choosing. To be true to their own nature, the Elves understood that they had to make a choice between the certainty of the past with all its known greatness and the uncertainty of the future with all its great unknowns. The trip over Sea was therefore the first step beyond regret and sorrow.

Chapter 2:
How the elves have changed

Some people have said there is no room for evolution in Middle-earth. That point of view overburdens Tolkien in the long-running dispute between Creationists and Darwinists. Tolkien's mythology does not participate in that dispute for, being a Philologist, he understood very well the inherent volatility that both languages and peoples experience across the centuries. We are different from our ancestors in many ways. And therefore changefulness is one of the primary characteristics Tolkien ascribes to Middle-earth, particularly when he speaks about the Elves and their choices.

In 1951, Tolkien wrote to the publisher Milton Waldman of Collins (now HarperCollins) about *The Lord of the Rings*. In that letter, Tolkien said that the Elves

> thus became obsessed with 'fading', the mode in which the changes of time (the law of the world under the sun) was perceived by them. They became sad, and their art (shall we say) antiquarian, and their efforts all really a kind of embalming -- even though they also retained the old motive of their kind, the adornment of the earth, and the healing of its hurts." Further on, in describing the Rings of Power, he said "the chief power (of all the rings alike) was the prevention or slowing of *decay* (i.e., 'change' viewed as a regrettable thing), the preservation of what is desired or loved, or its semblance -- this is more or less an Elvish motive....(*The Letters of J.R.R. Tolkien*, No. 131)

The Elves, therefore, fought against the natural evolution which occurred around them *and within them*. That is, change was natural to everything in their experience, including to themselves. They could not help but change. "Fading", as Tolkien describes it here, refers not to the eventual dissipation of the Elves' physical bodies (a very real fate he discusses in other writings), but rather concerns the loss of the world they love, as they perceive it. Legolas tried to explain this concept to his companions while they traveled down the Anduin in "The Great River":

Legolas stirred in his boat. 'Nay, time does not tarry for ever,' he said, 'but change and growth is not in all things and places alike. For the Elves the world moves, and it moves both very swift and very slow. Swift, because they themselves change little, and all else fleets by: it is a grief to them. Slow, because they do not count the running years, not for themselves. The passing seasons are but ripples ever repeated in the long long stream. Yet beneath the Sun all things must wear to an end at last.'

Legolas reveals a great deal about both himself and the Elves in these few sentences. He shares the Elvish experience as easily as can be, but he also shows that he himself has been cut off from part of that experience. Earlier in the book, in "The Ring Goes South", Legolas speaks of himself as a Silvan Elf. He is the son of Thranduil, a survivor out of Doriath who migrated east in the Second Age. But Legolas regards himself as a Wood-elf. The Wood-elf culture is very conservative and antiquarian. In fact, in a passage Christopher Tolkien cites in *Unfinished Tales*, J.R.R. Tolkien wrote of Legolas' grandfather Oropher (and the Sindar who followed him east) that:

...they were soon merged with the Silvan Elves, adopting their language and taking names of Silvan form and style. This they did deliberately; for they (and other similar adventurers forgotten in the legends or only briefly named) came from Doriath after its ruin, and had no desire to leave Middle-earth, nor to be merged with the other Sindar of Beleriand, dominated by the Noldorin Exiles for whom the folk of Doriath had no great love. They wished indeed to become Silvan folk and to return, as they said, to the simple life natural to the Elves before the invitation of the Valar had disturbed it.

Oropher's reactionary migration to Greenwood the Great was a counter-revolution, an attempt to de-evolve into a more primitive Elf. He abandoned much of the lore his people had acquired from Melian and the Dwarves, as well as the Noldor, in order to become more primitive, more natural. The Noldor represented both change and disruption. They had moved on to Aman, had dwelt within Valinor itself and communed with the Valar and Maiar on a scale incomprehensibly greater than the experience of the Sindar. And then the Noldor rebelled and returned to Middle-earth, but they brought their culture with them, rather than seek a return to their roots. The

Noldor were far from conservative when compared with the Teleri, many of whom had become Nandor out of a fearful conservativism.

Yet even Oropher's people could not stave off change. In time, they found themselves allied with the Noldor in the wars against Sauron. And they moved northward through Greenwood the Great until Thranduil at last established an underground fortress which reminded some people of Menegroth, the underground city of King Thingol of Doriath, and Nargothrond, the underground city of King Finrod (who was himself a Noldorin prince out of Valinor, though also Thingol's nephew).

The history of the Elven peoples is demarcated by change: change in location, change in culture, change in language. Tolkien shrewdly allowed his Elven peoples to evolve from very primitive clans into more sophisticated tribes, ultimately founding kingdoms and civilizations. The Elvish world order lasted for thousands of years, and though the Elves were almost consumed with preserving the past, or what they had once been, none of them seemed truly capable of avoiding their own inevitable evolution. Their choices forced them to change, even if only in reaction to unwanted change. There was nothing really static in Elvish nature. Rather, like glass, which is a liquid that seems to be a solid only because it moves very slowly, the Elves flow through time and changefulness at a pace which mere mortals can barely discern. The Elves pursue an illusion of stability which they can never make fully real.

In the beginning, according to the story of the First Elves (published in *The War of the Jewels*), there were only 144 Elves. These 144 constituted a whole community. But they were divided into three clans by the first three Elves to awaken: Imin, Tata, and Enel. This initial division had nothing to do with cultural preferences. The story tells us that the three Elf-fathers simply claimed groups of sleeping Elves to be their followers. Imin claimed the first group (of 6 couples) to be his special companions. Tata and Enel went on to choose the next four groups for themselves: 18 for Tata, 24 for Enel, 36 more for Tata, and 48 more for Enel.

The single community of Elves was predisposed to divide itself into three smaller communities. These smaller communities became the three clans: the Minyar (Firsts), Tatyar (Seconds), and Nelyar (Thirds). The Nelyar alone had a second name for themselves, Lindar (the Singers). When the Valar discovered the Elves and invited them to live in Valinor, the Elven communities were again divided. Although all of the Minyar accepted the invitation to settle in Valinor, only half of the Tatyar agreed. Slightly more than one third of the Nelyar insisted on staying behind.

After this second division, the Valinor-bound Elves became known as the Eldar, and they called the remaining Elves the Avari. For their part, the Avari did not reciprocate. That is, the Avari did not immediately assign new names to the two communities. They eventually migrated west but they became divided into smaller clans: the Kindi, Cuind, Hwenti, Windan, Kinn-lai, and Penni. The Penni may have been the only Nelyarin clan among the Avari. The essay "Quendi and Eldar" stipulates that the linguistic change from "*KWEN" to Telerin "*PEN" may have occurred before the division of the Elves into Eldar and Avari. If so, then the Penni would be the only self-named Avarin group descended from the Nelyar. The remaining self-named groups would all be of Tatyarin descent (all these clan names evolved from the word "Quendi", which was the Elves' original name for themselves).

The Eldar were divided into three groups (thus preserving the original divisions among the Elves): the Minyar became the Vanyar, the Tatyarin Eldar became the Noldor, and the Nelyarin Eldar became the Teleri. The Teleri were led by two brothers, Elwë and Olwë, who divided their people between them into two groups. As the Eldar moved westward, the Teleri began leaving behind sub-groups. The first such group were the Nandor, "those who turn away", the followers of Lenwë (and they came mostly from Olwë's group). The Nandor appear to have eventually become divided into many smaller, unnamed groups.

The Teleri who reached Beleriand became divided into three groups. The largest group followed Olwë to Aman, and there they became the

Falmari. Some of the Teleri who remained in Beleriand settled by the coastlands and took Cirdan (one of Elwë and Olwë's relatives) as their leader. The remaining Teleri were eventually reunited with Elwë (who had become separated from his people). Cirdan's people became known as the Falathrim and Elwë's people called themselves the Eglath. Eventually, the returning Noldorin Exiles called them all Sindar.

When Olwë's people finally reached Aman, the Elves had become divided into many peoples: the Vanyar, the Noldor, the Falmari, the Falathrim, the Eglath, the Nandor, and the Tatyarin Avari and Nelyarin Avari. In time, most if not all of these groups would become further sub-divided, but they also began to intermarry with each other. For example, the Noldor and Vanyar lived together in the city of Tirion for many years before the Vanyar began moving west into Valinor itself. And the Noldor helped the Falmari/Teleri build their city of Alqualondë on the northern shore of the Bay of Eldamar. The Noldor then began marrying Falmari. And some of the Avari eventually joined Nandorin groups.

The only Nandorin groups to be named came from the followers of Denethor. He was the son of Lenwë and he led many Nandor to Beleriand, where they settled in Ossiriand. After Denethor was slain in battle, his people became divided into two groups. Those who remained in Ossiriand became known as the Green-elves, although they continued to call themselves the Lindar (their most ancient name for themselves). Some of Denethor's people settled in Thingol's kingdom, however, and they became known as the Guest-elves. By this time, some of Thingol's people had migrated north. Cirdan's people had also expanded along the northern coastlands of Beleriand.

So, the Teleri of Beleriand (along with some Tatyarin Avari who had settled among Denethor's people) were now divided into seven or eight groups: the Falathrim of the two cities Brithombar and Eglarest; the Eglath of Thingol's kingdom; the Falathrim who settled in Nevrast; the Eglath who settled in Dorthonion and Hithlum; the Falathrim and Eglath who settled in the lands between Thingol's kingdom and the coasts; the Guest-elves of Arthorien (the southeastern region of

Doriath, located between the rivers Aros and Celon) in Thingol's kingdom; and the Green-elves of Ossiriand.

Not to be outdone, the Eldar of Aman began fragmenting in their own ways. The Vanyar scattered across Valinor. Although Tolkien never provided any names for their clans, they must have distinguished between families if not between larger groups in some way. For example, Ingwë, King of the Vanyar, settled on the slopes of Taniquetil. At the very least, he had a house there. But he is hardly likely to have lived alone. He must have had followers and relatives who lived close by (and the texts say that Indis, his sister or niece, lived in Ingwë's house until she married Finwe, King of the Noldor). But there were Vanyar who lived in the woodlands of Oromë, or in the plains of Yavanna. Simply because they lived apart from other Vanyar, these groups became distinct from the rest. And yet, we have no names for them (nor any history).

But, despite appearances, the Noldor did not all remain in Tirion, either. Some of them settled near the Halls of Aulë (apparently in central Valinor, and presumably housed in an unnamed group of hills or mountains). The only member of these Auléan Noldor to be named by Tolkien was Mahtan, father of Nerdanel, wife of Fëanor. Yet other groups of Noldor settled in Valinor, particularly on the western slopes of the Pelori (the huge chain of mountains separating Valinor from eastern Aman). And when Fëanor was exiled from Tirion, he, his sons, Finwe, and an unspecified number of followers settled in the fortress of Formenos in northern Valinor.

The Noldor also became divided into two philosophically opposed groups due to a change in language. The Noldor, seeking new knowledge, were the most prone among the Elves to deliberately change their language. They did so through changing sounds as well as through adding, altering, or abandoning words. Being very creative, the Noldor were predisposed to devise new names for things, as well as to alter the way they said things. But Fëanor led or inspired a conservative or traditionalist movement among the Noldor which opposed at least some of the linguistic change. His motivations are explained at length in "The Shibboleth of Fëanor", which was published in *The Peoples of Middle-earth*. Briefly, Fëanor insisted on retaining a pronunciation used in his mother's name, "Serindë", which the majority of the Noldor abandoned. The *shibboleth* (a word or sound which is used to distinguish between peoples through their different pronunciations) was the "thorn" sound Fëanor preserved, for which the Noldor substituted an "s" sound. That is, "Serindë" had originally sounded something like "Therindë".

Fëanor's prominence among the Noldor undoubtedly propelled some of the artificial distinctions between various groups into the forefront of Noldorin political life. He had the prestige and the position to assert his will in the face of public opinion. In effect, Fëanor and his followers isolated themselves from the larger Noldorin language. Their reticence proved to be the source of the first true political division of the Elven peoples. That is, until this point, politics really had nothing to do with determining who belonged to which group. You were an Avar because you (or your ancestors) refused to accept the Valar's invitation. You were a Nando because you (or your ancestors) turned aside from the Great Journey. You were a Noldo because you (or your ancestors) followed Finwe to Aman. What you believed was right or wrong regarding some controversy really had nothing to do with what people you belonged to.

But Fëanor's linguistic intransigence presaged his eventual political intransigence. For purely emotional reasons, Fëanor rebelled against the Valar and persuaded the majority of his people to leave Aman. Now, some of those rebels eventually turned back and rejoined the few who had refused to rebel. These Noldor, led by Fëanor's youngest half-brother Finarfin, took no special name for themselves, but we can call them Loyalists. The Loyalists would eventually outnumber the Exiles, if only because so many Exiles would be killed in the wars of Beleriand.

But before the Exiles left Aman, they became divided into two groups: those who followed Fëanor, and those who followed Fingolfin, Fëanor's other half-brother. The Fëanorians most likely included the majority of those Noldor who had held to Fëanor's linguistic conservatism. But they must also have included those Noldor who resided in Formenos with Fëanor and his family (there may be no distinction between these groups). The Fëanorians were the first Noldor to attack the Falmari in Alqualondë, and Fëanor ensured that his followers retained control over the ships they stole from Alqualondë. Fëanor cemented the unity among his followers by taking them to Middle-earth in the stolen ships and abandoning the majority of their people in Aman. Shame and shared disgrace bound the Fëanorians to their leader.

Fingolfin's people remained in Aman for the equivalent of many years of the Sun. Because of their great number, Fingolfin shared responsibility with his sons Fingon and Turgon. But Finarfin's eldest son Finrod also led part of the abandoned Exiles. One must infer that, when the Noldor first set out on their road, there were three groups: Fëanor's small band, Fingolfin's great following, and Finarfin's following. Finarfin and some of his people repented and returned to Tirion. Finrod thus assumed the leadership over his father's remaining followers. But while the abandoned Exiles remained in Aman, they all seem to have accepted Fingolfin as their king.

By the time Fingolfin reached Middle-earth, Fëanor was dead and his eldest son Maedhros was held prisoner by Melkor. The Fëanorian Noldor were not entirely leaderless (at least five of Maedhros' brothers were still alive), but they had lost the initiative. And yet, instead of rejoining Fingolfin's people, they remained a separate community. Fingolfin's people eventually became divided into three major kingdoms: Fingolfin's kingdom in Hithlum, Turgon's kingdom in Nevrast (later on, Gondolin), and Finrod's kingdom in Nargothrond. Both Turgon and Finrod enlarged their followings by absorbing many Sindar (mostly Falathrim) into their peoples.

Fingolfin's kingdom included many Sindar, too. But Hithlum and the March of Maedhros were remembered as Noldorin realms, with little connection to their Sindarin inhabitants. That is, in their own ways, both realms were purely Noldorin. Even Turgon preserved Quenya as a living language in his household, though his people in general used Sindarin as their daily language. But all three realms were eventually destroyed by Melkor's forces. Those Noldor who survived the fall of their lands were driven into a second or third exile. Some of Finrod's people, driven from Dorthonion, migrated south to the Isle of Balar, to join the remnant of Cirdan's Falathrim who had gathered there. Some of the Fëanorians settled in Nargothrond. And survivors from Gondolin helped to establish the havens in Arvernien.

The long Siege of Angband, during which the Noldor built up a great civilization and interacted with Dwarves, Sindar, and Men in nearly continuous peaceful relations, misleadingly implies that the Noldor avoided changefulness during much of their time in Beleriand. And yet, with each passing century they had to absorb some new aspect of Beleriandic experience into their culture: the ban on the use of Quenya by the Sindar, the disappearance of Turgon's kingdom, the migrations of Men into Beleriand, the growth of the Elvish populations.

But in the space of a few decades, at a pace which must have seemed exceedingly rash to the Elves, their great kingdoms vanished one by one: the March of Maedhros, Hithlum, the Falas, Nargothrond, Doriath, and Gondolin were all destroyed by enemies from without or within the Elvish culture. Ragged bands of survivors gathered in Arvernien, the forests of Ossiriand, or on the Isle of Balar. Even then the Fëanorians could not restrain themselves. They destroyed Arvernien as they had destroyed Doriath. Those Eldar who survived the fall of Arvernien fled to Balar and there waited until the world was made safe once again.

There must have been divisions on Balar, if for no other reason than that separate groups of Elves arrived at different times. Cirdan's people settled there first, followed soon after by Noldor (and Sindar) from Dorthonion. Eventually, Sindar (and perhaps some Noldor) from Hithlum made their way to Balar. Survivors from Nargothrond probably also found their way to the island. Each small group brought with it differences in language and experience, but they also brought with them memories of a fragmented past which would serve as the springboard for a new future.

When the Second Age began, Gil-galad established a new kingdom in what remained of Beleriand. This would be the last fully Eldarin civilization in Middle-earth. That is, Gil-galad's kingdom included both Noldor and Sindar. But the Eldar found they could no longer live together, for reasons which Tolkien never fully explained. Some of the Sindar left Beleriand and migrating east or south settled among Nandor or Avari to establish new kingdoms. Most of those kingdoms eventually disappeared, perhaps overrun in the wars with Sauron, or perhaps abandoned when their peoples decided to flee Middle-earth forever. And some of the Noldor, quite probably dominated by descendants of the Fëanorians, migrated east to establish Eregion.

Eregion's origin is clouded by the confused history of Galadriel and Celeborn. Perhaps they helped to establish the realm, perhaps not. No text speaks of a King (or Queen) of Eregion. In one disputed version of events, Celebrimbor seizes control over Eregion from Galadriel and Celeborn. Celebrimbor is the last living descendant of Fëanor, and he is the greatest craftsman among the Noldor in the Second Age. As Fëanor created the Silmarils, and so spawned a series of events which led to the destruction of the Noldor, so Celebrimbor led the Gwaith-i-Mirdain in creating the Rings of Power, thus spawning a series of events which led to the destruction of the Noldor again.

The Noldor could not help but tinker with things. They were driven to create, to alter, to change the world around them. And yet, it was their growing regret for the lost past which led them to create the Rings of Power. In seeking to arrest change, they introduced the greatest change of all. All the funny little names, the political movements, the linguistic arguments were rendered meaningless. The Noldor and Sindar ceased to be distinct peoples. They became the Eldar again, the Elves of the West once more. The Noldor remained the High Elves, but they arrested their own further growth when they created the Rings of Power.

Gil-galad's people established one last colony at the end of the War of the Elves and Sauron: Rivendell. Elrond had retreated there during the war with as many survivors from Eregion and nearby lands as he could gather. But if his people took a special name for themselves, they stopped using it. Rivendell became known simply as the home of Elrond Half-elven. In the Third Age, we are told, Elrond gathered many High Elves in Rivendell. It became their cultural center in Eriador. Lindon was ruled by Cirdan. While some Noldor must have remained there, Lindon became for all intents and purposes a Sindarin realm.

The changes brought on by history had altered the Elvish landscape in many ways. The Avari and Nandor vanished as distinct peoples. Their descendants, the Silvan Elves of Greenwood the Great and Lothlórien, were eventually joined by Sindar (and Noldor in Lothlórien). The ancient Elven communities of Eriador were replaced by human communities which were in turn crushed by their enemies. The Noldor maintained an outpost in Rivendell, but they no longer distinguished between isolated groups by politics or language. They had changed again, growing wiser with age, more tolerant of each other, perhaps. In the end, there would be no need to speak of Fëanorians or the followers of Turgon and Fingolfin. They were simply Noldor, more learned than their ancestors, more experienced, but in some ways just as uncomplicated by politics and prejudice.

Tolkien's evolutionary vision requires a twilight period for each civilization. Historical closure is only achieved after a people have risen to great heights and then tumbled down to their simpler roots. The Elves had lost their innocence. They could not become again the simple, naive creatures their ancestors had been at Cuiviënen. Not even the Wood-elves could escape the demands of Time. Legolas may not have identified with the Noldor, nor understood their ambitions. But he remained a descendant of the great adventurers of the past, and he possessed some of their best qualities: courage, loyalty, friendship, and curiosity. Yet he also inherited their longing for the Sea, and when Legolas heard the gulls crying out overhead, that longing awoke within him. His life was forever changed. Like all Elves, the changefulness he had sought to leave behind found him and overwhelmed him.

MICHAEL MARTINEZ

Chapter 3:
It's all in the family

The Elwëans and Ingwëans

Nothing is more confusing than trying to figure out who is actually supposed to be in the various family trees, and what their relationships to the three Eldarin kings are. Most people have only read *The Lord of the Rings*, and that book provides us with so few clues about the Eldarin families that all the cousins, brothers, aunts, and uncles who are named in *The Silmarillion* arrive as quite a shock. Why weren't these people mentioned in *The Lord of the Rings*?

Of course, their stories had come to an end thousands of years before Hobbits even arrived on the scene. So the princes of the Eldar were no longer of paramount historical importance. History in Middle-earth had shifted from being a primarily Eldarin course of events to a primarily Dunadan course of events, and even the Dunedain were in decline. Socially, the Eldar no longer mattered. So their great heroes, their ancient kings, all their noble families were forgotten by most of the peoples in Middle-earth. To hear the stories of ages lost in time's remote antiquity from people who had been there would have been an extremely special experience for the Hobbits who visited Rivendell. Their people had no knowledge of such stories, and Bilbo had accomplished something unique by awakening the desire to learn more about Elvish histories in his young nieces and nephews.

Naturally, Bilbo would be most interested in the tales of the relatives of Elrond and Aragorn, his special friends. Conveniently, their Elven ancestors just happened to be part of the extended families of Finwë and Elwë, some of whose members ruled various kingdoms in Beleriand. It would all be quite romantic (in the heroic and adventurous sense). But it would also provide an insight into the character and motivations of both Elrond and Aragorn for Bilbo to understand who their families were. It would be that Elvish sense of obligation. Elrond couldn't just leave Middle-earth until a resolution had been found for the problem of the Rings of Power. Aragorn, of course, had no opportunity to leave Middle-earth. But he had inherited the whole mess from his human ancestors.

The difficulty for us is that Tolkien never fully understood what he wanted to achieve with the Eldarin genealogies. Every now and then he would add a name to the lists and if he had time, perhaps years down the road, he would drop in some tantalizing comment that began the process of defining a new character. And in retrospect, he would delete names from the lists, too, if he felt the characters they referred to belonged in other tales, or didn't fit in at all. Hence, Indis begins as the sister of Ingwë and ends up as his niece. And Ingwiel, Ingwë's son, vanishes altogether. Such losses are regrettable, because they hint at untold stories which might be very interesting.

Ingwë, Finwë, and Elwë also present problems. Their histories as characters under Tolkien's hand evolved both together and separately. There can be no doubt that at one time Ingwë was the eldest of the Elves, the first to awaken. Finwë, too, seems to have been a first generation Elf for a while, as Fëanor was originally supposed to have been born during the Great Journey. And yet, these "facts" were discarded and the Elven families were pushed back. Tolkien constructed an elaborate social history for the Elves which explained their numerous divisions and apparently called for even more ancient Elves. Ingwë, Finwë, and Elwë subsequently become merely very ancient Elves, but not the most ancient of Elves.

In the children's tale of the First Elves ("Quendi and Eldar", in *The War of the Jewels*), there is no mention of Ingwë, Finwë, Elwë, or Olwë. The first three Elves to awaken are Imin ("one"), Tata ("two"), and Enel ("three"). Their appointed spouses lie sleeping beside them: Iminyë, Tatië, Enelyë. Clearly, since Finwë's first wife was Miriel and since Elwë only married Melian the Maia, Tata and Enel cannot be Finwë and Elwë. Also, because Elwë's brother Olwë is firmly established in the mythological canon, they must have had parents.

Yet some people insist that Imin must be Ingwë. After all, they argue, Tolkien doesn't say that Imin is *not* Ingwë. Which is the silliest possible argument of all, since it is completely lacking in logic. Tolkien's absence of denial for any given assertion does not make that assertion true, possibly true, or even possible. The distinction between Tolkien's imagination and our own is the boundary between what Tolkien wrote and what we write. It may seem convincing to believe that Imin is Ingwë, but Imin cannot possibly be Ingwë. In the children's tale, Imin is the undisputed leader of the Elves. He is the eldest. No one questions his place in their primitive society. And yet, Ingwë holds no station among the Elves until Oromë selects him to be an ambassador. From that point forward, Ingwë acquires an authority which Imin cannot claim: Ingwë is Oromë's chosen representative for the Minyar (the Firsts, the Elves descended from Imin's companions).

In "Quendi and Eldar", Tolkien wrote: "According to the legend, preserved in almost identical form among both the Elves of Aman and the Sindar, the Three Clans were in the beginning derived from the three Elf-fathers: *Imin*, *Tata*, and *Enel* (sc. One, Two, Three), and those whom each chose to join his following....It is said that of the small clan of the *Minyar* none became Avari."

What we learn from these statements is that all the Elves of Aman and Beleriand remembered the ancient divisions and told virtually the same stories about the three Elf-fathers. There is no indication that either Elwë or Ingwë were identified with Imin and Enel. In fact, the very absence of such identification works where the absence of denial fails. That is, if Tolkien didn't identify Enel with Elwë and Imin with Ingwë, we cannot assume that such an identification exists. The two absences don't cancel each other out. Rather, the statements of fact take precedence. Imin was an individual who awakened at Cuiviënen, and his wife Iminye lay beside him. Ingwë is no longer said to have *awakened* at Cuiviënen.

In preparing *The Silmarillion* for publication, Christopher Tolkien carefully side-stepped the entire issue. He says nothing about who among the three Elf-kings may have awakened at Cuiviënen. In "Of the Ruin of Doriath", which Christopher wrote with some help from Guy Gavriel Kay, Thingol proudly says to the Dwarves of Nogrod, "How do ye of uncouth race dare to demand aught of me, Elu Thingol,

Lord of Beleriand, whose life began by the waters of Cuiviënen years uncounted ere the fathers of the stunted people awoke?" Some people misread this passage, or elect to *interpret* it to mean that Thingol claims to have awakened at Cuiviënen. But the text doesn't say he *awakened* there. It only says his life began there before the Dwarf-fathers awoke.

Now, we don't know when the Dwarf-fathers awoke, but J.R.R. Tolkien's Elu Thingol most likely would not have made such a claim anyway. The original story from *The Book of Lost Tales*, "The Nauglafring", holds that Tinwelint (the precursor of Thingol) had fallen prey to Mim's curse on the hoard Urin (Hurin) had taken from Nargothrond. Tinwelint contracted with Dwarves to shape the gold and place the Silmaril in the Nauglafring. Ufedhin, a Gnome (the Gnomes of the Lost Tales were replaced by the Noldor in the later mythologies), arranged for the contract. But because Tinwelint had held him prisoner, Ufedhin asked the Dwarves to demand an insulting price for their work. The Dwarves made the request and Tinwelint had them and Ufedhin whipped. He then paid them common wages and forced them to pay for Ufedhin's food and lodging during the time he was a prisoner. The Dwarves and Ufedhin eventually left and plotted their revenge. They allied themselves with Orcs and attacked Artanor (Tinwelint's kingdom) while he was riding in the hunt, celebrating Beren's hunting of the wolf. Another Elf, overcome by lust for the cursed gold, helped Ufedhin enter Artanor without Gwendelin (Melian's) knowledge.

Although this story little resembles Christopher Tolkien's account of how Thingol came to be slain, Christopher's account does not resemble his father's brief notes. In an extended note explaining what material he had available for "The Ruin of Doriath" (*The War of the Jewels*, pp. 354-6), Christopher says that "in *The Tale of Years* [composed for the First Age] my father seems not to have considered the problem of the passage of the Dwarvish host into Doriath despite the Girdle of Melian, but in writing the word 'cannot' against the D version (p. 352) he showed that he regarded the story he had outlined as impossible, for that reason. In another place, he sketched a possible solution (*ibid.*): 'Somehow it must be contrived that Thingol is lured outside or induced to go to war beyond his borders and is there slain by the Dwarves. Then Melian departs, and the girdle being removed Doriath is ravaged by the Dwarves.'

Christopher adds:

> In the story that appears in *The Silmarillion* the outlaws who went with Hurin to Nargothrond were removed, as also was the curse of Mîm; and the treasure that Hurin took from Nargothrond was the Nauglamír -- which was here supposed to have been made by the Dwarves for Finrod Felagund, and to have been the most prized by him of all the hoard of Nargothrond. Hurin was represented as being at last freed from the delusions inspired by Morgoth in his encounter with Melian in Menegroth. The Dwarves who set the Silmaril in the Nauglamír were already in Menegroth engaged on other works, and it was they who slew Thingol; at that time Melian's power was withdrawn from Neldoreth and Region, and she vanished out of Middle-earth, leaving Doriath unprotected. The ambush and destruction of the Dwarves at Sarn Athrad was given again to Beren and the Green Elves (following my father's letter of 1963 quoted on p. 353, where however he said that 'Beren had no army'), and from the same source the Ents, 'Shepherds of the Trees', were introduced.

> This story was not lightly or easily conceived, but was the outcome of long experimentation among alternative conceptions. In this work Guy Kay took a major part, and the chapter that I finally wrote owes much to my discussions with him. It is, and was, obvious that a step was being taken of a different order from any other 'manipulation' of my father's own writing in the course of the book: even in the case of the story of the Fall of Gondolin, to which my father had never returned, something could be contrived without introducing radical changes in the narrative. It seemed at that time that there were elements in the story of the Ruin of Doriath as it stood that were radically incompatible with 'The Silmarillion' as projected, and that there was here an inescapable choice: either to abandon that conception, or else to alter the story. I think now that this was a mistaken view, and that the undoubted difficulties could have been, and should have been, surmounted without so far overstepping the bounds of the editorial function.

The correct story of Thingol's death is provided only in notes associated with the previously unpublished "Wanderings of Hurin", in which tale Hurin is released by Morgoth to sow a path of death and destruction among the last enemies of Angband. Hurin unwittingly reveals to Morgoth's spies that Gondolin lies in the Echoriath, and not in the distant south as everyone had supposed for hundreds of years. Hurin then goes to Brethil, and he meets up with outlaws from Hithlum who declare their loyalty to him. He finds Morwen as she is dying and he buries her, and then he demands an accounting from the people of Brethil. In doing so, Hurin awakens a civil war among the Folk of Haleth and the last heirs of Haleth are slain.

Hurin moves on to Nargothrond, where he finds Mim has seized Glaurung's hoard. Hurin slays Mim, who curses the treasure as he lays dying. With the help of the Hithlum outlaws and some of the former people of Brethil, Hurin takes the entire treasure (or a great part of it) to Doriath, and there insults Thingol. Melian heals Hurin, who then departs into the south with a great following of Men. Thingol is left with the treasure, and eventually he commissions the melding of the necklace and the Silmaril. At this point, Tolkien notes to himself, Thingol must be drawn out of the kingdom and slain, so that Melian will withdraw her protection and leave Doriath open to the Dwarves.

Yet there is no narrative for this story. There are no statements by Thingol even in cryptic marginal notes where he makes any sort of boast to the Dwarves about having begun his life at Cuiviénen. Thingol (Elwë) certainly began his life there. He was one of the three ambassadors Oromë chose to visit Aman. But there is nothing in *The Silmarillion* or its late sources which implies that Thingol was a first generation Elf. And, in fact, since there were no siblings (brothers and sisters) among the first generation Elves, we can safely remove Thingol from that crowd. It should not be doubted that he came from a later generation.

Finwë, because of his marriage to Miriel in Aman, cannot be identified with Tata. So, Finwë could not have been a first generation Elf, as they all awoke beside their spouses. Hence, we are left only with the question regarding a possible identification of Ingwë with Imin. And of Imin there is nothing said in *The Silmarillion*. "Quendi and Eldar" is a fairly late composition, dating to the late 1960s. It also departs from the "established" Silmarillion canon in a few ways, such as making Eol an Avarin Elf of the Tatyar (the second clan, from whom the Noldor were derived). In *The Silmarillion*, Eol is one of Thingol's kinsmen.

Cirdan is another of Thingol's kinsmen, as is Celeborn. If they are Thingol's cousins, then Thingol cannot even be part of the second generation of Elves. His parents would have to have siblings in order for him to have cousins. Hence, at the very least, Thingol would have to be a third-generation Elf. And that leads people to wonder what happened to his parents and grand-parents. In fact, we have no way of knowing how many generations lie between Enel and Thingol, nor even if Thingol is a descendant of Enel (he does not have to be). But Thingol is a contemporary of Finwë. They are friends. It seems that they must have grown up fairly close together, chronologically. So they may have been "young" but not immature Elves when Oromë selected them.

Would Ingwë have been a similarly "young" Elf? He must have been a bit adventurous. He was, after all, willing to make the trip to Aman with Oromë. The Elves were afraid of Oromë when he first appeared, for Melkor had apparently been abducting or slaying Elves since he had first discovered them. Furthermore, in "Laws and Customs Among the Eldar" ("Morgoth's Ring"), Tolkien writes: "Indeed, in their earlier days death came more readily; for their bodies were then less different from the bodies of Men, and the command of their spirits over their bodies less complete." It is entirely conceivable that Imin, Tata, and Enel had all perished by the time Oromë showed up. Conceivable, but not necessary. For, one assumption people make is that the eldest Elves must be the leaders.

Why should that be? Tolkien never says the eldest Elves are the leaders. What he says is that the ambassadors whom Oromë selected were afterwards kings. Imin could have been alive and he simply deferred to Ingwë's courage and wisdom. Ingwë was indeed very persuasive, for all of the Minyar agreed to follow him to Aman. *The Silmarillion* says, "The first host was led by Ingwë, the most high lord of all the Elvish race. He entered into Valinor and sits at the feet of the

Powers, and all the Elves revere his name; but he came never back, nor looked again upon Middle-earth. The Vanyar were his people; they are the Fair Elves, the beloved of Manwë and Varda, and few among Men have spoken with them."

Now, some people point to that phrase, "the most high lord of all the Elvish race", and argue that it refers to Ingwë's status among the Elves at the time the Great Journey began. But it is a descriptive phrase which reflects the indeterminate tense of the paragraph. The next sentence, for example, reads "He entered into Valinor and sits at the feet of the Powers". The mixture of past and present tense in a single sentence would surely merit a red mark for most people, but Tolkien is using the two tenses to imply a boundless life for Ingwë. Of the three ambassadors, he was the only one who was not slain. And we know (from late writings) that Finwë eventually elected not to return to life, so that Miriel could live again. Thingol may or may not have emerged from the Halls of Mandos. But Ingwë lives and sits at the feet of the Powers. So, although he is now "the most high of all the Elvish race", when did he become so? We don't know.

But we do know that Finwë married Ingwë's niece, Indis. In an earlier conception she was Ingwë's sister. Even if some doubt lingers about Ingwë's age, it is impossible to identify him with Imin because Ingwë has at least one sibling, a sister who is Indis' mother. Indis was originally described as "of the kin of Ingwë", and this passage was altered to "sister of Ingwë" (*Morgoth's Ring*, p. 207). Eventually, in "The Shibboleth of Fëanor", Tolkien notes that "she is said to have been the daughter of King Ingwë's sister" (*The Peoples of Middle-earth*, p. 343). In the final conception, therefore, Ingwë has a sister and he cannot possibly be identified with the sisterless Imin. At the very least, Ingwë and his sister must be second-generation Elves, and they could be further removed from Imin and Iminyë (and that assumes they were descended from Imin and Iminyë, which need not necessarily be so).

Of Ingwë himself, little more may be said. We are told he never returned to Middle-earth. The original Ingwë, from *The Book of Lost Tales*, led all the Elves back to Europe in a failed attempt to rescue the

Elves who had been defeated by Morgoth. In early versions of "Quenta Silmarillion", it was Ingwiel, finally Ingwion, Ingwë's son, who led the host of the Vanyar back to Middle-earth in the War of Wrath (*The War of the Jewels*, p. 246). We thus know of at least six members of Ingwë's family: his (unnamed) father and mother, the unnamed sister, Ingwë's spouse, their son Ingwion, and Indis, the daughter of the unnamed sister. Ingwë's family could indeed have been much larger. He could have come with assorted aunts, uncles, cousins, daughters, younger sons, etc. But because the Vanyar were less prone to rebellion than the Noldor, and therefore less bound up with tragedy, their stories are not preserved in the histories of Middle-earth.

One Vanya did travel into exile: Elenwë, Turgon's wife. People sometimes ask if she might have been related to Ingwë. If the naming convention requires that "in-" or "ing-" be utilized, then I would say that Elenwë came of a different Vanyarin family. But that is only conjecture, as Tolkien seems never to have considered the issue (and in any event she could have been related to Ingwë by marriage if not by blood). Glorfindel is another puzzling figure, and people are tempted (because of his golden hair) to ask if he might not have been a Vanya or half-Noldo/half-Vanya who followed Turgon. My feeling is that Tolkien's statement in the LoTR appendix about only the children of Finarfin having golden hair among the Noldor must be taken with a grain of salt. That statement was added to the Second Edition in 1965 and by that time Tolkien appears to have forgotten that the Elvenking of *The Hobbit* (Legolas' father Thranduil) and an unnamed Elf of Lórien both are said to have golden hair. The association of the Vanyar with golden hair appears to be a late idea, or one which Tolkien abandoned and returned to more than once. Idril Celebrindal had golden hair, too, and she was not of the House of Finarfin, but rather was Turgon's daughter by Elenwë.

Elwë's family produces a few mysteries, too. For example, in *Unfinished Tales* Christopher Tolkien mentions "Thingol's brother Elmo -- a shadowy figure about whom nothing is told save that he was the younger brother of Elwë (Thingol) and Olwë, and was 'beloved of Elwë with whom he remained'." Elmo was presumed to be the grandfather of Celeborn through a son named Galadhon. Celeborn had a brother, Galathil, who was the father of Nimloth, Dior's wife in *The Silmarillion*. Many years later, Tolkien decided that Celeborn was an Elf of Aman, a grandson of Olwë. Such a relationship would have made him Galadriel's first cousin, and such a marriage was supposed to be forbidden or at least disapproved of by the Eldar. Many people like to argue that this was Tolkien's final decision on Celeborn and therefore it should be accepted, but the problem is that Celeborn's ancestry in Aman does not fit with the published texts. There is, in fact, little explanation for how Celeborn and Galadriel should arrive in Middle-earth, and it's impossible to reconcile Galadriel's history as established in *The Road Goes Ever On* with this late conception of Celeborn, in which she and Celeborn had the Valar's permission to leave Aman before Fëanor launched his rebellion.

In *The Lord of the Rings*, Celeborn is presented as a Sindarin Elf, related to Thingol of Doriath. But this information came late, too. Celeborn was originally conceived as a Wood Elf, according to Christopher Tolkien. He may have been silver-haired like Thingol, but he was not an Elda at all. As the years passed and Tolkien developed the Silmarillion mythology more fully, Celeborn became an important validation of Thingol's family. That is, Thingol had to have relatives, so that it would be clear he was not all alone in the woods. *The Silmarillion* tells us that Thingol's friends and kinsfolk mostly stayed behind to search for him. Doriath must have been a pretty cozy little place the first thousand years or so, and it would have been hard to cheat at cards because everyone knew everyone else.

Hence, if Olwë had to take most of the Teleri over Sea, then Elwë Thingol had to have other relatives who stayed behind. Celeborn's ancestry was thus moved over to the Elwëans tree and he became Elwë's grand-nephew. Celeborn's wisdom was thus also transferred to the Eldar. Although some people smirk at Celeborn, who but for one reproach by Galadriel comes off as the wiser of the two in several critical areas, he is nonetheless Celeborn the Wise. Should a Wood Elf be as wise as an Elda, whose people have been tutored by the Valar and Maiar, which association the Wood Elves eschewed?

Cirdan is another of Elwë's kinsmen. Like Celeborn and Elwë, Cirdan is silver-haired (grey-haired in *The Lord of the Rings*). Ëarwen, the daughter of Olwë and Galadriel's mother, also has silver hair, and Celebrian (whose name begins with "celeb", "silver"), the daughter of Galadriel and Celeborn, may also be silver haired. Although Tolkien never assigns a significance to the silver hair, he uses it to bind Elwë's family together almost as a symbol of royalty. The silver hair seems to have been a mark of the family, and perhaps no other Elves would have had silver hair. But the trait does not always appear in the family lines. For example, in "Of Tuor and his Coming to Gondolin" (*Unfinished Tales*), Voronwë tells Tuor that he is the son of Aranwë (a Noldo, whom Voronwë later on claims is "of the House of Fingolfin") and a Sindarin lady who was related to Cirdan. Although we never hear of a Mrs. Cirdan, if Voronwë's mother is only related by marriage to Cirdan, then she need not be silver-haired. But if she is silver-haired, should Voronwë have the silver hair?

Cirdan's family is not further elucidated, although it seems to me that Tolkien missed a great opportunity to expand the legends of Beleriand. Cirdan could have had one or two sons who fell in the wars of Beleriand. Imagine a Cirdanwion making a valiant last stand as Brithombar was overrun by Orcs, and Cirdan had to watch his brave son fall beneath enemy swords while his ship, the last to leave the quays, moved out. Perhaps Tolkien would have had Cirdan's son leap onto the quays to sacrifice himself in a heroic holding action.

Of course, Cirdan was also a close friend to the Dunedain. He apparently spent a lot of time with Aldarion, who learned a great deal from Cirdan about constructing sea-walls and harbors. A son or grandson of Cirdan could have made an impact in the War of the Elves and Sauron, or even the War of the Last Alliance. But there seems little room for Cirdanic heroics in those two wars. Cirdan's personal moment of tragedy was probably the fall of the Falas. Everything after that was just an extension of his life toward the War of the Ring. Cirdan's mark in Beleriand was the Falas.

Eol is another Thingolian kinsman, at least in some conceptions. "Quendi and Eldar" supposes that Eol is a Tatyarin Elf, one of the

Avari, who resents the Noldor. In a note attached to the text, Christopher Tolkien writes: "It is curious that -- as in the original text of *Maeglin*, where he was 'of the kin of Thingol' -- in my father's very late work on the story Eol becomes again 'one of the Eldar'...." Eol is generally accepted as one of Thingol's relatives, but we only have it so because that is how Christopher compressed the story of Maeglin for *The Silmarillion*. "The Shibboleth of Fëanor", which appears to be the most authoritative treatment of the Finwëans genealogy, makes no mention of Eol (in fact, it appears to confuse Ireth, a name for Aredhel, with Idril in one passage).

If we put all the pieces together, we may contrive several family trees for Elwë and Olwë, but none of them are very satisfying. I doubt that Eol and Cirdan would have been brothers. They just seem to be too different in temperament and proclivities to have had much association with one another. Hence, I think there would have to be three branches of the family: the primary branch, consisting of Elwë, Olwë, and possibly Elmo (although the name doesn't seem to fit well with the styles of the other two) and their descendants; Cirdan (originally called Nowë according to an essay published in *The Peoples of Middle-earth*) and his "kin", perhaps a sister or several siblings and their descendants, including Voronwë; and Eol, who would not have had any siblings.

If we accept this as the working genealogy, there would have to be at least two generations missing from the tree. Enel and Enelya could have been the grandparents. Some people seem to be compelled to insist that would have to be so, and I know of no reason to argue otherwise. There would have to be at least three siblings, the eldest of whom would be the father or mother of Elwë, Olwë, and Elmo.

However, limiting the family to three generations like this makes Doriath seem awful empty. The text says that Thingol's friends and kinsmen stayed behind, but I get the impression that he had a lot of relatives. Now, I don't mean hundreds. But keeping Elwë in the third generation just makes it all too tight and cozy. A lot of time elapsed between the awakening of the Elves and the Great Journey. I think Tolkien eventually came to realize this and that is why he began making the genealogical explanations much vaguer. He was leaving himself room to fill out the family trees, or to at least introduce new cousins and kinsmen later on, if the need arose.

Even Beleg and Mablung could have eventually become kinsmen of Thingol (although I would not find that satisfying -- it's nice to know there are other families which can produce a few lords and heroes). And, too, some people like to see Oropher and his son Thranduil as kinsmen of Thingol who wandered into the eastern lands of Middle-earth hoping to revive the spirit of Doriath. Keeping them in the family would provide an adequate context for Celeborn's cryptic "Too seldom do my kindred journey hither from the North" in "The Mirror of Galadriel" (a statement which seems to clearly imply that Celeborn is a Wood Elf, since Legolas has already declared himself to be "of the Silvan Folk" in "The Ring Goes South").

So, if Oropher is another cousin, we either have to introduce a fourth sibling in the second generation (not really a problem, actually) or we have to insist on a four-generation tree leading down to Thingol and the boys.

Then there is the unnamed Sindarin lady whom Orodreth married. Adding her to the family of Elwë and Olwë is, in my opinion, a stretch. She came from northern Beleriand, apparently the region of Dorthonion, and must have been the daughter of the chief of the Sindar in that region. Such a leader would have been the Elvish equivalent of a clan-lord, perhaps himself a very ancient Elf or the son of one of the ancient Elves who made the Great Journey. When the Noldor first divided the empty lands of northern Beleriand among themselves, Finrod and his brothers were given the upper Vale of Sirion and Dorthonion.

When Thingol gave Nargothrond to Finrod, he moved south and Angrod moved into the Vale of Sirion, leaving Dorthonion to Aegnor. Angrod's wife was Eldalôtë (Sindarin Edhellos) and their son was Orodreth. Orodreth's children were Gil-galad and Finduilas. Finduilas had golden hair, like her foremother Indis, but Gil-galad does not seem to have been golden-haired or silver-haired. His most famous name,

"Gil-galad" (Star-radiance), refers to "his helm and mail, and his shield overlaid with silver and set with a device of white stars, shone from afar like a star in sunlight or moonlight and could be seen by Elvish eyes at a great distance if he stood upon a height."

The Finwëans

The central role of Tolkien's mythology is assigned to the family of Finwë, the first King of the Noldor. Unlike the Minyar (Firsts), all of whom migrated to Valinor and became known as the Vanyar, the Tatyar (Seconds) and Nelyar (Thirds) divided themselves into two groups. Those Tatyar who undertook the Great Journey became the Noldor, and Finwë was their leader. Those Nelyar who undertook the Great Journey became the Teleri, and the brethren Elwë and Olwë were their leaders. Hence, Finwë, Elwë, and Olwë were only kings over those members of their clans who followed them on the Great Journey. The remaining Elves, collectively known as the Avari, were ruled by other (unnamed) chieftains.

The significance of this distinction is that Finwë's isolation from the Tatyarin Avari reinforces Tolkien's emerging view that Finwë should not be a first generation Elf. Although Tolkien never says so, it would be respectful of Finwë's primacy if all the Tatyar were to accept his decision to go Aman. Since Ingwë, Finwë, and Elwë had to persuade their people to undertake the journey, we know that they did not have the autocratic power of Eldarin kings while all the Elves lived in Cuiviënen. The social structure of the primitive Elven culture must therefore have been substantially different from that of the Eldarin realms in later ages. Fëanor, too, had to persuade the Noldor to follow him into exile, but he was making an emotional appeal during a time of crisis while he was still under the ban of the Valar. His legitimacy as their king was questionable, since Fingolfin was technically still the acting king in Tirion. In Middle-earth, Turgon does not appear to have had to persuade his people to follow him when he moved from Nevrast to Gondolin. He simply made the decision and the entire kingdom moved.

It is thus evident that there was a process of evolution for the authority of the Eldarin leaders. It is certainly arguable that a less sophisticated society may not have provided the eldest Elves with the power of monarchs. But if that is the case, then the assumption that Finwë must be identified with Tata, the eldest of the Tatyar, is further weakened. Such identification need not be limited to identification of character with character. It is not apparent that Finwë has to be a descendant of Tata and Tatie. He could have come from any family and risen to prominence through his courage and wisdom.

Nonetheless, the Noldor, more than any other Elven people whose culture Tolkien wrote about, maintained a very patriarchal system. The Noldorin kings achieved a near absolute authority over their people, much like the authority Melkor wielded over his own subjects. In a way, the Noldor became a parody of the very thing they despised: Morgoth's realm. Their social structure must have been compelled toward such autocracy by ancient customs more than by experimentation. In fact, it is reasonable to infer from the names of several Avarin groups that the Tatyar were more prone to division than the Nelyar. If that is so, then Finwë's ability to retain the full loyalty of his people in Aman was remarkable. Fëanor was far less popular than his father.

So, whereas the autocratic authority of the later Noldorin kings implies that they may have inherited a primal authority from Tata, Finwë's personality may have played a greater role in establishing that authority than his heritage. That is, for the Noldor, descent from Finwë would be more important than descent from Tata. Which is not to say that the original chieftains of the Tatyar should not have been descended from Tata. It makes sense that, if Ilúvatar selected Tata to awaken first of the Elves, he would have the qualities of a natural leader Ilúvatar felt the Tatyar would require. Hence, Tata would (if he were a good father) raise his children to be good leaders, too. Leadership would have become the natural role of the family simply because the family exercised leadership. Hence, if Finwë had brothers or cousins who elected not to go to Valinor, they may have become the leaders of the Tatyarin Avari.

The issue of whether Finwë had other relatives is interesting though not necessarily critical to understanding the Noldorin culture. There were other princely houses among the Noldor. They may have shared a kinship with the royal house through common descent from Tata, but Tolkien never explores the subject in any published writing. There were princes in Gondolin, such as Glorfindel (whom Gandalf tells Frodo is descended of a house of princes). Unfortunately, the history of the Gondolin texts makes it impossible to determine how many princes there were in Gondolin, or what their relationship to the Finwëans (if any) may have been. Voronwë claimed kinship with the House of Fingolfin. A common descent from Tata might explain that apparent discrepancy. A descent through a daughter of Fingolfin (one of whom went into exile) might also explain Voronwë's claim. But some people argue that Voronwë's statement may only imply a feudal relationship between his family and Fingolfin's family (a highly improbable interpretation, since there is virtually no textual support for such relationships and nomenclature in Tolkien's works).

So Gondolin offers us no insight into the Noldor's complex social hierarchies. However, Nargothrond is a different story. There is at least one house of princes there who (apparently) do not claim kinship with the Finwëans. That is the family of Guilin, whose son Gwindor bore the chief responsibility for launching the disastrous attack that initiated the Nirnaeth Arnoediad. Gwindor also brought Túrin to Nargothrond, which ultimately led to the end of that kingdom. Tolkien says Gwindor is "a very valiant prince". Elsewhere Gwindor is "a lord of Nargothrond". His rank is therefore a noble one, but he is not a Finwëan. Whether Guilin's family was regarded as noble from the ancient times or had been elevated to that status by Finwë or one of the kings of Nargothrond is a mystery.

What we can be sure of, however, is that the Finwëans derived their special status from Finwë himself. The Noldorin monarchy began with Finwë, and all the legitimate kings of the Noldor claimed descent from him. Furthermore, no Noldorin prince outside the family ever established a realm of his own. The esteem with which Finwë's family was held by his people was strong enough that they limited their choices of kings only to his descendants. Hence, even if all the

Tatyarin chieftains were descended from Tata, such a heritage was insufficient to justify a royal prestige.

Finwë's charisma is also evident in the fact that more than one Elven woman loved him. In "Laws and Customs among the Eldar" (*Morgoth's Ring*, pp. 207-53), Tolkien writes: "The Eldar wedded once only in life, and for love or at the least by free will upon either part....Marriage, save for rare ill chances or strange fates, was the natural course of life for all Eldar....Those who would afterwards become wedded might choose one another early in youth, even as children (and indeed this happened often in days of peace)...."

If the Eldar's natural course led them to marry only once in life, then Finwë's ability to attract and love more than one wife was extremely unusual. His personality must have been extremely charismatic. It is not fair to say that something may have been wrong with Indis for loving Finwë even while he was married to Miriel. Her love was undoubtedly natural and pure. There is never a hint of any sign of shadow or corruption in either Finwë or Indis in the stories concerning their marriage. Rather, their marriage is recognized as a sign of healing in Finwë's grief over Míriel's death and refusal to return to life. Although the narrative says things would have been better for the Noldor in general had Finwë not remarried, the love he and Indis shared seems to have been as strong and natural as the love that any normal first marriage among the Eldar would have been founded upon.

The distinctive personality of Finwë must therefore have been conveyed to all of his children in one fashion or another. Growing up in the household of a leader whose people may have idolized him would have imbued Finwë's children with a sense of prestige. But seeing their father interact with his people as a leader, and undoubtedly hearing him lecture (as fathers are wont to do) on how to govern or lead people would have provided Fëanor, Fingolfin, and Finarfin with a spectacular education in the Noldorin equivalent of the personality cult. Finwë must have been very good at judging the moods of others and figuring out how to get what he wanted. The Noldor thus developed a very close relationship with their king, much closer (it would seem) than that between the Vanyar and Ingwë or the Teleri and Elwë and Olwë.

However, Tolkien added a bit of linguistically inspired political division to the environment which produced the Finwëans. That is, in "The Shibboleth of Fëanor", Tolkien documented the conscious transition most of the Noldor undertook in their daily speech between use of one sound (þ, called a thorn, phonetically related to *th*) and another (*s*, which replaced the older sound). The Vanyar, who adhered to ancient practice, retained the older sound. Fëanor adhered to it as a symbol of his love for his mother. Finwë, on the other hand, took up the new pronunciation, perhaps as a sign that he was moving on with his life. Indis took up the new pronunciation, too, because she felt she had joined the Noldor and should speak as they did.

Fëanor's intransigence was derived in part from the stubborn nature he had inherited from his mother. But the Valar's decision to forbid Míriel's return to life in order to allow Finwë and Indis to marry led Fëanor to conclude that Indis was the source of his unhappiness. He apparently did not attend the council where the Valar debated the pros and cons of allowing Finwë to take a second wife, so he did not understand that it was Míriel's intransigence which had led to the conundrum. The Valar wanted only what was just, and in their view (particularly Manwë's), Miriel was being too selfish. She had therefore forfeited all her rights as a living, incarnate being. All Fëanor saw was the fact that he was never to speak with his mother again, which would seem (in his grief and anger) like a broken promise from the Valar. After all, the Elves were supposed to live with the life of Arda. Miriel should have been restored to life eventually. That was the natural state for an Elf.

Thus, when Finwë and Indis married, Fëanor's resentment of her intrusion into his family assured that he would isolate himself from Finwë's new household. As Fëanor raised his sons, they questioned why their uncles and aunts spoke a different way from them. Fëanor's response was merely to deride the choices of his relatives. He and his family would respect the language of his beloved mother. Fëanor made it a personal issue, and in so doing alienated many of the Noldorin lore masters who would otherwise have accepted and supported his arguments against the linguistic shift. By comparison, consider how (in American idiom), many people today use the pronoun "myself" incorrectly (by the old rules). When speaking of another person and oneself, we should use "me" in the objective and "I" in the subjective. Yet many people have been rebuked by teachers and relatives for using "me" when they should use "I", so they substitute "myself" for "me".

In other words, instead of saying, "They were speaking to my sister and me", most people now say, "They were speaking to my sister and myself". "Myself" is, according to rules of grammar, a *reflexive* pronoun. It should only be preceded by "I" or "me", and not used alone. Now, imagine if Prince Charles were to launch a personal crusade to correct every person who uses "myself" incorrectly. How long would it be before people decided he was too arrogant to respect? And imagine that while Prince Charles is campaigning against the vulgar idiom, his mother the Queen begins to use "myself" incorrectly. The people's love and respect for a popular monarch will remain intact, because she speaks like they do and doesn't make a fuss over a small issue. That love and respect will not transfer to her son, though.

Fëanor thus elevated a minor scholarly disagreement to the status of a political agenda. All those Noldor who used "s" were against him, and all those who retained the thorn pronunciation were his supporters. Ironically, Fëanor ignored the Vanyar, who were practitioners of the thorn-pronunciation, and he pursued an alliance with the Teleri, whose speech was radically different from the Quenya spoken by the Noldor and Vanyar. Furthermore, Finarfin retained the thorn-pronunciation for his own purposes. The "Shibboleth" notes that Galadriel switched to the "s" pronunciation in part because of her animosity toward Fëanor.

All these life-threatening changes in pronunciation thus symbolized the polarization of Noldorin loyalties. But, more importantly, they underscored the transition between the primitive authority of the Elven chieftains to the autocracy of the Noldorin kings. Fëanor was going to have his language his way, and he gathered about him all the people who felt as he did. But because he was such a masterful person, he came to dominate the decisions of his followers. Their transition to almost political automata was completed by their willing participation in the attack on Alqualondë. They may have gone in thinking they were just stealing ships, but when the fighting started getting bloody, none of the Fëanorians appear to have stood aside and said, "Wait a minute! What are we doing?"

To a lesser extent, the division over the pronunciation must have influenced the other Noldor not merely to support Finwë and Fingolfin. It must have forced them into an "us and them" frame of mind. One either followed Fëanor or one followed Finwë and Fingolfin. Subsequently, Finwë's prestige among the Noldor must have been diminished. He was, after all, dishonoring his own son by not supporting Fëanor. It must have been a proud moment for the Fëanorians when Finwë departed from Tirion to live with his son in exile. Although Finwë's role in the dispute between Fëanor and Fingolfin is silent, it would be only a small leap of the imagination to color him vexed as, when he tries to restore peace between his sons, he finds the Valar have stepped in to deliver their own justice. Then, to add injury to insult, they exile his son, disregarding anything he may have said on Fëanor's behalf (not to mention Fingolfin's own attempt at reconciliation). Admittedly, drawing a sword on your brother in public is a pretty nasty piece of business. But Finwë's authority was compromised. He was not permitted to dispense justice within his own family, much less among his own people.

Finwë's act of rebellion was the true beginning of the rebellion of Fëanor, despite all the conflicts which had preceded it. Melkor's meddling may have inflamed the Noldor's pride, but it was ultimately the Valar's own decision to exile Fëanor from Tirion which set the final sequence of events into motion. Which is not to say the rebellion would not have occurred otherwise. Fëanor may eventually have been pushed over the edge regardless of what happened. Melkor's murder of Finwë threw Fëanor into the final deep funk which resulted in what could be characterized as his madness. Fëanor lost all rational perspective, and because he had been honing his powers of persuasion through the years, and because the Noldor were a nation grieving over the entirely unexpected death of their king and the loss of the Two

Trees, Fëanor had the perfect moment to infect his people with his madness.

The dynamic of the Finwëans' personality cult, as it were, was thus founded upon a strong emotional bond between the kings and the people. Fëanor had alienated most of the Noldor by the time Melkor murdered Finwë, but misery loves company and Fëanor had plenty of company after Melkor and Ungoliant killed the Two Trees and raided Formenos. All of Finwë's just and popular decisions through the equivalent of thousands of years had prepared the way for Fëanor's emotional appeal. He may have had the powers of an incredible motivational speaker to begin with, but Fëanor probably could not have swayed the Noldor to join him at any other time in their history. Finwë's death and the way Melkor had caught the Valar completely off guard in their own realm must have shaken the Noldor's faith in Manwë and Varda.

Yet, Fëanor did not have everything in his favor. Fingolfin, equally grieving for their father, and much loved and respected by the Noldor, argued against Fëanor. The debate lasted a long time. There must have been some harsh and bitter words. The sarcasm and ridicule may have rolled off Fëanor's tongue fast and furious. Fingolfin may have stopped holding back for a while and simply unloaded on Fëanor. All we are told is "fierce words awoke, so that once again wrath came near to the edge of swords." What lay at stake was not simply the fate of the Noldorin nation, nor even just the kingship of the Noldor. Personal issues were pressing forward and both Fëanor and Fingolfin were investing (or had invested) themselves in matters of prestige and personal power. That is, Fingolfin by this time felt he should be king of the Noldor. He was, in some ways, nearly as proud and arrogant as his brother.

Fingolfin's Machiavellian ambitions were awakened by Melkor's lies, which had sown dissent among the Noldor. It was when Fingolfin made an emotional plea to their father to restrain Fëanor that Fëanor drew his sword upon Fingolfin. Fëanor accused Fingolfin of harboring royal ambition. It may be that Fëanor was reading his brother's desires correctly. Fingolfin, after all, didn't speak funny the way Fëanor did.

Nor was he running around with swords, threatening relatives in front of the king and his people. He may have deemed himself a better candidate for kingship than his brother (although there was, at that time, no reason for anyone to be thinking about who should succeed their father). *Let the better prince rule* was the order of the day, but Fingolfin was apparently no better at avoiding Melkor's manipulations than Fëanor. Hence, when Finwë gave up his crown to share Fëanor's exile, Fingolfin had no choice but to humbly accept the weighty responsibility of ruling the majority of the Noldor in Tirion.

Ten years of kingship must be a very addicting tenure. Fingolfin might have restored the crown to his father, but he did not wish to give it up to Fëanor. When Melkor murdered Finwë, the Noldorin kingship fell into immediate dispute. Though the Valar had not yet restored to him to his place among the Noldor, Fëanor entered Tirion and summoned to the Mindon of Finwë. Such a summons was a clear usurpation of royal authority. More infuriatingly, Fëanor declared himself the rightful King of the Noldor. Fingolfin had not abdicated his own authority, however temporary that was intended to be. As Finwë had stood before the Tatyar ages before and offered them a new life in Aman, Fëanor now stood before the Noldor and made a similar offer of a new life in Middle-earth. The old social structure was rendered meaningless. Fingolfin had to respond to Fëanor, but if his hope was to restore Finwë's kingship under his own rule that proved vain. The majority of the Noldor wanted nothing more to do with the Valar and Valinor. Some of them were moved to join the rebellion despite a strong attachment to Valinor. And a small part of the nation refused to accept either Fëanor or Fingolfin if they were determined to lead the Noldor into exile, even if Fingolfin only went along just to make sure Fëanor didn't get everyone killed.

In the end, Finarfin proved to be the only son of Finwë with any real sense. He apparently never bought into the lies Melkor sowed among the Noldor. Whenever a great liar spreads confusion, there are usually a few people who stay above the discord, and Finarfin was that kind of individual. He, too, tried to persuade the Noldor not to follow Fëanor into exile. And, like Fingolfin, he went along reluctantly mostly because his children wanted to try their luck in Middle-earth, and because he feared what might happen to the people if they were left to the mercies of Fëanor's leadership. When the Noldor attacked Alqualondë and the Valar condemned them to a terrible fate, Finarfin quietly withdrew from the rebellion and sought the pardon of the Valar (and, hopefully, the Teleri, his kinsfolk by marriage). In the end, the kingship was bestowed upon Finarfin, whose hands were bloodless and whose heart had the least ambition among the sons of Finwë.

Other members of the Finwëan family who have received virtually no attention through the years are Finwë's daughters by Indis. Finwë had *daughters*? Well, that is what "The Shibboleth of Fëanor" tells us. Findis was, in fact, the first-born of the children of Finwë and Indis. She was apparently very much like her mother in temperament. Indis stayed in Tirion when Finwë joined Fëanor at Formenos. She played no part in the governance of the Noldor, it would seem, and Findis seems to have stayed close to her mother. When news came of Finwë's death, both Indis and Findis departed and returned to the Vanyar.

Originally, Finwë was to have three daughters by Indis. Christopher Tolkien mentions that, from 1959 through 1968, this was the case in the several genealogies his father prepared for the Finwëans. However, the second daughter, Faniel, is never mentioned in "The Shibboleth", and it may be that Tolkien intended to drop her from the family. As provided in the Shibboleth, Irien (originally called Irimë, the third daughter) was born between Fingolfin and Finarfin. She was also called Lalwendë, and it was this name which was Sindarinized into Lalwen. She and Fingolfin were very close and she accompanied him into exile. We hear nothing more of her, but some people have wondered if Aranwë, the father of Voronwë, might not gave been Lalwen's husband or son. Presumably, Lalwen settled in Hithlum and may have been slain or captured after the Nirnaeth. And since she was close to Fingolfin, she may have actively supported his claims to the kingship.

Fingolfin asserted his royalty by taking his father's name. Finwë had named all three of his sons after himself: Curufinwë (Fëanor), Nolofinwë (Fingolfin), and Aranfinwë (Finarfin). Fingolfin, it appears, initiated the custom of taking their father's name as a sign of royal authority. Hence, he called himself Finwë Nolofinwë, perhaps during the debate with Fëanor in Tirion, more likely after the attack on Alqualondë. The Shibboleth says: "Fingolfin had prefixed the name Finwë to Nolofinwë before the Exiles reached Middle-earth. This was in pursuance of his claim to be the chieftain of all the Noldor after the death of Finwë, and so enraged Fëanor that it was no doubt one of the reasons for his treachery in abandoning Fingolfin and the stealing away with all the ships."

Finarfin did not take the name "Finwë". Curiously, the Shibboleth says that Finrod himself created the name "Finwë Arafinwë", or "Finarfin", after the death of Fingolfin, at which time the Noldor became divided into separate kingships. Although this statement would seem to contradict *The Silmarillion* (which explicitly mentions the kings of the Noldor prior to Fingolfin's death), Tolkien's intentions are not clear. Still, the use of Finwë's name as a prefix became a royal prerogative. At some point, Finwë's name may have become synonymous with the word title of "king", and it would be appropriate to speak of the ruler of the Noldor as The Finwë. After the First Age, Gil-galad would have been the Finwë in Middle-earth.

The wives of Finwë's sons received little attention from Tolkien. Fëanor's wife, Nerdanel, was the daughter of a smith named Mahtan in *The Silmarillion*. Mahtan's family possessed brownish-red hair and he may have been the leader of a community of Noldor who dwelt close to Aulë's halls. Nerdanel had a ruddy complexion which her son Caranthir inherited from her. It may be that they were freckled. In a note appended to "The Shibboleth of Fëanor", Nerdanel's father is named *Aulendur* and *Urundil*, and *Aulendur* is said to have supplanted *Mahtan*, which nonetheless was the name Christopher used for him in *The Silmarillion*. Another name for this character, which Christopher is not sure of, may have been *Sarmo*. He wore a copper circlet around his head and was very fond of copper. Maedhros was apparently much like him in temperament and appearance, and also wore a copper circlet. When Fëanor became too contentious for Nerdanel to put up with him any more, she returned to her father's house. Aulë persuaded Aulendur and his family not to follow Fëanor into exile. Nerdanel asked Fëanor to leave their youngest sons in Aman, but he refused.

She then foresaw that the youngest would never set foot in Middle-earth.

Fingolfin's wife was Anairë. She was a Noldo but all we are told of her is that she was a friend to Ëarwen (Finarfin's wife) and that she refused to follow Fingolfin into exile "largely because of her friendship with Ëarwen". Ëarwen was the daughter of Olwë of Alqualondë. She had silver hair like other members of her family. In an early history of Galadriel published in *Unfinished Tales*, Tolkien wrote that Finrod "had also from his Telerin mother a love of the sea and dreams of far lands that he had never seen". It is not clear if Ëarwen was old enough to have been born in Middle-earth, but the text seems to imply that the Teleri of Alqualondë (or at least Ëarwen) were not wholly alienated from Middle-earth. The Teleri had spent a great deal of time living on the isle of Tol Eressëa before Ulmo commanded Ossë to teach them the craft of ship-building so they could finally sail to Aman and join the other Eldar there.

Fëanor and Nerdanel had seven sons, as *The Silmarillion* tells us: Maedhros, Maglor, Celegorm, Curufin, Caranthir, Amrod, and Amras. The Shibboleth says their father-names (given in Quenya) were Nelyafinwë ("Finwe Third", as in Finwe III, Finwe the Third), Kanafinwë, Kurufinwë (spelled Curufinwë in *The Silmarillion*), Morifinwë, Pityafinwë ("Little Finwë"), and Telufinwë ("Last Finwë"). Maedhros is said to be the most handsome of the sons, and Curufin was their father's favorite because he was most like Fëanor in spirit and skill. Curufin also resembled his father more closely than the other sons. Their mother-names were Maitimo, Makalaure, Tyelkormo, Atarinke ("Little Father"), Carnistir ("Red Faced"), Ambarusso and Ambarusso. The two Ambarussos were twins and Fëanor asked Nerdanel to give one of them a different name. She chose Umbarto ("Fated"), which Fëanor changed to Ambarto ("Exalted"), and he gave that name to the youngest.

"The Shibboleth of Fëanor" says that Nerdanel asked Fëanor to leave her the twins, or at least one of them, when he was preparing to lead the Noldor into exile. He refused, rebuking her for following Aulë's advice instead of her husband's will, and Nerdanel foretold that one of the sons would not reach Middle-earth. When Fëanor burned the stolen ships at Losgar, he assembled his sons on the shore and only found six of them. Then Ambarussa told him that Ambarto had slept on his ship. "That ship I destroyed first," Fëanor replied. "Then right you gave the name to youngest of your children," Ambarussa replied, "and *Umbarto* 'The Fated' was its true form." An end note says that Ambarussa's name became Amros in Sindarin (not Amrod, as recorded in *The Silmarillion*). Wherever *The Silmarillion* speaks of Amrod and Amras after the burning at Losgar, it is more correct to understand that only Amros was present.

Of Fëanor and Nerdanel's sons, only three took wives: Maglor, Curufin, and Caranthir. In Note 7 appended to the essay "Of Dwarves and Men" (*The Peoples of Middle-earth*, pp. 295-330), Christopher cites a note his father made in 1966 after the second edition of *The Lord of the Rings* was published. There, Tolkien decided that Celebrimbor (named lord of Eregion in the appendices) must be the son of Curufin, for Maedhros and the twins had no wives. Curufin, inheriting the greatest part of his father's skill among the seven, passed this skill (and presumably much lore) on to Celebrimbor, who disapproved of his father's behavior in Nargothrond. When Celegorm and Curufin were driven out of Nargothrond, Celebrimbor stayed behind. Curufin's wife elected not to follow her husband into exile, so she remained in Aman among the people ruled by Finarfin (and was, therefore, presumably a Noldo). There is no mention of any other grand-children of Fëanor and Nerdanel, and the fates of the wives of Maglor and Caranthir are not given.

Fingolfin and Anairë had four children: Findekano (Fingon), Turukano (Turgon), Irissë (Aredhel), and Arakano (Argon). Although Anairë remained in Valinor when Fingolfin went into exile, all their children followed Fingolfin. Fingon led the vanguard of Fingolfin's host, and he rushed to help Fëanor's Noldor against the Teleri of Alqualondë when he learned there was a battle at the haven. Turgon led a third of the Noldor of Fingolfin's host, and he was accompanied by his wife Elenwë of the Vanyar. Irissë was close to Turgon as their aunt Irien (Lalwen) was close to Fingolfin. Irissë remained with Turgon's people until she persuaded him to let her visit Fingon in Hithlum. Instead, after leaving Gondolin, she fled from her escort and wandered east into Nan Elmoth. There she married Ëol and bore him a son, Maeglin, with whom she returned to Gondolin many years later.

Arakano emerged relatively late, probably after the second edition of *The Lord of the Rings* was published. He is described as "the tallest of the brothers and the most impetuous". Tolkien found it difficult to assign him a role in the generally complete history, and at first he devised deaths for Arakano in Aman. But eventually Tolkien decided that Fingolfin's host would be attacked by an army of Orcs as the Noldor passed south along the coast of Middle-earth. There Arakano would both distinguish and sacrifice himself for his people:

> When the onset of the Orks [sic] caught the host at unawares as they marched southwards and the ranks of the Eldar were giving way, he sprang forward and hewed a path through the foes, daunted by his stature and the terrible light of his eyes, till he came to the Ork-captain and felled him. Then though he himself was surrounded and slain, the Orks were dismayed, and the Noldor pursued them with slaughter.

Arakano's name was thus never formally changed into Sindarin, "but the Sindarin form *Argon* was often later given as a name by Noldor and Sindar in memory of his valour" (*Peoples of Middle-earth*, p. 345).

Fingon was also impetuous. He not only rushed to Fëanor's aid, he led the counter assaults against Morgoth's forces, whenever Hithlum was attacked. And when Gwindor led his company of Nargothrondian soldiers against Morgoth's army at the Nirnaeth, Fingon could no longer contain himself. Instead of waiting for Maedhros, as he should, he donned his helmet, mounted his horse, and charged off toward glory, death, and defeat. Fingon was undoubtedly one of the greatest warriors of the Eldar, for it required more than one Balrog to slay him in the end, and his recorded personal accomplishments on the field of battle out-numbered those of other Elven princes.

Turgon was undoubtedly the wisest of Fingolfin's children, and for a reason not disclosed he was one of Ulmo's favorites among the

Noldorin princes. It may be that, since Turgon took up rule over the Sindarin Elves of Nevrast, Ulmo felt Turgon would be most sympathetic to the sea. In the end, Turgon was the only Noldorin king to commission the building of ships for the purpose of seeking aid from Aman. The Shibboleth records that Turgon's wife, Elenwë, perished in the Helcaraxë. She and their daughter, Itaril, fell and Turgon rescued Itaril but Elenwë was crushed by falling ice. It would appear, from a cryptic remark in the Shibboleth, that Irissë and Elenwë were very close friends.

When Fingolfin named Findekano, he did not necessarily use the stem for "Finwe", an ancient Elvish name given at a time when names were bestowed for the way they sounded. Nor, the Shibboleth tells us, would it have been necessary. The use of a similar word honored the ancestral name. Findekano is described as wearing "his long dark hair in great plaits braided with gold". Tolkien was of several minds about Findekano's personal life. Although *The Silmarillion* tells us that Gil-galad was his son, Christopher Tolkien admits in both *The War of the Jewels* and *The Peoples of Middle-earth* that he was in error when he incorporated Gil-galad into the book as Fingon's son. Christopher mentions that all the genealogical tables provide Fingon with an unnamed wife and two children: *Ernis* (later *Erien*) and *Finbor*. But this family was stricken from the final genealogy and Tolkien wrote a note saying Fingon "had no child or wife".

It would undoubtedly have been necessary to construe some depressing fate for both Erien and Finbor, as Finbor would have to be Fingon's heir. It served Tolkien's purpose to move Gil-galad to the family of Finarfin. Hence, the High Kingship passed from the childless Fingon to Turgon, and then from Fingolfin's family (the male line of which ended with Turgon) to Finarfin's.

The children of Finarfin and Ëarwen were Findarato Ingoldo (Finrod), Angarato (Angrod), Aikanaro (Aegnor), and Newendë Artanis (later called Altariel, Galadriel). *The Silmarillion* places Orodreth (Artaher or Arothir) among Finarfin's sons, but the final decision was to make him the son of Angrod and Eldalôtë (*Eþellos*, *Edhellos* in Sindarin). She was a Noldo, and Arothir was born in Aman. *The Silmarillion* says that Orodreth stood beside Finarfin in pleading with the Noldor not to follow Fëanor into exile. It would not be entirely inconsistent with the final genealogy for Arothir to retain that role. He was a reluctant warrior-king, and only gradually allowed himself to be swayed by Túrin's aggressive policies.

Tolkien's final decision on Finrod was puzzling. In August 1965, he wrote a brief explanation of Gil-galad's descent. The text says "Finrod left his wife in Valinor and had no children in exile". Finrod's (here unnamed) wife must be Amarië of the Vanyar (mentioned in *The Silmarillion* as a love he left behind in Valinor). But the sentence could mean one of three things: that Finrod and Amarië had children who remained in Valinor, that they had no children, or that they had children after he was restored to life by the Valar. It is tempting to rationalize the claim of Gildor Inglorion, whom Frodo, Sam, and Pippin meet in the Shire, with this rather ambiguous statement. That is, Gildor told Frodo that he was "of the house of Finrod". So far as we know, there was only one Finrod. Originally, the name Finrod had been given to the father, and the prince who founded the realm of Nargothrond was named Inglor. But while revising *The Lord of the Rings* for the second edition, Tolkien changed Finrod to Finarphir (later it became Finarphin, Finarfin) and Inglor to Finrod. But he did not change Gildor's name.

If Gildor is truly a descendant of Finrod, he must have been born in Valinor. But if that is the case, how did he arrive in Middle-earth, and when? Tolkien seems to have overlooked Gildor completely. And people are quick to point out that Gildor names himself an Exile (or, rather, he says, "We are Exiles"). How could Gildor be an Exile if he was born after Finrod was restored to life? The answer to that question is simple: any of the children of the Noldor who went into exile, and who were living in Middle-earth, would be Exiles (a sub-group of the Noldor) as much as they were still Noldor. Yet there is no text which associates Gildor with the renamed Finrod/Finarfin or the renamed Inglor/Finrod (other than his own name, which means "scion of Inglor").

A further difficulty arising from connecting Gildor with Finrod is that, if he were alive in Middle-earth when Gil-galad perished, should he not have been eligible to claim the High Kingship over the Noldor? It may be that such a claim would be deemed invalid, since the kingship had passed to Orodreth's line (just as it had passed from Fëanor's line to Fingolfin's and then to Finarfin's). The kingship could go down the line of descent but not up to a previously abandoned branch of the family. Yet that is unsatisfying. It could also be that Gildor would have arrived with one of the Istari, although only Glorfindel is said to have ever arrived in Middle-earth after the Downfall of Númenor. In fact, there is a note associated with the Shibboleth which states that "little has been ever heard in Middle-earth of Aman after the departure of the Noldor. Those who returned thither have never come back, since the change of the world. To Númenor in its first days they went often, but small part of the lore and histories of Númenor survived its Downfall."

Here again we have a frustratingly ambiguous statement. "Those who returned [to Aman] have never come back, *since the change of the world.*" What is the change of the world, however, if not the event where Ilúvatar made the world round, removing Aman from the circles and destroying Númenor? The following sentence seems to imply that the Noldor (of Tol Eressëa) only sailed as far east as Númenor in its early years. Still, the passage does not completely rule out the possibility of an eastward passage by someone of a younger generation. In fact, in one of his final notes on Glorfindel, Tolkien decided that he had indeed returned to Middle-earth by way of Númenor in the middle of the Second Age, when Gil-galad was preparing for Sauron's assault in the 17th century (the War of the Elves and Sauron lasted from 1695 to 1701).

Whatever Gildor's true relationship to the Finwëans may be, he cannot be a descendant of Finwe who passed into exile with Fëanor and Fingolfin. Nor can he be a son of Finrod born in Middle-earth. If he is a *descendant* of Finrod, though he might originally have been Finrod's *son*, his name as preserved in the canon of *The Lord of the Rings* implies there must be an Inglor, who could perhaps be Finrod and Amarië's son born in Valinor after Finrod was restored to life. But such speculations, lacking any textual support, go no further.

Galadriel's history is as convoluted and puzzling as Gildor's ancestry. Tolkien changed her history more than once, and in doing so altered her relationships with both Celebrimbor and Celeborn. Celeborn was originally a Wood Elf, but in time he was changed to a Sindarin Elf related to Elwë through a younger brother Elmo. Yet, in the last year of his life, Tolkien decided that Celeborn should be a grandson of Olwë, born in Alqualondë. It seems that Tolkien had forgotten about the ancient (in terms of his life) Eldarin restriction against marriage between first cousins (which principle is referred to in the story of Maeglin, although as published in *The Silmarillion* that story is mostly the work of Christopher's editing and compression of older materials).

Nonetheless, we can be sure that Galadriel was a daughter of Finarfin and Ëarwen, and that she was never on good terms with Fëanor. And yet, despite her feelings toward Fëanor, Galadriel shared Finrod's dreams of other lands, and she was as ambitious as any of the younger princes of her day. She wished to rule her own realm. Regardless of whether she followed Fëanor into exile or (as is told in the late story from 1972) preceded him with Celeborn, Galadriel was swept up into the doom of the Noldor. Like her people, she was forbidden to return to Aman. It also remains certain that Galadriel somehow became closely associated with Melian in Doriath for a time, and that she and Celeborn passed over the Ered Lindon before Nargothrond and Gondolin were destroyed.

Galadriel's departure from Beleriand is not mentioned in *The Silmarillion*. I suspect it would have occurred sometime between the Dagor Bragollach (455) and the Nirnaeth Arnoediad (473). Many northern Sindar fled east over Ered Lindon during or immediately following the Dagor Bragollach. The best opportunity for Galadriel and Celeborn to leave would be when these Sindar were forsaking the war. Galadriel and Celeborn would have been welcomed among them, and Galadriel's disapproval of the Noldorin policies may have induced her to get out of Beleriand while the getting was good.

Angarato (Angrod) brought his wife, Eldalôtë (Edhellos), and son, Arothir (Orodreth), into exile. They settled in Dorthonion with Aikanaro (Aegnor), who never married. Angrod possessed great strength and he earned the *epesse* (a nickname) "Angamaitë" (iron-handed). Angrod perished in the Dagor Bragollach, but Arothir escaped and fled south to join Finrod in Nargothrond.

Aikanaro (Aegnor) is said to have been "renowned as one of the most valiant of the warriors, greatly feared by the Orks: in wrath or battle the light of his eyes was like flame, though otherwise he was a generous and noble spirit. But in early youth the fiery light could be observed; while his hair was notable: golden like his brothers and sister, but strong and stiff, rising upon his head like flames." Aegnor took no wife, but it emerges in "Athrabeth Finrod ah Andreth" (found in *Morgoth's Ring*) that he fell in love with Andreth, a Bëorian wise woman, while she was quite young. And though he wished to marry her, he had apparently confided in Finrod (or Finrod understood implicitly) that he had foreseen his own death in battle, and he did not wish to leave her widowed, or any children she might bear him orphaned. Andreth grew quite old and may have lived until the Dagor Bragollach, although her death date is not recorded.

The Finwëan genealogy winds down to a few stray names in the following generations: Celebrimbor, son of Curufin; Idril (Itaril), daughter of Turgon; Arothir (Orodreth), son of Angrod and Eldalôtë; and Celebrian, daughter of Galadriel and Celeborn. Idril married Tuor and bore a son, Ëarendil. She was wise enough to foresee the need of a hidden escape path out of Gondolin, and her hair was as golden as her Vanyarin mother's hair. Arothir (Orodreth) remained close by Finrod and was among the few nobles who supported Finrod when he felt compelled to repay his debt to Beren (Beren's father Barahir had saved Finrod's life in battle). Finrod made Arothir his steward in Nargothrond, and when word came of Finrod's death, Arothir drove Celegorm and Curufin out of the kingdom.

Arothir married a northern Sindarin lady, although her name is not recorded. Their children were Ereinion (scion of kings) and Finduilas. Finduilas was golden-haired, and Arothir himself must have been golden-haired. Although she loved Gwindor, when she met Túrin she could not help but fall for him. And yet Túrin did not return her feelings. Finduilas was taken prisoner when Nargothrond fell to

Glaurung and his Orcs, but the Orcs slew her and other prisoners when they were waylaid by Men from Brethil.

Ereinion escaped the sack of Nargothrond and made his way south to the Mouths of Sirion. From there he reached Cirdan on the isle of Balar, and when word came of Gondolin's fall Ereinion was named High King of the Noldor-in-Exile. His mother named him Gil-galad.

The royal authority of Finwë ended with Gil-galad. But the ambitions of the Finwëan princes appear to have stopped with Gil-galad as well. For though he established a mighty kingdom in Lindon which lasted more than 3,000 years, he apparently took no wife. Ëarendil left Middle-earth forever, and the ambitions of his ancestors seem to have been realized only by his son Elros, who when given a choice between mortality and Elven-kind elected to become the first King of Númenor (and therefore mortal). His brother Elrond chose to be of Elven-kind but never established his own kingdom. He governed Imladris as an outpost of Gil-galad's kingdom in the Second Age and maintained it as a stronghold of Eldarin power in the Third Age. But Elrond never took the title of king. It may be that, legally, he felt he could not claim a kingship, since Ëarendil was the son of a mortal man and not an Elf king.

But perhaps Elrond recognized that the time of the Elvish Finwëans had come and gone. For four thousand years they ruled mighty kingdoms in Middle-earth, and defied their enemies. Despite their faults, the Finwëans imparted great wisdom to Men, and through Idril's marriage to Tuor they bestowed an ancient and noble heritage upon the lordly houses of Númenor and its successor realms. As the Eldarin princes vanished, one by one, their Númenorean cousins ascended to center stage and assumed the central role in the ongoing play of Middle-earth's history.

Chapter 4:
Of thegns and kings
and rangers and things

Maybe only once have I ever seen anyone on the Internet ask how many Rangers would have been guarding Sarn Ford the day the Nazgul showed up. And then no one was able to provide a satisfactory answer. It's a tough question because, so far as we know, J.R.R. Tolkien himself never tried to answer it. And in trying to answer that question for ourselves, we quickly get drawn into digressions and tangents.

Any attempt to figure out how many Rangers were stationed there inevitably gets bound up in an effort to calculate how many Rangers there must have been altogether. An interesting question which also occasionally gets asked is, where did they all go during the War of the Ring? And were the thirty Rangers whom Halbarad led to Rohan the last of their kind? Halbarad's words to Aragorn, "I have thirty with me; that is all of our kindred that could be gathered in haste," seem to imply there were more Rangers who stayed home.

But if Halbarad couldn't gather them all in his haste, where were the other Rangers? They certainly weren't guarding the Shire any more, because Saruman's ruffians were in the process of taking over. They weren't guarding Bree, because Bree was having its own problems with Saruman's ruffians.

The Rangers are a mysterious group. Tolkien never gives us an explicit history of the organization. Nor does he tell us how they managed to survive as a people. It seems most likely that the Rangers were merely a special group supported by the larger Dunadan tribe or nation. When Aranarth decided not to re-establish the Kingdom of Arnor, he took the title of *Chieftain of the Dunedain*, but he also retained the title of *Lord of the Dunedain*.

Since Tolkien left no word unturned, but used them all in both innovative and traditional ways, it may help to examine where the words *chieftain*, *lord*, and *ranger* come from, or at least how they are integrated into Middle-earth's mythology. Tolkien believed that a good mythology was interwoven with the language which expressed that mythology.

> ...It was just as the 1914 War burst on me that I made the discovery that 'legends' depend upon the language to which they belong; but a living language depends equally on the 'legends' which it conveys by tradition. (For example, that the Greek mythology depends far more on the marvellous aesthetic of its language and so of its nomenclature of persons and places and less on its content than people realize, though of course it depends on both. And *vice versa*. Volapuk, Esperanto, Ido, Novial, &c &c are dead, far deader than ancient unused languages, because their authors never invented any Esperanto legends.) So though being a philologist by nature and trade (yet one always primarily interested in the aesthetic rather than the functional aspects of language) I began with language, I found myself involved in inventing 'legends' of the same 'taste'....(*The Letters of J.R.R. Tolkien*, No, 180)

The fruits of Tolkien's labors in forging a confluence between language and mythology are apparent to anyone who has perused "The Etymologies" in *The Lost Road and Other Writings*, or "Quendi and Eldar" in *The War of the Jewels*. To those who are familiar with this material, it may be overreaching to postulate that he derived the legend of the first Elves from the three numbers *min*, *atta/tata*, and *nel*; but then again, who is to say what went through his mind when Tolkien devised the names of the first three numbers? The words would have to have meaning to the Elves who used them, and in that usage they would have to accrue new meanings and associations through the generations. What if the mythology of the Elves had explanations for the earliest meanings?

But the process of developing legends for the languages didn't stop with Elvish. Tom Shippey likes to point out that the place-names in Rohan all have significance with respect to the geography of Rohan. The Emnet, for example, is appropriately named (in Anglo-Saxon), representing literally the kind of name the Rohirrim would have given to the grasslands in their own language: "The first Rohirric place-name we hear is 'Eastemnet', followed soon by 'Westemnet'. An 'emnet' is a thing in Middle-earth, also a place in Norfolk [England], also an asterisk-word [reconstructed, hypothesized] *emnmaeth for 'steppe' or 'prairie', also the green grass which the Riders use as a touchstone for reality." (T.A. Shippey, *The Road to Middle-earth*).

In fact, what Tolkien does, Shippey says, is give "*The Lord of the Rings* a dinosaur-like vitality which cannot be conveyed in any synopsis, but reveals itself in so many thousands of details that only the most biased critical mind could miss them all." And he concludes by adding that "everything Tolkien wrote was based on fusions like that, on 'woses' and 'emnets' and *eoreds*, on 'elvish' or *orthanc* or *panaches*." (Ibid.)

In essence, every noun and verb Tolkien uses has a capacity for telling us something about Middle-earth: we can learn about its past, its cultures, its races, even its geography by examining the vocabularies. One need not be a linguist to see the value in understanding the etymology of the words. The transformational processes studied by the linguists don't reveal much about who the people are, as much as the development of root-words and derivatives. But it is evident that even the English words chosen by Tolkien represent the integration of language and mythology. His unique fiction of offering the reader a *translation* of a long-lost work is closer to reality than we suspect. That is, the translation comes from Tolkien's imagination, from the original expression of this imaginary time in our past, and is not merely a faux attribution of his creativity.

The world exists, grows, and recedes in Tolkien's mind as he writes about it. The long, painful process of working out the geography, races, and history of Middle-earth must be viewed as distinct from the final product. The revisionism Tolkien introduced was a process of clarification, sometimes born of purely non-literary needs, but which optimized the development of the translation and capitalized on the rich depth that preceded it.

In short, we can probably figure out a few things about the Rangers simply by looking at the facts we are given. The word itself, *ranger*, is a good, old-fashioned Middle English word which stems from a French root, which in turn goes back to ancient German, even Anglo-Saxon, roots. Ultimately, it is traceable back to a postulated Indo-European root-word. The modern meaning of the word is not clearly defined. It could denote a specific type of soldier, or merely a wanderer.

And Tolkien does say that Aragorn's people were "a wandering folk" who dwelt in the wilds east of Bree. But was that really all he intended the word *ranger* to convey, or was there more? Actually, we are first introduced to the Rangers in "At the Sign of the Prancing Pony", as Tolkien introduces the reader to Bree: "In those days no other Men had settled dwellings so far west, or within a hundred leagues of the Shire. But in the wild lands beyond Bree there were mysterious wanderers. The Bree-folk called them Rangers, and knew nothing of their origin....They roamed at will southwards, and eastwards even as far as the Misty Mountains; but they were now few and rarely seen."

The name *Rangers* is thus associated with *wanderers*, but they are never referred to by an Elvish term, such as *randiri*. That is a curious omission from a story which seeks to marry the Dunedain to Sindarin traditions. Their names are Sindarin (Aragorn, Halbarad, Arathorn) in origin. The names of their kingdoms (Arthedain, Rhudaur, Cardolan) are usually Sindarin. Even their cities (Fornost Erain, Tharbad) are often named in Sindarin. So why are the Rangers not referred to by a Sindarin term, even by the Elven-folk, who seem to name everyone in their own language? And why do most readers believe that Aragorn's people lived some sort of nomadic life?

Well, the answer to that last question is found in Appendix A to *The Lord of the Rings*, in the section titled "Of the North-kingdom and the Dunedain". This essay provides the only background information on Aragorn's people that is available to most readers. After the history of Arnor has been related, up through the defeat of Angmar, the essay notes:

'When the kingdom ended the Dunedain passed into the shadows and became a secret and wandering people, and their deeds and labours were seldom sung or recorded. Little is now remembered of them since Elrond departed....'

The use of the single quote marks (') implies that the passage is a translation from the original *Red Book of Westmarch*. This paragraph, therefore, is a part of the primary mythology, a continuation of the narrative of the story and not the author's own intrusive commentary. It's an explanation by the mythology of the mythology itself. And since the passage insists that most of what was known about the Dunedain of the north has been lost or forgotten by the time the *Red Book* was composed (sometime in the second century of the Fourth Age), we are not expected to trust the literal explanation. It may be erroneous.

The veracity of the Hobbit historians cannot be wholly discounted, but the function of the word *ranger* may shed more light on their role in Eriadorian society than we have previously considered. Although a *ranger* may indeed be nothing more than a wanderer or a rover, he may also be "a member of an armed troop employed in patrolling a specific region" (note: the preceding definition, and those following, is from Merriam-Webster's *dictionary.com* web site). Now, that sounds very much like Faramir's Rangers, who worked together to maintain Gondor's claim to Ithilien, but it could also describe Halbarad's thirty hastily gathered Rangers.

On the other hand, there are other meanings for the word. For example, "One of a body of mounted troops, formerly armed with short muskets, who range over the country, and often fight on foot." Now, this sounds a bit more like Halbarad's Rangers, although their *ranged* weapons were bows instead of muskets. However, Halbarad seems to imply that they didn't normally work together as a company.

So one must consider the possibility that Tolkien had something like the forest ranger in mind: "The keeper of a public park or forest; formerly, a sworn officer of a forest, appointed by the king's letters patent, whose business was to walk through the forest, recover beasts that had strayed beyond its limits, watch the deer, present trespassers to the next court held for the forest, etc. [Eng.]"

Aragorn's rangers do, in many ways, resemble sworn officers of the forest. But were all of his people in fact Rangers? In seeking the hidden location of Aragorn's people, readers have speculated on which regions of Eriador might have provided a relatively safe and comfortable haven for them. The Emyn Uial, north of the Shire, and the North Downs are popular suggestions. The South Downs are also considered a possibility. But Tolkien actually made a note, now filed among his papers at Marquette University, which stated that Aragorn's people lived in the Angle, between the Bruinen and Mitheithel rivers. The Mitheithel river, as it turns out, does lie about 100 leagues (or 300 miles) east of the Shire.

So if Aragorn's people lived in the Angle, they could hardly have been wandering all over Eriador. The true wanderers were the Rangers themselves, and it would seem reasonable that the Rangers were only a small corps of special officers or soldiers charged with patrolling Eriador, specifically with policing the highways. The Dunedain could not maintain a court and prison system, but they could ensure that local justice received their support. Furthermore, by maintaining the Rangers, the Dunedain continued to assert a royal claim to all of Eriador.

That is, Aranarth seems to have realized that if he simply abandoned Eriador, his descendants would never have the legal authority to re-establish the Kingdom of Arnor. But if at least some of the services of the Kingdom of Arnor were maintained by the Dunedain, then they would have the legal authority to re-establish their realm. The local populations, protected by the Dunedain, would have no reason to oppose the restoration of royal authority. It may even be that Aranarth consulted with Tharbad, the Shire, and Bree (and any other surviving communities) and shared his plan with them. And then, a thousand years later, people had simply forgotten the whole deal, except for the Dunedain.

As a special corps of officers charged with patrolling Eriador, the Rangers would represent the rightful King. But without a court system, they could not really enforce the King's Law. Unlike the Rangers of medieval England, therefore, they would not be protecting the King's Land, but instead were protecting the legacy of the kingdom. All of Eriador's inhabitants were therefore, perhaps, free to settle where they would. Tradition, ties to family and friends, and economics kept the Hobbits and Bree-folk from spreading too far.

Aranarth's appointment of royal officers would derive from his authority as *Lord of the Dunedain*. A *lord* has legal authority over a region. A *chieftain*, on the other hand, is either the leader of a tribe or clan, or "a captain, leader, or commander; a chief; the head of a troop, army, or clan".

As *Chieftain of the Dunedain*, Aranarth may have established his authority as their captain, rather than as their tribal leader. He was already their *lord*, which title Aragorn inherited from Aranarth. And though it may be that Tolkien intended the two words to be used interchangeably, I believe he was implying a distinction between the two offices that Aranarth retained. When the Battle of the Pelennor Fields was over, Aragorn said to Eomer and Imrahil:

> Behold the sun setting in a great fire! It is a sign of the end and fall of many things, and a change in the tides of the world. But this City and realm has rested in the charge of the Stewards for many long years, and I fear that if I enter it unbidden, then doubt and debate may arise, which should not be while this war is fought. I will not enter in, nor make any claim, until it be seen whether we or Mordor shall prevail. Men shall pitch my tents upon the field, and here I will await the welcome of the Lord of the City.

Now, while Eomer and Imrahil recognized the wisdom of Aragorn's conservative approach to Minas Tirith, they also felt he deserved better than to "remain like a beggar at the door". To which Aragorn replied, "Not a beggar. Say a captain of the Rangers, who are unused to cities and houses of stone."

Aragorn's assertion has always seemed like a dissimilation, but that would be uncharacteristic of him. In fact, it would be contrary to his purposes for him suddenly to reverse course and distance himself from the royal claim he had just asserted (through the display of royal emblems on his standard). Although Aragorn expresses some uncertainty earlier in the story, he is by now resolute and committed to the course of action he has taken. He is not going to back down. So his claim to be a captain of the Rangers implies that he is merely asserting one of his titles. He would never lie about something like that, nor would it be necessary for Aragorn to rely upon a generic application of a word with such special meanings.

Which is not to say that Tolkien doesn't use the word *chieftain* in the sense of a tribal or clan leader. That usage occurs throughout the book, from the Prologue, where he speaks of the Hobbit chieftains of the Shire who elect their Thain, to the chieftains of the Haradrim. Some of the uses, however, appear to be similar to the way Aragorn speaks of himself. There is the orc-chieftain in Moria who attacks Frodo. Later on, Aragorn tells his companions that the "Orcs will often pursue foes for many leagues into the plain, if they have a fallen captain to avenge."

The Lord of the Nazgul, referred to as the Black Captain, and the Captain of Mordor, is also the Chieftain of the Nazgul. So how is the reader to know whether Tolkien is speaking of a clan or tribal leader, or of a military leader? The distinction seems to be defined only by the application of both words to a given character. There are no captains among the Hobbits. There are captains among the Orcs. There are both captains and chieftains among the Rohirrim. So a chieftain among the Hobbits is a traditional leader of a people or clan; yet a chieftain among the Orcs or Dunedain, or in Sauron's direct service, is a captain. Among the Rohirrim, a chieftain of a local people (such as Dunhere, the "chieftain of the folk of Harrow-dale") may be appointed a captain within the Muster of Rohan, although Tolkien's description of the Muster of Rohan in *Unfinished Tales* does not allow for the placement of captains within the formal structure. He seems to use the term generically to refer to the military leaders of the Rohirrim, the officers of the Muster are its captains, but they are not *Captains*.

Therefore, a distinction between captain and chieftain, if it exists, supplies an entirely new meaning to Faramir's speech to the people of Gondor before Minas Tirith, when Aragorn formally presents his claim to the throne to the people of the South-kingdom:

> Men of Gondor hear now the Steward of this Realm! Behold! One has come to claim the kingship again at last. Here is Aragorn son of Arathorn, chieftain of the Dúnedain of Arnor, Captain of the Host of the West, bearer of the Star of the North, wielder of the Sword Reforged, victorious in battle, whose hands bring healing, the Elfstone, Elessar of the line of Valandil, Isildur's son, Elendil's son of Númenor. Shall he be king and enter into the City and dwell there?

Now, it's entirely reasonable to argue that Aragorn's title of *Chieftain of the Dunedain of Arnor* means nothing more than that he is the leader of the northern Dunedain. When Elrond introduces Aragorn to Boromir, the Lord of Rivendell says, "He is the Chief of the Dúnedain in the North, and few are now left of that folk". But Aragorn's claim to the kingship of Gondor may have been asserted as one of a successful captain in war.

Another question readers often ask is why none of Aragorn's ancestors ever tried to claim the throne of Gondor. Arvedui tried to claim the throne, of course, but his claim was rejected by the Council of Gondor. Since Arvedui had asserted his claim as the Heir of Isildur, no Heir of Isildur would ever again be able to claim the throne of Gondor. Aragorn's claim was asserted as the Heir of Elendil. When Boromir confided in Elrond's Council about Gondor's troubles, Aragorn asked him, "Do you wish for the House of Elendil to return to the land of Gondor?"

When the Company of the Ring debated what course of action they should take, Aragorn was thrown into doubt. "His own plan," the narrative tells the reader, "while Gandalf remained with them, had been to go with Boromir, and with his sword help to deliver Gondor. For he believed that the message of the dreams was a summons, and that the hour had come at last when the heir of Elendil should come forth and strive with Sauron for the mastery."

When Galadriel gave the green Elfstone to Aragorn in Lórien, she told him, "In this hour take the name that was foretold for you, Elessar, the Elfstone of the house of Elendil!" He called himself "the heir of Isildur Elendil's son of Gondor" when he introduced himself formally to Eomer, who in turn recognized Aragorn as "the heir of Elendil". When Aragorn revealed himself to Sauron, he somehow conveyed the knowledge to Sauron that he was Elendil's heir (probably by showing the sword Anduril to Sauron).

And, finally, when Faramir spoke with Eowyn about why she remained in Minas Tirith despite Eomer's repeated requests that she join him at Cormallen, Faramir guessed "you do not go, because only your brother called for you, and to look on the Lord Aragorn, Elendil's heir, in his triumph would now bring you no joy."

It should therefore not seem a mistake that Faramir refers to Aragorn as "Chieftain of the Dunedain of Arnor". Faramir was very familiar with Aragorn's titles, and he understood that Aragorn was presenting his claim as Elendil's heir of Gondor (a phrase Aragorn himself had used in Rohan). In fact, why would the people of Gondor care about Aragorn's position as a tribal leader in the north? They had had no contact with Arnor for a thousand years. On the other hand, Aragorn had already established his position as the captain of the Rangers of the north. The Rangers were all Dunedain of Arnor. Arnor no longer existed, but as a royally commissioned force, the Rangers represented the legal authority of the kingdom of Arnor.

Furthermore, the last time Gondor awarded the crown to a claimant, he had been a victorious captain in war. Ëarnil, descendant of Telumehtar Umbardacil, had been Captain of the Southern Army of Gondor during the war with the Wainriders and their allies. When King Ondoher and both his sons died in battle, Ëarnil, already victorious in the south, rushed north and assumed command of the Northern Army. He routed the enemy and saved Gondor. Ëarnil was eventually awarded the crown of Gondor at least in part because of his victory.

A precedent had therefore been established whereby a claimant of royal blood might be chosen on the basis of his military achievements on behalf of Gondor. Aragorn had entered Gondor as the captain of his small force of Rangers. He had used his authority as the Heir of Isildur (one of Gondor's first kings) to summon the army of the Dead Men of Dunharrow and defeat the Haradrim and Corsairs. He had then taken command of the freed slaves on the ships, expanding his forces. When Angbor of Lamedon and other men of Gondor arrived at Pelargir, they joined Aragorn's growing army.

When Aragorn arrived at Minas Tirith he came as a victorious captain of war in charge of Gondorian forces. He then led the Army of the West in its march upon Mordor. So, when Faramir recounted Aragorn's military pedigree for the people of Gondor, he put Aragorn's title of "Chieftain of the Dunedain of Arnor" first, and followed it with "Captain of the Host of the West". Aragorn's military credentials were thus impeccable under Gondor's tradition. He had led Gondorian troops in war, but also came to Gondor as a captain in his own right. He was the captain of the Rangers of the north.

So, in essence, Aranarth's legal contrivances had prepared the way for Aragorn. Aranarth couldn't restore the kingdom of Arnor. He had too few people to do that. But he preserved the royal authority of the Kings of Arnor through his title *Lord of the Dunedain* (in "The Tale of Aragorn and Arwen", Aragorn introduced himself as "Aragorn, Arathorn's son, Isildur's Heir, Lord of the Dunedain"). And Aranarth also took the title *Chieftain of the Dunedain*, which may have denoted a diminution in the status of the Dunedain of Arnor. But it seems possible that the title was in fact a self-appointed military rank.

By extension, one must ask if the title, or rank, of *chieftain* inducted all the Dunedain (including women and children) into a formal military order. That is not really necessary. Instead, Aranarth became their captain in war, and his descendants inherited the office. But the Rangers were probably not the principal military force of the Dunedain. That is not to say that the Dunedain maintained a standing army. Rather, it may be that they initiated the custom of maintaining a *muster*, and the *chieftain* was the captain of the muster. The Shire-folk appointed their Thain "to hold the authority of the king that was gone."

It's a curious expression to use for a hereditary leader who was replacing a king, but the word *thain* appears to be a derivative of *thane*, from Anglo-Saxon *thegn*. A *thane* was "a freeman granted land by the king in return for military service in Anglo-Saxon England". Or, a thane was "a dignitary under the Anglo-Saxons and Danes in England. Of these there were two orders, the king's thanes, who attended the kings in their courts and held lands immediately of them, and the ordinary thanes, who were lords of manors and who had particular jurisdiction within their limits. After the Conquest, this title was disused, and baron took its place."

The Shire's Thainship therefore established a hereditary military office with some civil duties. "The Thain was the master of the Shire-moot, and captain of the Shire-muster and the Hobbitry-in-arms," Tolkien notes in the Prologue. A moot was "an ancient English meeting, especially a representative meeting of the freemen of a shire." Tolkien used the word *moot* in other ways, such as in the Entmoot and the Folkmoot of Brethil (the latter term is used only in reference to a meeting of the Folk of Haleth in "The Wanderings of Hurin," published in *The War of the Jewels*).

So, instead of appropriating the royal authority for themselves, the Shire chieftains (most likely the clan or family leaders) in fact acted to *preserve* the royal authority. They expected, or hoped for, the return of the king. Aranarth was the rightful king, and the Thain was elected in 1979, four years after Aranarth took the title of *Chieftain of the Dunedain*. The Thainship must therefore have been appointed to the Shire-folk by Aranarth. In essence, he established a feudal relationship with them. They continued to recognize his royal authority, but they also enacted a practical measure for their own defense, which the Dunedain were no longer able to provide for directly.

Tolkien doesn't tell us when Aranarth's people settled in the Angle. It may have been generations before they migrated to that region, and their purpose in doing so is not entirely clear. But what is clear is that Aranarth (or one of his descendants) established the Rangers as a special service to maintain the authority of the king throughout Eriador. Bree and Tharbad may have had similar local military offices which were eventually lost, either as the populations of those regions diminished, or as the Rangers gradually cleared Eriador of most of its evil intruders.

Technically, Arnor ceased to function as a kingdom or nation. There was no king to govern the people or to act on their behalf in dealing with other nations. But the last rightful king bequeathed to his heirs the authority over all military forces in Eriador, as well as the claim to nobility and royal prerogatives. The kingship became dormant, passing into a sort of regency under which the rightful heirs of the kings acted as their own regents. However, the symbols of Arnor's kings, the Sceptre of Annúminas and the Star of Elendil, were given to Elrond. Elrond was therefore appointed the trustee of the royal authority of Arnor, holding its emblems in escrow until such time as an Heir of Isildur proved able to reestablish the kingdom.

Rather than dissolve Arnor and divest himself of the kingship, Aranarth simply created a public trust to hold the kingdom in perpetual abeyance. Everyone recognized that the kingdom of Arnor still existed, but only in a legal state of suspension. In this way Arnor's surviving peoples became autonomous but remained subjects of the crown. And yet Tolkien writes that "after Arvedui the North-kingdom ended." That is, the North-kingdom ceased to exist as a state, and it neither enforced its laws nor enacted new ones. But some of its institutions survived, or were preserved through inheritance by new institutions.

It thus seems most likely that Rangers constituted only a small part of the male population of the Dunedain of Arnor. Elrond was not wrong to say there were now few Dunedain left, but they probably numbered in the thousands, rather than the hundreds. When Frodo sat upon Amon Hen and beheld visions of a world moving toward war, he saw that "the Misty Mountains were crawling like anthills: Orcs were issuing out of a thousand holes". Most of those Orcs probably attacked the Beornings and Woodmen, or Lórien. But some of them had to turn toward Eriador. And it would have fallen to the Dunedain to defend Eriador against invasion. In such a time of need, the Rangers would have been called back to defend the homeland and patrol the frontier.

Halbarad's ability to muster a company of Rangers would therefore have been hampered not by fewness of men, but by the necessity to leave his people (and Rivendell) defended.

Some people are quick to point out, however, that Elrond had summoned Arwen back to Rivendell in order to protect her from the perils encroaching upon the Vales of Anduin. True, but Lórien was threatened by greater forces than Rivendell should have faced. Dol Guldur and the Misty Mountains presented formidable threats to Lórien and neighboring lands (and peoples), and Sauron controlled all the lands between Mirkwood and Mordor, as well as many lands to the east. Lórien was thus in considerably greater peril than Rivendell. Sauron's ability to threaten Eriador was thus limited, but it was not non-existent. Gandalf pointed out to Frodo that Rivendell, the Shire, and similar enclaves would "soon become islands under siege, if things" were allowed to continue as they were proceeding prior to the Council of Elrond. One area which still caused Rivendell (and the Rangers) some grief was the Ettenmoors, north of Rivendell, where Trolls (and perhaps other evil creatures) still lived.

Later on, after the Company of the Ring failed to cross over the Misty Mountains via the Redhorn Pass, Gandalf held out the prospect of returning to Rivendell. But he pointed out that "to go back is to admit defeat and face worse defeat to come. If we go back now, then the Ring must remain there: we shall not be able to set out again. Then sooner or later Rivendell will be besieged, and after a brief and bitter time it will be destroyed." So Rivendell was not a safe haven for anyone. It was simply farther removed from the front lines than Lórien. It therefore seems reasonable to infer that most of the Dunedain capable of wielding arms were busy during the War of the Ring, and the Rangers had been summoned to reinforce what was probably a capable but at best semi-professional folk-muster.

Finally, if the Rangers were in fact a standing force of road and forest-wardens, how were they organized? If the nine Nazgul were unable or unwilling to face the Rangers stationed at Sarn Ford in broad daylight, how large a body of men had Aragorn stationed there? It's not like there would have been a fort just beyond the border of the Shire with a sign above the door saying "Ranger post number 4". But Aragorn had doubled the guard on the Shire at Gandalf's request, and presumably that included doubling the guard at Sarn Ford. The Rangers assigned to the ford may have numbered in the tens or dozens, and perhaps were briefly reinforced as scouts and sentries fell back to the Baranduin to warn the main body of the approach of the Nazgul.

"The Hunt for the Ring" in *Unfinished Tales* tells us that:

> Night was waning on the twenty-second day of September when drawing together again [the Nazgul] came to Sarn Ford and the southernmost borders of the Shire. They found them guarded, for the Rangers barred their way. But this was a task beyond the power of the Dunedain; and maybe it would still have proved so even if their captain, Aragorn, had been with them. But he was away to the north, upon the East Road near Bree; and the hearts even of the Dunedain misgave them. Some fled northward, hoping to bear news to Aragorn, but they were pursued and slain or driven away into the wild. Some still dared to bar the ford, and held it while day lasted, but at night the Lord of Morgul swept them away, and the Black Riders swept into the Shire....

Boromir's account of how the Lord of the Nazgul defeated his force at Osgiliath indicates that even a small army of several hundred men probably would not have prevailed against the Nazgul at night, when they were all together and led by their captain. So it's not necessary to suppose that there were many Rangers at Sarn Ford. But there were probably more than twenty, though most likely less than fifty. A company similar in size to Halbarad's troop may have been assigned to patrol the Shire's southern border. A similar number of Rangers could have been assigned to watch the Shire's western border, and perhaps another company may have patrolled the lands around Bree.

Some Rangers had passed near Weathertop a few days before Aragorn and the Hobbits arrived there, probably before Gandalf had shown up. They left wood piled behind a rock in the little dell that Aragorn selected as a camp for the party. It seems there must have been roving patrols which watched over the lands east of Bree, between Bree and the Angle, in fact. These patrols probably went as far north as the ruins of Fornost Erain (where Gandalf told Barliman the Rangers visited on occasion) and as far south as Tharbad. There may have been no more than three hundred Rangers in all, not necessarily organized into companies of thirty, but patrolling assigned regions. The Rangers may always have kept some men close to home for emergencies, as well as to replace troops in the field on some sort of rotating basis.

The function of the Rangers could not be to take and hold territory like an army. Instead, they would report on the intrusions of evil creatures and probably gather whatever forces would be necessary to repel roving bands of Orcs and Trolls, evil men, or packs of wolves. They may also have helped keep the roads clear of bandits, thus ensuring the safe passage of merchants and travelers. The Rangers were as close to a police force as Eriador had, and were undoubtedly an elite force of soldiers who were highly motivated, well-trained, and well-equipped. The thirty who accompanied Halbarad were all dressed in uniform attire, and they possessed similar weapons: swords, bows, and spears. Their somber discipline (observed by Legolas, Gimli, and Meriadoc at Helm's Deep) similarly implies they were professional warriors.

In the end, attempting to answer the question of how many Rangers guarded Sarn Ford leads to unsatisfactory guesses and yet more questions. But the quest for an answer reveals some interesting implications about the relationships between the Dunedain and other inhabitants of Eriador. It also illuminates just exactly how Aragorn was able to formally claim the crown of Gondor and re-establish the Kingdom of Arnor without having a large population of Dunedain to empower him. We may also have a better understanding of how Eriador maintained a semblance of civilization throughout the last thousand years of the Third Age.

Chapter 5:
Simple Hobbits have lots of friends

One of my pet peeves through the years has been the injection of thieves guilds and other role-playing motifs into Middle-earth. I once watched in disbelief as a mailing list of gamers defined Tharbad to be a din of iniquity, dominated by a thieves guild, without any apparent regard for the way Tolkien's world actually worked. I should say, "without any apparent regard for the way I believed Tolkien's world actually worked."

It took a silly movie to make me think about Tolkien and thieves' guilds in a new way. I'm referring to Eddie Murphy's "Dr. Doolittle 2", in which the doctor (who hardly resembles the now less-famous literary doctor of yesteryear) is recruited by the animals of an endangered forest to help them save their turf.

The movie is cute, filled with jokes and gentle jabs at the Mafia. The endangered forest is secretly run by a beaver who sends out a possum (that's Opossum for those of you who like silent vowels) and a raccoon as his messenger boys. "When you meet the beaver, you should treat him with the respect he deserves," the raccoon tells the doctor at one point. "Listen, when the beaver offers you a fish, you take it!" he admonishes in another scene. "I am just a simple fisherman who is blessed with a lot of friends," the beaver tells Murphy's character.

Not exactly a thieves guild, but there are certain elements of the Mafia mystique which have crept into role-playing games. A well-designed thieves' guild always has a mafia-like atmosphere. You don't just casually break into the guild and demand to see the bosses. They're busy people. They have wives and children to support. They need their space, just like everyone else.

Now, Tolkien never mentions a thieves guild. In fact, he rarely mentions guilds at all, and when he does he isn't talking about typical medieval bakers guilds. But there is something mafia-like in the way Tolkien depicts Lotho Sackville-Baggins' takeover of the Shire. I mean, think about it. He uses his money to buy up a lot of farms and plantations in the Southfarthing. And then he establishes a trading relationship with Isengard.

Or was that the other way around? Maybe "Pimple" Sackville-Baggins was rich, but not rich enough to achieve his dreams. So he went looking for friends in new places, and he found Isengard ready and willing to help. Isengard sent him money, wagon-drivers, carpenters, and bully-boys. With all due respect to the members of our hard-working labor unions, the connections between the mob and labor unions have been documented through the years in our courts, and exploited through the years in novels, movies, and television shows. So maybe Southfarthing Wagon-drivers Local No. 2 was just a front for the organization.

When Frodo Baggins returns to find that "Pimple" has taken over control of the Shire, he makes the comment that maybe it's time the Family dealt with the annoying little upstart. It's reported to Pippin Took that his father said, "If anyone is going to play boss around here, it should be ME." Clearly, there is an undertone to these Hobbit families and their financial arrangements that we haven't explored before.

The real Mafia was started by rebel Sicilians in the 9th century (or was that the 13th century?). They were a secret society who resisted the Arab conquest (or was that the Norman French conquest?). Through the centuries, the organization built up its tradition of family trust and honor, and maintained great secrecy. They began sending pictures of black hands to wealthy Sicilians in the 1700s, demanding money in exchange for protection. The consequence of withholding payment was to be targeted for kidnappings, murder, vandalism, etc.

Mafia dons began fleeing to the United States to escape imprisonment starting around the year 1901. By 1924, Benito Mussolini decided to stamp out the Mafia, and Mafiosi fled to the United States in droves. The United States stumbled upon the Mafia in the late 1800s in New

Orleans, when New Orleans Police Chief David Hennessey investigated the murder of an Italian immigrant and was subsequently assassinated. 12 men were hung by a vigilante organization in retaliation for the assassination, and President Harrison compensated the families of the men for the lynchings.

Saruman's emblem was the white hand. The white hand does not appear inside the Shire, but it does reach out and entangle itself in Shire politics and economics in Mafia-like secrecy. Saruman seized control over Dunland, had at least one highly-placed spy in the Rohirric government, and established contacts and a foothold in the Shire. One might ask if he was also shaking down the simple fishermen of Anfalas and controlling the trade (or lack thereof) coming down Anduin. Isengard was in a position to influence a lot of people and places.

Like the Mafia, who were originally bands of freedom fighters (or thugs, in some people's opinions) resisting foreign invaders, Saruman established himself in Isengard as a force for good, resisting Sauron's efforts to take control over all of Middle-earth. But when one begins to acquire power and gain influence over people, it can become a very intoxicating experience. Power corrupts, and people are corruptible. Saruman gave in to temptation and began building up his own organization. He made contact with one or more local bands of Orcs and recruited them into his scheme. He organized the Dunlendings and set about building them into a powerful army.

But Saruman ran afoul of the law, so to speak. That is, he turned against the White Council and the Free Peoples of Middle-earth. When his henchmen started beating up on the local trees, the Ents formed a vigilante committee and set out to lynch Saruman and his bururum, his Orcs. Well, they took down Isengard's outer wall but the Ents couldn't get to Saruman himself. All they could do was lay siege to the tower of Orthanc and wait him out. In the meantime, Rohan, once rid of the Isengard menace, turned its attention to Sauron and forgot about Isengard.

But Saruman's contacts in the Shire weren't extinguished. Undoubtedly, cut off from Isengard, Lotho went on a rampage. There may even have been a brief period of gang warfare. Drive-by swordings and late-night massacres of Saruman's most trusted henchmen as they partied with local Hobbit girls most likely helped ensure Lotho's control over the Isengarder organization.

In the meantime, the local families were slow to figure out what was going on. They never expected new blood to come in from Isengard and Dunland. They had been running the Shire since the 1900s, and had a pretty good deal. They were landowners now, respectable, and didn't really think about organizing bands of resistance fighters as in the old days when the Realm of Angmar was sending armies to overrun the Hobbits.

But the Shire had its own Mafia-like history and organization. The original Mafiosi fled to the hills of Sicily when the Arabs (or Norman French) showed up. They fought back secretly, and they eventually seized control over the Sicilian government. The Shire families, led by their chieftains, moved into the hills. When Angmar attacked they resisted. Eventually, the chieftains got together and elected a Thain to lead the local bully-boys and resistance fighters. But things settled down after that and the Shire families prospered. They even became aristocratic. But they stayed close together. Some of the families, like the Tooks and Brandybucks, adhered to the Old Ways.

The Brandybucks had once been called the Oldbucks, and they had controlled the Shire for generations. But in what was obviously a turf war (probably over control of wine production in the Southfarthing) the Tooks ran the Oldbucks out of the Shire. The Oldbucks settled across the Baranduin (Brandywine) river in what became known as Buckland. There in Brandy Hall the Master of Buckland continued to exercise considerable influence in the Shire. It's said that many people in the nearby Marish continued to look to the Master of Buckland as their leader. Undoubtedly some of the fees of the Buckleberry Ferry and the Stone Bridge made their way into Brandybuck coffers.

The Tooks settled down in the heart of the Shire and let the Hobbits think they had a nice, quiet little country. The Hobbits even elected a Mayor every seven years who oversaw the Postal Service and the Shirriffs and Bounders. The Bounders were useful in keeping the Brandybucks and other riffraff out of the Shire proper, except for occasional visits by the highest members of the Brandybuck family. But the Shirriffs were limited in number, undoubtedly to prevent them from getting too ambitious and launching investigations into the Tooks' financial arrangements. The Mayors were therefore mostly for show, and it may be that the Tooks didn't even care who was elected Mayor as long as he knew his place and applied himself mostly to feasting.

The Baggins family obviously had its ups and downs. They were closely allied with the Tooks and probably dominated the legal profession. The law firm of Burrowes, Burrowes, and Grubb was a front for Baggins family money-laundering schemes. Baggins and Took adventurers occasionally went off and brought back huge fortunes in "hush" money. Supposedly, Bilbo Baggins helped take out a dragon in distant lands. So it may be that the Baggins family supplied the Tooks with their hit men. It may be that Frodo's journey to Mordor was simply a contract killing intended to take out this Sauron wiseguy who was starting to threaten to take over the local action.

It just so happened that one part of the Baggins family, miffed at losing control over the family business, decided to branch out on its own. They made contact with the Isengard organization and began carving out their turf in the Southfarthing. Things proceeded quietly. Rumor has it that many of the locals were paid off quite well. So the Tooks had no idea of what was coming. They didn't think about calling a Shire-moot and weeding out the traitorous riffraff in their midst. In fact, they couldn't have accomplished anything that way at all. The Baggins family had to deal with its own, and Frodo, head of the Baggins family, was away on a mission.

The Hobbits' own secrecy was their downfall. Their blind devotion to family, honor, and tradition prevented them from taking action. Even when the Isengard gangs started showing up, cutting down trees, and gathering and sharing (mostly gathering from the Hobbits to share for themselves), Paladin Took, the Thain, decided he'd wait for Frodo to come back and take out the little upstart Pimple. So what if Pimple called himself, "Boss"? Paladin knew who the real Boss was. And he had the Took army to back himself up. So he closed off the borders of Tookland and kept the Isengarder gangs out.

Lotho made a mess of things, though. He clearly didn't root out all the opposition when he took over the Shire. When Saruman showed up a few months later, the ruffians and Half-orcs flocked to his side and returned to their old boss. Most likely Saruman had been more generous with the wine and the pipeweed. Reports say that Isengard was well-supplied with these items. Lotho, having little experience in running the family business, was not prepared for the counter-coup. Saruman sent his own messenger boy, Grima Wormtongue, to take out the little dweeb.

The Isengard organization then started to munch down on the Shire. Shakedowns became the order of the day. Saruman simply took control over the puppet government and expanded its law enforcement services to ensure that his laws were obeyed. The Shirriffs became a terrorizing army of thugs controlled by the Isengarders. Things looked pretty grim.

And then Frodo returned.

If there's one thing Tolkien understood, it was that any Hobbit who could take out a Dark Lord shouldn't have any trouble dealing with the nitwit who had lost his own organization down south. Saruman may have been bigger than Lotho Sackville-Baggins, but he wasn't half the Hobbit that Frodo Baggins was. As soon as Frodo returned the Hobbit families began to organize. A new resistance was born. The Tooks started taking back their old turf. Frodo himself oversaw the hit on Saruman.

It wasn't long before the Shire was safely back in the hands of the Old Families. And the old way of life was quickly restored. But the good days weren't destined to last long. There was now a King, and he began sending people north to put his affairs in order. Frodo, the best hit man the Hobbits ever had, read the writing on the wall and he booked passage on the next ship over Sea. The Shire was never the same after he left. The King realized that Hobbits and Men just didn't mix very well. An investigation into Shire family businesses revealed that they controlled the pipeweed trade, and that Shire weed was preferred even in Bree. Worse, the Hobbits' ability to run gangsters from Isengard out of the woods proved to be alarming. What if they got ambitious?

Well, all that may seem a bit of an overread, but it occurs to me that perhaps the gamers' desire to impose a couple of local thieves' guilds on Middle-earth isn't all that out-of-line after all. Tolkien was obviously a wiseguy who wanted to blow the lid off a corrupt and intransigent organization. He obviously changed the names to protect the innocent, but it's easy enough to show that The Lord of the Rings is heavily influenced by the medieval origins of the Mafia, and that it's just an allegory about the perils of living in a society where organized crime has taken control.

Chapter 6:
The men who would be steward

Guardianship is the mark of the Stewards of Gondor. They are guardians, wardens, keeping an ancient trust placed in their hands by a family of kings which, at the end of the Third Age, no longer exists. Gondor's Ruling Stewards are a curious example of how authority combined with tradition can produce a subtle irony in power and position.

The Elvish word for "steward" is *Arandur*, "King's servant". The name implies that the Stewards began their long career as something less than government officials. They may have been the personal servants of Gondor's early kings. At some point in Gondor's history, the Aranduri may have assumed special duties which led to their elevation in station and authority. Eventually, they succeeded to the royal authority of the kings, although they never displaced the House of Elendil in Gondor's formal government.

Some people have observed a parallel between Gondor's history and the history of early medieval France. The Major Domos of early Frankish dynasties eventually displaced the kings and assumed royal authority. Charles Martel, renowned as the Major Domo who defeated the Moors in southern France, founded a new dynasty.

But the problem with comparing the Frankish Major Domos to Tolkien's Ruling Stewards is that their history provides a *Frankish* model. Tolkien was not very fond of France, or of French words. In fact, few of the important titles or names in *The Lord of the Rings* are derived from French words.

For example, the term *Major Domo* is usually translated as "Mayor of the Palace" by historians discussing the Pepinid dynasty (Charles Martel is believed by some people to have been descended from Pepin of Landen, who became the Mayor of the Palace in Metz under King Chlotar II of Neustria). The Frankish Major Domos were in some ways like Tolkien's Stewards, in that they governed Frankish nations in the names of their kings, but the Major Domos eventually became kings. They were powerful men who controlled money, armies, and royal appointments. The kings who appointed the Major Domos had very little real power. It proved to be only a matter of time before the Pepinids replaced the descendants of Clovis as rulers of the Franks.

Tolkien uses nothing like "mayor of the palace" or "major domo" in Middle-earth. The Mayor of Michel Delving is about the only example of an official whose title derives from a French title. The term "Steward", on the other hand, is a good, old-fashioned Anglo-Saxon word for "sty warden", the guardian of the animal compound. How a beast-keeper should rise to become an important royal officer (and eventually King of Scotland, as in the royal Stewart/Stuart family) is an interesting bit of history.

The reason for the importance of stewards lies in the architecture used by northern Europe's early peoples. They lived in long houses (going back thousands of years) which eventually evolved into the halls of Norse and Germanic song and legend. Heorot, the golden hall of Hrothgar, King of Denmark (in the poem "Beowulf") is a typical if idealized northern hall. The hall-warden would have been the most important servant of the lord, looking after the animals and managing the lord's affairs in his absence.

The hall-warden and sty warden were virtually the same person, since animals were commonly kept in the ancient long houses. As the power of the northern chieftains grew and they became kings of early Anglo-Saxon peoples in England, their Sty Wardens assumed more important duties. Eventually, Stewards were as important to the Anglo-Saxon kings as Major Domos were to the Frankish kings. But the Anglo-Saxon kings managed to retain their power.

Walter Fitz-Alan, a Norman knight, founded the Stewart Clan which eventually assumed the throne of Scotland. He served King David I in Scotland's wars with the Vikings. Walter's great-grandson Alexander became Lord High Steward (Stewart) of Scotland. Sir John Stewart, a descendant, married Marjory, daughter and only child of Robert Bruce.

Their son Robert became Robert II, King of Scotland, and the Stewart Kings of Scotland and England were descended from him.

Thus, one of the first apparent ironies stems from the fact that Tolkien's choice of title for the "temporary" rulers of Gondor, the Stewards, is derived from the Anglo-Saxon surname of an Norman-Scottish family. The Normans were responsible for destroying the ancient English nobility, along with suppressing their English literature and language with which Tolkien had fallen in love.

Despite history's examples, Tolkien clearly wanted his Stewards to keep their place. They were not destined to assume the throne of Gondor, although at least one member of the family had royal aspirations. Boromir, elder son of Denethor II, asked his father how long it would take for a Steward to become King. "Few years, maybe, in other places of less royalty," Denethor told him. "In Gondor ten thousand years would not suffice." The comment seems to be a poke in the eye to the Pepinids, who supplanted the rightful heirs of Clovis as Kings of the Franks.

Boromir obviously chafed at the confinement tradition (and law) had placed upon him. As he grew up, he could only expect to become the faithful steward to a long-dead line of kings. He undoubtedly felt his family was wasting its time, waiting for the impossible return of a king who could not possibly exist. In contrast, the Pepinids chafed under the rule of weak Merovingian kings (Merovech was the grandfather of Clovis, and the dynasty is named after him). The Merovingians occasionally tried to curb the power of their Major Domos, and eventually the Major Domos simply got rid of them. Tolkien's Stewards thus proved to be more reliable than the Frankish Major Domos.

When Boromir reached maturity, he became his father's servant. We know from his own testimony in Rivendell and comments made by Faramir and Denethor that Boromir was a captain of Gondor. Tolkien uses the word "captain" (a *French* word derived from Latin) in various ways throughout *The Lord of the Rings*. The only specific titles attributed to Boromir are *High Warden of the White Tower* and

Captain-General (of all Gondor's forces). "Captain-General" is an actual royal title of the British monarchy, and denotes the station of the monarch as commander-in-chief.

Although it might seem imprudent or even hypocritical for the Stewards to assume such a title, *The Peoples of Middle-earth* says that "the *Hurinionath* were not in the direct line of descent from Elendil, [but] they were ultimately of royal origin." Boromir, therefore, was a descendant of Elendil, a fact not provided in *The Lord of the Rings*. Descent from Elendil may have provoked Boromir's ambitions, but it also may have served as the foundation for Denethor's jealousy of Aragorn, whom he had known in his own youth as Thorongil. In any event, since Gondor needed a commander-in-chief, the office and its title were assumed by the Stewards (and presumably conferred upon a son or nephew being groomed to take up the Stewardship later in life).

Hurin of Emyn Arnen was the Steward of Minardil, King of Gondor from 1621 to 1634. Minardil died in battle at Pelargir, fighting the Corsairs of Umbar (who were led by his cousins Angamaitë and Sangahyando). Minardil was twenty generations removed from Meneldil, son of Anarion. There is no indication in any of the published texts about where Hurin of Emyn Arnen's family branched off from the royal line. He himself may have been the son of a royal princess.

One possibility for Hurin's ancestry would be the daughter of Eldacar, the half-Dunadan/half-Northman King of Gondor who was driven from the throne for ten years by Castamir the Usurper. Eldacar's elder son Ornendil was slain in the Kin-Strife, and Eldacar was eventually succeeded by his younger son Aldamir. But Aldamir was Eldacar's third child. Minardil was Aldamir's grandson, so Hurin of Emyn Arnen could have been Aldamir's grand-nephew and Minardil's second-cousin. Hurin could not have been more closely related to Minardil, and he could, perhaps, have been more distantly related.

A descent from Eldacar would prevent the Stewards from claiming a purer bloodline than that of the Kings. Bloodlines, however, are not as important to Tolkien as they are to many of his failed characters. That is, the Kin-Strife was fought between Gondorians who believed the royal house should remain pure and Gondorians who believed that mingling the royal family with other kindreds of Men would do no harm. So, it is not necessary for Tolkien to show from whom the Stewards descended. Nonetheless, Eldacar remains, in my opinion, the best candidate for their most immediate royal ancestor. At the very least, he is the only king said or implied to have a daughter (in "The Heirs of Elendil", a chapter in *The Peoples of Middle-earth* which provides a great deal more information about the leading houses of Gondor than *The Lord of the Rings*).

Boromir's perspective would have been shaped, at least in part, by his own family's historical experience. Whereas the kings had all been descended of the male line in Anarion's house, the Stewards were more liberal in their choices. At least one Steward came from a daughter's family. Denethor I (2435-77) was the son of Rian, sister of Dior (2412-35), the 9th Ruling Steward. If he didn't have to come from the male line to be Ruling Steward, then why should he not be king? Boromir seems to have felt that the Hurinionath had earned their place on the throne, and it wasn't like they weren't descended from Elendil anyway.

Denethor II's reply to his son's inquiry might seem a bit rude and short-sighted. "Shut up, son, and do as your forefathers have done." But the Stewards had effectively eliminated themselves from the succession. It was in the power of the council of Gondor to make new law, but not to undo ancient law. In the year 1944, King Ondoher and both his sons fell in battle with the Wainriders. Neither son left behind any male heirs. Gondor was in a quandary, for by this time the royal house had become a victim of its own suspicions. Pure-blooded men of the royal house either foreswore their heritage and took wives outside the Númenorean community, or if the kings became jealous of them they fled to Umbar.

Arvedui, prince of Arnor, had married Ondoher's daughter Firiel in 1940. He claimed the throne of Gondor in Firiel's name but the council, led by the Steward Pelendur, rejected his claim. They wanted only a prince descended in the male line from Anarion. Even

Arvedui's son, Aranarth, would not be acceptable, though he was also the son of Firiel and a descendant of Anarion. By excluding Isildur's line from claiming the throne, Pelendur effectively excluded himself and his heirs from making similar claims. A thousand years later, Pelendur's descendant Boromir, son of Denethor II, would ask why he was not destined to be King of Gondor. The answer was that Pelendur had made it impossible for his family to ascend the throne.

Pelendur did actually have at least one good candidate left in the Line of Anarion. Eärnil II, who had led the Southern Army of Gondor to victory against the Wainriders, claimed the throne in 1945. He was as pure-blooded as any descendant of Eldacar could be. As a victorious captain, he was popular and thus well-accepted by the people. Unfortunately, Eärnil's son Eärnur never took a wife. When he vanished in 2050, Gondor was left without any acceptable claimants to the throne.

The Stewards were thus left in a peculiar state. Eärnur doesn't seem to have left any instructions about what should happen if he failed to return. Mardil Voronwë ruled in his name for many years, and though Gondor's council probably debated how to choose a new king, the fear of a new Kin-Strife prevented them from choosing a new monarch. Technically, there is no reason to believe that the Line of Anarion really ended with Eärnur. That is, there must have been men descended of the male line whose forefathers had married women from non-Númenorean families. But their ancestors had foresworn their heritage, and the tradition-bound Gondorians would not allow those families to repudiate the choices of their fathers.

The root of such an iron-clad adherence to tradition must lie in the choices made by Elrond and Elros at the beginning of the Second Age. When Elros chose to be of mortal kind, he bound his descendants to that choice forever, even though some of them later decided they would rather be Elves. The Faithful Númenoreans who founded Arnor and Gondor longed for perpetual youth and immortality, but they accepted the choice of Elros (in fact, most of them probably weren't descended from Elros, but their leaders were). The Faithful would thus have brought with them an understanding that the choice of a father affected all his descendants. Hence, in any matter of law, a family's fate was decided by its current generation. Unborn generations were given no leeway.

And that is the truth Boromir had to face, when his father pointed out to him that he was not royal enough to be king. It wasn't that he was deemed to be less of a man, whether by virtue of blood or deeds. Rather, Boromir's ancestor had made a choice which bound all future generations of the family. Boromir may have resented that choice. In one letter, Tolkien referred to Boromir as Faramir's "bossy brother". Boromir's bossiness does reveal itself in numerous passages throughout the text. For example, when the Company of the Ring is trapped in the snow on Caradhras, it is Boromir who takes the initiative and decides that he and Aragorn will forge a path through the snow for the others. When the Hobbits despair of following that same path, Boromir decides that he and Aragorn will carry them.

He asserts himself again when the Company is outside of Moria's West-gate. When it becomes apparent that Gandalf has no clue about how to get into Moria, Boromir orders Sam not to let Bill the Pony go just yet. Aragorn is silent on both occasions. Why is that?

It would seem that Boromir had to be a very compelling man, perhaps a very charismatic man. His people loved him, including his stern father, his scholarly brother, and the brave men who served under him in war. Aragorn seems to have respected Boromir's opinion enough not to argue with him. And perhaps Aragorn was himself a bit intimidated by Boromir, who was after all the heir of the ruler of Gondor. Aragorn was the rightful King of Gondor, but his right had not been recognized by Gondor. Boromir seems a bit tyrannical at times, but it may be that he was simply being himself -- a leader of men, making decisions swiftly and reasonably (within the bounds of his experience). He did give pretty good advice, on occasion. For example, it was Boromir who suggested the Company of the Ring take bundles of wood up onto the mountain.

For his part, Aragorn was deferring to Gandalf's leadership while Gandalf traveled with the company. But he may also have been winning Boromir's trust. Boromir would have been in a position to sway the people of Gondor toward Aragorn's claim, but why should he do so? When Frodo told Faramir (in Ithilien) that Boromir was satisfied of Aragorn's claims, Faramir pointed out that Boromir and Aragorn had not yet become rivals in Gondor's wars. Aragorn needed to be Boromir's friend. He needed Boromir to trust him, at least to the point where Boromir might say nothing when Aragorn pressed his claim. Were Boromir to denounce Aragorn after reaching Minas Tirith, things would not have gone well for Aragorn.

But Boromir, for his part, had accepted Aragorn's companionship on the road. Furthermore, he recognized his obligation to let Aragorn make his case to Gondor. After Elrond introduced Aragorn to Boromir, Aragorn asked him bluntly: "Do you wish for the House of Elendil to return to the land of Gondor?" Boromir immediately denied any such request: "I was not sent to beg any boon," he replied, "but to seek only the meaning of a riddle." Nonetheless, he quickly added: "Yet we are hard pressed, and the Sword of Elendil would be a help beyond our hope -- if such a thing could indeed return out of the shadows of the past."

Boromir's concession is very grudging at best. He is not saying, "Yes, you are the heir of Elendil, come and make your claim to the throne." Rather, he is saying, "The throne awaits the return of a true king, as it has for a thousand years." Boromir does not yet believe that Aragorn is really Elendil's heir. He knows Elrond is an ancient lord among the Elves, but Elrond's words just cannot ring quite true to a man whose family has awaited the return of a king merely as a formality for so many centuries.

Boromir's opinion of Aragorn begins to shift ever so slightly during the rest of the council. Aragorn speaks for himself, and the details of the journey from Bree to Rivendell are discussed at length. Eventually, Boromir suggests that the Ring can be used against Sauron, but Elrond rebuffs him, and both Elrond and Gandalf flatly refuse to take up the Ring. In the face of such rebuke, Boromir is humbled. It is not that he politely bows his head when he says, "So be it. Then in Gondor we must trust to such weapons as we have." Rather, his humility allows him to confess, "though I do not ask for aid, we need it."

Boromir is honest enough to recognize his weaknesses. A good commander must be able to do so. So Faramir's words many months later, when he learns that Boromir had tried to take the Ring from Frodo, reveal an especially bitter observation: "Alas for Boromir! It was too sore a trial!" But why was the trial too sore for Boromir, and not for Faramir? For his part, Faramir implies that his own vow has fortified him: "We boast seldom, and then perform, or die in the attempt," he reminds Frodo and Sam. "*Not if I found it on the highway would I take it*, I said." Boromir had made no such vow. It might have gone better with him if he had.

But, in truth, Boromir's test was not as easy as Faramir's. Faramir was indeed tempted by the Ring, once he understood it was in his presence. Faramir had a brief moment of intense reaction to that knowledge, and then he passed the test and moved on. But for Boromir the test did not pass so quickly. He expressed an immediate interest in using the Ring at Elrond's council, and though he was rebuffed, he did not renounce his desire. "So be it" is not the same as "I fear to take the Ring to hide it. I will not take the Ring to wield it," which is what Elrond says. "Nor I," Gandalf chimes in, although he has already refused the Ring in Bag End.

Even Aragorn had already refused to take the Ring. "If I was after the Ring, I could have it -- NOW!" he declared in the Prancing Pony, when he was trying to persuade Frodo to accept his company. There followed a brief moment in which Aragorn stood up and scared the Hobbits with his stern and commanding nature. As when other people handled the Ring, or were tempted by it, a light gleamed in his eyes. But the moment passed and Aragorn affirmed that he was who he said he was, and he swore to save Frodo.

When Boromir says, "So be it," in reply to Elrond, he is not renouncing the Ring or any claim to it. Nor is he placing himself in direct opposition to the Ring's power and purpose. Rather, he leaves his options open, and that proves to be a fatal mistake. But it is the kind of mistake that one should expect of a master tactician. Boromir is used to thinking in terms of how to win battles, and how to persuade others to follow his will. His experience at dealing with conflicts undoubtedly includes working with his father's council. "So be it" is a safe, non-committal reply. It betrays Boromir because he does not understand what he is dealing with.

And Boromir should not be faulted for that. The Ring represents an opportunity to him, and Boromir looks at the opportunity, not at the risks. He is an optimist who doesn't allow himself to become trapped. He plans ahead and reacts swiftly to danger. Not only does Boromir advise the Company to carry extra wood up onto Caradhras, he immediately changes his mind about going to Moria when the Company of the Ring realizes that wargs are tracking them in Eregion. Boromir isn't simply an optimist, he is a pragmatist. He not only believes there is a solution to every problem, he is willing to do whatever it takes to get the job done. Whatever works, as long as it does the job, is good enough for him.

And if there is one thing the Ring of Power can do, it's give a leader of armies a winning edge in a war. Boromir has no ambition to rule the world or to conquer other lands. He just wants to find a way to defeat Sauron. The Ring seems to be a tool which can give him (or someone) that victory. It is difficult to believe that the victory would come at so great a cost that no one should want it. In fact, for Boromir, it is impossible to believe such a thing. There is nothing in his experience which allows him to accept that some victories should not be sought.

Boromir's wisdom is firmly rooted in the common wisdom of the people of Gondor. He is practical, not thoughtful. Solutions present themselves to Boromir. He does not seek them out. When Boromir shares some of the lore he has learned in Gondor, he draws upon common knowledge, not esoteric knowledge. For example, when Gandalf points out that Isildur "did not march away straight from the war in Mordor, as some have told the tale," Boromir replies with: "Some in the North, maybe. All know in Gondor that he went first to Minas Anor and dwelt a while with his nephew Meneldil, instructing him, before he committed to him the rule of the South Kingdom."

And later, when the Company of the Ring is struggling up Caradhras and the snow is coming down heavily, Boromir says out loud: "I wonder if this is a contrivance of the Enemy. They say in my land that he can govern the storms in the Mountains of Shadow that stand upon the borders of Mordor. He has strange powers and many allies." In expressing this thought to his companions, Boromir undoubtedly speaks for them all (or most). But he reveals a knowledge or familiarity with the enemy, which is the mark of a good war leader.

And yet, Boromir's wisdom has its limits. When Celeborn warns the Company to avoid Fangorn Forest, Boromir says: "Indeed we have heard of Fangorn in Minas Tirith. But what I have heard seems to me for the most part old wives' tales, such as we tell to our children." Celeborn then admonishes him: "Do not despise the lore that has come down from distant years; for oft it may chance that old wives keep in memory word of things that once were needful for the wise to know."

Boromir has no real use for old wives' tales. He needs solid, credible information upon which to base his decisions as a leader. His attitude thus strikes some people as a bit arrogant. But he is true-hearted in his own fashion, pursuing a goal which he feels is noble and worthwhile. He is the Captain-general of the one nation which stands between Sauron and the complete domination of Middle-earth (or so he believes). He is the heir of Gondor's Ruling Steward, destined to one day be Steward himself. He naturally evaluates every situation and reaches his own conclusions, and he is used to expressing his ideas and commanding others. He is, as Tolkien says, *bossy*, but that is because he was raised to be bossy.

Boromir's flaws are a reflection of the flaws of the Stewards. He legitimizes their values. Even Denethor is stubborn and quick to judge both others and situations he is involved with. Rather than wait for confirmation of his conclusions, for example, after he has beheld the fleet of ships sailing up the Anduin, Denethor gives in to despair and kills himself. Denethor has passed on his resolute and determined nature to his elder son. But somewhere along the way, the Stewards have lost their true wisdom. They are no longer masters of lore.

Among the Elves, the most renowned loremasters are their kings and princes. Tolkien does not say so directly, but it would seem that the Númenorean loremasters also come from their kings and princes. The Stewards are thus charged with both preserving and understanding the ancient lore they have inherited from the kings. It is not enough simply to retain control over ancient lore. One must ensure that it is not left in the care of old wives or, worse, left to rot in some library where everyone forgets about it.

As Boromir distrusts the old wives' tales, Denethor leaves scrolls unread in his library until Gandalf comes searching for them. It appears that, by the time Gandalf returns to Minas Tirith with Pippin Took, Denethor has begun piecing together all the clues which are available to him. He has given long thought to the rhyme which troubled the dreams of both his sons and eventually led to Boromir's death. He has probably deciphered the scroll of Isildur, to learn what Gandalf had sought. He has figured out that his old rival, Thorongil, was probably the Heir of Isildur, leader of the Dunedain of the North. Hence, knowledge comes to Denethor eventually, but not wisdom. And the same is true for Boromir.

Just as Denethor realizes that Aragorn intends to claim Gondor's throne, and that Gandalf has sent the One Ring to Mordor, so Boromir eventually concludes that his only chance for greatness is to accomplish something even Aragorn cannot do. As Boromir and Aragorn travel together, Boromir has as much opportunity to assess Aragorn as Aragorn has to assess Boromir. Aragorn relies upon Gandalf's judgement, and he is respected by the Elves, who must seem like creatures out of old wives' tales to Boromir. Aragorn bides his time and complies with Boromir's immediate commands, but when the true leadership of the Company is cast into momentary doubt by the loss of Gandalf, Aragorn immediately says, "I will lead you now." He leaves no opportunity for Boromir to assert himself as Gandalf's successor.

It is not that Boromir hesitates at the crucial moment. Rather, it is simply not his moment. Boromir's concern is not with leading the company, but with returning to his people. Boromir often looks ahead, but he overlooks the immediate tasks which lie before him. He is so troubled by the dream both he and Faramir have had that he sets aside his duties in Gondor and undertakes a heroic journey to seek the meaning of the riddle. Boromir admits to the council that Gondor's situation is desperate. He has already been defeated in battle. He has no plan for defeating the enemy when the final assault comes.

Yet Gondor likes victorious captains. Maybe the people will rally around a leader who can only say, "We have done the best we can, and we will fight bravely until the end." But if someone else arrives who speaks of hope and defeating Sauron, Boromir's career will be over. Especially if that someone claims to be the rightful King of Gondor. Such concerns, though far away from Rivendell, should be clear to Boromir. During the months which follow the Council of Elrond, Boromir's thoughts must be in conflict. On the one hand, he has a duty to his people. On the other hand, the Council has decided to overthrow Sauron once and for all. If their plan succeeds, all of Middle-earth will be saved. But Gondor may be called upon to make a tremendous sacrifice. And what will Aragorn do? He has a more legitimate claim to the throne than the House of Hurin.

Were Boromir to use the One Ring against Sauron, he would deprive Aragorn of the chance to win popular acclaim. The decision regarding the return of the House of Elendil would be deferred indefinitely. While in his heart Boromir undoubtedly is not pursuing such a plan, the Ring seems to be offering exactly that to him. Boromir's resolve is weakening in Lothlórien, the night before the Company of the Ring bids farewell to the Elves. Boromir suggests it would be folly to throw the Ring away. He also becomes more adamant about persuading the Company to go to Minas Tirith with him, even though everyone knows Minas Tirith lies outside the path the Ring must take.

It is an unrealistic ambition, and a faux hope. Nonetheless, the torment of knowing that his people are doomed if the Ringbearer's quest fails, or if it takes too long, must frustrate Boromir. As it becomes more evident with each passing day that no one is really powerful enough to face Sauron directly, despair gnaws at Boromir's mind continually. Despair eventually leads his father to conclude that all is lost, and that there is no further point in living. Despair leads Boromir to believe that he can take the Ring and use it. Only after he fails both the test and to take the Ring is Boromir freed from the torment at last, and he understands what he has done.

In fact, Boromir inherits the burden of a thousand years spent waiting for a future no one thought would ever come. The Stewards have become complacent about their situation. They no longer expect a claimant to the throne to turn up. Gondor is theirs, in their eyes, but not theirs to claim. Generations of sons of Stewards must have asked the same question, time and again: "Why are we not the kings, if we rule the land?" The ancient oath of office, whereby the Steward takes up rule of the land "until the king returns", suddenly rings true in Boromir's ears. He has a duty to examine Aragorn's claim, and to present it to Gondor, if it seems to be legitimate. In the end, that duty falls to his brother Faramir, who succeeds Denethor as the last Ruling Steward of Gondor.

Faramir needs time to reconcile himself to Aragorn's claim. When he first learns of that claim from Sam and Frodo, he is doubtful. "So great a claim will need to be established, and clear proofs will be required," he points out, before Gondor considers Aragorn's petition. From that time forward, until he is awakened from his illness by Aragorn, Faramir has no opportunity to meet and appraise the man who would be king. And yet, Faramir recognizes Aragorn immediately upon awakening. He has certainly had plenty of time to consider Frodo's story. In fact, Faramir knows Gondor's history better than Boromir. Whereas Boromir casually relays what the common people know or believe about the past for his companions, Faramir gives Sam and Frodo a concise lecture on Gondor's history. It may be that Faramir has had time to think about Thorongil, the mysterious Dunadan warrior who served his grandfather, Ecthelion, for a few years.

By the time Aragorn arrives at Minas Tirith, it seems everyone but Denethor himself is ready and willing to acknowledge Aragorn's claim. Prince Imrahil, whose fief lies beyond the authority of the Stewards, declares for Aragorn openly. And Faramir does so as well. Eomer, King of Rohan, also supports Aragorn's claim, though the

Rohirrim have no power or authority to intervene in Gondor's affairs. Their recognition nonetheless swells Aragorn's reputation. But the only clear proof Aragorn provides of who he is can be his sword, which is the sword Elendil had borne and which broke beneath him. All other heirlooms have either been lost, withheld, or given away.

It requires a Steward's recognition for Aragorn to become King of Gondor. A Steward must judge him and proclaim his worthiness to the people of Gondor. That would have been Boromir's task, and Boromir knew Aragorn far better than Faramir. But what would Boromir have done? The question is unanswerable. Boromir was conflicted, and he only found peace through sacrificing his life for others. He was guided by his ambition, and to some extent his forefathers were guided by similar ambitions. When Gandalf asked Denethor how he would order things, if he could have his own way, Denethor replied: "I would have things as they were in all the days of my life, and in the days of my longfathers before me: to be Lord of this City in peace, and to leave my chair to a son after me, who would be his own master and no wizard's pupil."

The Stewards did not view themselves as caretakers. They were lords and princes. Even Faramir felt this way, when he met Frodo and Sam in Ithilien. When Frodo said that Aragorn alone would be able to claim Isildur's Bane for himself, if any had the right to do so, Faramir asked: "Why so, and not Boromir, prince of the City that the sons of Elendil founded?" Soon afterward, when Sam angrily confronts Faramir over the way he questions Frodo, Faramir points out: "I am commanded to slay all whom I find in this land without the leave of the Lord of Gondor."

For a thousand years, the Stewards *have* been the lords of Gondor. To suddenly learn that a claimant to the throne is on the way is a bit unnerving. And perhaps there have been false claimants to the throne in the past. Their way of life must be utterly and irrevocably changed when a new king sits upon the throne. And what will be left for the Stewards in the aftermath of such an event? When Faramir greets Aragorn in formal procession before the city of Minas Tirith, he lays aside his office as Steward. Technically, there is no law requiring

Aragorn to restore that office to Faramir. In fact, there is no law requiring Faramir to acknowledge Aragorn as king. Just as Aragorn subtly alters his claim, naming himself Elendil's Heir rather than Isildur's Heir (as the Isildurian claim had already been rejected), so Faramir avoids naming Aragorn as Isildur's Heir. He names Isildur in Aragorn's lineage, but leaves Elendil's name for last.

Faramir could easily have said, "Well, the Line of Isildur has already been considered and rejected. Gondor will not revisit that issue." Instead, he accepted the assertion that only an heir of Elendil would be acceptable to Gondor. By implication, Aragorn's claim was reuniting Gondor with Arnor. Faramir's decision thus ensured that Gondor's power would be extended far to the north.

If the Stewards were indeed descended from Anarion, then Faramir's recognition of Aragorn was the final action by the family of Anarion. Aragorn was indeed descended from Anarion through Arvedui's wife Firiel, but the last vestiges of the Line of Anarion ceased to exist under the law. All claims were laid aside in favor of the House of Elendil. In effect, Faramir laid to rest ancient conflicts which, like the Dead Men of Dunharrow, had to wait through the centuries for an Heir of Isildur to give them release. He brought closure to the ancient question of succession, and in doing so discharged the final obligations of his office. The Stewards' peculiar role in Gondor's history ended on a much more graceful note than that on which it had begun.

Had Tolkien truly modeled his Stewards on the historical Pepinids, Faramir would have rejected Aragorn's claim, and he would have taken the throne for himself. But eventually Gondor would have been divided among his descendants, and the ancient realm his family had been entrusted with would have ceased to exist. That, of course, was what actually happened in Arnor. The High Kingship was set aside and the northern realm divided into three lesser realms. Denethor's remark to his son about "other places of less royalty" was thus a subtle rebuke to the northern kings who set aside their heritage. But it also emphasized the fact that, despite all its tribulations, Gondor had survived. It had proven itself worthy of the rightful king, should he return to claim the throne. And it had done so under the rule of the

Stewards. They had proudly remained humble, curbing their ambitions. And they did so because they were Stewards, not men who would be kings.

MICHAEL MARTINEZ

Chapter 7:
Legolas Greenleaf

Through the years I have been writing about Middle-earth, few topics have proven to be as popular as Legolas. The two Legolas essays have been read by more people than I can hope to count. "Legolas, you're just so darn...CUTE" has been copied (pirated) on so many Web sites I had to stop asking people to give me proper credit. I couldn't keep up with the unauthorized reproductions. (Fortunately, enough Web site operators agreed to give me credit that the others quickly followed suit -- so, I am at least widely acknowledged as the author of the essay, an abbreviated version of which is included here). I wrote the essay in response to the tremendous amount of e-mail I received in the first month after the "Fellowship of the Ring" movie was released (December 2001). As of this writing, only one other essay has proven to be more popular than the Legolas essays.

Speaking of Legolas...

I decided to set myself a challenge and write something about Legolas which hasn't been said before. There seems to be a lot of curiosity about this Elf. People want to know all sorts of things about him, such as what color was his hair, who was his mother, when was he born, was he at the Battle of Five Armies?

If someone were to produce a television series based on the Fellowship of the Ring (the company, not the book), they would have to come up with their own history for Legolas. The inevitable exploration of each character's background would result in episodes where Gandalf first learns that Middle-earth is dangerous even for Maiar (say, within a year after he steps off the boat); where Aragorn tracks down his first Orc; where Gimli learns to cope with being the son of Gloin; where Frodo remembers the day his parents drowned; where Pippin watches as his sister Pearl takes Lalia the Fat for her last ray of sunshine; where Merry goes into the Old Forest for the first time; where Sam capers about with Rosie Cotton and her brothers, and he first realizes he loves her; and where Boromir tries to come to terms with the fact that he'll never be King of Gondor.

What would Legolas' past conflict be? What sort of experience would an immortal Wood-elf have such that it would help define the character of Legolas as he revealed himself to the Fellowship? There is really only one moment of doubt for Legolas in the story that Tolkien did tell us. That was when he recognized the Balrog. That is not to say Legolas was always sure of what to do. In typical Elf fashion he does not give Aragorn clear advice on what to do when they and Gimli are pursuing the Orcs which have seized Merry and Pippin. "My heart bids me go on," he says. "But we must hold together. I will follow your counsel."

Legolas' moment of doubt before the Balrog was a defining event. He panicked. He recognized the Balrog for what it was and lost heart. "Ai! Ai!" wailed Legolas. "A Balrog! A Balrog is come!" He dropped his arrow to the ground, rather than shoot the thing. Nonetheless, the encounter may have better prepared him for confronting the flying Nazgul over Anduin. Legolas had leaped up the bank and drawn an arrow, seeking a target. "*Elbereth Gilthoniel!*" he cried when he sensed the approach of the flying Nazgul. He was startled and moved by fear, but now he had greater courage.

Such a growth in Legolas' character is good, but it reminds me of the silly premise that went into Lieutenant Commander Data in the "Encounter at Farpoint" storyline. Supposedly, he had been serving in Starfleet for something like 27 years. In all that time he had learned virtually nothing about humans and human emotion. What did they do, assign him to serve only with Vulcans until Captain Picard signed him up on the Enterprise?

Legolas refers to his companions as children, and when he, Gimli, Aragorn, and Gandalf are approaching Meduseld he says that the leaves have fallen five hundred times in Mirkwood since the Rohirrim came out of the north. He also makes it sound as though he had lived through all five hundred years. Elsewhere he says he has watched many an acorn grow up and die as a hoary old oak tree. As Elves go

Legolas is probably not ancient, but he seems to have been around for a while. And yet, Lórien is a mysterious place to him. Legolas has never visited there. It seems strange that he should not know anything about a land of Silvan Elves.

We may thus suggest that Legolas may have been born after his father left the Emyn Duir (the Mountains of Mirkwood) and led his people north to settle along the Forest River. That would have been shortly after Sauron rose again and established himself on the hill of Amon Lanc, building the fortress of Dol Guldur. And yet, one of the peculiar inconsistencies in Legolas' character is that he knows the Lay of Nimrodel. The lay itself had to have been composed sometime after 1981, the year in which Nimrodel and Amroth left Lórien. Who wrote it? How did the story get back up to Mirkwood so that Legolas could learn it?

The most likely answer seems to be that during Sauron's absence from Dol Guldur (the years of the Watchful Peace, TA 2063 - 2460) the Elves of Mirkwood went abroad and traveled as far as Gondor. Calenardhon's population was declining in these years but Gondor was still able to hold the Anduin against its enemies. Celeborn and Galadriel took up rule in Lórien after Amroth's departure and it may be they did not enact their policy of secrecy right away. So some of Thranduil's people may indeed have traveled to Lórien in those years and learned the lay. Legolas says merely, "It is long since any of my own folk journeyed hither back to the land whence we wandered in ages long ago, but we hear that Lórien is not yet deserted."

That's a curious thing to say. From whom did they hear the land was not deserted? Probably from Elrond's folk. And Legolas did learn the Westron translation of the lay in Rivendell, apparently. So it seems that Legolas was young enough not to have ever been in Lórien, or even to have approached it while its people were still active in the broad world. It may be, therefore, that he was born sometime in the Watchful Peace, and perhaps towards the end of it. He would thus be quite old even by comparison with the long-lived Gimli and Aragorn.

Yet again Tolkien sets an apparent inconsistency before us. When Aragorn and Legolas discuss Celeborn's warning about Fangorn Forest, Legolas professes to know nothing, save only that old songs speak of the Onodrim, the Ents. He has not traveled as far as Aragorn. Yet later on, when they enter Fangorn to look for the missing hobbits, Legolas says, "It is old, very old. So old that almost I feel young again, as I have not felt since I journeyed with you children."

That's a rather strange comment from an Elf who hasn't traveled far. Mirkwood is an ancient forest in its own right. But Mirkwood, unlike Fangorn, has been home to creatures which cut down trees, clear paths, and do other things which strip the age from forests. Elves, Men, Orcs, and even the giant spiders all make Mirkwood a very different forest. Perhaps Legolas was experiencing the sense of wonder that any child would feel upon first stepping out into the wider world.

Legolas may have visited Rivendell more than once. He doesn't seem to be unfamiliar with Elrond's people. The journey from Mirkwood to Rivendell would not have been very perilous for many years after the Battle of Five Armies (since most of the Orcs of the Misty Mountains were killed in that battle). Some people have wondered if Legolas might not be a younger son of Thranduil. His role as messenger to Elrond, and Thranduil's later granting permission to Legolas to lead some of their people to Gondor seem to indicate Legolas may not have been his father's heir. Of course, Thranduil may only have been bowing to the inevitable as far as letting Elves leave for Gondor.

If he were barely more than 500 years old at the time of the War of the Ring, Legolas would have lived through several significant events. He would recall the coming of Smaug to Erebor, and the destruction of the kingdoms of Dale and Erebor. He would remember the Long Winter, and probably would have been one of the Elven lords defending Thranduil in the Battle of Five Armies. He thus would have known some dangers and hardships, and so was well able to care for himself. He seems to fight the Orcs well enough at Parth Galen and later at Helm's Deep to show he is an accomplished warrior. He threatens Eomer's life on Gimli's behalf with all the confidence of a veteran.

Since Tolkien doesn't mention Legolas in the scanty accounts of the War of the Last Alliance most people seem willing to accept that Legolas was probably born in the Third Age. But it may seem radical to some to suggest he was probably born late in the Third Age, perhaps even well into the Watchful Peace. But there is precedent for a "relatively young" elf to rise to prominence. When the Noldor fled into Exile, Turgon and his wife Elenwë probably did not have any children. Their daughter, Idril, was still a child when Elenwë was lost during the crossing of the Helcaraxë. Idril therefore grew up in Middle-earth.

Orodreth was also apparently born and raised in Middle-earth, being the son of Angrod (according to *The Peoples of Middle-earth*). Orodreth's children were Gil-galad and Finduilas, who would have been even younger at the fall of Nargothrond than Legolas seems to have been during the War of the Ring. Voronwë, Tuor's friend, was the son of Aranwë of the Noldor and a Sindarin Elf who was related to Cirdan. And Maeglin, the son of Eol and Aredhel, was only a couple hundred years old when he died in the fall of Gondolin.

Thranduil may have had three or four children, and Legolas could easily have been the baby of the bunch. Hence, to him the events of the First Age and even the story of Nimrodel and Amroth would seem far away. He would be a stranger in Lórien and because of the perils inhabiting Middle-earth he might not have begun leaving his father's kingdom until after the Battle of Five Armies. It may be the Battle of Five Armies was the first true defining event in Legolas' career.

Certainly when the Elvenking of *The Hobbit* set out with his army he didn't expect a battle. Smaug was dead and there was hardly anyone else around to bicker over the dragon's hoard. Except for the fact he was a king going after a large hoard of gold and jewels, he should not have felt much need for an army. So it would make sense if he brought his youngest child with him.

All that said, we are still left with questions about Legolas. We cannot, alas!, be sure of anything concerning his past. He probably knew Aragorn and Gandalf before the Council of Elrond, but there is no sign of recognition. He probably had been to Dale and Erebor, but he and

Gimli don't seem to have really known each other before the Council of Elrond. Of course, they traveled together for some weeks before they began bonding. Legolas seems to have made the first overtures of friendship when he tried to soften his words about the history of the Balrog on the borders of Lórien.

Of course, Legolas also lost his temper when Gimli refused to go blindfold alone into Lórien. That was the only time Legolas ever became cross with anyone. Was he speaking as a proud Elven prince, or as a young Elf-lord who had not yet burned out his youthful fires? Legolas was still curious about the world, following Aragorn all the way to Gondor, seeking the hidden secrets of Fangorn, and allowing himself to become absorbed in the beauty of Aglarond.

Perhaps most Elves would have appreciated the sights Legolas encountered on his journey, but there is something youthful and refreshing in the way he glances back at the spirits following Aragorn's company. "...Legolas turning to speak to Gimli looked back and the Dwarf saw before his face the glitter in the Elf's bright eyes...."

There is something playful in the way Legolas engages in a deadly game with Gimli at Helm's Deep. Can anyone picture Elrond counting coup on Orcs in the midst of a very serious struggle over the future of Rohan? Or what of Fëanor? Filled with fury though he was, at the end of his life he was still the stern and measuring father. Whatever mirth he might have known in youth had long since fallen away. So, too, was the mirth of Fingolfin long since shorn from him when he rode forth to challenge Morgoth to battle. And even Maedhros who chided his angry brothers with laughter over Thingol's cession of empty lands to the Noldor became a grim and determined lord who, by the end of the First Age, was consumed with weariness and the burden of guilt.

Legolas seems rather impetuous when he and Gimli are riding through the "herd" of Huorns and Ents who have saved the Rohirrim at Helm's Deep. He can barely contain himself as they ride through the trees, and when he discovers eyes looking out at them, he turns back from the road and starts to enter the strange wood. Only Gandalf's caution brings Legolas out of his curious Elvish euphoria. It is hard to imagine Celeborn or Galadriel being so overcome with curiosity they would abandon their mission to find out more about the eyes in the wood.

The character of Legolas is not so much compelling as confounding. I think many people wonder about him because he seems such a paradox, both old and young, both wise and yet inexplicably ignorant of the wide world around him. Legolas is a subtle stroke of Elvish youth at the end of the Elder Days. It may be there were few young Elves around at the time, and his may have been the last great adventure for a young Elf in Middle-earth. When Celeborn finally sailed over Sea, Tolkien notes, the last living memory of the Elder Days went with him. But when Legolas built his ship and departed, it may be that the last sparkle of youthful Elvendom vanished from Middle-earth, too.

Legolas, you're just so darn...CUTE!

When I first saw Orlando Bloom dressed as Legolas, I said to myself right then and there, "That is the DEFINITIVE Legolas." A lot of people complained about the blond hair. Why is he blond? Almost overnight, the Great Hair Color Debate raged across the Internet. What color should Legolas' hair be?

The book doesn't say and, quite frankly, I never really cared that much, although I always pictured him as being dark-haired myself. Why? No idea. That's just the way I saw him...until Orlando Bloom (who is himself dark-haired) stepped into the pointy shoes of nearly every Tolkien fan's favorite Elf (in the movies).

Lúthien has always been my favorite Elf, but I liked Beleg, too. Of course, my favorite Tolkien story is the tale of Lúthien and Beren. But Legolas is an enigma. A lot of people have devoted a great deal of time to trying to figure him out. The color of his hair isn't the only question people have asked about him. How old is he? Is he married? Does he have any brothers or sisters? And (again), was he at the Battle of Five Armies?

The answers to all these questions are: Don't know. What do you think? and Whatever you want the answer to be.

Tolkien at one point said of Legolas that, of all the members of the Fellowship, the Elf had achieved the least. Many people have disagreed with Tolkien about that assessment. After all, Gimli didn't bring down any flying Nazgul. Nor, for that matter, did Aragorn or Boromir. Even Meriadoc only earned honorable mention for sneaking up behind the Lord of the Nazgul and stabbing him in the rear of the leg. Of course, Legolas didn't kill the Nazgul (he was dead already) -- just the flying steed.

And speaking of Legolas...oh, yes. Orlando plays a character named Legolas in these movies Peter Jackson put together for him. How much like Tolkien's Legolas is Peter Jackson's Legolas? I've been asked that, actually. I noted in my review of "The Lord of the Rings: The Fellowship of the Ring" how spectacular Sir Ian McKellen is as Gandalf. I think he's absolutely fantastic as Gandalf. Well, I can honestly say the same thing about Orlando Bloom. He's absolutely fantastic as Legolas.

I think he comes as close to portraying a Tolkien Legolas as any actor alive today would be capable of doing. Are there differences between the film character and the book? Yes. Legolas in the movies is not quite as reserved as Legolas in the book. The Legolas in the book is a bit playful and mischievous. The whole quest thing is almost like a holiday for him.

The movie Legolas is so darned serious. I can see why all the girls like him. They want to soothe his brow, massage his shoulders, help him relax. And yet, he moves with the grace of a cat. And that walk is something Orlando says he practiced. He put a lot of time and thought into figuring out what Legolas' movement should be like. It was time well-spent.

But let's not forget that Legolas is strong, loyal, dedicated, and he kills Orcs really, really fast.

Legolas is a very violent character in the movies. He's deadly, cold, and calculating when he confronts Orcs. But he also has some interesting reactions. One of the odder parts of "The Lord of the Rings: The Fellowship of the Ring" occurs in the council of Elrond, when all the Elves and Dwarves start yelling at each other. There is nothing like this in the book. No Tolkien Elf or Dwarf would behave that way. Not under such circumstances.

But when that little guy steps forward and offers to accompany Legolas on his heroic journey (or was it the other way around?), Gimli offers his axe. And just at that moment, you see the Look on Legolas' face. He realizes that this really isn't HIS movie. He actually seems to panic for the briefest moment.

Well, people thought it was a funny look, and obviously all the shouting was intended to give Orlando an opportunity to ham it up in his movie. I think he did a good job.

I wish I did know how old Legolas was supposed to be. For the movies, they decided he was 2931 years old. Where did they come up with that age? No idea. It has no relevance to any published Tolkien text of which I am aware.

But, I doubt anyone will care much.

Chapter 8:
The wars of the Glorfindels

J.R.R. Tolkien created a lot of "throw-off" characters, characters who appear for a story or only part of a story, never to re-emerge fully again. And of all these throw-offs the one which garners nearly as much attention and discussion as any of the primary characters is Glorfindel. Or would that be, the Glorfindels? Was there one or two of the guy? Enquiring minds want to know (or do they just want to argue forever and never actually know?).

Why is Glorfindel so cool? He shows up near the end of "Flight to the Ford", is seen but not heard in "Many Meetings" (oh, Gandalf and Frodo talk about him briefly), participates in "The Council of Elrond" long enough to confound and confusticate Bombadilian-related topics, and then vanishes until Arwen arrives in Gondor to marry Aragorn in "The Steward and the King". Except for putting Frodo on his white Elven horse and lighting up like a Christmas tree when the Nazgul try to cross the Ford of Bruinen, what does Glorfindel do that is so special? His one real claim to fame comes in an anecdote in "Gondor and the Heirs of Anarion" (included in Appendix A, *The Lord of the Rings*) where his arrival with an Elven army in Angmar helps defeat the Witch-king (in the north) once and for all.

Of course, no Glorfindel discussion is complete (and few are started) without someone asking, "Was the Glorfindel of Gondolin related to the Glorfindel of Rivendell?" Sometimes one is tempted to respond with something like, "Yes, they were twin brothers, and the evil one killed the good one and took his place in the family. The Elves have yet to catch on to the truth."

It may be fairly said that the relationship between the two Glorfindels is not obvious. In fact, it's really not clear to many people who have studied the matter for decades. For some reason, the revelation in *The Return of the Shadow* that "years later, long after the publication of *The Lord of the Rings*" J.R.R. Tolkien decided after much thought that

Glorfindel of Rivendell was actually Glorfindel of Gondolin returned from the dead, just doesn't carry much weight with some people. Why? Because the decision to connect the two characters this way was made *years later*, after *The Lord of the Rings* had been published. By implication (or inference, depending on which way you choose to examine the issue) Glorfindel of Rivendell was not originally conceived of as Glorfindel of Gondolin.

Well, that's fair enough. In fact, originally, Tolkien had written "Glorfindel tells of his ancestry in Gondolin" in a note which outlined events for the Council of Elrond. Clearly JRRT was intending to connect Glorfindel of Rivendell with Glorfindel of Gondolin, although at this time (the early 1940s) hardly anyone other than J.R.R. Tolkien, C.S. Lewis, and a few close friends even knew about the Glorfindel of Gondolin.

In any incarnation, Glorfindel(s) had hardly blazed a trail across the pages of Tolkien's imagination. A Glorfindel appears in one story in *The Book of Lost Tales*, and that is "The Fall of Gondolin". There he doesn't even make his appearance until the battle for the city is raging on, and he arrives with the battalion from the House of the Golden Flower. His "house" bore a device of "rayed sun upon their shield", but Glorfindel himself "bare a mantle so broidered in threads of gold that it was diapered with celandine as a field in spring; and his arms were damascened with cunning gold."

Of the eleven lords of houses of Gondolin (who served King Turgon), Glorfindel is the only one whose personal device is described. Glorfindel was one of the smarter lords. He didn't rush out and get slaughtered with all his warriors, but most of them died nonetheless defending Turgon. The warriors of the House of the Harp (whose lord Salgant had held back out of fear) saved Glorfindel and some of his warriors when they were almost overwhelmed. From that point forward Glorfindel stayed close to Tuor, but he didn't really accomplish much until Tuor began fleeing the city with all the women and children he could gather together. Then Glorfindel took the rearguard and fought off dragons, Orcs, and Balrogs with his dwindling force of warriors.

Tuor retreated from the city to the mountains and there the column of exiles, nearly a thousand strong, was ambushed. Orcs had been sent to the hills and mountains to prevent any escapes from the city, and they threw rocks upon the column from high cliffs while troops attacked the head of the column and its rear. And with the attack on the rear came a Balrog. Thorondor and his eagles stopped the Orcs who were throwing rocks, but the Balrog pressed in on Glorfindel's warriors and he finally attacked it alone. Glorfindel's battle with the Balrog was brief but he managed to kill it. He ended up going over a cliff with the creature, and so died himself, and the Elves made songs about his victory and death long afterward.

There is something moving about Glorfindel's sacrifice, and I cannot help but wonder if Tolkien wasn't projecting something of his friends Rob Gilson and Geoffrey Bache Smith, both of whom were killed in World War I, into the early Glorfindel's character. Gilson had fallen in battle at La Boiselle, leading a contingent of British soldiers into battle on July 1, according to Tolkien's biographer, Humphrey Carpenter. Smith wrote a letter to Tolkien, who himself survived unscathed 48 hours of front-line combat at Ovillers. When Tolkien's company was relieved and he returned to quarters he found Smith's letter.

One cannot say enough in a few brief sentences what Tolkien's early friends meant to him: he, Smith, Gilson, and Christopher Wiseman had formed the core of a small clique they called the Tea Club, Barovian Society (T.C.B.S.) when attending school. These four were particularly close, and all of them served in war in some capacity. Tolkien and Wiseman lived through the experience. When he replied to Smith's letter about Gilson's death, Tolkien wrote "I do not feel a member of a complete body now. I honestly feel that the T.C.B.S has ended." Smith wouldn't allow that to happen, however. "The T.C.B.S. is not finished and never will be," he said. By the end of that year Smith himself would be dead. On December 16, 1916, Christopher Wiseman wrote to his friend Ronald Tolkien, "I have just received news from home about G.B.S., who succumbed to injuries received from shells bursting on December 3rd. I can't say much about it now. I humbly pray Almighty God I may be accounted worthy of him."

Smith's spirit must have been infectious to Tolkien, as was Gilson's. Gilson's father had been the headmaster of King Edward's School in Birmingham, and it was the elder Gilson who had encouraged Tolkien to pursue the study of classical linguistics. It was with the T.C.B.S. that Tolkien became entranced with "Beowulf", "The Pearl", "Sir Gawain", and "Volsungsaga". Carpenter says that Smith, a late member of the T.C.B.S., was so knowledgeable and influential with the others that they "began to wake up to the significance of poetry -- as indeed Tolkien was already doing."

One of the last letters Smith had written to Tolkien contained the following:

> My chief consolation is that if I am scuppered tonight -- I am off on duty in a few minutes -- there will still be left a member of the great T.C.B.S. to voice what I dreamed and what we all agreed upon. For the death of one of its members cannot, I am determined, dissolve the T.C.B.S. Death can make us loathsome and helpless as individuals, but it cannot put an end to the immortal four! A discovery I am going to communicate to Rob before I go off to-night. And do you write it also to Christopher. May God bless you, my dear John Ronald, and may you say the things I have tried to say long after I am not here to say them, if such be my lot.

In the next year Tolkien would fall ill with Trench Fever and his part in the war would come to an end. But he would immortalize its tragic sense of loss and despair in the first of a series of stories that eventually came to be *The Book of Lost Tales*: "The Fall of Gondolin". Carpenter says that Tolkien did not model the story on any prior event or tale, but that is not entirely true. Gondolin owes a great deal to the story of Troy. The idea of a lost city, destroyed by an overwhelming force despite the heroic efforts of its defenders -- doomed to betrayal and treachery -- is a powerful motif that is seldom revisited in ancient literature. Homer's Troy is symbolic of the despairs and insanities of war, from Achilles' fretting over a slave girl to Menelaus' ridiculous insistence on winning back Helen no matter what the cost.

The story of Gondolin is not the human story of Troy retold. Gondolin is an Elven city, and though Tolkien's conception of Elvish values and philosophy had yet to emerge, those who mourned the fall of Gondolin were Elves, not Men. Gondolin is to the Elves as Troy is to Men: the inspiration for great songs and literature. And it is that to Tolkien, as well. Some of his greatest prose in the years 1917-25 is found in "The Fall of Gondolin", the first full Elvish tale he ever wrote. And when he incorporated the story into his book of Lost Tales, one of his narrative Elves says of "The Fall of Gondolin" that "it is the greatest of the stories of the Gnomes [the Gnomes became the Noldor in later mythologies], and even in this house is Ilfiniol son of Bronweg, who knows those deeds more truly than any that are now on Earth."

At this time in Tolkien's life there was no story more important to his emerging mythology. "The Fall of Gondolin" represented the near fulfillment of the long promises of his youth and of the Gnomic legends. Bright Ëarendil would survive the fall of Gondolin to become the savior of Elves and Men, much as Aeneas survived the fall of Troy to become the ancestor of Rome. Tolkien survived the fall of the T.C.B.S., and he set about the task of ensuring that its dreams would live on, even as G.B. Smith had foretold.

But such a tragic story cannot be told without some great sacrifice. And Tolkien had many examples of sacrifice to choose from. He needed to refine the theme and produce a character who was untouched by corruption, unscathed by the loss of hearth and home. A character who, despite the intrusion of death upon his life, would determine that Gondolin should continue. Death could not destroy Gondolin, nor exile. That was Glorfindel's contribution. Gondolin had been founded by Noldoli (Gnomes) who survived the Battle of Unnumbered Tears. When Gondolin itself was destroyed, a remnant of its people escaped, and they carried on. It was much the same with the T.C.B.S. Geoffrey Smith had determined that death and loss should not dissolve the group. The survivors would carry on, and at least one of them would tell great stories, revitalizing English literature in a way few men could hope to.

So Glorfindel becomes a tragic figure who alone among a host of tragic characters is memorable. There is something deep and moving about Glorfindel's sacrifice. Echoes of the heroic fight with the Balrog would be passed down to later works such as the "Quenta

Noldorinwa" and the "Later Annals of Beleriand". But the story of Gondolin itself was to languish and fall by the wayside. Tolkien never returned to the battle for the city, but he returned to Glorfindel.

As mentioned previously, while writing "The Council of Elrond", Tolkien at one point considered having Glorfindel speak of his ancestry in Gondolin. Something of Gondolin was thus to be carried forward into the new Hobbit book. But Tolkien dropped the idea. Glorfindel of Rivendell became simply Glorfindel, and there was no reference to an earlier Glorfindel or an earlier story. The transformation of Glorfindel may represent nothing more than an author's need to tell a concise story. He would, after all, remove material concerning the romance of Aragorn and Arwen to an appendix.

So the tale of Glorfindel would go on, and in fact Tolkien enlarged it several years later when he wrote the material for the appendices. There now appeared the account of Glorfindel's arrival on the field of battle with an Elven army, completing the Gondorian victory over the Witch-king of Angmar and in a way rebutting Melkor's crushing defeat and enslavement of Gondolin. Where darkness ruled, Glorfindel brought light. But his light would soon fade and the Elves would return to their haunts, eventually to sail over Sea in great numbers, fleeing Middle-earth. Glorfindel would remain, but he was an exceptional elf, and the exception would haunt Tolkien's thoughts in later years.

Who, then, was Glorfindel, and what was he doing in Middle-earth? He wasn't much of an enigma for the fans. In 1958 Rhona Beare asked Tolkien (on behalf of other fans) why Asfaloth, Glorfindel's horse, had a bridle and bit "when Elves ride without bit, bridle, or saddle?" Tolkien responded quickly that he should have written "headstall", and this change was eventually made to the text. And that (but for the request of the use of Glorfindel's name for a cow) represents the sum total of early fannish interest in Middle-earth's most enigmatic Elf.

The Glorfindel legend subsided. Tolkien attempted to rewrite the story of Tuor and Gondolin, but he only got as far as having Tuor look across the plain of Tunladen upon Gondolin for the first time. Glorfindel briefly appeared in the story of Aredhel and Maeglin as one of the lords Turgon appointed to escort her, but Tolkien decided that Glorfindel, Egalmoth, and Ecthelion were inappropriate choices for Elven lords who would become so dismayed by Nan Dungortheb they would turn back in despair and so lose their charge. He decided it would be best not to name them in the story. This decision, and a note concerning Elven death and possible resurrection accompanying "Athrabeth Finrod ah Andreth", represents an elevation of Glorfindel's stature in the churning cauldron of Tolkien's thought.

The question of who Elrond's Glorfindel should be diminished in importance as the fame of Gondolin's Glorfindel increased...in Tolkien's mind. The readers had no idea these issues existed for the author. Glorfindel was more important to J.R.R. Tolkien than he was to *The Lord of the Rings*. But to find a place for Glorfindel in the mythology Tolkien had to be consistent with what Gandalf had said of the Elf in "Many Meetings":

'What about Rivendell and the Elves? Is Rivendell safe?'

'Yes, at present, until all else is conquered. The Elves may fear the Dark Lord, and they may fly before him, but never again will they listen to him or serve him. And here in Rivendell there live still some of his chief foes: the Elven-wise, lords of the Eldar from beyond the furthest seas. They do not fear the Ringwraiths, for those who have dwelt in the Blessed Realm live at once in both worlds, and against both the Seen and the Unseen they have great power.'

'I thought I saw a white figure that shone and did not grow dim like that others. Was that Glorfindel then?'

'Yes, you saw him for a moment as is upon the other side: one of the mighty of the Firstborn. He is an Elf-lord of a house of princes. Indeed there is a power in Rivendell to withstand the might of Mordor, for a while: and elsewhere other powers still dwell....'

Glorfindel is therefore an Elf who has dwelt in Aman. So the published text makes it virtually impossible for him to be descended from an Elf of Gondolin. He could have lived in Gondolin, but could not have been born there or afterward among the Exiles of Gondolin. Hence, the decision not to make Glorfindel a descendant of the *other* Glorfindel was really a very early choice, made prior to the publication of *The Lord of the Rings*. But that doesn't mean that Glorfindel was meant to be the Glorfindel of Gondolin.

Despite common misconceptions, Tolkien did not mind reusing names among the Elves. Although no two Elves in *The Lord of the Rings* bear the same names, one (at least) bears the name of an earlier Elf: Rumil, one of the march-wardens of Lórien, is given the name of the Noldorin Elf who created the first Tengwar (and the earlier Rumil is mentioned in Appendix E). But another name from Gondolin appears in Elrond's council: Galdor, the Elf from the Havens, Cirdan's emissary. Christopher Tolkien reaches the conclusion that this cannot be the same Galdor who led the vanguard of Tuor's column of refugees in "The Fall of Gondolin." Galdor of Gondolin not only lived, he returned to Aman at the end of the First Age and never returned to Middle-earth.

So there are peculiar cases even in *The Lord of the Rings* where Tolkien reused Elven names, and he was not entirely clear on whether the usage was appropriate. Years later, while considering the history of Cirdan, JRRT noted to himself that Galdor of Gondolin could have survived the fall and remained in Middle-earth, thus never acquiring the wisdom Glorfindel obtained in the West. Christopher is quick to point out that his father phrased the speculation in such a way as to indicate he wasn't sure, and Christopher concludes that his father could not have located the manuscript for "The Fall of Gondolin" to check and therefore would merely have been suggesting a possibility to himself (for future reference, perhaps).

In *The Peoples of Middle-earth*, Christopher published for the first time two essays concerning Glorfindel which his father had written around the time of 1972. The first essay is incomplete, its opening page missing, but it seems that JRRT had decided that several Elves had been sent back to Middle-earth with the Istari "as guards or assistants." One of these was Glorfindel, attached to Gandalf. This essay supposes that Glorfindel, because of his great sacrifice, was released from Mandos early, and he was restored to the natural innocence of the Elves. Living with the Maiar and among Elves who had never rebelled, he probably became a friend to Olórin (Gandalf) and grew in wisdom and power.

But after having written out these thoughts, Tolkien changed his mind. In a note Christopher only refers to, his father decided soon after writing the first Glorfindel essay that the Elf had more likely returned to Middle-earth in the Second Age. Thereupon Tolkien wrote the second essay concerning Glorfindel and he decided finally that the two Glorfindels were the same person, who having been purged of his sins in Mandos was released and allowed to live in Aman. But then he returned to Middle-earth to help Gil-galad prepare for the wars with Sauron.

The fact that Glorfindel of Rivendell had lived in the Blessed Realm at some point forced Tolkien to consider how he might have gotten there. Glorfindel's arrival in Middle-earth was not so firmly mandated, but Tolkien doesn't really say why Glorfindel had to return in the Second Age, except to say in the second essay that such travel by the Elves would have been forbidden after the Downfall of Númenor. Hence, the Istari could not have been accompanied by the guards and assistants of the first essay.

The restriction on travel from Aman to Middle-earth *is* attested in his letters, so Tolkien was not simply adding another element to the story to rationalize his choice. Rather, he was ensuring that the choice was consistent with what he had already told other people.

The final issue, that of Glorfindel's apparent great power, is dealt with by suggesting that as a reconstituted Elf he would have become closer to a Maia in power than any normal living Elf. The mystery of Glorfindel's power in Middle-earth is therefore explained. Not just any Elf can send the Nazgul fleeing. One Nazgul, alone in the Shire, withdrew before the company of Gildor Inglorion (himself an Exile). But the Nine of them were willing to face Elrond and Glorfindel together if they must when it seemed certain Frodo would escape them after all. So Glorfindel's being sent out to find Frodo was a decision which reflected a great faith in his abilities.

If we accept that Glorfindel returned to Middle-earth in the Second Age, probably at the time of the War of the Elves and Sauron (which Tolkien suggests is the most likely event to trigger his return), then Glorfindel must have been very active in defending Lindon and Eriador against Mordor. After the war he might have accompanied Galadriel and Celeborn on some of their travels, or perhaps would have been Gil-galad's emissary to other Elven realms (such as there still remained: Oropher's kingdom in Greenwood, Amdir's in Lothlórien, and the haven of Edhellond are all we know about for sure, though some people insist that the mysterious land of Dorwinion, located on the northwestern shore of the Inland Sea, must also have been an Elven realm).

And then Glorfindel would have marched with the army of Lindon and Imladris in the War of the Last Alliance. Elrond was Gil-galad's herald, a role which would have afforded him little time to command armies, as he would have been vital to Gil-galad's relations with the other alliance leaders, and also would have been delivering proclamations to Sauron's forces. Gil-galad would have had Celeborn, Cirdan, and Glorfindel to call upon to act as captains of his various forces. Of course, other Elven lords would have served as seconds-in-command, lesser captains, advisors, etc. There would have been a horde of Elven lords. Glorfindel's status in the War of the Last Alliance is by no means certain.

Yet it was Glorfindel who led the armies of Rivendell and Lothlórien to the last combat with the Witch-king of Angmar. Should his status have been elevated so much in the Third Age? Why didn't Amroth lead his own army? Was he even present at the battle, or did he stay home in Lothlórien to tend to the kingdom? That Glorfindel led the combined armies seems to imply he was a person of great stature among the Elves, a very great and noble lord indeed.

Tolkien tells the reader just enough about Glorfindel in *The Lord of the Rings* to imply that he was a very important Elf lord, but no more. It's not until we get to *The Silmarillion* and read about his great sacrifice that we learn about Glorfindel's tragic history. And yet even the Gondolin story leaves something to be desired. The account in *The Silmarillion* is a pastiche assembled by Christopher from "The Fall of Gondolin" and "Of Tuor and his Coming to Gondolin". It doesn't really say the great things that "The Fall of Gondolin" attempted to say. Other than commanding one of Turgon's flanks in the Nirnaeth Arnoediad, Glorfindel isn't mentioned anywhere else in *The Silmarillion*.

He had to be one of the Exiles, moved by Fëanor's demand that the Noldor follow him back to Middle-earth. He probably did not take part in the Kinslaying at Alqualondë, since of Fingolfin's host only Fingon's people helped the Fëanorians directly. Turgon, presumably, came after his father's group of Noldor. So Glorfindel survived the crossing of the Helcaraxë, and he was there with Fingolfin when the greater part of the Noldor marched on Angband with no effect. And he must have sat by as the greater princes of the Noldor convened their council in the wake of Fingon's rescue of Maedhros.

Glorfindel is always there, in the background, a face amid the nameless legions of characters who make up the ancient hosts of the Noldor. What's odd is that *The Silmarillion* sparked more questions about Glorfindel's ancestry than about his personal history. Was he one of the Vanyar? Was he only part Vanyarin? Why did he have golden hair, if (as Tolkien says in *The Lord of the Rings*) only the descendants of Finarfin and Ëarwen have golden hair among the Noldor?

Golden hair is supposed to be a rare thing among the Elves, and yet the Elven-king of northern Mirkwood has golden hair in *The Hobbit*, some nameless Elf warrior of Lothlórien is golden-haired in *The Lord of the Rings*, and Glorfindel and Idril Celebrindal both have golden hair. Idril, at least, is a descendant of Indis, second wife of Finwe, who came of the Vanyar, and Idril's own mother Elenwë was from the Vanyar. Tolkien's ideas on Elven physical attributes must not have been fully-developed when he made the statement that only Finarfin's descendants had golden hair among the Noldor.

But that doesn't explain Glorfindel's ancestry. Who were his parents? Was he part Vanya, like Idril? It seems quite likely he must have had one some Vanyarin blood. People feel that the Vanyar were above rebellion, but Elenwë's decision to join Turgon in exile is an indication they were not. If one wife was moved to follow her husband, then why not others? And it may be that Elenwë went only because she and Turgon had not been married for very long. Idril was only a child when Elenwë was lost in the ice. So Idril was born during the sojourn through Araman, after the Kinslaying.

Few if any of the "elder" Noldor seem to have gone into exile. Nerdanel, Fëanor's wife, did not go with him. Nor did her father Mahtan, or any member of their family (except the sons of Fëanor and Nerdanel). So Glorfindel probably could not have been an "elder" among the Noldor at the time of the rebellion. He may have been the son of a Noldorin lord and Vanyarin lady who had befriended Turgon, and as one of Turgon's friends may have followed him out of loyalty and sense of youthful adventure.

Another possibility is that Glorfindel was the son of a Vanyarin lord and a Noldorin wife. Less likely would be a more remote Vanyarin ancestry. Few of the Vanyar appear to have been living in Tirion upon Tuna at the time of Fëanor's rebellion. Most of them had moved on to the slopes of Taniquetil or the woodlands of Valinor or the area of Valmar. If he came from the Vanyar, Glorfindel's family must therefore have had close ties to the Noldor.

In the final analysis Glorfindel remains as much a mystery as ever. We know virtually nothing of his place within Eldarin society, who his relatives were (apparently all or most had died in Middle-earth, as Tolkien mentioned he was the first of his family to be released from Mandos in one of the two Glorfindel essays), or even what his specific relationship to Turgon was (except as a follower in the hierarchy of Gondolin's nobility).

And Glorfindel's history is far from complete. We can only trace his movements in the most general fashion. Perhaps he spent a fair amount of time with Gandalf, wandering around the northern lands. It would be hard to imagine a book written solely about Glorfindel, though he and Gandalf would make quite a pair of adventurers. Perhaps in the year 2061 or thereabouts a television series concerning the two will be launched, and Tolkien fans will at long last get to explore some the fascination this character holds for them.

MICHAEL MARTINEZ

Chapter 9:
Gil-galad was an Elven-king...

And that is where we all agree.

Gil-galad's ancestry hasn't yet become a nuclear topic among Tolkien fans, but time will tell if it does. As little information as we have on Tolkien's most famous Noldorin king, people have found reason to write huge editorials about him (and I'm no exception).

Who was Gil-galad's father, Fingon or Orodreth? J.R.R. Tolkien says Orodreth, but millions of fans seem to disagree with him. After all, *The Silmarillion* says it was Fingon. "That Gil-galad was the son of Fingon (*The Silmarillion* p. 154) derives from the late note penciled on the manuscript of [Grey Annals] ($157)," Christopher Tolkien tells us in *The War of the Jewels* (p. 243 of my Houghton Mifflin edition), "stating that when Fingon became King of the Noldor on the death of Fingolfin 'his young son (?Findor) [*sic*] Gilgalad he sent to the Havens.' But this, adopted after much hesitation, was not in fact by any means the last of my father's speculations."

This tantalizing hint fired the first of the Gil-galad debates. If Fingon wasn't his father, and Finrod Felagund couldn't be (earlier discussion showed that idea had been abandoned), then who *was* the father of Gil-galad? Some people stood squarely by *The Silmarillion*, stating it must be canon, as it was faithfully produced by Christopher Tolkien according to his father's wishes. But this is not true.

Elsewhere in *The War of the Jewels*, and in several other volumes of *The History of Middle-earth*, Christopher points out where he departed from his father's vision (mostly through inadequate research, given that he was working under pressure and didn't have access to all of his father's papers). In particular, he says of "The Ruin of Doriath" that:

> To have included ["The Wanderings of Hurin" in *The Silmarillion*], as it seemed to me, would have entailed a huge reduction, indeed an entire re-

telling of a kind that I did not wish to undertake; and since the story is intricate I was afraid that this would produce a dense tangle of narrative statement with all the subtlety gone, and above all that it would diminish the fearful figure of the old man, the great hero, Thalion the Steadfast, furthering still the purposes of Morgoth, as he was doomed to do. But it seems to me now, many years later, to have been an excessive tampering with my father's actual thought and intention: thus raising the question, whether the attempt to make a 'unified' *Silmarillion* should have been embarked on.

In a further explanation of how "The Ruin of Doriath" was written later in the book, Christopher says:

This story was not lightly or easily conceived, but was the outcome of long experimentation among alternative conceptions. In this work Guy Kay took a major part, and the chapter that I finally wrote owes much to my discussions with him. It is, and was, obvious that a step was being taken of a different order from any other 'manipulation' of my father's own writing in the course of the book: even in the case of the story of the Fall of Gondolin, to which my father had never returned, something could be contrived without introducing radical changes in the narrative. It seemed at that time that there were elements in the story of the Ruin of Doriath as it stood that were radically incompatible with 'The Silmarillion' as projected, and that there was here an inescapable choice: either to abandon that conception, or else to alter the story. I think now that this was a mistaken view, and that the undoubted difficulties could have been, and should have been, surmounted without so far overstepping the bounds of the editorial function.

This repudiation of his most significant contribution to *The Silmarillion* shows that Christopher Tolkien does not present it as a canonical work. That is, he never intended the published *Silmarillion* to represent his father's vision. He was cautionary in the foreword to the *Silmarillion* itself, noting that

...to attempt to present, within the covers of a single book, the diversity of the materials -- to show *The Silmarillion* as in truth a continuing and evolving creation extending over more than half a century -- would in fact lead only to confusion and the submerging of what is essential. I set myself therefore to work out a single text, selecting and arranging in such a way as seemed to me to produce the most coherent and internally self-consistent narrative....A complete consistency...is not to be looked for, and could only be achieved, if at all, at heavy and needless cost....

We therefore have solid reason, provided by Christopher Tolkien himself, to question the validity of any statement in *The Silmarillion*. But that is not to say that everything in the book should be thrown out as non-canonical. Rather, since we now have the source materials available for our own study, we can determine (especially with the aid of Christopher's explicit commentary) where the original stories were altered or not used, and why.

In the case of Gil-galad's parentage we have a more certain declaration from Christopher than the one above. In *The Peoples of Middle-earth* he devoted a brief commentary to the parentage of Gil-galad on pages 349-51. It appears that the true genealogy of Gil-galad places him as the son of Orodreth, who himself was the son of Angrod, and not one of the children of Finarfin. "There can be no doubt that this was my father's last word on the subject," Christopher tells us. His final statement reads: "Much closer analysis of the admittedly extremely complex material than I had made twenty years ago makes it clear that Gil-galad as the son of Fingon *(see XI. p. 56, 243) was an ephemeral idea."

What a revelation! Saying that Gil-galad as the son of Fingon was "an ephemeral idea" lit the fires of controversy almost overnight. People have argued back and forth through the years on what the right parentage for Gil-galad should be. And yet we have it from Christopher Tolkien that there can be no doubt concerning his parentage: he was the son of Orodreth.

Furthermore, Christopher admits to changing Gil-galad's name in the text of the letter published as part of "Aldarion and Erendis" in *Unfinished Tales*. Where the book shows "Ereinion Gil-galad son of Fingon" JRRT had actually written "Finellach Gil-galad of the House of Finarfin". In another passage of the story Christopher also changed "King Finellach Gil-galad of Lindon" to "King Gil-galad of Lindon".

So why do people continue to doubt the word of Christopher Tolkien, the man who published *The Silmarillion*, admittedly with the intention of providing "a single text", who selected and arranged the material to produce a consistent and coherent narrative (a goal he did not fully achieve, by his own admission)? I think answering that question would require an analysis on the order of a dissertation. The refusal to accept Christopher Tolkien's authoritative statements on any number of issues is a sociological phenomenon.

But we can examine Gil-galad in the context of the correct story and determine a few things about his character which were never revealed in *The Silmarillion*. That is, we can deduce something of his personal history.

Orodreth was probably born in Valinor. His mother was Eldalótë, a Noldorin lady whose name was easily converted to Sindarin Edhellos. When Finrod built the hidden city of Nargothrond, he commended rule over Tol Sirion and the adjoining lands to Angrod, while Aegnor retained command over the heights of Dorthonion which overlooked Ard-galen. All this contradicts what we are told in *The Silmarillion*, of course.

When the Dagor Bragollach erupted and the Noldor were thrown back Finrod rushed north to reinforce his brothers, but he was too late. Aegnor's people were overwhelmed, and though Angrod's people held out on Tol Sirion for a while Angrod himself was eventually slain and Orodreth retreated from the island, fleeing to Nargothrond. He took with him his wife, a Sindarin lady from the northern lands, and his son (Rodnor Gil-galad) and daughter (Finduilas).

Gil-galad didn't stay in Nargothrond for very long. He would have settled there at the very earliest around the year 455 (the year of the Dagor Bragollach), and Christopher cites a note from his father which states that "Gil-galad escaped and eventually came to Sirion's Mouth and was King of the Noldor there". His escape would have to be from the destruction of Nargothrond, which occurred in the year 495.

During those 40 years we hear nothing of Gil-galad, but we can infer that he may have been present at the great debate when Beren asked for Finrod's help in the quest of the Silmaril. He, of course, was not one of the twelve faithful lords who accompanied Finrod on the quest, but presumably Gil-galad would have been deemed too young or too important to join the quest (in fact, he had not even been conceived of in Tolkien's thought when the fullest version of Beren's story was written in the 1930s). Gil-galad did not march with Gwindor's company to the Nirnaeth Arnoediad, and he doesn't seem to have been one of the soldiers in Orodreth's army which was defeated by Glaurung's army at the Battle of Tumhalad.

It would make sense for Orodreth to leave Gil-galad behind to defend Nargothrond. Gil-galad might only then have just been reaching full maturity. And Orodreth was usually a cautious ruler, having only given in to pressure from Túrin and the impatient Noldorin lords who favored Túrin's counsel to abandon Nargothrond's policy of hidden defense.

Thus when Glaurung came up against the city and its defenders proved to be too few and weak to withstand the dragon, the young prince must have become separated from his family. We don't know the fate of his mother, though she was probably killed or taken prisoner, but Finduilas was captured and taken with other Elf-women to Brethil by the Orcs. There she was mortally wounded despite the best efforts of the wood-men to free the captives.

Making his way south Gil-galad reached the Mouths of Sirion. The community of Elves and Men which would later found the realm of Arvernien under Ëarendil did not yet exist, but many Noldor (and Sindar) had been fleeing south for years, hoping to join up with Cirdan, whose people had abandoned the Falas after the Nirnaeth Arnoediad in 473 and fled to the Isle of Balar. Annael, leader of the group of Sindar who fostered Tuor, eventually reached the Mouths of Sirion.

So Gil-galad established a community of Elves there, or found one and was acknowledged its leader. This community, however, must have eventually moved to Balar, probably at Cirdan's invitation, thus ensuring that the House of Finwë would survive.

Gil-galad was at this time *merely* a king of the Noldor, not their High King. The High Kingship had passed on Fingon's death to his brother Turgon, and now we know why. Fingon had no children, and the kingship therefore went to his closest male relative of the male line of descent from Finwë. When Gondolin was destroyed in the year 510, and Turgon killed, the High Kingship passed to the House of Finarfin, of whom the last male line descendant was Gil-galad.

Throughout the rest of the First Age Gil-galad remained on Balar. He and Maedhros were the last Noldorin kings to live in Beleriand, but it appears that Gil-galad never met Maedhros. He would have known Celebrimbor, the son of Curufin, who stayed in Nargothrond after Celegorm and Curufin were banished by Orodreth. Celebrimbor was not a king, and had no realm to inherit, although he technically should have become leader of the Fëanorians upon Maedhros' death and Maglor's departure.

When the War of Wrath ended and the Host of Valinor departed back into the West, many of the Noldor and Sindar of Beleriand went with them. The handful of Finwëans left (Gil-galad, Celebrimbor, and Galadriel) along with the chief lords of the Sindar (Celeborn and Cirdan) elected to stay in Middle-earth. Galadriel's history is very confused, but it appears she left Nargothrond sometime before 495 (probably before the Nirnaeth in 473). So she and Celeborn must have come west when Eönwë summoned all the Elves of Middle-earth to sail over Sea.

In 'The Road Goes Ever On' J.R.R. Tolkien writes that Galadriel "was the last survivor of the princes and queens who had led the revolting *Noldor* to exile in Middle-earth. After the overthrow of *Morgoth* at the end of the First Age, a ban was set upon her return, and she had replied proudly that she had no wish to do so. She passed over the Mountains of *Eredluin* with her husband *Celeborn* (one of the *Sindar*) and went to *Eregion*...."

Galadriel's position among the Eldarin lords of Middle-earth was thus unique, and she doesn't seem ever to have fit in well with Gil-galad's kingdom. In another history, published in *Unfinished Tales*, Galadriel and Celeborn first settled in Eriador near Lake Evendim early in the Second Age, and there they were acknowledged Lord and Lady of the Elves in Eriador. Nonetheless, *The Lord of the Rings* tells us that Celeborn was Gil-galad's vassal in Harlindon for a while after the Kingdom of Lindon was established.

Elrond, in choosing to remain with the Elves, became a counselor and apparently close friend to Gil-galad. His pedigree all but ensured Elrond a high place in the new Elven realm. Born amid the survivors of Gondolin and Doriath, a descendant of Turgon and Thingol, Elrond was captured while still a child by the Fëanorians, and he and his brother Elros were fostered by Maglor. Elrond thus developed a special relationship with the Fëanorians.

Gil-galad's realm at first must have included Elves from every part of the former Beleriand: survivors from the Falas and Hithlum, survivors from Nargothrond, survivors from Gondolin and Doriath, Fëanorians, and probably even a few Laegrim from Ossiriand and whatever remained of the Avari who had reached Beleriand. Although all was supposed to be forgiven among the Elves, it doesn't seem they could really set aside ancient griefs. The Doriathrim seem to have accepted Gil-galad's rule at first but it was they (apparently) who led the great migration of Sindar away from Lindon.

Sindar began migrating eastward early in the Second Age, but we don't know how early. And their first movements may have been only to settle in western Eriador. Population pressure may have been part of the reason for why they left Lindon. The Elves continued to have families throughout the Second and Third Ages. But it may also be that Gil-galad was influenced by Noldorin policies enough that the Sindar may have felt his realm wasn't for them. Cirdan and the Falathrim had always been friendly with the Noldor, and were in some ways Noldorinized in Beleriand (Finrod had helped to rebuild their cities, for example). The Sindar of Hithlum and Nargothrond would also have been Noldorinized.

It was the Sindar of Doriath who would be most reluctant to adopt Noldorin customs and culture. And they would also have the hardest time overlooking past griefs, having fought the Fëanorians directly not once but twice. Virtually all the grievances of the Sindar over what they had lost could have been laid at the feet of the Noldor, if it were in them to place blame. So their eastward migration was probably also the result of some antipathy toward the Fëanorians.

The first phase of Sindarin migration had probably been completed by the time Númenoreans reached Middle-earth and began visiting Lindon. By this time the haven of Edhellond had been established far to the south and many Sindar had settled among the Nandor and Avari of Eriador. Gil-galad's people retained contact with the Elves of Eriador, and had come into contact with the Edainic peoples still living there as well. These Men sent twelve of their leaders to meet with Vëantur and his Númenoreans after asking Gil-galad to arrange the meeting.

So, just as his realm seemed to be coming apart, Gil-galad was thrust upon the stage of world history by Númenor. And Sauron began stirring in Middle-earth once again. Word came to Gil-galad of some distant power which was not friendly to Men and Elves. He knew nothing for certain, but his doubts and concerns gradually increased. When the young prince Anardil (later Tar-Aldarion) began adventuring in Middle-earth Gil-galad befriended him, and the Númenorean prince made many journeys on Gil-galad's behalf, visiting Men throughout the north-western lands of Middle-earth.

Gil-galad seems to have formed a policy of establishing closer ties with Men. Perhaps he was only interested in Men of Edainic descent, since the Elves distrusted Men of other kindreds. But the Edainic peoples had spread far and wide. They could be found as far south as the Mouths of Sirion and as far east as the Carnen river and the Iron Hills.

The establishment of the Noldorin realm of Eregion may also reflect, in part, Gil-galad's policies. Although Eregion acted on its own initiatives, Gil-galad did not abandon the people of Eregion during the

War of the Elves and Sauron. And he may have been instrumental in deciding that the Noldor should establish a colony near Khazad-dum so as to have access to mithril. In this way the Elven civilization would be assured of control over the Eriadorian trade routes.

When Sauron began approaching Elven realms in the guise of Annatar, Lord of Gifts, feeling them out concerning their doom to eventually fade, Gil-galad and Elrond suspected the motives of Annatar and refused to treat with him. Annatar/Sauron was not admitted to Lindon, and he turned his attention to Eregion. There Celebrimbor, lord of the Gwaith-i-Mirdain, listened to Annatar, and he dreamed of making Middle-earth into an Elven paradise much like Valinor. The Elves were facing a real problem in that they had their own form of death to contend with: fading. They would lose their bodies. Their spirits would remain, conscious, aware, but incapable of interacting with the world.

Gil-galad undoubtedly understood this problem as well as anyone. But he made the innate choice not to meddle with nature. The Elves lived with the life of Arda. That is, their spirits would not leave the circles of the world as Men's spirits would. So for them "life" was not simply a biological function but was also a spiritual one. They wondered if their spirits would continue to exist beyond the existence of Time. They felt Men were assured of continued life, and weren't as concerned about the death of the body as Men were. So Gil-galad did not want to hold back the effects of Time.

And yet, when the Rings of Power were made, and Sauron revealed himself to the Ring-makers when he put on the One Ring, the Elves were unable to bring themselves to destroy the Rings. Celebrimbor gave two of the greatest Rings to Gil-galad, and Gil-galad also couldn't destroy them. Why? Was it that he felt there would be no point in trying to undo what had been done? Would it have irreparably harmed Celebrimbor, sole maker of the Three, for the Rings to be destroyed? Or had Gil-galad found reason to change his mind in the centuries after rejecting Annatar's overtures?

The Three Rings worked their magic on the Elven realms even though no one wore them throughout the rest of the Second Age. Tolkien wrote that they would still hold back the effects of Time, so the Elves were assured of not fading while the Rings of Power existed. Gil-galad's policies then became more manipulative. When he was sure Sauron would invade Eriador Gil-galad asked Númenor to help defend the Elves and Men who lived there. But he didn't tell the Númenoreans what the war was about. One can only imagine what arguments must have raged in the highest Elven councils before the call to arms went out. Was it fair to withhold vital information from the Men who would be risking their lives on behalf of the Elves, who had dared to meddle with nature?

When the war finally came Númenor stood by the Elven-realm, no doubt for the sake of ancient friendship, and because anyone who knew the ancient legends and histories of the Wars of Beleriand knew Sauron was a bad guy. That he must have been using Orcs and Trolls in his armies, and that the Gwathuirim with whom the Númenoreans had been having trouble went over to Sauron, would only encourage the belief that it was right to support the Elven-folk. The issue had become one of survival for all Elves and Men. The Rings of Power were hidden from Númenor as well as Sauron, and their secret maintained for centuries.

Gil-galad may have come to feel vindicated in his decision not to share all with his allies in the centuries which followed the war. Sauron was defeated and driven back to Mordor, and his power to threaten Eriador was diminished. He turned his attention to the eastern lands of Middle-earth, where he decided he could build up a great empire capable of challenging Númenor and Gil-galad. But starting around the year 1800 the Númenoreans began to exhibit new behavior. The War of the Elves and Sauron had shown them they were strong, and this strength was now turned to dominating and enslaving other Men, rather than helping them.

It would be dangerous to reveal the existence of the Rings of Power to this new Númenor, for soon the Dunedain began to question their fate, and to long for the lifespan of the Elves. How much of this reached Gil-galad's ears we can only guess, but after the Númenoreans became divided into the camps of the Faithful and the Kings' Men, and only the Faithful continued to settle in or visit north-western Middle-earth, it must have been obvious that the Kings of Númenor had set themselves upon a path of self-destruction.

Gil-galad for his part had his own problems. Many Eldar left Middle-earth after the War of the Elves and Sauron. It probably seemed like only a matter of time before Sauron grew powerful enough again to challenge Gil-galad and the wayward Númenoreans. So Gil-galad's power was diminished and the Elves remained under constant attack even during the centuries when Sauron's attention was turned to the east. When the Númenoreans began conquering portions of Middle-earth they would eventually come into conflict with Sauron's realm. The wars of conquest might relieve some of the pressure on the Elves, but their Days of Flight seem to have continued until Ar-Pharazôn's fateful decision to wrest control over Middle-earth from Sauron.

Technically, Númenor may still have been allied in some capacity with the Elves. Pelargir, the royal garth of ships (essentially a naval base), had been founded near the Mouths of Anduin in 2350. Although it became the chief haven south by the Faithful Númenoreans, the city's name implies that it was built with royal sanction, and may have served as a base of operations in conflicts with Sauron's realm. The power assembled by the Númenoreans at Pelargir through the centuries may have served to challenge and provoke Sauron, although Mordor would at that time have been more of an outpost of Sauron's empire than its heart.

Gil-galad took no action when Ar-Pharazôn brought an armada to Middle-earth. Umbar, where Ar-Pharazôn landed, was probably too far south for Gil-galad to march or sail to, and Ar-Pharazôn most likely didn't want any Elvish help anyway. He was come to claim his place as the King of Men, and no Elf should be required to help him assert his authority. In any event, Ar-Pharazôn's army was so great that Sauron's allies abandoned him. The One Ring failed Sauron once again. So Sauron left Mordor and surrendered to Ar-Pharazôn, allowing the king to take him back to Númenor.

Sauron's departure seems to have brought an effective end to the wars with the Elves. Over the course of the next 57 years Gil-galad was able to extend his influence throughout the northern world, even into the upper Vales of Anduin. When Elendil and his sons brought nine ships of survivors from the disaster of Númenor to Middle-earth in 3319 Gil-galad befriended them and helped them establish the realms of Arnor and Gondor. The Elven-king built three towers overlooking the Gulf of Lune for Elendil, and these may have been the Dunadan king's first home in Middle-earth. But though he ceded vast authority to Elendil over Eriador, Gil-galad still said nothing (it seems) about the Rings of Power.

It would not be until the year 3429, when the reconstituted Sauron felt strong enough to attack Gondor, that Gil-galad would be faced with the moral dilemma of the Rings. He had kept Narya and Vilya hidden for more than 1,000 years. Neither he nor any other Elf had worn or actively used the Rings in that time. They dared not do so. But they had still benefited from the Rings' ability to hold back the effects of Time. It must have become obvious to Gil-galad that the Elves had only deferred the inevitable decision to destroy the Rings. He may not have been convinced of the need to do so, or that they would fail if the One Ring were unmade, but as long as Sauron remained a threat to Men and Elves there was no hope of the Elves ever realizing the full benefit from the Rings they had retained control over.

So Gil-galad seems to have revealed all to Elendil and his sons. Now at last the Elves fessed up to their own sins, and they resolved with the Dunedain to undertake a final war against Sauron that should have resulted in his complete defeat. They had the military power to achieve this end. Gil-galad's people had grown numerous again, but he had also established relations with the peoples of the Vales of Anduin, including the much more numerous Silvan Elves ruled by Oropher and Amdir. Elf, Man, and Dwarf came together with a common purpose and they raised the greatest army Middle-earth had seen since the end of the First Age.

But Gil-galad's persuasive arguments don't seem to have endeared him with Oropher, who as a Doriathrin Elf was by one account unfriendly to the Noldor. It may only have been Gil-galad's relationship to Thingol and the pressing need to do something about Sauron, who had ravaged the lands east of the Misty Mountains as well as Eriador, that drove Oropher to ally himself with Gil-galad. Oropher nonetheless refused to march under Gil-galad's banner.

It took three years for Gil-galad and Elendil to prepare their armies. They had to recruit and train their soldiers, and apparently make arms and armor. But they must also have spent a considerable amount of time building up a preparatory strategy: scouting the lands, testing Sauron's defenses, perhaps sending reinforcements to Gondor to ensure Anarion wasn't overcome. There may also have been considerable debate over how to attack Sauron. Should a northern force attack Mordor while the main army thrust over the mountains, or should the main assault come from the north?

In 3431 Gil-galad and Elendil crossed the Misty Mountains and marched south. They were joined at some point by armies from Khazad-dum, Lórien, and Greenwood. The strategy they had selected was to drive straight toward Mordor. It may have been necessary to take this path for several reasons, not the least being their armies were too large to transport to Gondor easily. But Sauron seems to have built up his defenses in the upper vales of Anduin, so Lórien and Greenwood were directly threatened. Gil-galad's move would have freed those realms from any immediate perils.

The first major battle occurred in the lands south of Greenwood where the Ent-wives had built their gardens. The fate of the Ent-wives was never learned, although they may have been destroyed when Sauron burned the lands to prevent the Last Alliance from acquiring any help there. The Ent-wives at the very least could have supplied food to the Last Alliance. Sauron retreated south and the Last Alliance followed him. They overtook his army on the Dagorlad, and there inflicted a severe defeat upon Sauron. But Amdir and the army of Lórien were cut off in the Dead Marshes, and more than half the Silvan Elves of Lórien perished. Gil-galad may have been influenced by the devastating losses suffered by Amdir's people to hold up.

The Last Alliance arrayed its forces before the northern entrance to Mordor (where the Morannon would later stand), but Gil-galad could not restrain Oropher, who launched an assault against Sauron's defenses prematurely. Tolkien doesn't say how the battle went, but Gil-galad most likely followed in the footsteps of Fingon thousands of years before at the Nirnaeth Arnoediad. He most likely put his helmet on and charged into battle on the heals of Oropher's attack, too late to save Oropher, who died early on. The Last Alliance won the day, however, and pushed its way into Mordor.

Whatever remained of Sauron's forces must at this time have retreated or been annihilated, and Sauron was confined to Barad-dur. Now Gil-galad settled down to the age-old Elven policy of besieging a dark lord in his fortress. Gil-galad took up a position on Orodruin, near the Sammath Naur where the One Ring had been forged. Gil-galad could have destroyed the Three Rings then, perhaps, but he either chose not to or else the Rings had not been carried into war. He must have fortified the mountain, though. Tolkien notes there were many sorties during the next seven years, and after six years of siege Sauron was still able to lob stones out from Barad-dur, for Anarion was slain in that year by one of the stones.

Gil-galad's strategy had thus changed radically. The Last Alliance no longer tried to take Sauron by force, and the war dragged on. They could only hope to so wear down Sauron's forces through attrition that in the end Sauron would capitulate. But Sauron became so desperate he formed a different plan. He sought out Gil-galad on Orodruin and attacked him. Elrond tells the people in Rivendell that only Elendil stood near Gil-galad, and that only he (Elrond), Cirdan, and Isildur saw what happened. Sauron's body was so hot it burned Gil-galad, and slew him, but Elendil rushed up and delivered a death-stroke against Sauron. The Dark Lord was nonetheless able to retaliate, and he threw Elendil down. And Elendil's sword broke beneath him.

The final strategy against Sauron worked, but probably not as Gil-galad hoped. Would he really have intended to do battle with Sauron alone? He seems to have been a cautious king throughout his career. To prepare for the War of the Elves and Sauron Gil-galad built up his defenses along the Baranduin river. He gave Elrond command of a small army that attempted to reinforce Eregion but it was driven back and forced to retreat north. Sauron forced his way across the Baranduin and Gil-galad was only barely able to hold the Lune against him. So the Elven-king's resources were limited and the limits of his resources may have dictated his policy.

But he quickly helped Elendil establish the kingdom of Arnor, which became the most powerful realm in the north. Why was it important to make a large kingdom of Men? Was it important to Gil-galad to recall the greatness of Númenor, or was his policy of dealing with Men through Men a conservative, perhaps xenophobic decision? Gil-galad had no problem in treating with Edainic peoples, but anyone else had to go through his Númenorean proxies.

The only time Gil-galad went on the offensive was when he and Elendil formed the Last Alliance of Elves and Men. By this time it must have been obvious that Sauron would be able to rebuild his power with the One Ring every time someone defeated him. Gil-galad's goal must have been to find and take Sauron prisoner, and then to somehow wrest the One Ring away from him. Gil-galad may not have known the secrets of the Ring-makers, but he must have been able to learn enough to understand the true peril that the One Ring presented. One must wonder if Gil-galad would ever have used the Three Rings, or permitted their use, had he lived and Isildur still taken the Ring from Sauron. Prudence would have counseled the Elves not to use their Rings after Isildur vanished in the north. But though he was wise, Elrond did not follow the path of prudence.

MICHAEL MARTINEZ

Chapter 10:
Much ado about Arwen: Elven Princess

Let's stop and talk about Arwen a little bit. There doesn't seem to be much to say about Arwen at first glance, but then, you have to wonder *why* she gave it all up for Aragorn. I mean, here she was, the hottest Elf-babe in Middle-earth, and she went and fell for a down-on-his-luck *Ranger*. Aragorn may have had the *right* to be king of both Arnor and Gondor, but he wasn't actually king of anything. He was chieftain of the Dunedain of Eriador. Any Hobbit girl marrying into the Took or Brandybuck clans would have ended up with more money, land, and relatives than Arwen figured to receive if she were to go against her father's will.

When Elrond discerned Aragorn's love for his daughter, he summoned the young man to him and said:

> "You shall be betrothed to no man's child as yet. But as for Arwen the Fair, Lady of Imladris and of Lórien, Evenstar of her people, she is of lineage greater than yours, and she has lived in the world already so long that to her you are but as a yearling shoot beside a young birch of many summers. She is too far above you. And so, I think, it may well seem to her...."

Elrond certainly tried to let Aragorn down easily, but the plan may have backfired on him. Or perhaps Elrond's doubts were irrelevant. Aragorn had grown up in Elrond's household. He knew Elrond's ancestry. Arwen would not have been the first Elf woman to love a mortal man, if her heart turned toward him. Of course, many people think quickly of Lúthien and Beren, and of Idril and Tuor. But there were other Elf women who loved mortal men: Nellas, the mysterious Elf maiden of Doriath who watched over Túrin as he grew up in Doriath; and Finduilas, the Elven princess who fell in love with Túrin after he settled in Nargothrond. Nimloth married Dior, mortal son of Beren and Lúthien. One can only wonder what Elf-man relationships developed in the largely forgotten Second Age. Did young Númenorean men pine for lovely Elven women from Tol Eressëa?

Relationships among the Elves were deep and more fully committed than those among men. Even among the Dunedain it was not unknown for a man to have more than one spouse (Túrin I, 6th Ruling Steward of Gondor, was married twice). Rare though it may seem, men were far more likely to take second wives than were the Elves. In fact, among the Eldar, only Finwë was known to have taken a second spouse. That is not to say that the Dunedain couldn't love each other as fully and deeply as the Elves. But apparently the Elvish custom was deeply rooted in a mating of souls, as much as in a mating of bodies.

It should therefore be unusual that an Elf would want or love a mortal in that fashion. Perhaps even unnatural, in the sense that the Elven souls were predisposed to seek out mates which were likely to spend the full span of time with them, rather than souls which would fleetingly pass by, leaving behind only a few memories. The great tragedy of Tuor and Idril's relationship is that there is no clear disposition of their ultimate fate. They sailed off into the West, and men said Tuor must have been joined to the Noldor, but I think he was premature in that respect. The choice of fates could only be appointed to the Half-elven, Ëarendil and his wife Elwing. Tuor and Idril must have parted bitterly at the end, or else been drawn into some enchanted island where they would await the end of Time, according to Ilúvatar's grace.

The fates of Nimloth and Dior are more clear, however. Manwë decreed that all children born of Elf-Man unions were by nature mortal though long-lived. This mortality meant that eventually their souls would follow the path appointed to Men, and seek elsewhere for their ultimate destiny. Dior, therefore, had no hope of being rejoined with Nimloth after his death. Would she in time have emerged from the Halls of Mandos, healed and ready to take up a new love with some Elf lord, or would she live in grief-stricken remembrance for age after age? Perhaps she, like Finwë and Miriel, would not wish to rejoin Elvenkind because of her special loss.

The broken hearts weren't all among the ladies. Aegnor, brother of Finrod, fell in love with Andreth. She was a Bëorian woman, related to Beren though not closely so. When she was young she captured the heart of an Elven prince, but he didn't marry her. Instead he attended to the long war between the Noldor and Morgoth, and he seemed to have forgotten her. But in truth he had foreseen that he would soon die, as the Elves accounted such matters, and for that reason he forbore inflicting any greater grief on Andreth. The tragedy of their love was that he didn't understand how much she would have preferred to have been his wife if only for a few years, than a lonely woman unsure of what had gone wrong. They were in the end separated for all Time because of their fates, and they didn't even have the shared memories of one night as husband and wife.

Arwen must have known all these stories. She didn't just grow up in the house of Elrond, she lived there for thousands of years. Although she may have had special duties among the Yavannildi (the Maidens of Yavanna, who grew and harvested the special corn from which Lembas was made), Arwen seems to have been in a position to earn the greatest of Elven educations. Elrond was not simply the chief master of lore among the Third Age Elves, he was the central figure of Eldarin scholarship in Middle-earth. Many great and wise Elves visited or settled in or near Imladris. Arwen would have had access to the greatest Elven minds of her age: Elrond, Galadriel, Cirdan, Celeborn (yes, *Celeborn*), Glorfindel, and others. She would have heard first-hand accounts of Elvish sorcery, warfare, and scholarship.

And the lady traveled around. She must have crossed the Misty Mountains dozens of times to visit her grand-parents after Celeborn and Galadriel settled in Lórien. Did she, perhaps, also visit Lindon? With her family background and likely education, Arwen may well have been high in the councils of the Eldar. She was probably considered one of the Wise. Does that mean she might have been a member of the White Council itself? Why not? She was a politically savvy Elf-princess. After all, she made that banner for Aragorn.

And Aragorn's banner is not just a jewel-encrusted flag waving in the wind. Think about it. Aragorn unfurled the banner at Erech but there was no visible device upon it. It just seemed black to his living companions. But apparently it helped convince the Dead that he was indeed who he was. What would a banner made by an Elven princess mean to an army of ghosts?

Elves were enchanters. They made things the old-fashioned way: magically, as far as mortals were concerned. Arwen's pedigree for sorcery was no less impressive than her noble lineage. She was the great-granddaughter of Lúthien Tinúviel, the Half-Maian princess who was regarded as the greatest of all Elven enchantresses. ALL of them. Lúthien and Lúthien alone was able to put Morgoth to sleep deep inside his own fortress of Angband. No Elven king or prince ever saw the inside of Angband except as a prisoner. Only Lúthien's mom, Melian, performed a greater feat, surrounding Doriath with a "girdle" of enchantment which protected the realm from Morgoth and his servants.

Arwen was also descended from Galadriel, whose daughter Celebrian married Elrond. Galadriel's enchantments were nothing to be ignored. Where Lúthien was remembered for tearing down the walls of Sauron's fortress on Tol Sirion, Galadriel laid bare the pits of Dol Guldur, Sauron's ancient fortress in southern Mirkwood. Lúthien wove a cloak from her own enchanted hair which made her invisible, so she could escape from her guards. Galadriel didn't weave any cloaks of invisibility, but she used a silver basin to spy on Sauron and watch events unfold in the world outside Lórien, and she captured light from the star of Ëarendil in a phial of water for Frodo.

Arwen had also spent many years among the Elves of Lórien. Should one wonder if she didn't learn to put her thoughts into all things she made, as they said they did when Pippin asked about the Elven cloaks which were given to the Fellowship? Those grey cloaks were undoubtedly the same kind of enchanted clothing worn by the Grey-Elves of Mithrim, whom the Noldor met first upon their return to Middle-earth. So Arwen probably put a lot of thought into that banner for Aragorn, and perhaps it had something to do with inspiring his followers when it was displayed.

Arwen did watch over Aragorn from afar, according to Tolkien, and she could see deep into the hearts of others. Both abilities seem to be inherited from Galadriel, who studied under Melian (and undoubtedly Lúthien). When Frodo was preparing to leave Gondor, Arwen bestowed upon him the courtesy of taking ship with Bilbo when her father finally chose to leave Middle-earth. In one of his letters (*The Letters of J.R.R. Tolkien*, No. 246), Tolkien wrote that "it was Arwen who first thought of sending Frodo into the West, and put in a plea for him to Gandalf (direct or through Galadriel, or both)".

Imagine the goings-on in Gondor after the royal wedding. Here are Elrond, Galadriel, Celeborn, and many other great Elves come to celebrate the marriage of Aragorn and Arwen. Aragorn is busy putting his realm into order, arranging treaties with foreign nations, and so forth. What is Arwen doing during all that time, sitting by the White Tree and singing it into good health and blossoming? No. She is meeting with Galadriel and Gandalf, asking for a special gift for the Ringbearer. What other pleas did she make? Was she perhaps instrumental in persuading Thranduil to give Legolas leave to bring part of their people south to live in Gondor? Arwen became Queen of Men and Elves, not just Queen of Gondor.

Surely not contented with being an enchantress, mover, and shaker, Arwen also practiced something of the healing arts, and she seems to have raised horses. She gave Aragorn his horse, Roheryn (the name means "horse of the lady") and she gave Frodo a small white gemstone on a silver chain which helped to comfort him when he had fits of painful remembrance of his past wounds and loss (of the Ring).

"But she doesn't wield a sword in the stories!" people say. No, Tolkien never put a sword in Arwen's hand. This is the most grievous blow to the legends of Middle-earth, it seems. That Arwen, daughter of Elrond, who undertook dangerous journeys across the Misty Mountains, and who engaged in secret arts to help her beloved gain the throne of Gondor, and then helped him rule Gondor and Arnor for over 100 years, should in "The Lord of the Rings: The Fellowship of the Ring" movie be seen with sword in hand, facing down the Nazgul upon the road from the Shire to Imladris. Whatever is the world coming to?

Arwen should not be regarded as a frail and helpless flower guarded in secret dells and meadows. Elrond was concerned for her safety, that is true, and she would have not have journeyed alone, but like her mother before her would have been accompanied by Elven warriors and perhaps Rangers. She was often compared to her foremother Lúthien, not just because she *looked* like Lúthien, but because she was wise and well-learned in the lore of the Elves. Arwen's role in the book may seem small but it is crucial to the final outcome of the story. She is the means of Frodo and Bilbo's salvation. Her sacrifice is essentially unrewarded, for in the end she loses all that she has gained: love, life, and Middle-earth.

If therefore Peter Jackson has put a sword in her hand, I don't think J.R.R. Tolkien -- who wrote of the armed and armored Idril, who sent Lúthien on the perilous journey into Angband in quest of a Silmaril, who carefully recorded the attack on and capture of Arwen's mother Celebrian as she journeyed through the Misty Mountains -- would greatly object to the portrayal of a skill she probably possessed in his own conception. The changes in story were inevitable. But this change in character may not be as catastrophic as some people had believed.

Chapter 11:
If I only had a Bombadil...

By now everyone knows that, in the movie "The Lord of the Rings: The Fellowship of the Ring", Peter Jackson did not include the part of Tolkien's story which includes Tom Bombadil and the Hobbits' journey through the Old Forest. In fact, Jackson seemed to make it clear long before the movie's release that he didn't think Bombadil important to the story.   Early on I had hoped to perhaps see a Bombadil sequence in the extended version of the DVD of the movie. Alas, it was not to be so. But could there have been any incentive for him to do a Bombadil sequence for it?

Well, let's dispense with all the "faithful to Tolkien" themism and consider that a Bombadil sequence would have afforded Jackson an opportunity to extend his vision of Middle-earth to include the Old Forest and the Barrow-downs. Regardless of who howls and gnashes their teeth over the absence of Tolkien's beloved spirit of the vanishing Oxford countryside, the Old Forest and the Barrow-downs themselves are vital parts of the literary story. The Old Forest, like Sam's revelation of a walking tree in the Northfarthing, prepares the reader for the Ents and Huorns later on in the literary story. I suppose one could ask if there is any need to prepare the viewing audience for walking trees. I dunno. We already have some vague idea of how the story ends. Why bother preparing us for that with films 1 and 2?

The Barrow-downs is a more complicated episode. In the literary story, Gandalf noted that this was the most dangerous escapade Frodo experienced on his journey to Rivendell. People often wonder how this could be (well, in my email they do -- just like they wonder if that walking tree was an Ent, and no, sorry, I don't know). Why is the Barrow-wight a worse evil than the Nazgul at Weathertop? I would say that's because the Wight actually *had* Frodo and the Ring in its power. The Nazgul went in with a half-baked plan to stab Frodo and turn him into a wraith. Of course, they had to make it up as they went along. Strider (Aragorn) had thrown them for a loop, and it was only a guess that he would head to the ancient hill overlooking the great road. Undoubtedly, when they found Gandalf there days before (and I'm talking about the literary story right now), they were reassured that their guess was correct. That's why five of the boys sat around watching the road after Gandalf took off.

My guess is that the Nazgul always intended to stab Frodo. If Khamul had found Frodo in Hobbiton, he probably would have come back after dark and nabbed our dear Hobbit. How else should they have been able to take him back to Mordor anyway? Peter Jackson's story required the Nazgul to come across as terrifying and dangerous creatures. The audience had to feel somehow that if Jackson's Nazgul were to get Jackson's Frodo, they'd haul him back to Mordor. So, one must ask the question, would have including the Barrow-wight diminished the effect of the Nazgul?

Something we learn from Bombadil is that the Barrow-wights were sent by the Lord of the Nazgul to infest the mounds of Tyrn Gorthad. Okay, what the reader is told is that "A shadow came out of dark places far away, and the bones were stirred in the mounds." Where is the mention of the Lord of the Nazgul? Well, "Eriador, Arnor, and the Heirs of Isildur" (included in Appendix A, *The Lord of the Rings*) says "It was at this time [1636, the year of the Great Plague] that an end came to the Dunedain of Cardolan, and evil spirits out of Angmar and Rhudaur entered into the deserted mounds and dwelt there." The Lord of the Nazgul was ruling Angmar and Rhudaur at the time.

Okay, all one need do is turn to the Appendix to see where the Wights came from. Of course, the reader doesn't know to do that during the chapter "In the House of Tom Bombadil", and movies don't have appendices (but DVDs could!).

Bombadil basically recounts the entire history of Arnor from its founding up to its fall. So much is lost on the reader, and I believe this is intentional. I think Tolkien wanted to slip the history lesson past us so that when Aragorn whips out his broken sword at Imladris and Elrond recounts his lineage the reader can be surprised without feeling cheated. It's not like we weren't warned about that. In "Fog on the

Barrow-downs", Bombadil continues the history lesson after rescuing the Hobbits:

> 'Old knives are long enough as swords for hobbit-people,' he said. 'Sharp blades are good to have, if Shire-folk go walking east, south, or far away into dark and danger.' Then he told them that these blades were forged many long years ago by Men of Westernesse: they were foes of the Dark Lord, but they were overcome by the evil king of Carn Dûm in the Land of Angmar.

> 'Few now remember them,' Tom murmured, 'yet still some go wandering, sons of forgotten kings walking in loneliness, guarding from evil things folk that are heedless.'

> The hobbits did not understand his words, but as he spoke they had a vision as it were of a great expanse of years behind them, like a vast shadowy plain over which there strode shapes of Men, tall and grim with bright swords, and last came one with a star on his brow. Then the vision faded, and they were back in the sunlight world. It was time to start again. They made ready, packing their bags and lading their ponies. Their new weapons they hung on their leather belts under their jackets, feeling them very awkward, and wondering if they would be of any use. Fighting had not before occurred to any of them as one of the adventures in which their flight would land them.

This passage is very important to the story of the Ringbearers for several reasons. First of all, it represents a rite-of-passage for Frodo and his companions. They have just emerged from the Barrow-wight's lair, but they have also learned that they will be responsible for getting themselves out of future scrapes. They cannot count on meeting friends like Bombadil along the way (and he had, in fact, been asked to keep an eye out for them by Gildor and the Elves).

Secondly, Bombadil is reinforcing his history lesson here, but though Tolkien reveals a little more this time, the history remains vague in detail for the reader. Bombadil is also reinforcing Gandalf's history lesson from "The Shadow of the Past", however. There, after revealing the fiery letters Sauron had etched into his One Ring millennia before, Gandalf tells Frodo that the Ring had once been taken from Sauron.

...The strength of the Elves to resist [Sauron] was greater long ago; and not all Men were estranged from them. The Men of Westernesse came to their aid. That is a chapter of ancient history which it might be good to recall; for there was sorrow then too, and gathering dark, but great valour, and great deeds that were not wholly vain. One day, perhaps, I will tell you all the tale, or you shall hear it told in full by one who knows it best.

Gandalf's "one who knows it best" is undoubtedly Elrond, but Bombadil knows part of the tale and he shares what he knows with an inattentive Frodo (and inattentive readers).

A third reason for why the sword-giving passage is very important is that it gives us our first glimpse of Aragorn. Well, our second, really. Gandalf has already mentioned Aragorn -- named him fully -- in "The Shadow of the Past". But that discussion is long forgotten by now, and Frodo doesn't remember the name of Aragorn. Nor do most readers, it seems. And Bombadil and Aragorn seem to know each other quite well, though Bombadil doesn't reveal Aragorn's identity to either the Hobbits or the reader. He only prepares the Hobbits to meet the leader of the Rangers. I believe that Bombadil's vision of Aragorn's family line implants a certain sense of trustworthiness in the Hobbits. Maybe it only takes root in Frodo, but that is sufficient. When the time comes, it is only Frodo's opinion of Aragorn which matters, and he alone decides to accept Aragorn's offer of help and guidance upon the road.

Bombadil in fact plants other seeds in Frodo. For example, the second night the Hobbits stay in Bombadil's house, Frodo dreams of "sweet singing running in his mind: a song that seemed to come like a pale light behind a grey curtain, and growing stronger to turn the veil all to glass and silver, until at least it was rolled back, and a far green country opened before him under a swift sunrise."

Frodo's dream concerns Valinor, and his eventual passage over Sea. Frodo suddenly wakes up and there Tom is, outside the window, whistling. On the first night in Bombadil's house, Frodo dreams of Gandalf, trapped in Isengard; Pippin dreams of the Old Willow; and

Merry dreams of water spreading all round Bombadil's house. Merry's dream seems to be a foreshadowing of the Black Breath. Pippin's dream might just as easily be a foreshadowing of his and Merry's eventual encounter with the Ents. Frodo's dream is simply a prophetic revelation of events which have befallen his friend and counselor. It's a warning, perhaps, to all three that grave danger lies ahead of them.

When Bombadil tells the Hobbits they will need swords if they travel east or south, they don't seem to understand that he is foretelling their journey for them. They are deaf and dumb to all his wisdom, and really pay little heed to it, though his words seem to enrapture them. Bombadil in fact has a deceptively reassuring effect on the Hobbits. They feel safe with him, but he doesn't necessarily feel they will be safe if they remain with him. He is no master of the Nazgul, whom he knows come from Mordor. And he is no master of the One Ring, which cannot master him, either. But he cannot stand between Frodo and his destiny, nor forestall the inevitable.

In discussing the symbolic importance of Bombadil, Tolkien writes:

Bombadil is not an important person -- to the narrative. I suppose he has some importance as a 'comment'. I mean, I do not really write like that: he is just an invention (who first appeared in the *Oxford Magazine* about 1933), and he represents something that I feel important, though I would not be prepared to analyze the feeling precisely. I would not, however, have left him in, if he did not have some kind of function. I might put it this way. The story is cast in terms of a good side, and a bad side, beauty against ruthless ugliness, tyranny against kingship, moderated freedom with consent against compulsion that has long lost any object save mere power, and so on; but both sides in some degree, conservative or destructive, want a measure of control. But if you have, as it were taken 'a vow of poverty', renounced control, and take your delight in things for themselves without reference to yourself, watching, observing, and to some extent knowing, then the question of the rights and wrongs of power and control might become utterly meaningless to you, and the means of power quite valueless. It is a natural pacifist view, which always arises in the mind when there is a war. But the view of Rivendell seems to be that it is an excellent thing to have represented, but that there are in fact things with which it cannot cope; and upon which its existence nonetheless depends. Ultimately only the victory of the West will allow Bombadil to continue, or even to survive. Nothing would be left for him in the world of Sauron.

He has no connection in my mind with the Entwives. What had happened to them is not resolved in this book. He is in a way the answer to them in the sense that he is almost the opposite, being say, Botany and Zoology (as sciences) and Poetry as opposed to Cattle-breeding and Agriculture and Practicality. (*The Letters of J.R.R. Tolkien*, No. 144)

This is one of the most often-cited and most misunderstood passages in all of Tolkien's writings, when it comes to discussing Bombadil. All too frequently people cite the first sentence and stop reading with the period: "Tom Bombadil is not an important person -- to the narrative." One need only read a few sentences further to see that Tolkien is not speaking about the plot of the story, or the progression of Frodo's adventure: "...he represents something that I feel important...." And a little further on: "The story is cast in terms of a good side, and a bad side, beauty against ruthless ugliness, tyranny against kingship, moderated freedom with consent against compulsion." Bombadil is the "natural pacifist view" who has "renounced control" when "both sides...want a measure of control."

How can someone who is "not important...to the narrative" also represent "something [the author feels] important"? That makes no sense, except when presented as discussion of what the story is about, not of how the story progresses from beginning to end. The story is about "tyranny against kingship". Tom is neither a tyrant nor a king because he has "renounced control". So J.R.R. Tolkien never suggests that Tom Bombadil is not an important part of the story. Quite the contrary, he "would not have left [Bombadil] in, if he did not have some kind of function."

What is that function which Tolkien felt was so important? To another reader, Tolkien wrote:

I don't think Tom needs philosophizing about, and is not improved by it. But many have found him an odd or indeed discordant ingredient. In historical fact I put him in because I had already 'invented' him independently (he first appeared in the Oxford Magazine) and wanted an 'adventure' on the way. But I kept him in, and as he was, because he represents certain things otherwise left out. I do not mean him to be an allegory -- or I should not have given him so particular, individual, and ridiculous a name -- but 'allegory' is the only mode of exhibiting certain functions: he is then an 'allegory', or an exemplar, a particular embodying of pure (real) natural science: the spirit that desires knowledge of other things, their history and nature, *because they are 'other'* and wholly independent of the inquiring mind, a spirit coeval with the knowledge: Zoology and Botany not Cattle-breeding or Agriculture. Even the Elves hardly show this: they are primarily artists. Also T.B. exhibits another point in his attitude to the Ring, and its failure to affect him. You must concentrate on some part, probably relatively small, of the World (Universe), whether to tell a tale, however long, or to learn anything however fundamental -- and therefore much will from that 'point of view' be left out, distorted on the circumference, or seem a discordant oddity. The power of the Ring over all concerned, even the Wizards or Emissaries, is not a delusion -- but it is not the whole picture, even of the state and content of that part of the Universe. (Ibid., No. 153)

To Tolkien, therefore, Bombadil represents a symbolic part of the whole, necessary and vital to the completeness of the World. Without Bombadil Middle-earth is not what Tolkien intends it to be. Bombadil may seem playful and goofy, but he is a guardian and mentor to the Hobbits. He restrains the Old Forest, which had once attacked the Hobbits (and Merry notes when he leads the others into the Old Forest that "something makes paths. Whenever one comes inside one finds open tracks..."). Bombadil also watches over the Bree-folk, whose land is very close to the Barrow-downs, and who might be threatened by the Wights were they not held in check. And Bombadil preserves the knowledge of Aragorn's people, while he interacts with them and with the Elves. He recalls the beauty of an ancient Númenorean lady of Cardolan, and takes her brooch for Goldberry so they can honor her, and he fulfills Gildor's request to help Frodo and the Hobbits on their journey.

Well, that hardly makes the case for including Bombadil in a DVD. But it's easier to make a case for including Bombadil in the whole story. After all, Tolkien included him. And Bombadil's resonances are felt throughout the books, all the way to "The Grey Havens". The story has to be substantially altered to get rid of Bombadil. Let's recap the key scenes in the books where his influence is felt:

1. The barrow-blades. These are the most obvious impact that Bombadil has on the storyline itself. The barrow-blades are significant in scenes at Weathertop, the Ford of Bruinen, the Chamber of Mazarbul, Parth Galen, the Hornburg, Minas Tirith, Cirith Ungol, the Battle of the Pelennor Fields, and the Battle of the Morannon.

2. The Ents. People seem to forget completely that part of Treebeard's conversations with Merry and Pippin concerned Bombadil and the Old Forest. In fact, Merry and Pippin discuss the Old Forest with Treebeard as he takes them to Wellinghall.

3. Aragorn. Aragorn doesn't just overhear Bombadil's last conversation with Frodo and the lads, he fulfills Bombadil's prophecy. Bombadil is the bridge between Gandalf's all-too-brief history lesson and Bilbo's verse in Gandalf's letter, which ends with "the crownless again shall be king." The clues are there for the reader to put together. Bombadil is staying abreast of events. And his knowledge of the Ring matches Gildor's. It seems everyone knows about the Ring, though no one bothers to inform Frodo of their own awareness. Bombadil's knowledge provides the reader with an important bridge between foreshadowings and fulfillments.

4. Gandalf. Bombadil and Gandalf have a history, and when Gandalf brings the Hobbits home he turns off to visit Bombadil. It's a convenient means of getting rid of the Wizard so that the Hobbits can take care of their own problems at home.

5. The Grey Havens. Frodo is given a glimpse of what lies before him in Bombadil's house. Bombadil represents hope in the darkness.

6. The Barrow-wight. Although the Wight never returns to trouble Frodo, it is Frodo's first serious exercise in asserting his own will. Frodo gradually becomes a different person because of his resistance to the Ring, but his development in that respect begins with the Wight.

7. The ponies. This is the least important part of the story, but Bombadil eventually hears about the problems in Bree and he sends the ponies to Barliman Butterbur. (Out of curiosity: from whom did Bombadil get the news about events in Bree?)

8. The Old Forest and the Barrow-downs. At the beginning of this essay, I mentioned that including the Old Forest and the Barrow-downs would afford Peter Jackson an opportunity to show more of Middle-earth. Why not show us the Old Forest? It isn't just about trees that move around, you know. It's a piece of Hobbit culture. In particular, it's part of what makes the Buckland the Buckland. Hobbits in the Shire don't have to maintain a High Hay to keep the trees out. Shirefolk say the Bucklanders are strange; different. And to a Hobbiton Hobbit, the Bucklanders *are* different. And then there are the Barrow-downs. This is the only region of Eriador where Aragorn's people once lived that we actually get to see any Númenorean ruins. Weathertop doesn't count. That's supposed to be just a ring of stones on a hill-top, an old fortress.

But Bombadil is important in other ways as well. It is Bombadil who shows that the Ring cannot master everyone, and if it cannot master everyone then there is reason to hope that Frodo can withstand its influence for at least a while. He has to struggle with the Ring more and more as he gets closer to Mordor, but the Ring only wins in the final struggle, as Frodo stands before Sammath Naur. Even so, when Frodo succumbs to the Ring's influence in Bree and at Weathertop the reader is reminded that Frodo, too, has his limits. He is not as powerful as Bombadil, not as sure of himself as Bombadil. Bombadil is a catalyst who sets up the conflict between Frodo and the Ring in a way that Gandalf cannot. Gandalf is himself afraid of the Ring. Tom isn't.

The step from Buckland to Bree may seem rather simple, but in terms of advancing the story Bombadil provides the means for Frodo to sidestep the net which has been laid for him. The full scope of the search for the Ring is only made apparent in *Unfinished Tales*, where we are told that the Lord of the Nazgul is responsible for waking the Willow and arousing the Barrow-wights. Recall that when Tom first meets the Hobbits he is surprised to learn that the Willow is awake and active. "You let them out again, Old Man Willow! What be you a-thinking-of? You should not be waking. Eat earth! Dig deep! Drink water! Go to sleep! Bombadil is talking!"

The Willow and Wight are important to the plot because they help underscore just how perilous Frodo's escape from the Shire really is. He is no longer safe anywhere, as Gildor points out. The Nazgul have found his home in Hobbiton, they are tracking him through the Shire, and they are on horseback. How are four Hobbits supposed to outrun four Nazgul on horseback? They can't. So getting the Hobbits from the Shire to Bree forces a hard choice upon the screenwriters. The escape has to be acceptable, and it can't drag on.

The most oft-cited reason for not including Bombadil in the movie is that there simply isn't time to include everything. Quite true. Yet if Bombadil is dropped in order to save time, that means that the plot has to be altered, or else a gap left in the storyline. Removing Bombadil surgically is simply impossible. You either leave in a lot of stuff which goes unexplained (such as the Hobbits' swords) or you change the story to eliminate the discrepancies.

So what we see in Peter Jackson's movie is the latter option: changes in the storyline, some of which seem relatively inexplicable to a large part of the viewing audience, such as Aragorn's sudden appearance at Weathertop with an armful of swords for Frodo and the boys. It appears there is nothing particularly special about the movie swords, whereas in the book Aragorn points out that they are "wound about with spells for the bane of Mordor".

Regardless of how this was handled in the first movie, removing Bombadil forced other changes in the story as well. In "The Lord of the Rings: The Two Towers", Merry tells Pippin that "something makes paths" in the Old Forest beside Buckland. He implies there are Ents living in the Old Forest. Ents, but no Bombadil. But then, the point of the movies is to tell the journey of the Ringbearers, not to document Bombadil's every silly song. We've already seen changes in Arwen's larger role in the movies, as well as even more significant changes in "The Two Towers" (such as Aragorn's faux death, Eomer's exile from Rohan with a large part of its army, and the arrival of an army of Elves at the Hornburg).

Okay, the point is, the story has been changed. Its now much too late to 'save' Bombadil and add him into the DVD. But it sure would have been nice to see Robin Williams capering across the landscape singing "Hey dol a merry dol!".

One of the greatest scenes in "The Wizard of Oz" movie (in my humble opinion) is the Jitterbug sequence. What's that? You don't remember the Jitterbug sequence? I'm not surprised. It was cut from the movie. But not everything connected to the scene was cut. When the Wicked Witch of the West sends the flying monkeys to capture Dorothy and Toto, she tells their leader, "They won't give you any trouble! I've sent a little bug ahead to take the fight out of them." (I should perhaps mention that there was no such sequence in the original book by L. Frank Baum, who wrote about Dorothy's adventures long before the Jitterbug dance was devised.)

For about 23 years I wondered what the heck the witch was referring to. And then I bought the fiftieth anniversary commemorative video. Mamma mia! What fantastic footage was revealed on that tape. And, sadly, the notes which accompanied the tape revealed that other scenes had been filmed and lost. The Jitterbug sequence only survives because the choreographer made a home movie of it (fortunately, he used color film). So, you not only get to see Judy Garland, Ray Bolger, Burt Lahr, and Jack Haley doing the Jitterbug, you also see one of the tree operators (yes, the Jitter Trees in the Haunted Forest had people inside them) coming out for a breath of fresh air.

Sadly, we never actually get to see the Jitterbug, although it was there in the original movie as an animated pink and blue insect. And the dance number required five months of rehearsals and filming. The deletion of this scene was a crime against all film-making.

"The Wizard of Oz" is a great movie, and one of my all-time favorites. It's almost nothing like the book. Well, there's a tornado, and Toto too. People can enjoy both the book and the movie (I loved the book when I read it). Or not. But we can also hope the final "Lord of the Rings" DVD collection offers at least as much extra magic as the Wizard's 50th anniversary video. Because, you know, Bombadil is important to the story no matter how much it gets changed. *He is*.

Chapter 12:
The Sauron Strategies

Footsteps into Failure

Sun Tzu points out the wisdom of the "divide and conquer" strategy, but he also advocates the use of massive, overwhelming, superior force whenever it is available. The art of war is indeed an art, for both sides in any given war have the potential to learn and adapt. One of the notable qualities of Middle-earth history is Sauron's mutability. He alters his strategies.

In the First Age, Sauron was just one of several captains serving Morgoth. Sauron's generalship is never really explored. We learn more about his cunning ability to ferret out enemies, and his willingness to engage in personal combat at considerable risk to himself. Morgoth, on the other hand, relies upon stealth and massive, overwhelming, superior numbers. It seems to be Morgoth's perpetual weakness that he confuses numbers with force.

Of course, Morgoth pulled off a few major victories. In fact, he crushed the Eldarin civilization in Beleriand and reduced the Dwarves of Nogrod and Belegost to sideline players. But Morgoth missed the big picture. While he dithered around in the north with the Noldor, most of Middle-earth escaped his attention. The Valar took advantage of Morgoth's intense interest in Beleriand and the Noldor to isolate him there and inflict the final defeat upon him.

The outcome of the War of Wrath was that Morgoth was captured and his forces reduced to probably no more than a few vagabond groups of Orcs, Trolls, and Men. At most, only a handful of the corrupted Maiar probably escaped, and at least a couple of the winged dragons as well (since a breeding population of dragons survived into the Third Age and beyond). Of the Maiar, we can be sure that two were Sauron and the Balrog of Khazad-dûm. The Balrog withdrew from all political entanglements for over five thousand years.

Sauron, on the other hand, was apparently apprehended. "Of the Rings of Power and the Third Age" (published in *The Silmarillion*) tells us that Sauron "put on his fair hue again and did obeisance to Eönwë, the herald of Manwë, and abjured all of his evil deeds." But Eönwë could not pardon Sauron, and instead commanded him to return to Valinor and await the judgement of Manwë. To that Sauron would not consent, and he remained in Middle-earth when Eönwë returned into the West.

For the next five or six hundred years, Sauron vanished from history. It is unlikely that Sauron "slept" in the sense that the Balrog seems to have curled up under a conveniently huge mountain and dreamed of past debaucheries for the next several thousand years. More likely, Sauron retreated into far eastern Middle-earth and there he could have done anything, such as plant a garden or found a monastery to teach ancient Elves, Dwarves, and Men the Way of Peace. Whatever he did, after a few hundred years Sauron realized he wasn't going to accomplish much -- or else that he could probably get away with doing whatever he wanted, so he launched a new initiative.

Sauron's gradual emergence into the affairs of Middle-earth did not go unnoticed, and it may be that the catalyst for his return was the eastward migration of Sindar. Tolkien observed that, "seeing the desolation of the world, Sauron said in his heart that the Valar, having overthrown Morgoth, had again forgotten Middle-earth; and his pride grew apace."

In the "notes on motives in the Silmarillion" essay (published in *Morgoth's Ring*), Tolkien wrote: "[Sauron] did not object to the existence of the world, so long as he could do what he liked with it. He still had the relics of positive purposes, that descended from the good of the nature in which he began: it had been his virtue (and therefore also the cause of his fall, and of his relapse) that he loved order and co-ordination, and disliked all confusion and wasteful friction."

Sauron fundamentally believed that he could set the world in order, bring it out of the chaos that Morgoth and his wars with the Valar and Eldar had created, and restore it to its original purposes. But, because of his pride, "his 'plans'...became the sole object of his will" (ibid.).

Sauron forgot why he wanted to bring order to the world, and simply focused on bringing order to it.

He clearly saw the Elves as potential instruments of his will. They had the sub-creative abilities to affect the wider world in ways that other creatures, such as Men, apparently lacked. Dwarves don't seem to have figured broadly in Sauron's designs, and that may be due to either a lack of knowledge about them on Sauron's part (such a perspective is reinforced by the fact that Sauron failed to convert any Dwarves into Ringwraiths) or to their lesser abilities (although we have too little information about Dwarven capabilities to compare them with the Elves in that way).

However, Sauron at first began organizing the remnants of Morgoth's creatures. They would have been easy for him to recruit into his service -- he would have known them well and they might have remembered him -- but he seems to have worked slowly and subtly at first. Gil-galad suspected that a servant of Morgoth had begun organizing peoples or creatures in the east before the year 1000 in the Second Age.

According to "Aldarion and Erendis: The Mariner's wife" (*Unfinished Tales*), Gil-galad recruited Anardil, prince of Númenor (later the king Tar-Aldarion), to serve as an ambassador to men living in northern and western Middle-earth. At the time, Gil-galad seems to have striven to collect information and to build up goodwill among peoples dwelling near his kingdom, which lay upon the northwestern shores of Middle-earth, in the last remnant of eastern Beleriand. Anardil's activities in Middle-earth, and the growing presence of Númenoreans in the coastlands (through voyages of exploration and seasonal camps or temporary colonies such as Vinyalondë), induced Sauron to select a permanent base of operations around the year 1000 (according to Appendix B, "The Tale of Years", in *The Lord of the Rings*).

We can infer from the settlement of Mordor that Sauron had no permanent secure base in the east. He must have had one or more fortresses from which he directed his growing empire, but he apparently believed that he needed to be closer to the westlands in order to devise and implement a new strategy. This strategy was founded upon Sauron's hope of inducing the Eldar to accept him as a teacher and guide. Hence, either he initially populated Mordor with servants not likely to instill alarm in the Eldar, or else he suppressed knowledge of his presence in the region.

Sauron's diplomatic missions to the Eldar appear to have occurred in the brief period of a single year. The entry for 1200 in the Second Age of "The Tale of Years" reads: "Sauron endeavors to seduce the Eldar. Gil-galad refuses to treat with him; but the smiths of Eregion are won over." He probably never visited the other Elven realms, where the Eldar were few or had adopted the ways of the less sophisticated Silvan Elves. Clearly, Sauron was going after the heart of Elven power.

Since his objective was to impose an order upon the world (presumably to repair the hurts done by the war in Beleriand, and to eliminate or reduce the chaos which had replaced Morgoth's regime at the end of the First Age), Sauron had to appeal to the Eldar's own innate desire to bring order to the world about them. The Elves, in Tolkien's view, "wanted to have their cake without eating it." Or, more precisely, the Eldar "wanted the peace and bliss and perfect memory of 'The West', and yet to remain on the ordinary earth where their prestige as the highest people, above wild Elves, dwarves, and Men, was greater than at the bottom of the hierarchy of Valinor" (*The Letters of J.R.R. Tolkien*, No. 131) .

So, early on, Sauron's own desire to dominate Middle-earth was rivaled by the Eldar's (growing) desire to achieve a similar status. Both Sauron and the Eldar were seeking *control*, and *influence*. Rather than pursue an outright war, however, Sauron elected to bring the Eldar into his community through subterfuge. By appealing to their strengths, he believed he would take advantage of a vulnerability he perceived. Yet, was that vulnerability really there? Could Sauron have succeeded with the Elves?

Probably no more than he did. That is, Sauron seems to have underestimated the Elves' powers of perception and understanding. He did not anticipate the Elven-smiths' awareness of his actions, when he created the One Ring and placed it upon his finger. At that moment, the Elves were aware of him, his true nature and designs, and they removed their Rings. Sauron never had the opportunity to begin influencing them as he had hoped to.

I have often wondered why it took almost 100 years from that point (Second Age 1600) for Sauron to launch the war with the Eldar. It would seem he just sort of waited around, allowing the Eldar and Númenoreans to build up their defenses. But most likely Sauron himself lacked the power to launch a massive campaign against the West. He knew fully well the capabilities of the Eldar. He had fought them in Beleriand, and had witnessed more than one Elven victory against overwhelming numbers.

The 90 years of preparation for war with the Elves would have afforded Sauron time to increase the ranks of his Orc-soldiery, but it would also have provided him with time to learn how to use his Ring to gain better control over his servants. Sauron must have used the One Ring to extend his influence over many peoples at that time, but it is apparent from the aftermath of the war that he did not fully control eastern Middle-earth. He was working with limited resources.

According to the essay "Dwarves and Men" (published in *The Peoples of Middle-earth*), the Orcs had been driven from the northern lands by an alliance of dwarves and Men early in the Second Age. If Mordor was the only region where the Orcs dwelt in the year 1500, they could not have been very numerous. Sauron's preoccupation with the Eldar in Eregion from circa 1200 to 1500 suggests he paid little attention to the Orcs. They may have sustained their numbers but were not permitted to increase to a point where they would become unmanageable. That is, Sauron's strategy at the time did not call for unleashing hordes of Orcs upon the world. We can be reasonably certain of this because he did not launch an immediate invasion of the north in 1600.

If the Orcs required 90 years in which to increase their numbers, would Sauron have utilized that time to make inroads with other peoples? For example, how did he gain the trust of the Gwathuirim (a name the Númenoreans gave to the ancestors of the Bree-men and Dunlendings in the Second Age, according to "Dwarves and Men") , especially those living in Enedwaith and Minhiriath? These Men helped Sauron during the war, but did they simply flock to his banner when he showed up with an army of Orcs, or did he perhaps spend time among them, winning their trust and playing to their fears and resentments. The Gwathuirim felt threatened by the Númenorean settlements and timber industries. The had been raiding Númenorean lands along the Gwathlo river (between Eriador and Enedwaith) since Anardil (Tar-Aldarion) first built Vinyalondë in the late 800s.

90 years would also have provided Sauron time to scout out the lands east of the Misty Mountains. In "Dwarves and Men", we are told that Sauron overran the lands of the Edainic peoples who dwelt in the Vales of Anduin and east of Greenwood the Great, bringing down their ancient alliance with the Longbeard Dwarves. His objective in launching the war therefore appears to have been to destroy all possible resistance to his rule in Middle-earth. It would not have been sufficient for Sauron to seize Eregion and the Rings of Power. He wanted to eliminate all possible rival powers.

Hence, the Longbeard Dwarves themselves must have posed a considerable threat to Sauron's plans. Their kingdom had been strengthened early in the Second Age by an influx of Dwarves emigrating from the Ered Luin. These were mostly Belegostian Dwarves, former allies of the Eldar in Beleriand and enemies of Morgoth. Khazad-dum, the chief city of the Longbeards, provided a key avenue of supply and reinforcement between Eregion and the Vales of Anduin. Considerable trade must have passed through the Longbeards' hands. But more importantly, the Longbeards were the traditional central power of Dwarvendom. They were the guardians of Gundabad, where the Dwarven peoples had communed for countless years.

If the Eldar posed a threat to Sauron's control over Middle-earth, the Dwarves were at the very least an obstacle in his path. They would not have accepted his domination and they were, in the westlands, allied with the Eldar and the Edainic peoples who were friendly with the Eldar. Sauron well knew what the Edain were capable of, for he had fought them in Beleriand. Among Men, the Númenoreans may have presented the greater threat, but their homeland lay far beyond Middle-earth. Relatively few Númenoreans dwelt in Middle-earth. The Edainic peoples provided Gil-galad and his allies with a tremendous resource.

Therefore, Sauron's assault on the lands east of the Misty Mountains makes sense. While he besieged Eregion, Khazad-dum's priorities were divided. Sauron may not have anticipated the assault that Durin III launched against the invaders from Khazad-dum's west-gate (mentioned in "The History of Galadriel and Celeborn", published in *Unfinished Tales*), but clearly the Dwarves were too weak to defeat Sauron's army. Or else Sauron intended the battles in the east to draw off a great part of Durin's strength, thus ensuring that Durin could not help save Eregion. The eastern Edainic peoples were driven from their lands, and most were apparently killed. The survivors fled into the mountains, where the Dwarves could protect them, or the deeper woodlands, where they were isolated from other peoples. Most of them probably fled into the far northern lands anyway. But the end result was the ruin of the ancient alliance between Dwarves and Men.

The Silvan Elves probably suffered terribly. They may have been incapable of mounting or sustaining the kind of war which the Eldar could achieve, but they were more numerous than the Eldar and, in some lands, were led by Eldarin princes. It may be that several smaller realms were wiped out or their peoples driven to seek refuge in Greenwood the Great and Lothlórien. Yet Sauron's failure to destroy the realms of Amdir (father of Amroth) and Oropher (father of Thranduil) implies that he lacked the resources to fight a woodland war. He must have had few if any troops trained for warfare under the trees. Or else he simply could not afford to concentrate as many forces on the eastern lands as he brought against Eregion.

A failure to capitalize on his victories in the east may have been the reason for why Sauron decided to burn the forests of Eriador. His eastern armies must have cleared the open lands of Men and Elves and been stopped in the forests. Either the eastern forces were wiped out in pitched, desperate battles, or else they withdrew when they could go no further. If Durin's attack on Sauron's western forces in Eregion was completely unexpected, and Sauron could have realized that if he took his army through the great woodlands of Eriador, the Eldar and Edain would ravage his troops and supply lines.

Hence, after crushing Eregion, Sauron sent enough troops northward to ensure that Elrond's army was pinned down, and then he proceeded to eradicate the whole of Eriador. In a way, the devastation Sauron wreaked upon the world would serve as a statement, a sort of declaration of sovereignty. "This is mine to do with as I please." He would be telling the Elves in no uncertain terms that he, and not they, would control Middle-earth. The cake was his, not theirs. The Elves must have understood this, too.

After the war was over, and Sauron had been defeated, there apparently was no talk of marching into Mordor and taking Sauron down a peg. Many Elves fled Middle-earth and Gil-galad elected to establish a new outpost at Imladris, which was farther north (and distant from Mordor) and more defensible than Eregion had been. The army or armies which had pursued Sauron back to Mordor must not have had sufficient resources to force their way into the land. So the implication of their withdrawal is that the Eldar and Númenoreans ran into something they were not ready to deal with.

Mordor, surrounded by high mountains, was very defensible, and undoubtedly Sauron chose to make it his fortress because of the advantages offered by the geography. But Gil-galad had few if any resources for maintaining a lengthy siege so far from Lindon. Númenor had no bases in the area (Pelargir would not exist for another 600 years), and the only peoples in the area were unfriendly (except possibly for the Ent-wives, who may have been willing to support the cause, but might also have stood aside).

"The Tale of Years" says that, beginning around the year 1800, Sauron extended his power eastward. It would seem that Sauron, like the Eldar and Númenoreans, felt it was time for a change in policy. Rather than take on the Eldar directly, he elected instead to build up his power among other peoples (presumably among the Men of eastern Middle-earth, whose ancestors had once been loyal or friendly to Morgoth). The evolution of Sauron's goals emerges as a consequence of his several failures: he failed to accept responsibility for his rebellion and refused to go to Valinor; he failed to seduce the Eldar to his full service; he failed to crush the Eldar and eliminate them as potential rivals for control over Middle-earth.

Gil-galad's lack of ambition was Sauron's saving grace. While Gil-galad probably concentrated on healing the lands and peoples Sauron had nearly destroyed in the war, Sauron invested his time in developing new resources. And he did not forget the Dwarves. Having seized the Nine and the Seven Rings of Power from the Gwaith-i-Mirdain in Eregion, Sauron perverted the Rings and gave them out to Men and Dwarves. Three of the Rings were given to Númenoreans, possibly to captains or lords who led new colonization efforts in Middle-earth. Although the Númenoreans had begun making permanent havens around the year 1200, they began "establishing dominions on the coast [of Middle-earth]" around the year 1800 ("The Tale of Years").

By dispensing Rings of Power to Men and Dwarves in the east, where he already had influence, Sauron probably achieved ironclad control over many lands very quickly, within the space of a few years or generations. Although the Men who received Rings eventually became wraiths, the Dwarven lords could not be so corrupted. And yet, "Dwarves and Men" implies that all the eastern Dwarven peoples may have fallen into evil. If Sauron could not have dominated the Dwarves through their Rings, he may nonetheless have won influence and friendship among them through the bestowal of such gifts.

The Rings given to the western Dwarves are a more complicated issue. There is no indication that any of them ever fell into evil. Their Rings may have been the foundation of great hoards (and the implication of that tradition, recorded in "Durin's Folk", in Appendix A, *The Lord of the Rings*, is that the kingly houses of the Ered Luin not only survived but thrived in the Second Age). How did Sauron manage to give Rings of Power to the Dwarves? And when? He clearly did not visit them in the capacity of his former persona. Durin III, at least, should have resisted any such attempts at bribery.

The whole business with redistributing the stolen Rings of Power smacks of a poorly thought-out "Plan B". Sauron did not quite know what to do. He needed more powerful servants through whom to conquer Middle-earth, but those servants did not present him with advantages over the Elves. In fact, although Sauron continued to attack the Elves throughout the next 1300 years or so, he never again mounted the kind of massive campaign against the Eldar that he had attempted in the war of 1695-1701. Why?

The Númenoreans certainly began to take on a larger role in the affairs of Middle-earth. As the centuries passed, new Númenorean strongholds and havens were established along the coastlands. Númenorean power slowly marched northward toward Mordor's borders. So Sauron found himself confronted by two rivals: the Eldar in the north and Númenor in the south. And yet, with the destruction of Eregion, all ambition seems to have fled the Eldar. As long as the Rings of Power existed, of course, the Elves would have some protection against fading. So their chief objective had been accomplished. But they appear to have had the stuffing beaten out of them. There would be no more great Elven realms in Middle-earth.

Sauron may have built up his strength, but he seems to have devoted more than 1,000 years to dueling with the Númenoreans over various minor regions. His strategy floundered as he pondered what to do about the two problems. Sauron's flexibility undoubtedly ensured that his realm survived. By changing directions and pursuing more easily obtained goals in the east, he established an empire capable of withstanding most of the incursions of Númenor. But he appears to have held back in confronting Númenorean power. There is no mention of massive assaults on any Númenorean fortresses (which is not to say they did not or could not have occurred in some places-- the chronologies only record major, history-altering events with strategic importance). Once Umbar was established, it remained in Númenorean control. Once Pelargir was built, Númenor had a permanent foothold along the lower Anduin.

However, it may be that Sauron stumbled early on, and his apparent reluctance to launch a second massive war was due to a realization of his mistakes in the first war. When the Elves realized that they had been betrayed, Sauron seems to have given in to anger and pride. He demanded that they surrender their Rings of Power to him. Of course, they refused to do so. Hence, Sauron reacted angrily and launched a war against them. Although he might have cooled off after a few dozen years, any setbacks he suffered early on in the war (such as losing his eastern armies, or at least failing to destroy the woodland realms) may have reignited or fed his anger. It would not be until Sauron and his bodyguard returned to Mordor, soundly defeated, that he may have calmed down enough to figure out that he wasn't going to seize all of Middle-earth through war.

Hence, the ensuing centuries where Sauron sparred with the Númenoreans for control over what must have been relatively minor territories (probably mostly in the south) may have been time well spent in Sauron's opinion. That is, he was able to probe the Númenoreans for weaknesses, and he must have studied them. It may be that Sauron studied the young prince who eventually became Ar-Pharazôn, realized that here was an individual who could be manipulated, and eventually enticed Ar-Pharazôn (from afar) to challenge him for mastery over Middle-earth.

If that was indeed Sauron's goal, he blundered. For Ar-Pharazôn brought such an immense army out of the west that Sauron's allies deserted him. Of course, Sauron resorted to subterfuge, surrendering himself so that he could be taken to Númenor as a prisoner. There he gradually won the king's confidence and seduced the vast majority of Númenoreans, many of whom were already rebellious toward the Valar, into worshipping Morgoth and defying the Valar. "Akallabeth" implies that Sauron hoped to destroy Númenor all along, but it also records that he was astounded at what he found in Númenor, for the achievements of the Dunedain surpassed all his expectations.

Sauron's change in plans preserved Mordor as a base of power and opened up for him an opportunity to undermine the Númenorean civilization. He was clearly acting opportunistically, and perhaps entirely making up things as he went along. But his sojourn in Númenor was a fresh approach, and one which, though resulting in temporary setbacks (Gil-galad was able to extend his own power during Sauron's absence from Middle-earth), helped Sauron achieve one of his goals: the destruction of Númenor.

With Númenor out of the way, Sauron returned to Middle-earth, wounded but not greatly weakened. He may have contemplated turning his full attention upon Gil-galad, but he would have quickly learned that Númenorean survivors led by Elendil were establishing two new kingdoms in the north. Although many of the Númenorean colonies would now support Sauron, the Faithful Dunedain were helping Gil-galad to consolidate his power in the north. In effect, Sauron had replaced an immensely powerful Númenor, which he could not overcome militarily, with an immensely powerful alliance of Elves and Men.

Sauron attacked Gondor without warning, but "Númenor" in Appendix A, *The Lord of the Rings*, says he "struck too soon, before his own power was rebuilt; whereas the power of Gil-galad had increased in his absence." "Of the Rings of Power and the Third Age" (published in *The Silmarillion*) is less pessimistic: "When therefore Sauron saw his time he came with great force against the new realm of Gondor, and he took Minas Ithil, and he destroyed the White Tree of Isildur that grew there." Although Minas Ithil fell, Anarion held out in Osgiliath and eventually drove Sauron back to the mountains. Sauron thus seems not to have fully integrated all his former allies back into his realm, or else he didn't wait long enough for their armies to arrive.

The attack on Gondor is similar in scope to the attack on Eregion. Sauron was selecting strategic targets and seeking to isolate them from allied powers. He succeeded partially with Eregion: Elrond was unable to break through Sauron's lines, although Durin III rescued some of Eregion's people. The assault on Gondor was a failure, and it underscored the weakness in Sauron's approach: he allowed his enemies to work for the benefit of each other, even if they could not coordinate their efforts against him. Elrond and Durin both saved a portion of Eregion's people because Sauron was focused on seizing the

Rings of Power. Gondor withstood his attack because he was too eager to launch his war. He failed to isolate Gondor or to divide the realm into smaller, more easily conquered regions.

Isildur was able to sail north and rouse Elendil and Gil-galad. The alliance they assembled proved to be strong enough to destroy Sauron's realm. In fact, they raised a larger army than Ar-Pharazôn had brought to Middle-earth nearly 200 years before. If Sauron's allies were incapable of facing Ar-Pharazôn's army, it is to his credit that they stayed by him during the final war of the Second Age. But they were no match for the Last Alliance.

Through war after war, Sauron allowed his enemies to support one another and sometimes to work together. It would not be until Barad-dur was besieged and Sauron's plans lay dashed in blood across the landscape that he finally figured out what he was doing wrong. He needed to isolate his enemies from one another. He launched a final, desperate attack against Gil-galad and slew the Elven-king, but Elendil stood close by and was able to strike a mortal blow to Sauron. The last combat on Orodruin may have been more an act borne of frustration than anything else. Even without Gil-galad, the Last Alliance had won the war. Sauron's empire was dismantled. His personal realm of Mordor was occupied.

A second death gave Sauron a much-needed respite. Middle-earth settled into a long period of peace in which Men would forget the Dark Lord and the Elves could only hope he did not return. Sauron had plenty of time for reflection upon his mistakes, and when he finally returned he had a new strategy, one which encompassed millennia and took into consideration all the variables he had not considered well enough in the Second Age.

One war to win them all, except...

In the First Age, Morgoth attempted to overwhelm his Eldarin foes by throwing everything possible at them. Usually, his armies met with mixed success. Even the Nirnaeth Arnoediad proved to be so costly a victory that Morgoth could not fully capitalize on the defeat of the

Elven armies and their allies. He seized Hithlum and the March of Maedhros, restored his troops to Dorthonion, and took full control over the upper Vale of Sirion. But the Falas, Nargothrond, Doriath (and Brethil, which was technically a part of Doriath), and Gondolin each had to be dealt with separately.

In the Second Age, Sauron attempted to duplicate Morgoth's dubious successes with sudden onslaughts, hoping to achieve crushing military victories. Yet, he lacked Morgoth's advantages. Whereas most of Middle-earth was under Morgoth's control, Sauron had to continually engage in empire building. And whereas Morgoth's chief fortress of Angband was closely ringed about by his enemies, Sauron positioned himself in Mordor with the intention of deploying agents and forces to work against both the Eldar in the north and the Númenoreans in the south.

Númenorean settlements had not advanced very far north by the time Sauron forged the One Ring around the year 1600. The great fortresses of Pelargir, on the lower Anduin, and Umbar would not be established for more than 600 years. Númenorean power was at best a promise of future conflict. But when Gil-galad called upon Númenor to help prepare Eriador for the coming war, the Númenoreans invested nearly 100 years in fortifying positions along the Gwathlo and Lhun rivers. By the time Sauron began to move his forces north, his enemies had multiple lines of defense.

Which is not to say that Sauron should have been repulsed. The histories ("The History of Galadriel and Celeborn" in *Unfinished Tales*, "The Tale of Years" in *The Lord of the Rings*, "Of the Rings of Power and the Third Age" in *The Silmarillion*) make it clear that Sauron seized Tharbad and pushed his way into Eregion with relative ease. Ost-in-Edhil (the chief city of Eregion) held out for a while, possibly as long as a year. Elrond's attempt to reinforce Eregion failed and he had to retreat north. Sauron sent an army to keep Elrond out of the way. And, apparently, at the same time he was destroying Eregion, Sauron sent an army east of the Misty Mountains to root out the Elven and Edainic peoples there, the latter of whom had long been allied with the Longbeard Dwarves of Khazad-dum.

So, Sauron not only gave his enemies a long time to prepare for the war, he spread his forces thinly when he attacked his foes. Gil-galad was able to consolidate most of his surviving forces at the Lhun after being pushed back from the Baranduin river. Sauron overran Eriador, but Tolkien notes that Sauron killed or drove off the Men and Elves living throughout the region. Those who were driven off fell back to Elrond's encampment in Imladris or Gil-galad's kingdom. The two regions were thus strengthened by Sauron's advancing campaign. And Sauron had to allocate part of his own forces to keep Elrond pinned down at Imladris.

Ultimately, it required massive intervention from Númenor to defeat Sauron, but the lesson he learned from the war was that Númenor was going to be more trouble than Lindon. Tolkien tells us that war never ceased between the Elves and Sauron after that time, yet Sauron altered his strategic goals. He began conquering more territory in the east. And, gradually, as Sauron extended his power southward he came into conflict with the Númenorean colonies along the southern coasts of Middle-earth. Númenor had been colonizing Middle-earth since around the year 1200, but about the year 1800 the Númenoreans began establishing fortresses, levying tribute from local peoples, and conquering occupied lands (Cf. "The Tale of Years"). Númenor became a rival power with which Sauron had to contend. In fact, it proved impossible for Sauron to defeat Númenor in the field, and he finally overcame the Númenoreans through a subterfuge which brought about Númenor's destruction and the death of most of its people.

And yet, despite the fall of Númenor, Sauron had not rid himself of the Númenorean threat. Elendil and the exiled Faithful Dunedain established the kingdoms of Arnor and Gondor in northern Middle-earth. Though but a remnant of the once mighty nation which had humbled Sauron militarily, the Faithful Dunedain were too powerful to be overwhelmed quickly. Sauron learned this when he took Minas Ithil but was driven back from Osgiliath. One can almost hear him thinking, "Uh, oh. This didn't go as planned." Had he waited another 100 years, both Arnor and Gondor would have become more powerful, but Sauron might have re-established full control over his network of allies and subject states. He would have had far greater resources to call upon than he possessed when he attacked Gondor in 3429.

Waiting too long, acting too soon -- these were the mistakes Sauron committed in the Second Age. He permitted his enemies to grow strong while he himself dispersed his forces and waged war on many fronts. After his defeat, Sauron had 1,000 years to reflect upon his failures and weaknesses. When he became strong enough to re-embody himself, he understood that in order to seize control over Middle-earth, he needed to work slowly, carefully. He needed to build up his power while wearing down his enemies.

The first step was to select a safe haven. Mordor was occupied by Gondor, which in the 11th century of the Third Age had nearly reached the height of its power. There was no hope of wresting control of Mordor away from the Dunedain at this point in time. And yet, Sauron needed to be close to his enemies. Greenwood the Great therefore offered an attractive position. The dense woodlands would offer relative secrecy and some defense, and the commanding height of Amon Lanc, long abandoned by the Elves, would be easy to fortify.

Becoming the Necromancer of Dol Guldur (the new name the Elves gave to Amon Lanc), Sauron built up a cadre of evil servants who spread through the forest. Greenwood the Great became so terrifying that Men renamed it Mirkwood. And as Orcs, Trolls, Wargs, Spiders, and other creatures gathered around Dol Guldur, Sauron renewed contact with some of the eastern peoples who had once served him. Inducing some of the Easterlings to migrate to southern Mirkwood, Sauron set into motion a wave of migrations which rolled into Eriador. The Hobbits, having dwelt in the Vales of Anduin for many centuries, grew fearful as the influx of Easterlings threatened their neighbors, and began departing for safer lands in the west.

Around the year 1300, Sauron sent the Lord of the Nazgul north to establish the realm of Angmar (Cf. "The Tale of Years"). Angmar served two purposes. First, it was a remote base of operations which worked against Arnor's people in close proximity. Sauron did not have to worry about establishing and protecting long supply lines. Secondly,

Angmar would seem like just another enemy land to Elves and Dunedain. An implacable single enemy state would draw too much attention. But if hostile realms rose up in several places, no one could be sure of exactly what was happening. Had Sauron returned, or were some of his former servants simply becoming more ambitious and powerful? Inspiring doubt and delay in his enemies purchased time for Sauron to grow stronger.

But though Angmar could take advantage of the divisions which had arisen in Arnor (which the Dunedain had divided into three smaller realms in 863), Dol Guldur itself became isolated from the east. About the time Sauron must have been contemplating what he could do to the northern kingdoms, Minalcar settled Gondor's differences with the Northmen and Easterlings by attacking the lands near southern Mirkwood ("Gondor and the Heirs of Anarion", Appendix A, *The Lord of the Rings*), lands to which Gondor had long laid claim, but which had become home to many Easterlings and some treacherous Northmen. Minalcar destroyed or drove the Easterlings well beyond the Sea of Rhun, and he allied himself with the kingdom of Rhovanion, east of Mirkwood, then ruled by Vidugavia.

Minalcar's failure to attack Dol Guldur is curious. Quite possibly, Sauron was using the Easterlings as a screen, and the Necromancer of Dol Guldur may have struck Minalcar as being little or no threat to Gondor. Still, Sauron had to wait for the Easterlings to recover their numbers. But it may also be that he felt a new kind of Easterling culture needed to be developed. In later centuries, Tolkien tells us, there would be wars among the Easterlings (Cf. "Gondor and the Heirs of Anarion"). Sauron's control over the eastern peoples may not have been complete, or else he felt that the best warriors would be those who survived dreadful feuds and wars.

But Gondor was also very powerful. Even when the Kin-strife broke out, and Eldacar eventually drove his enemies south, Sauron was in no position to take advantage of the conflict. He was too far away from Umbar, where the defeated rebels sought refuge, to make contact with the dissidents. Though it was a safe haven, Dol Guldur was very confining. The Great Plague of 1636, which Sauron unleashed in the east and sent westward, opened up new opportunities for him. Gondor lost so many people it could no longer sustain the garrisons in Mordor. When the Dunedain left, Orcs and other creatures loyal to Sauron moved in. But rather than return there himself, Sauron merely used Mordor as a corridor for further expansion. He probably began sending agents south at this time to make overtures to the Haradrim.

200 years after the Great Plague, the Wainriders attacked the Northmen and Gondor. The western peoples were defeated and Sauron achieved complete control over the lands between Mirkwood and Mordor. The Lord of the Nazgul soon afterward brought about the final overthrow of Arthedain, the last of the northern Dunadan realms. But though Lindon and Imladris remained in the north, and had both played significant roles in the defeat of Angmar, Sauron turned his attention to Gondor, whose intervention was responsible for the destruction of Angmar. The northern lands had not been entirely ruined, but they became less of a threat.

Also, when the Dwarves of Khazad-dum released the Balrog in 1980, they unwittingly shifted the balance of power in the north. Although Khazad-dum had not (apparently) taken an active role in the wars with Angmar, it had stood with the Last Alliance of Elves and Men against Sauron, and might yet again oppose Sauron. The Balrog's destruction of the Dwarven civilization, and the subsequent flight of many Elves from Lothlórien, virtually ensured that Sauron would have almost no enemies of significant power in the north. Tolkien suggests (in "The History of Galadriel and Celeborn", *Unfinished Tales*) that it was because of the Necromancer's presence in southern Mirkwood that Galadriel decided to intervene in Lothlórien. Had she and Celeborn not restored order to the Elven realm, there would have been no one left to oppose Dol Guldur except for a few woodmen and the still small people called the Eotheod, who were themselves only a remnant of Vidugavia's once great Northman kingdom of Rhovanion. Thranduil's realm in northern Mirkwood remained strong, but he had not participated in a major war since the end of the Second Age.

The 20th century of the Third Age proved to be a tumultuous period for both Sauron and his allies. The loss of Arthedain and Khazad-dum must have alarmed the Eldar and the Istari. Gondor's losses to the Easterlings and the final retreat of the Eotheod to the Vales of Anduin ensured that the West no longer possessed the manpower to stem the flow of peoples and resources to southern Mirkwood and Mordor. And the emergence of the Nazgul in 2002, when they laid siege to Minas Ithil, which fell after only two years, was a sign that the evil defeated in the north had only suffered a minor setback.

Nonetheless, Dol Guldur, though evil by reputation, seems to have displayed little ambition through this period. The kings of Arnor and Gondor had concluded in the mid-20th century that a single will was orchestrating their declines for an undisclosed purpose. By the mid-21st century, the Wise (the Istari and the lords of the Eldar) must have concluded that the power in Dol Guldur was the most likely candidate for the role of Master Enemy. But just who was the Necromancer? The Wise suspected it may have been a Nazgul. After all, the Lord of the Nazgul had been the Witch-king of Angmar. The Nazgul had just taken Minas Ithil. Nazgul were obviously active in Middle-earth. But some, probably including Galadriel and Gandalf, feared the Necromancer was Sauron himself. Hence, in 2063 Gandalf investigated Dol Guldur and Sauron retreated eastward.

Over the next 400 years, which the Wise referred to as the Watchful Peace, Sauron prepared new forces. The Balchoth, related to the Wainriders, rose to prominence in the east. The Uruks were bred in Mordor. Umbar, destroyed by Gondor in the 19th century, was reinvested by forces undoubtedly loyal to Sauron, and he finally began to challenge Númenorean control over the seas. At the same time, Sauron's influence among the Haradrim increased.

When he deemed the time right, in 2460, Sauron returned to Dol Guldur with new forces, and Minas Ithil unleashed the Uruks upon Ithilien. Sauron sent Orcs and Trolls to colonize the Misty Mountains. And the Corsairs of Umbar began to attack Gondor. The return to Dol Guldur, however, implies that Sauron still feared the union of his enemies. He did not yet feel strong enough to declare himself openly in Mordor. Gondor might still be able to rally the western peoples against their ancient nemesis. The Eldar were still numerous. The

Longbeard Dwarves were growing strong again. The Eotheod were becoming more numerous, and there were other Edainic peoples in the Vales of Anduin who might ally themselves with Gondor. Lothlórien remained as a bulwark of Elven power, and Thranduil controlled northern Mirkwood. Sauron must have wanted to keep his northern enemies off balance while the Nazgul, Balchoth, and Corsairs whittled away at Gondor's resources. By this time, Gondor had clearly become the key to defeating the West. It was the strongest nation remaining among the free peoples.

But Sauron was also probably drawn back to Dol Guldur by another factor: the One Ring. He long believed it had been destroyed. Yet in time he came to realize that this could not be so. He had invested the greater part of his strength in the Ring. If it had been destroyed, then he should have been rendered much too weak to become powerful again. His strength continued to return, though, and century by century he was able to exert his will over more people, more creatures. At some point, the Ring's survival had to become an obvious fact to Sauron. He hadn't merely survived his downfall. He was recovering from it.

It therefore became imperative that Sauron find the Ring before his enemies found it and used it against him. He never conceived of anyone trying to destroy the Ring, but there remained in Middle-earth powerful Eldar who might, if they came into possession of the Ring, try to use it to build up their power again: Cirdan, Elrond, Galadriel, Celeborn. They were all relatives of the ancient Eldarin kings, and were accounted mighty in lore and power. And what did Sauron know or suspect of the Istari? They were obviously immortal. They had been around for more than 1,000 years. If he suspected they were emissaries from the Valar, then he would have realized they could wield the Ring with greater effect than any Elf.

When Sauron eventually learned about Isildur's end, he was well positioned in Dol Guldur to seize control over the region of the Gladden Fields so that his servants could search for the Ring. But Sauron would not learn for many centuries yet that the Ring lay on the far side of the river, or that it was found before he even began looking for it by a Stoor named Deagol, whose cousin Smeagol murdered him and took the Ring.

The Balchoth's attack against northern Gondor in 2510 thus may have had two purposes: first, to wear down Gondor; second, to clear the way for Sauron's search for the Ring. Gondor's northern border lay too close to Dol Guldur for much secrecy. Sauron's objectives suffered a reversal, however, when Eorl led an army of Eotheod out of the north to Gondor's aid. The Battle of the Field of Celebrant was not a crushing defeat for the Balchoth. They remained an effective fighting force for Sauron, but control over the Undeeps passed from Gondor to the Eotheod, rather than to Sauron. Gondor and Lothlórien thus continued to pose a great threat to Sauron's plans.

Thus, when Cirion ceded Calenardhon to Eorl and his people, Sauron had to alter his strategy once more. Cirion consolidated his forces in Anorien and Ithilien, and Calenardhon came under the control of a strong northern people over whom Sauron had no hope of gaining control. The Rohirrim, as Eorl's people came to be known, could not simply be ignored. And an opportunity to deal with them arose in the 28th century. Helm, King of Rohan (as Calenardhon was now called), consolidated his power over the western lands by killing the upstart lord Freca and outlawing his family. Freca's son Wulf allied himself with the Dunlendings, whose ancestors (the Gwathuirim) had served Sauron in the Second Age.

In 2758, Wulf launched an attack against Rohan from Dunland. At the same time, Corsairs from Umbar or other parts of the Harad attacked Rohan from the west, and Balchoth or other Easterlings attacked Rohan from the east. Gondor itself was attacked and thus prevented from sending aid to Rohan. The Rohirrim were defeated in open battle and driven into the mountains. Wulf took possession of most of the land. Sauron undoubtedly planned the assault, and the extended period of cold, called the Long Winter, ensured that the people of Rohan (and Eriador) suffered terribly. But if it was Sauron's goal to destroy the Rohirrim in this conflict, he failed. Although Helm himself perished during the Long Winter, his nephew Frealaf defeated Wulf and his allies the next spring with help from Gondor, which repulsed the attacks in the south. But the conflict produced one other setback, which Sauron most likely did not see coming. (Cf. "The House of Eorl", Appendix A, *The Lord of the Rings*.)

In 2590, the Longbeard Dwarves re-established the Kingdom under the Mountain in Erebor, which lay to the east of northern Mirkwood. While Erebor posed no threat to Dol Guldur, it allied itself with the Northman Kingdom of Dale. The two realms increased in wealth, fame, and power. In 2770 the dragon Smaug came out of the distant north and destroyed both Erebor and Dale. The surviving Dwarves went into exile and the royal family ended up in Dunland. In 2990, Thror, who had been King under the Mountain, decided to return east. He was murdered by Azog, a chieftain of the Orcs in Khazad-dum, who decapitated Thror and mutilated the Dwarf-king's head.

Thror's son Thrain assembled an alliance of all the Dwarven peoples for a seven-year war against the Orcs of the Misty Mountains. Although the Dwarves suffered grievous losses, they nearly wiped out the Orcs. Sauron's control over the Misty Mountains was effectively destroyed in that war. Coupled with his failure to destroy or seize control over Rohan, losing the Misty Mountains diminished Sauron's chances of destroying Lothlórien or of finding the One Ring. (Cf. "Durin's Folk".)

Not to be thwarted for long, Sauron may at this time have begun retrieving the other Rings of Power he had given out in the Second Age. The Dwarves had the Seven and the Nazgul had the Nine. Commanding the Nazgul to surrender their Rings would be no problem. But Sauron had to hunt down the Dwarf-kings one by one and take their Rings from them. And of those kings, only three still possessed their Rings. Four of the Rings had apparently been destroyed by dragons (Cf. Gloin's report in "The Council of Elrond", *The Lord of the Rings*, and Gandalf's comments). Thrain was the last Ring-keeper to fall into Sauron's hands (so he claimed, when Gandalf found him in Dol Guldur). Although Tolkien offers no explanation for why Sauron took back the Rings of Power, it may be that he used them to enhance his own strength. Or perhaps he intended, at some point, to distribute them again to potential new slaves. Gloin reported that

Sauron had offered three Rings to King Dain II, although we cannot say that Sauron would actually have restored the Rings to the Dwarves.

At the urging of the White Council, which Galadriel had convened among the Istari and lords of the Eldar after the Watchful Peace ended, Gandalf returned to Dol Guldur in 2851. There he finally confirmed that the Necromancer was indeed Sauron returned, and Gandalf discovered that Sauron was gathering the Rings of Power once again, as well as seeking for the One (Cf. "Of the Rings of Power and the Third Age"). Such news proved alarming to Saruman, who had settled in the former Gondorian fortress of Isengard after the Long Winter. Saruman had by this time come to believe that the One Ring could indeed be found, and he wanted it for himself. He began recruiting Dunlendings and Orcs to serve him, and sent spies to search for the Ring near the Gladden Fields.

Although Saruman presented little immediate threat to Sauron, the search for the Ring took on new urgency. Whereas Arnor had been completely destroyed (or so Sauron believed -- he did not realize that descendants of Isildur had survived in the north), Gondor was proving to be much more resilient and versatile, thanks to the alliance with the Rohirrim. The rise of a rival power in Isengard could complicate matters, but if Sauron could find the One Ring he would quickly be able to achieve mastery over many peoples.

By 2941, Sauron was probably convinced the One Ring was no longer in the region of the Gladden Fields. The White Council moved against him and he retreated from Dol Guldur. Mirkwood is said to have become a cleaner, more wholesome place for a time. Such a transition implies that Sauron did not simply retreat from Dol Guldur. It suggests that there was a wholesale migration eastward of Orcs, Men, and whatever other creatures were directly under his control. While some people argue that the White Council's action may have consisted of some sort of magical attack, it is more likely that Lothlórien sent an army into Mirkwood. The Istari and the Lords of the Eldar may have challenged the Necromancer's sorcerous power directly, but Sauron pulled back and thereby preserved a great part of his forces (as well as leave his enemies in doubt about how strong he had become militarily).

The retreat suggests that Sauron was no longer willing to risk his primary armies in open combat, or to allow them to act by proxy. On the other hand, in the north, Bolg (son of Azog) launched a campaign against the small company of Dwarves, led by Thorin Thrain's son, who returned to Erebor. After the death of Smaug, Elves, Men, Dwarves, and Orcs all converged on the mountain to seize the treasure which Smaug had guarded there for 170 years (Cf. *The Hobbit*). Was Bolg acting on Sauron's orders, or had Sauron lost control over the Orcs of the Misty Mountains? If Sauron approved of or permitted Bolg to launch the attack, then he allowed considerable resources to be committed to an action which might have secured a base in the north Sauron could use against Thranduil. But it also left Sauron without close support from the Misty Mountains. Had Bolg gained control over Erebor, Sauron would have been in a position to crush Thranduil and bring reinforcements against Lothlórien without hindrance. But when Bolg drew off the Orc armies, Lothlórien had a window of opportunity in which to take action.

If Bolg was therefore to be Sauron's proxy in the north, Sauron would himself be able to return to Mordor with all the forces of Dol Guldur. Instead of spreading his resources across three major bases (Mordor, Dol Guldur, and Erebor), Sauron could have consolidated his strength in two very defensible regions, both of which could be easily reinforced and resupplied from the east. Hence, because he had not risked everything, Bolg's defeat at Erebor only delayed Sauron's plans. Tolkien says that three-quarters of the Orcs of the north perished in the Battle of Five Armies. It would require several decades for them to recover their numbers. In the meantime, as the Northmen rebuilt the Kingdom of Dale and the Longbeard Dwarves rebuilt the Kingdom of Erebor, Sauron returned to Mordor.

Sauron declared himself openly in 2951. He now felt confident enough, despite his failure to recover the One Ring, to withstand any assault the West might launch against him. The psychological effect of "I have returned" upon the Elves cannot be underestimated. Many of the Eldar simply lost hope. Perhaps most of them believed that Sauron had recovered the One Ring, or that he was on the verge of recovering it. By the year 3,000 Dwarves began moving west, and they brought out of the east reports of the movements of peoples, of predatory wars, and of Sauron's increasing power. Many of the remaining Eldar joined a massive wave of migration over Sea, leaving Middle-earth forever (Cf. Sam's comments in "The Shadow of the Past", *The Lord of the Rings*). The Silvan Elves remained steadfast, but Lindon and Imladris could no longer raise armies (according to Elrond in "The Council of Elrond", Ibid.).

As the Orcs of the Misty Mountains recovered their numbers, new enemies threatened the eastern borders of Dale. Mordor forged new alliances with Easterlings and Haradrim, and Saruman fell under Sauron's influence when the wizard used the Palantir he had found in Isengard to spy on Mordor. Although Saruman's allegiance to the West had already vanished, he had until this time opposed Sauron. It therefore served Saruman's purpose to help the White Council drive Sauron from Dol Guldur in 2941. He wanted to search for the One Ring freely. By the time of the War of the Ring, Saruman had found Isildur's remains, but not the Ring (which, of course, had left Smeagol and been found by Bilbo Baggins, who took it to the Shire).

Gondor had continued to decline under the repeated attacks from Mordor and Harad, but Gondor's military strength was no longer vital to Sauron's strategy. The Ring itself became Sauron's chief priority. He finally learned the fate of the One Ring from Smeagol, and in 3018 he sent the Nazgul to the Shire to seize the Ring and bring it back to him. Although he was preparing for a war no one believed he could lose, Sauron needed to ensure his enemies would not use the Ring against him before he launched that war. His captains might shift allegiances if someone powerful enough to wield the Ring rose up and took possession of it.

The vast array of kingdoms and tribes Sauron had assembled assured him of ultimate victory in any war where no one used the Ring. The recovery of the Ring would have assured him of undisputed control over Middle-earth. The Eldar who remained were no longer powerful enough to challenge him. The Dunedain had dwindled and were too few in number to raise the powerful armies they had commanded at the height of their power. And the Northmen, though strong in places like Dale, the upper Vales of Anduin, and Rohan, were divided into many realms and incapable of forming an alliance powerful enough to challenge him.

In 3018, Sauron was poised to crush Dale and Erebor, roll through northern Mirkwood, and sweep the Vales of Anduin clear of Men, Elves, and Dwarves. Even Lothlórien probably would not have survived for long. Gondor, on the other hand, possessed sufficient strength, especially if reinforced by Rohan, to withstand at least one massive assault. Saruman's assigned role was to prevent or delay Rohan's reinforcing Gondor. The Orcs of the Misty Mountains could attack the Beornings, the Woodmen, and Lothlórien, and undoubtedly Imladris and Eriador. Dol Guldur, now reinvested, would keep Thranduil at bay. There was no hope of the northern peoples forming a last-minute alliance and coming to Gondor's aid. All the pieces were in place. Victory was assured. It was a good time to be a Dark Lord.

Gandalf's analysis of Sauron's intentions and priorities (as revealed at the Council of Elrond in 3018 and in the last debate of the Captains of the West in 3019) offers insight into Sauron's changing strategies in the Third Age. When he awoke and assumed a physical shape again, Sauron believed he had been wounded deeply through the destruction of the One Ring. Determined to avenge himself upon his enemies, and perhaps to regain control over Middle-earth, he set about the task of dividing and weakening his foes. His lieutenant brought about the destruction of Arnor. The Balrog (either at Sauron's direction or through fortuitous circumstance) destroyed Khazad-dum and almost eliminated Lothlórien. The Easterlings, Corsairs, and Haradrim wore down Gondor, reducing it from a very powerful empire to a shriveled state, still proud but fearful and imbued with a sense of dread and doom. And most of the remaining Eldar fled Middle-earth when they saw the final conflict was about to begin.

Despite occasional setbacks, by 3019 Sauron was confident of his ability to achieve complete victory over his foes. He had learned that the One Ring still existed, and he knew who possessed it. He feared that someone would take the Ring and use it against him. The greatest peril, in Sauron's view, lay in the possibility that division and strife might arise within his armies. The forces he had assembled could be used against him. Aragorn and Gandalf therefore concluded that the best chance for Frodo's quest to destroy the Ring depended upon Sauron's fear. They let him believe that a new Ringlord, presumably Aragorn, was emerging. Keenly aware of what delay had cost him in the Second Age (and perhaps feeling he would not be acting too soon), Sauron launched a massive attack against Gondor in the hope of capturing the Ring. And when that assault failed, he unleashed everything he had left in a savage assault he believed would quickly bring the Ring to him.

How devastating must the realization have been to Sauron, when Frodo claimed the Ring from within the chamber of the Sammath Naur, that he, the master manipulator, had been played for a fool. All his careful planning and maneuvering for two thousand years had been for nothing. Massive force, overwhelming power, and the most subtle strategies were all undermined by Sauron's complete misinterpretation of the facts he had gathered. He believed his enemies would seek to become like him. Had he understood that they would simply wish to be rid of him and all Dark Lords forever, he might have become more defensive. In such a world, Sauron would have been stalemated for a time. He would still have to fear that someone might seize the Ring and use it against him. But he would also have to fear that someone might succeed in destroying it. He would have had to devise a new strategy. It should not be doubted that he would have done so, and that the Council of Elrond rightly concluded that they had one and only one opportunity to defeat Sauron.

MICHAEL MARTINEZ

SECTION II:
THE SECOND AGE
OF MIDDLE-EARTH

MICHAEL MARTINEZ

Chapter 13:
Before the Númenoreans came

Things in Middle-earth changed radically as a result of the War of Wrath. The war lasted about 42 years, beginning in the year 545 of the First Age and ending in the year 587. During that time huge parts of Middle-earth -- Beleriand, the far northern lands, the inland sea of Helcar -- were ruined or reshaped. In *Morgoth's Ring* Christopher Tolkien presents a previously unpublished essay by his father which ponders the motives of the various forces in the *Silmarillion*.

In the first and second parts of the essay JRRT explains how Melkor diminished himself gradually by incarnating

> himself (as Morgoth) permanently. He did this so as to control the *hroa*, the 'flesh' or physical matter, of Arda. He attempted to identify himself with it. A vaster, and more perilous, procedure, though of similar sort to the operations of Sauron with the Rings. Thus, outside the Blessed Realm, all 'matter' was likely to have a 'Melkor ingredient', and those who had bodies, nourished by the *hroa* of Arda, had as it were a tendency, small or great, towards Melkor: they were none of them wholly free of him in their incarnate form, and their bodies had an effect upon their spirits.

This remarkable conclusion (itself but a proposition for further conclusions reached later in the essay) was decided or perhaps weighed by Tolkien in the late 1950s and/or early 1960s, less than ten years after the publication of *The Lord of the Rings*, and approximately contemporarily with the texts which formed the basis for much of the published *Silmarillion*. It is therefore reasonable to accept the explanation which follows the above citation as the motive behind the Valar's reluctance to act against Melkor in the published *Silmarillion*:

> But in this way Morgoth lost (or exchanged, or transmuted) the greater part of his original 'angelic' powers, of mind and spirit, while gaining a terrible grip upon the physical world. For this reason he *had* to be fought, mainly by physical force, and enormous material ruin was a probable

consequence of any direct combat with him, victorious or otherwise. This is the chief explanation of the constant reluctance of the Valar to come into open battle against Morgoth. Manwë's task and problem was much more difficult than Gandalf's. Sauron's, relatively smaller, power was *concentrated*; Morgoth's vast power was *disseminated*. The whole of 'Middle-earth' was Morgoth's Ring, though temporarily his attention was mainly upon the North-west. Unless swiftly successful, War against him might well end in reducing all Middle-earth to chaos, possibly even all Arda. It is easy to say: 'It was the task and function of the Elder King to govern Arda and make it possible for the Children of Eru to live in it unmolested.' But the dilemma of the Valar was this: Arda could only be liberated by a physical battle; but a probable result of such a battle was the irretrievable ruin of Arda....

The assault upon Morgoth thus had to begin with an assault upon Middle-earth itself, really. Morgoth would have been able to use the very land to fight the Host of Valinor. And the Valar would have had to destroy the land in order to diminish Morgoth's strength. So it makes sense that the Host of Valinor landed as far to the north as possible, as close to Angband as possible. They would be bypassing the greater part of Morgoth's disseminated strength. More importantly, they would be closer to Morgoth's physical incarnation, which was essentially the goal of their war.

The War of the Jewels for all intents and purposes ended with the assault upon Gondolin. The Elves never again mounted a campaign against Morgoth and he never again took direct action against them. With the fall of Gondolin the Elves were reduced to three relatively small and ineffectual enclaves: Ossiriand, where a few Fëanorians had taken refuge with the Green-elves, Arvernien, where refuges from Doriath and Gondolin established a new colony with some of the Edain; and Balar, where refugees from Hithlum (Sindar such as Annael), Nargothrond, and the Falas had established a colony after the Nirnaeth Arnoediad.

Many other Elves wandered through Beleriand, outcasts or Avari, or were enslaved in Angband. Some of these Elves, it may be supposed, eventually reached Arvernien, and from there made their way to Balar. But when the Fëanorians destroyed Arvernien in the year 538, a significant number of Elves died. The free Elvish population of Beleriand was reduced to its smallest size. From the Fëanorians, the Balarians, and the Ossiriandic Elves were eventually drawn the Eldar who established the realm of Lindon in the Second Age.

The Valar and Maiar, with their Amanic allies of Vanyar and Noldor, were aided by the Bëorians and Marachians of Hithlum. By 545 these Edain had lived in slavery for more than 70 years, nearly three of their generations. Virtually no one should have been left alive who could remember the Nirnaeth Arnoediad. Absolutely no Men should have been left alive who would have had contact with the Edain of Estolad, those Bëorians and Marachians who fled east over the mountains in or soon after the year 455, the year of the Dagor Bragollach, when Morgoth broke the Siege of Angband.

At least 90 years after Edainic refugees entered Eriador from the west carrying tales of the victories of Morgoth over the Eldar and Men of Beleriand, Edainic men rose up against their Easterling masters and joined the Host of Valinor. It was this service in the final war against Morgoth which ensured that the Edain of Hithlum (and whatever Edain from Brethil may have joined them) would be rewarded by the Valar with the gift of the island in the Sea that became Númenor. But it was also this service which would ensure that the western Edain would lose contact with their eastern cousins.

Eriador had become very crowded in the fifth century. Easterlings of various types had wandered into the region, settling (it appears) in a buffer zone between the older Edainic peoples (mostly Bëorians) who lived in the hills of Tyrn Gorthad, the Weather Hills, and the North Downs and the Dwarven and Elven lands around the Ered Luin. The northernmost Easterlings were akin to the Folk of Bor (the tribe of Easterlings who remained faithful to the Eldar in the Nirnaeth Arnoediad, but were wiped out by their enemies). They were farmers and appear to have been friendly or at least not hostile with the Edainic peoples. But other Easterlings eventually moved on to settle in Beleriand and strengthen Morgoth's forces.

The Elves of Balar and Ossiriand had to know the war was being fought. They would have seen the tremendous upheavals which gradually ruined Beleriand and caused much of the land to sink beneath the sea. The sundering of the Ered Luin so that a great gulf was created there would have announced the fact of the war to the peoples of Eriador. Elves and Men alike must have fled further east, probably beyond the Baranduin, to find a region of land which was relatively stable. The Easterlings in the north may have suffered great losses as those lands began sinking into the Sea.

Tolkien doesn't explain why or how the sea of Helcar was destroyed, but it may be that the lands were raised up so that the waters flowed north and hence around the northern edge of Middle-earth to help inundate the sinking lands in Beleriand. It may be that Morgoth attempted to use the waters to stall the advance of the Host of Valinor. The effect would have been catastrophic for the Elves, Dwarves, and Men living in the eastern portions of Middle-earth. But perhaps there were no longer that many Men living in those lands. After all, Morgoth had concentrated his power in the North-west. He needed all the help he could get when the War of Wrath came.

With the defeat of Morgoth's forces a few evil creatures were able to flee eastward. One Balrog made it to the Misty Mountains, and there hid itself for more than 5,000 years. At least two dragons (apparently a male and female) fled to the Withered Heath and presumably there established a breeding ground which eventually allowed dragons to trouble the world again. Orcs and Easterlings also fled east, and they settled in the northern mountains. The Orcs took Gundabad from the Dwarves, who eventually formed an alliance with the Edainic Men of Wilderland.

In short, the War of Wrath must have produced two waves of migration: one coming from the east to the west as new lands rose up and destroyed the Sea of Helcar, one coming from the west to the east as people and evil creatures fled the destruction of Beleriand. Caught in the middle would have been the Nandorin Elves, Dwarves, and Edainic Men of Eriador and Wilderland.

In the three years following the War of Wrath Eönwë traveled throughout Middle-earth, summoning Elves once again to pass over Sea to the West. Many of the Elves seem to have heeded his call. Of those who remained, the majority appear to have become (or to have been) the Silvan or Wood Elves of the Vales of Anduin. These Elves were descended from Avari and Nandor who had mingled together.

But Gil-galad and Cirdan must have somehow become reconciled to the remaining Fëanorians during the final three years of the First Age. It must have been at that time that the Elves abandoned Balar. Did the island sink or did Gil-galad and Cirdan simply feel it was time to return to the mainland, now that Morgoth was gone? We'll never know.

The Edain of Beleriand also migrated east, but they settled in Lindon along the new coastlands. They apparently never attempted to communicate with the Edain of Eriador. In *Unfinished Tales*, the third note to "Aldarion and Erendis" says that the Númenoreans believed "that the Men left behind were descended from the evil Men who in the last days of the war against Morgoth had been summoned by him out of the East." The Edain of Beleriand must therefore have lost all memory of their more distant kinsfolk in the east, and that loss implies that all their lore-masters must have perished in the wars. The generations which grew up in slavery must have learned very little of their origins, and the Elves could probably tell them very little.

This sundering of Edain had a profound effect upon their cultures. When the Númenoreans returned to Middle-earth in the year 600 of the Second Age, "they looked upon...Men who could have walked in Númenor and not been thought aliens save in their clothes and their arms." To the Edain of Eriador the Númenoreans "resembled rather Elvish lords than mortal Men in bearing and apparel". The early Edain had been welcomed to Númenor by the Eldar of Tol Eressëa, survivors of Beleriand, who brought the Edain many gifts and taught them new lore. But the Edain had also been taught by Eönwë in Middle-earth.

In fact, the Edain lived in Lindon for about 35 yeas before they began to set sail across the Sea, and the migration to Númenor is said in *The*

Peoples of Middle-earth to have lasted at least 50 years. So the Edain of Lindon migrated over Sea from about SA 32 to SA 82. During that time they were enhanced by the Valar, and tutored by Eönwë and perhaps other Maiar. But they seem to have had no contact with their kinsmen in the east.

The first fleet to set sail to Númenor consisted of at least 150 ships, perhaps as many as 300. Each was piloted by one of Cirdan's mariners, who presumably returned to Lindon when their voyage was finished. One must wonder what became of the ships when the Elves were finished transporting the Edain over Sea. Some, no doubt, were used by Eldar to sail to Tol Eressëa, but the rest must have become incorporated into the new economy of Lindon. The ships were small, holding between 30 and 40 passengers with goods and animals. How long did it take the Elves to build the ships, one must ask? Did Cirdan have to train new mariners?

As the Edain left Lindon the Dwarves of Belegost began leaving Ered Luin and migrating to Khazad-dum. These Dwarves most likely reinforced the Longbeard Dwarves (Durin's Folk) in their renewed wars with the Orcs, who coming from the ruin of Angband seemed numerous to Durin's Folk. If a reason for the Dwarvish migration must be sought, it may be supposed that the Longbeards invited the Belegostians to join them as a result of the Orcish invasions.

The Dwarf migration must have impoverished Eriador, however. The Edain there would have had Nandor to trade with, but few Dwarves. So it may be that their cultural development proceeded along different paths from that of the Edainic Men of Wilderland, many of whom became allied with the Dwarves and benefited from Dwarven trade. It would seem that one difference between the (mostly) Bëorian Edain of Eriador and the (mostly) Marachian Edain of Wilderland was the use of horses. The Marachians raised horses even in Beleriand, but the Bëorians seem not to have used them.

The Edain of Eriador settled in the Hills of Evendim, the North Downs, the Weather Hills, and the lands between them as far west as the Baranduin river. According to both *Unfinished Tales* and *The*

Peoples of Middle-earth, the Edain sometimes wandered into the lands beyond Baranduin but that was Elvish country and they did not settle there.

The Elves between Baranduin and Lhun must have been mostly Nandor. The Noldor settled in Forlindon with Gil-galad and Elrond. These were probably mostly descended from the Noldor of Gondolin and the folk of Angrod (from northern Nargothrond), many of whom had fled to Balar. Virtually none of the Hithlum Noldor should have survived the Nirnaeth Arnoediad, or if they did they must have been enslaved. So the remaining Noldor must have been derived from the handful of Fëanorians who survived the third Kinslaying and any refugees who escaped the fall of Nargothrond.

Although Cirdan's people settled in the twin havens of Mithlond, the Sindar of Doriath and the Green-elves of Ossiriand settled in Harlindon. But many of these Elves eventually migrated east to the Vales of Anduin. Tolkien only says they left "before the building of Barad-dur" (which Sauron began around the year 1000). Many people believe the Sindarin migration must have occurred before the Noldor established Eregion (circa 700-750). Because Sauron began taking action against Elves around the year 500 (apparently stirring up Men from the east to harass the Elves), it may be that the Sindarin migrations inspired him to do something. (It should be noted that in an early draft of the Tale of Years for the Second Age, the Sindarin migration coincided with a Noldorin migration to Imladris and Eregion.)

The Elvish populations in Lindon increased, and they most likely grew as rapidly as the populations of Beleriand had grown. That is, from the time of the reconciliation of the Noldor in Beleriand early in the First Age until the Dagor Bragollach, the Noldor and Sindar increased their population considerably. A comparable period of time without any Orcish intrusions as occasionally happened during the Siege of Angband elapsed between the departure and the return of the Númenoreans.

Gil-galad's kingdom, therefore, should have become wealthier and more powerful. Cirdan's mariners may have continued sailing across the seas. Why not? They had the ships, they had the skill. Tolkien never says that they visited Aman, but northern Aman, at least, would have been easily within their reach. And it would not have been much of a journey to sail from Númenor to Tol Eressëa while they were conducting the Edain over Sea.

At some point Gil-galad's people came into contact with the Edain of Eriador. These Men, thinking that their western cousins had been destroyed, never asked about them when visiting the Elves. And the Elves, having lost contact with the Númenoreans, never thought to inform the Eriadorians that some of their kinsfolk had survived. If we assume that an average generation among the Edain lasted 25-30 years, then anywhere from 24 to 29 generations passed among the Eriadorians after Estolad was abandoned until the Númenoreans returned to Middle-earth.

There was apparently no interaction between these Edain and the Men of Minhiriath, whom the Númenoreans named the Gwathuirim (Cf. "Dwarves and Men", *The Peoples of Middle-earth*, and "The Port of Lond Daer" in "The History of Galadriel and Celeborn", *Unfinished Tales*). From these people had come the Folk of Haleth in Brethil, and so they were also "Edainic" peoples, but they spoke a different language from that of the Bëorians and Marachians. The Men of Bree, many thousands of years later, were descended from the Gwathuirim, but it appears that Bree wasn't founded until sometime after the War of the Elves and Sauron.

The peoples of Eriador must have been relatively isolated during the first few centuries of the Second Age. The Elves kept mostly to themselves beyond the Baranduin but they were friendly with the Edainic Men. Gil-galad followed the policies of the Eldarin kings of Beleriand in maintaining a separation between Elves and Men. There was no war to speak of which should have driven them together. The Elves must have become inwardly focused, refining their civilization until population and the prospect of commerce with Khazad-dum became great enough to launch the eastward migrations.

The Gwathuirim lived quietly in their forests. In the east, the Dwarves and their Edainic allies built up a great civilization. But the occasional mention of interaction suggests that a vast network of some sort existed between all these peoples. Gil-galad eventually heard rumors of some dark power which was inimical to Elves and Men. When the Longbeards discovered Mithril, the Noldor decided to establish a colony in Eregion to engage in trade with Khazad-dum, and the relationship between the two peoples was so strong that the Dwarves tunneled all the way through the mountains to create a west-gate for the use of the Elves.

The question of when this network arose may never be settled. It's possible that the Dwarves always maintained their ancient contacts, and that for the first few centuries of the Second Age they conveyed news between east and west, Elves, Dwarves, and Men. It may also be that the Nandor who wandered through Eriador eventually made contact with Gil-galad's realm and carried news westward. And perhaps the Edain themselves traded freely with each other and the Dwarves, bringing news and wealth westward from Khazad-dum.

We know that twelve Edain were brave enough to meet with Vëantur and his Númenoreans in the year 600 (Cf. Note 3 to "Aldarion and Erendis"). And we know that the Edain of Beleriand had held at least one great council where their leaders convened to discuss the war with Angband. It may be that similar councils were occasionally held among the Eriadorians, and that perhaps the twelve men were leaders or chieftains from as many clans or tribes. A council of Eriadorian chieftains may imply that the Bëorians and Marachians had developed a sophisticated culture, cooperating with one another in time of need. Such a confederation of peoples would have been strong enough to discourage or repulse invasion, and may explain why the Easterlings and Orcs did not settle in central Eriador, and why the Gwathuirim did not pass farther north than the edge of their forests.

The encounter with Vëantur implies that the Eriadorians still spoke the same language as the ancestors they shared with the Númenoreans, and yet that language had in more than 700 years begun to drift away from the Adunaic the Númenoreans brought with them. So the inference that the Eriadorian Edain had maintained or developed a cultural unity is a strong one. They would have freely exchanged stories and songs, retained the same traditions and memories, practiced the same customs, and probably continued the ancient Edainic custom of marrying their sons and daughters (at least among their chieftains) to families from other communities in order to build or maintain strong bonds.

These Edain buried their dead in mounds, and most likely lived in fortified towns and villages, raising sheep, cattle, and (very possibly, the few Marachians in Eriador) horses. They would be mostly farmers and woodsmen, supporting a small cadre of craftsmen. They would have been ripe for learning new skills and trades from the Númenoreans. They should have seemed very much to the Númenoreans like their ancestors in Beleriand, and Eriador may have provided curious adventurers like Aldarion a glimpse into the past.

Chapter 14:
Have island, will rebel

Nearly all that we know about Númenor's geography and history is provided in *Unfinished Tales*. "Akallabeth", published in *The Silmarillion*, is more concerned with the motives if Númenor's rulers than with the lay of the land or the ways of its people. But the essays, notes, and stories provided in Unfinished Tales reveal a fascinating picture of Tolkien's Atlantis. Númenor must have seemed a very strange place compared to Middle-earth. The first people to dwell there were Men, not Elves or Dwarves. And there were no Dwarves, or Hobbits, and few Elves (who may have actually dwelt in the huge garden-region of Nisimaldar that they helped to cultivate) for any length of time. Númenor was for all intents and purposes a "Mannish" state and society.

Of course, Tolkien says the Eldar of Tol Eressëa visited the island almost from the very start, and the Elves taught the Dunedain many things. What things? Why didn't the Eldar teach the Edain all these neat ideas during the 140 or so years of relative peace that the Edain enjoyed in Beleriand before the Dagor Bragollach?

Well, there was the art of ship-building. Not that the Númenoreans needed ships at first (Cirdan's folk had transported the fathers of the Númenoreans to their island), but the greater part of the population lived along the coasts in towns and villages which supported a great fishing industry. It just seems sort of odd that the Dunedain whose ancestors had lived happily in the highlands of Dorthonion and the woods of Brethil would have taken to life on the seashore.

Of course, every Dunadan family had to eat, and fishing should have been one of the easiest ways for the early arrivals to provide for themselves. You weave a few nets, carve out some boats, make a few spears, and go skidding across the waves to find a good shoal where the local fishies haven't figured out that Men are not good things (for the fishies, that is).

Tolkien tells us that most of the Dunedain lived in the eastern regions of Númenor, in fact the greatest population was in the Arandor, the Kings land. The Dunedain must have been brought to shore by Cirdan's mariners approximately where Romenna lay, and from there colonists moved inland and gradually spread throughout the island. The westernmost peoples appear to have been primarily of Bëorian descent, and it was from them whom many of the Faithful centuries later claimed descent.

The early society of the Dunedain must have been rather clannish, perhaps even multi-tribalish. In the essay on Númenor (*Unfinished Tales*), Tolkien writes that "the King and most of the great chieftains possessed swords as heirlooms of their fathers; and at times they would still give a sword as a gift to their heirs." Who were these "great chieftains"? Undoubtedly there must have been families of prominent men who became leaders in their communities in the absence of their rightful lords, whose families were finally represented only by Elrond and Elros.

For more than 50 years the vast majority of the Dunedain were separated from their rightful lords. Tuor was never raised among his people, although he spent three years as a slave among them after he had been captured. When Tuor finally left Hithlum, never to return, Túrin was already a man set upon his doomed path. Tuor's deeds as an outlaw after his escape from slavery must have become legendary, for the Easterlings set a high price on his head.

So, at least two generations of Edain were raised in slavery after Tuor's departure. A lot can happen in the course of two generations. The slaves would develop leaders who would become important to them in some fashion. And from these leaders would have emerged their first commanders when they finally joined the Host of Valinor in the War of Wrath. Presumably Elrond and Elros also joined the army of Valinor, for how else could Elrond have recalled the Breaking of Thangorodrim (Cf. "The Council of Elrond", *The Lord of the Rings*)? And why would Elros have been able to contemplate a kingship over the Edain?

The War of Wrath lasted for 42 years, and for another 35 years Elros prepared his people for eventual departure over Sea. Somewhere in those years the Edain of Beleriand became the Dunedain, and their leaders must have gathered about them various factions of people. Elros undoubtedly must have gathered his own following, people who had come to admire him and to serve him willingly. These would have included his captains and their families, and his chief warriors. Perhaps the bravest of the Dunadan warriors were all led by Elros by the end of the war.

The Edain of Dor-lomin consisted of Marachians and Bëorians. The Marachians were the most numerous people, and the Bëorians were the second most numerous folk. The Folk of Haleth had become scattered after the last of their rightful chieftains, Manthor, died. "The Wanderings of Hurin" (published in *The War of the Jewels*) says that "lesser men ruled in Brethil in the time that was left", but we also learn there that many of the Folk of Haleth chose to go with Hurin and his outlaws. The "Narn i Chin Hurin" (published as "Narn i Hin Hurin" in *Unfinished Tales*) tells us that other members of the Folk of Brethil had gradually spread southward from the forest.

In time there must have been small communities of Edain living scattered throughout Beleriand. And their leaders would have provided at least some of the chieftains who led the Edain to Númenor with Elros. Elros led from five to ten thousand Edain in the first wave of colonization, but many thousands of other Edain came later. Most of these were probably absorbed into the population of Arandor, but one can well imagine the Bëorians and Folk of Haleth moving westward to seek out the highlands and forests which would have been most like their older homes in Beleriand.

Yet these bands of colonists were not necessarily crude barbarians waiting to be culturally elevated by the Elves of Tol Eressëa. Tolkien notes in the essay on Númenor that "the Edain brought with them to Númenor the knowledge of many crafts, and many craftsmen who had learned from the Eldar, besides preserving lore and traditions of their own." Obviously there was plenty of opportunity for the Edain to learn from the Eldar during the War of Wrath and the years afterward, but the notion that they had preserved knowledge from before implies that their craftsmen must have been valued by the Easterlings.

And if the Easterlings had used slave craftsmen, then quite possibly Hurin did not lead all the men of Dor-lomin to war. We know from "The Wanderings of Hurin" that he was able to recruit a band of outlaws, some of whom had fought in the Nirnaeth. So the forces of Dor-lomin had been partially scattered. But older men and boys too young to fight had to have been left behind. From these men would have emerged the craftsmen whom the Easterlings preserved as slaves (Turin's old companion, Sador, would have been one of these).

One can imagine that a sort of master-apprentice schooling must have developed as the aged men passed on their knowledge. Edainic society, regardless of what it had been like before the Nirnaeth, had to be fundamentally altered by the generations of slavery. Hence, organized "schools" or "guilds" could not have existed, although perhaps the slaves would have maintained some secret groups for various purposes.

The idea of guilds may be a purely Númenorean convention, but was it necessarily developed along the same lines as medieval European guilds would have been? For inspiration they could have been exposed to or even tutored by the Eldarin "schools" (such as the Lambengolmor, the masters of tongues, the "school" of linguists established by Fëanor in Aman). Elros, in particular, must have learned something of Noldorin culture from Maglor, his foster father, even though the Noldorin civilization had been destroyed. Elros could have prevailed upon all the craftsmen he found to come together to share knowledge and help build cities.

Hence, Romenna and Armenelos would have been founded quickly. Romenna with its great harbor would have received the ships of the Eldar, and Armenelos would have become the center of exploration and colonization for the rest of Númenor. It must also have been a center of great learning, and though no mention is made of one, Armenelos must have eventually (if not in Elros' time) have established a great library to preserve the lore of the Númenoreans. A road was built which ran from Romenna all the way to the haven of Andunië in northwestern Númenor, passing first through Ondosto, a region or city which Christopher Tolkien speculates was used for stone quarries. Trade and commerce thus existed within Númenor, as well.

But only two Númenorean guilds are actually named: the Guild of Weaponsmiths and the Guild of Venturers. The latter guild was founded by Aldarion while he was still just a prince (Cf. "Aldarion and Erendis: The Mariner's wife"), and it was a society devoted to exploration and travel. There seems to be no real evidence that the Guild of Venturers was anything like a medieval craft guild. The Guild of Weaponsmiths, on the other hand, was responsible for making the tools used by Númenor's craftsmen, and in the early centuries at least they spent more time making tools than weapons. It may be that the guilds were in fact sponsored by the kings, or other wealthy leaders.

If royal patronage gave a guild its income, the guild would have to take royal direction as well. Hence, Elros could decide where the cities would be built, where the mines would be dug, where the quarries would be established. All of early Númenor seems to have been laid out according to some well-conceived plan, and the logical conclusion is that Elros, who reigned in Númenor for 410 years, must have devoted a great deal of time toward organizing the kingdom.

And yet he doesn't seem to have been an arbitrary ruler, as his descendants were not all arbitrary rulers. Tar-Meneldur, Aldarion's father, did not act as an autocrat. In an end-note to "Aldarion and Erendis", Christopher Tolkien writes that "In a note on the 'Council of the Sceptre' at this time in the history of Númenor it is said that this Council had no powers to govern the King save by advice...." And yet when Tar-Meneldur announced his intention to abdicate, he told his council that he would defer the action for a while if they insisted. The Council was drawn from the leading men of various regions of Númenor, and these were not always descendants of Elros.

So it appears that Elros must have governed by a sort of consensus at first, winning the support and acclamation of the various chieftains who agreed to sail over Sea to Númenor, but establishing where necessary whatever guilds were utilized in building the Númenorean civilization, which literally rose up under Elros' guidance. Royal patronage or at least royal charters and direction must have brought about the profound and broad powers of the kings.

And yet the members of the Council of the Sceptre appear to be wealthy men themselves. Where did their wealth come from? If they were the descendants of the original chieftains, those men may have organized lesser guilds, or established control over local economies. The people of Emerië (a region in south-central Númenor, part of a larger region called Mittalmar) were shepherds, and vineyards were grown in eastern Hyarnustar (the southwestern peninsula of the island). Hyarastorni, another region in Mittalmar (perhaps bordering Emerië on the west), seems to have been a farming and sheep-raising region. Hallatan, son of Hallacar, was able to pass himself off as a shepherd when he was courting Ancalimë (who had disguised herself as a shepherdess in order to escape the pressures and obligations of her heritage).

The Council members were able to prevail upon Ancalimë to take a husband, and in one anecdote it is suggested that the Council tried to find Ancalimë when she was in hiding, even though Aldarion worked to distract them. The Council members seem to have a measure of independence and influence that the kings could not simply ignore even if the laws of Númenor and the actual governance of the realm flowed directly from the throne. When Sauron was taken prisoner to Númenor by Ar-Pharazôn, the king was reluctant to move against Amandil (Lord of Andunië and a member of the Council) in part because Amandil was still popular and held in great esteem by the people. Council members, at least in Tar-Meneldur's day, were selected because they were respected by the people in their regions.

So a reasonable inference is that the various regions of Númenor were led by a few families, the leaders of whom were the "chieftains" of the Dunedain, and from the most prominent of these families developed the eventual hereditary lordships. The Lords of Andunië, for example, were descended from Valandil, son of Silmarien, eldest daughter of Tar-Elendil the fourth king. Silmarien married Elatan of Andunië, who may have been a descendant of Bëor from a lesser line. Erendis' father, Beregar, was a Bëorian descended from Beleth, the sister of Baragund and Belegund, the nephews of Barahir, Beren's father.

Elatan's son may have been elevated to the lordship of Andunië because he was a king's grandson, but it could also be that Elatan was the most respected leader in Andunië and would himself have been made lord of that region if there had been a need for one. That Valandil was made the first Lord of Andunië seems to imply there weren't many people in that region until his day, or perhaps Tar-Meneldur expanded his council, or established the first Council of the Sceptre. Unfortunately, Tolkien doesn't say much about Númenorean history, because most of its historical records are supposed to have been lost in the Downfall.

Since at the end of Tar-Meneldur's reign only two members of his council (Valandil and Hallatan of Hyarastorni) were descendants of Elros, it may be that the various regions of Númenor were developed under the auspices of the wealthier chieftains. The initial wealth of these families could have come from land-grants made by the kings (Tar-Meneldur specifically gave extensive lands in Emerië to Erendis as a wedding gift), but it may be that Elros allowed men to claim lands they broke and settled. Any man who could establish a community would become its leader, and the leaders may have been the chief farmers, ranchers, and herdsmen in their regions. It would eventually become necessary for these chieftains to select a representative to speak for them on the Council of the Sceptre.

The idea that the lordships developed in part from independent chieftainships may help explain why Amandil and his predecessors could extend help to the Faithful Dunedain while retaining the good will of the Kings. The various lords must have obtained a degree of autonomy. Ar-Pharazôn's reign may therefore have represented a remarkable period in which his personal charisma overcame the barriers of autonomy. That is, he established himself as a great captain in Middle-earth and thus won renown and widespread support from other Númenorean lords.

Hence, when Tar-Palantir died, Ar-Pharazôn could take the sceptre and force Tar-Miriel to marry him because he already had the popular support of many of Númenor's lords. An appeal to their conservative values (only men should wield the sceptre in these dark times) or perhaps a simple declaration of "I should be the King!" might be all he required. Tar-Miriel would have found herself without sufficient support to gainsay Pharazôn's ambitions. Worse, she may have lacked the personal wealth necessary to raise an army to assert her own power, or to patronize the guilds. She was the rightful Queen, and should have become the Ruler of Númenor, but precedent established in Tar-Ancalimë's time required that she marry or give up the Sceptre.

Hence, Ar-Pharazôn's ambition was buoyed by the ancient laws. Númenor needed a ruler who was wed, and if Tar-Miriel didn't marry him he should have become the rightful king (because his father, Gimilkhad, was Tar-Palantir's younger brother). At least as Pharazôn's wife Tar-Miriel ensured that her father's line continued and she may have hoped to influence Ar-Pharazôn (though in the end she didn't, and it's doubtful she even lived with him, since they had no children). That Tar-Miriel could have married someone else is only briefly dealt with in some material published in *The Peoples of Middle-earth*, but Ar-Pharazôn seems to have been powerful enough to prevent that from happening.

If the lords of Númenor were largely autonomous then much of their later history would be easily explained. In time there would have been too few lands to bestow through inheritance or gift upon leading men in Númenor, either by the kings or the lords and chieftains. And Tar-Meneldur feared that the Guild of Venturers would encourage men to seek far lands outside of Númenor. Even when Aldarion was the Guild's chief patron and leader there were other captains who sailed to Mithlond, though these adventures seemed small by comparison with Aldarion's own voyages. To counter the wanderlust he feared might sap away Númenor's strength, Tar-Meneldur may have bestowed gifts of land upon worthy men in order to retain their interest in Númenor. But such a policy would quickly use up reserves of unclaimed lands.

The initial efforts to colonize Middle-earth, therefore, may have resulted from the various noble families sending younger sons over Sea, funding expeditions. The potential for dissension among Númenor's wealthier families would thus have been reduced, and the Kings would have retained considerable power and influence because there would be less competition for their patronage over the essential guilds. It may be that economic power coincided with political power in Númenor because political power would depend on economic power.

The effect of the Númenorean colonization policies from Second Age 1200 onward would thus be to preserve the royal power and prevent the absolute dilution of royal prerogatives. Capetian France all but disintegrated the royal power because the kings had to continually bestow lands upon their supporters in order to retain their loyalty. The kings ended up with less land and economic power than many of their great magnates, who were themselves as powerful and influential as the kings, or more so. By the late 1100s, the so-called Angevin Empire allowed the Kings of England to directly govern about half of France because they were also the Dukes of Normandy; and Henry II of England married Elanor of Aquitaine. Assorted other, smaller regions of France had been collected by the family over the generations, including Anjou, from which Historians derived the phrase "Angevin Empire".

Númenor must therefore have produced an immense surplus population through the centuries, and the Kings allowed or encouraged the adventurous people to sail to Middle-earth. The early colonists may have been led by lords whose families were paying for the ships and supplies required to establish the colonies. In return, the families may have set up special trade routes whereby they retained exclusive control over traffic between their colonies and the homelands. By finding opportunities in Middle-earth for younger sons, the families avoided the necessity of breaking up their lands. Nothing like feudalism should ever have developed in Númenor, especially since the kingdom had no enemies which required strong local defense.

Royal prerogatives outside of the maintenance of Vinyalondë, the haven founded by Aldarion near the mouth of the Gwathlo river in Eriador, must have been extremely few overseas until the Númenoreans began to see how powerful they were in the War of the Elves and Sauron (1695-1701). From the period 1800 onward the Númenoreans began to conquer large territories in Middle-earth. But who commissioned the armies and authorized the conquests?

The answer must be the kings themselves. If their contemporary aristocracy were breaking new lands in Middle-earth peacefully, the kings must have realized that they were gradually being overtaken by their peers in wealth and prestige. What better way to reassert royal prerogatives than by commissioning military expeditions and wars of conquest? The younger sons of the noble families would be recruited into the navy and army and would serve the kings, not their families. The families might actually have welcomed or even encouraged the change in policy as the conflicts with Sauron would have made the breaking of new lands more difficult. So competition for opportunity in Middle-earth between sons coming from Númenor and sons born in Middle-earth would have arisen. Now the Númenoreans would advance into Middle-earth as liberators and defenders of their colonies, but in reality the Kings might have been setting limits to the expansion of the autonomous nobles. The Kings must have controlled the core guilds in Númenor, so they could decide whose armies were equipped and whose fleets were built.

Nonetheless, the extension of royal power into the Númenorean circles of Middle-earth may have alarmed some families. Perhaps this is why Sauron was able to ensnare several Númenorean lords with Rings of Power. The Eldar didn't bother to tell the Númenoreans why they were fighting a war with Sauron. Ignorant of the Rings of Power and the perils they represented, the Númenoreans could be seduced by Sauron into rebelling against their rightful kings, or at least in abandoning their places in Númenorean society. "Of the Rings of Power and the Third Age" says that those (nine) men who accepted the Rings "became mighty in their day, kings, sorcerors, and warriors of old."

Now younger sons of powerful families, whose ambitions had been dispossessed by kings eager to increase their own wealth and influence, would have been enticed to strike out on their own. They could have raised wealth and armies with the aid of their Rings, undoubtedly kept secret from the kings and their own families. At least three areas of Númenorean Middle-earth must have suddenly noticed rival powers rising up without explanation. The new kingdoms could have been used by Sauron to slow or check Númenorean progress.

In fact, it's conceivable that Sauron would have used the nine men (to whom he gave Rings of Power) at first to bar or impede Númenorean aggression throughout Middle-earth. Hence 9 sorceror-kings must have risen fairly quickly, in lands close to the boundaries of Númenorean expansion. The various wealthy families would be proud of their successful sons and refuse to take up arms against them. In the long run they might have lost control over the colonies simply because the kings needed to ensure the new kingdoms didn't encroach upon Númenorean territory.

The autonomy of the nobles would explain why Amandil often acted with impunity, aiding the Faithful and eventually sailing west to try and rouse the Valar. He would have expected to be able to conduct his own business without much interference from the King. That would also explain why Ar-Pharazôn would not have taken action against Elendil's fleet in Romenna harbor. The withdrawal of Elendil and his people might have been viewed as a mild form of rebellion, a sort of statement that they would rather seek their fortunes elsewhere than take part in the changes sweeping across Númenor. Tradition would have forbidden Ar-Pharazôn from taking direct action against the Elendili. After all, he must have still owed something by then to the great families which had supported him.

The establishment of the fortress of Umbar and the city of Pelargir ("Royal garth of ships") within 100 years after the first appearance of the Nazgul seems to imply that Númenor felt it necessary to oppose Mordor militarily. The earlier kingdoms established by Sauron's Ringwraiths may have vanished or passed into the hands of other rulers. Now the Nazgul might more effectively serve their lord as captains of his armies, vassals in buffer regions between Mordor and the Númenorean colonies, and emissaries sent abroad.

Númenorean captains such as Ar-Pharazôn had been in his youth were achieving victories against Sauron's armies in Middle-earth. The implication is that Númenor made territorial gains or repelled invasions launched by Sauron against the colonies. It would appear that Númenor's ability to finance large overseas expeditions prevented a feudal breakdown of authority. The Kings of Númenor became true imperials. Their wealthy aristocratic families, therefore, must either have become confined to traditional, non-expanding spheres of influence or else were incorporated into a growing Númenorean bureaucracy and military machine. The Kings would need administrators for their colonies and they would need auditors to make sure they got their taxes and fees from all enterprises in Middle-earth.

Ar-Pharazôn effectively stripped Amandil of his lands and title. This reduction in autonomy, or increase in royal authority, could arguably be traced directly to Sauron's influence. Ar-Pharazôn may have been the first and only King to set aside ancient traditions and boundaries, at least on the scale on which he acted as indicated by "Akallabeth" and related texts. But even where Amandil was concerned Ar-Pharazôn may have had some precedent derived from events in Middle-earth. What if the autonomous families did resent the intrusion of the kings into the colonial world? Perhaps the kings, as they became more aggressive and militaristic, found reason and "just" cause to remove some colonial lords from their domains. The Númenoreans seem to have been very serious about following established precedent.

The adherence to precedence and tradition would have been a balancing factor in the early generations. Elros Tar-Minyatur was King of Númenor but he founded the kingdom with the help of Edainic peoples who had hundreds of years of traditions behind them. The Folk of Haleth, for example, had held folkmoots to decide great matters. Their chieftains led them in war, called the moots, and acted as judges, but they were not autocratic rulers. The lords of Dor-lomin and Ladros, on the other hand, were appointed vassals of Elven kings. They seem to have been given some autonomous rights in order to retain a division between cultures (and that was why these lordships were established, because the Elven kings felt that Men and Elves should not always live closely together).

The Lords of Ladros ended with Beren, technically, though he never governed his people, who had all left Dorthonion during his father's time. These Bëorians became incorporated into the societies of Brethil and Dor-lomin, the latter group thus taking the Lords of Dor-lomin as their leaders. Had Barahir gone with his people to Dor-lomin, would he perhaps have been accepted as an equal by Galdor of Dor-lomin, or would Fingon have established a second lordship for Men in his kingdom? The implications of such a move would be serious. Beren would probably have never met Lúthien, Dior would not have been born, Doriath would have survived, but Hithlum might still have been overcome in the end. What, then, would have become of the heirs of the dispossessed lords?

As matters progressed, however, the Edain of Hithlum were cut off from their rightful lords for generations, and in the absence of those lords they may have developed leaders who would have become strengthened in their prerogatives by custom and tradition. Hence, Elros would have needed to win the respect and support of these leaders, and he could not have ruled as autocratically as Ar-Pharazôn eventually did. The Edain took to Númenor the custom of the folkmoot and the tradition of being led by many chieftains of smaller peoples. Somewhere in the process of building his kingdom, Elros seems to averted the necessity of recognizing numerous separate "peoples" (as developed in Anglo-Saxon England, each leader giving his name to the community he founded) while retaining and perhaps enriching the folk traditions that provided for autonomy.

The retention of autonomous traditions may at first have been a stabilizing force in Númenorean society, but inevitably it seems to have led to a degree of instability. Tar-Meneldur was concerned that Aldarion's Guild of Venturers would foster ambitions for the conquest of foreign lands in the Númenoreans, but it seems that the inevitable competition between the Kings and the various aristocratic families would have brought on such colonization efforts anyway. The Guild of

Venturers may have opened the door, but they could not have forced the Númenoreans to walk through it. So the dissensions which arose centuries later as the Kings and their supporters began to turn away from the Valar in resentment of their mortality may owe something to the autonomy enjoyed by the leading families. They were free to some extent to speak and live as they pleased. By the time Ar-Pharazôn established near absolute control over Númenor, the Faithful had mostly fled to Middle-earth, where centuries of colonization afforded them a friendly base of support and the means of continuing their civilization in despite of the King's ill will.

Chapter 15:
Seeking the wayward
children of Númenor

Something should be said about the founding of Arnor and Gondor, but it's not easy to assign the establishment of the Dunadan realms in exile their proper place in the Tolkien legendarium. JRRT wrote to Dick Plotz of the Tolkien Society of America in 1965, saying, "...Of all the mythical or 'archetypal' images this is the one most deeply seated in my imagination, and for many years I had a recurrent Atlantis dream: the stupendous and ineluctable wave advancing from the Sea or over the land, sometimes dark, sometimes green and sunlit." (*The Letters of J.R.R. Tolkien*, No. 276)

One gets the impression that Tolkien was immensely moved by this legend, and yet only the year before he had told Christopher Bretherton, "Another ingredient, not before mentioned, also came into operation in my need to provide a great function for Strider-Aragorn. What I might call my Atlantis-haunting. This legend or myth or dim memory of some ancient history has always troubled me. In sleep I had the dreadful dream of the ineluctable Wave, either coming out of the quiet sea, or coming in over the green inlands. It still occurs occasionally, though now exorcized by writing about it. It always ends by surrender, and I awake gasping out of deep water. I used to draw it or write bad poems about it...." (Ibid., No. 257)

Here again he admits to being moved by it, and yet concedes that it only entered the world of Middle-earth as a resolution for his "need to provide a great function for Strider-Aragorn." The incorporation of the Atlantis legend was easy enough in that respect. Tolkien had already written an early version of the Downfall ("The Drowning of Anadune") and he had the primary characters defined. But he had yet to contrive the aftermath of the Downfall, and to work it fully into Middle-earth. Elendil's kingdom, for example, started out in Beleriand (more of which had survived in early efforts to map out this strange new world than Tolkien eventually decided upon for the published stories).

A common though occasional question asked by Tolkien readers is how many people Elendil could have fit upon his nine ships. In "Akallabeth" it is made clear that Elendil and his people stayed in ships in the harbor of Romenna for some considerable period of time.

> But Elendil did all that his father had bidden, and his ships lay off the east coast of the land; and the Faithful put aboard their wives and their children, and their heirlooms, and great store of goods. Many things there were of beauty and power, such as the Númenoreans had contrived in the days of their wisdom, vessels and jewels, and scrolls of lore written in scarlet and black. And Seven Stones they had, the gift of the Eldar; but in the ship of Isildur was guarded the young tree, the scion of Nimloth the Fair. Thus Elendil held himself in readiness, and did not meddle in the evil deeds of those days; and ever he looked for a sign that did not come. Then he journeyed in secret to the western shores and gazed out over the sea, for sorrow and yearning were come upon him, and he greatly loved his father. But naught could he descry save the fleets of Ar-Pharazôn gathering in the havens of the west.

Elendil's people had to have lived on those ships for weeks or months. How could they do so, if they had filled the ships with their wives and children, and their heirlooms, and great store of goods? They must have had a pretty good waybread recipe, or else were taking food from the mainland every now and then. But the impression one gets is that there weren't that many people on the ships. Suppose each ship was large, but carried only 100 families or so. At best Elendil might have had about 4500-5000 people with him.

So where did the rest of the populations of Arnor and Gondor come from, if they weren't all on those ships? The answer is clearly that there were people already living in the lands which became Arnor and Gondor. And this fact troubles some readers, because it seems to them that Númenorean survivors are too few to give rise to the immense numbers of Dunadan soldiers who fill the stories of the later history. And how could the culture of Númenor have such an impact if it's imposed on the inhabitants of Middle-earth by so few refugees?

A less obvious fact escapes the notice of many readers, it seems. There were already many Númenoreans living in northern Middle-earth, members of the Faithful who had fled there previously, or their descendants, some of mixed blood, some of pure Númenorean descent. These Númenoreans and mixed-Númenoreans must have vastly outnumbered Elendil's few thousand refugees. They had been settling and flourishing in Middle-earth for the equivalent of generations.

Númenor in fact had three havens in northern Middle-earth: Pelargir, Lond Daer Ened (originally known as Vinyalondë), and Tharbad. Pelargir began as a royal haven, probably a naval base of some sort, an extension or assertion of Númenorean power. Situated so close to Mordor its chief strategic purpose is obscure, but may have been intended to help shield the Elves of Edhellond from the threat of Sauron's power. When Gil-galad first called upon Númenor for aid, soon after the Elves realized Sauron had made the One Ring, the Númenoreans built lines of forts along the Gwathlo and Lhun rivers. Númenor thus had a long tradition of helping to defend Elvish lands.

In the War of the Elves and Sauron (S.A. 1695-1701), most of the Gwathlo forts were bypassed and ignored by Sauron (Cf. "The History of Galadriel and Celeborn", *Unfinished Tales*). Their garrisons must have been small and ineffectual, but they assured the Númenoreans of a measure of "stealth" when Ciryon, the admiral in command of the Númenorean relief fleet, sent a force up the Gwathlo to Tharbad. The Lhun forts ensured that Lindon remained free. Sauron carried his campaign all the way to the river, but the stubborn resistance of the Eldar and Dunedain prevailed and Sauron was unable to cross the river.

Númenoreans had been settling in Middle-earth for nearly 500 years by this time. Although it's conceivable (perhaps even probable) that most of those settlements had occurred neared the Elvish lands, the Númenoreans must have been devastated in the war. It would not be long (circa 1800) before Númenorean colonists became Númenorean conquerors, establishing great fortresses along the coastlines and carving out dominions.

Pelargir was founded in 2350, about 100 years after Tar-Ancalimon became King of Númenor (Tar-Atanamir took the scepter in 2251 according to "The Tale of Years" in *The Lord of the Rings*, but according to "The Line of Elros" in *Unfinished Tales*, Tar-Ancalimon took it in 2221 -- in *The Peoples of Middle-earth* Christopher Tolkien shows that the "Line of Elros" is correct). It was in Tar-Ancalimon's time that the Númenoreans became divided into the Faithful and the Kings Men.

It was also in Tar-Ancalimon's time (2221-2386) that Númenor began to establish the great fortress-havens along the coasts and to extract tribute from the men of Middle-earth. The fortress of Umbar was built in the year 2280. The Nazgul had already appeared in Middle-earth in some undescribed fashion, most likely as the leaders of Sauron's armies or his emissaries.

The initial differences between the Faithful and the Kings Men must have been philosophical, differences of intellectual discourse, rather than violent. All the Númenoreans were still loyal to their king. So the establishment of Pelargir as a royal haven doesn't necessarily preclude the possibility that it was always a refuge for the Faithful. Imagine a lord of Númenor who would be sent to Pelargir to defend the Anduin and extend Númenor's protection to Edhellond. How likely was he to be one of the Kings Men, jealous and envious of the Eldar, or one of the Faithful, reverent toward the Eldar and the Valar?

The public appointment of a commander sympathetic toward the Faithful and Eldar could have sparked immediate and long-term interest in Pelargir among the Faithful. Tolkien never explains why Númenoreans would want to leave Númenor as early as the year 1200 (when they began establishing permanent colonies) but the Faithful may have wanted to get away from the bickering and gradual estrangement of the Númenoreans from the Eldar.

And yet, Lond Daer Ened and Tharbad were closer to the Elves of Lindon and Imladris. If the Faithful wanted to live close to the Eldar, why didn't most of them go farther north? The answer must be that there was less room for settlement in the north. The implication of the gradual drift of the Faithful toward Pelargir is that the peoples of Eriador made a relatively swift recovery from the devastations of the War of the Elves and Sauron. *Unfinished Tales* indicates that Sauron overran Eriador, slaying or "driving off" most of its people. A lot of those people must have been driven across the Lhun, or into Imladris with Elrond (who is said to have gathered many Elves and Men there).

There were many different groups of Men living in Eriador in the Second Age.

There were Edainic peoples mostly of Bëorian descent (but also some Marachians). There were Gwathuirim, who were related to the Folk of Haleth in Beleriand and thus to the Númenoreans. There were in the far northern lands Men related to the Folk of Bor, the swarthy men who had settled in Lothlann in the late Second Age and allied themselves with Maedhros. And there were "evil Men", living in the eastern lands, presumably the ancestors of the hill-folk of Rhudaur and the Men of Angmar in the Third Age who served the Lord of the Nazgul.

There were at least two kinds of Men living along the Anfalas and in the Ered Nimrais, not including the Druedain. Some of these men were Gwathuirim, the ancestors of the Dead Men of Dunharrow and many of Gondor's people in the Third Age. These Gwathuirim inhabited the mountains or the lands adjacent to them and are occasionally referred to as the "wild men of the dales" (Cf. "Of the Rings of Power and the Third Age", *The Silmarillion*). The other men are an unnamed group who lived along the coasts. They appear to be swarthy (dark-skinned) and very unlike the Númenoreans in appearance.

Perhaps because of the proximity of the Elves and Mordor there weren't many men living in the lands near Pelargir. Many of the Gwathuirim worshiped and served Sauron, and that would give the Númenoreans reason not only to fight them but to take their lands. They would have retreated to the higher dales. The men of the coasts either submitted to Númenor or withdrew farther west and south. That left the lands of Belfalas and Lebennin open to colonization.

A natural consequence of the tendency of the Faithful to settle in or near Pelargir would also be a division of the Faithful Númenoreans into an "old blood" group and a "new blood" group. That is, the majority of the families in the northern lands were probably descended from early colonists. The majority of the families in the south were probably constantly infused with new bloodlines emigrating from Númenor.

Despite the animosity of the Gwathuirim, the northern Dunedain seem to have become better adjusted to living in and among many different peoples. They didn't drive other Men out of their lands, and probably due to the influence of Gil-galad's kingdom enjoyed greater peace and security. The southern Dunedain lived with the threat of war from both the mountains and Mordor.

Of course, for many centuries Pelargir must have been able to depend upon support from Umbar and other Númenorean fortresses farther south. If the constant influx of peoples wasn't enough to help keep the region securely in Númenorean hands, reinforcements were close by. So Pelargir must also have taken on the status of a frontier province or provincial capitol. Its importance wasn't just strategic but also political and economic. The city must have been the source of many goods which the colonists couldn't make for themselves. It should also have become a trading hub.

Emigration from Númenor need not have been very heavy. In fact, only a few hundred colonists need have arrived in Pelargir or Eriador a year. After many centuries the populations of both regions would have been considerably increased by Númenorean families. The half-caste families are hard to explain. Were they the descendants of concubines of conquering Númenorean warriors or powerful Númenorean lords, or were they the product of adventurers who, advancing beyond the frontiers of Númenorean colonization, took wives from among the native peoples? It seems unlikely many Númenorean women would have wandered out into the wilderness to find husbands, so the majority of the mixed families must have been started by Númenorean men.

Who were these men? Why couldn't or wouldn't they find wives among their own people? The answer must lie in part in the story of Aldarion and Erendis. He was an archetype among his people, an adventurer who couldn't quite let go of Númenor but who loved the sea and Middle-earth. Aldarion's adventures caused the failure of his marriage, and Erendis' bitterness was inherited in part by their daughter Ancalimë. She put off marrying for as long as possible, until forced to make a choice by the Council of Númenor, and even then her marriage despite its fairy-tale beginnings ended in grief. And Ancalimë abandoned the policies of her father, turning her back on Middle-earth. (Cf. "Aldarion and Erendis: The Mariner's wife", *Unfinished Tales*)

Although Ancalimë was still reigning Queen when the Númenoreans began to colonize Middle-earth, she gave up the scepter in 1280. The colonizations may have been undertaken without her blessing, and perhaps her son Anarion was a man of different mind and mood. But one possible implication of Ancalimë's indifference toward or dislike of Middle-earth may be that her father's Guild of Venturers became so ill-favored they started wandering away from Númenor. The division of the Númenoreans into the Faithful and the Kings Men may have been preceded by a more subtle division into the Wanderers and the Stay-at-homes.

If the early colonists were the more adventurous Númenoreans, there may have been few women among them who felt inclined to go to Middle-earth. Perhaps many of these women only went reluctantly, and insisted on settling in lands near the Eldar so they could at least find some comfort in the strange and wild mortal lands. The difference between the colonists of Pelargir and the colonists of Eriador, therefore, may also be that the early families of the north were more pure-blooded than the early families of the south. So the families of mixed descent may have been more numerous in the south.

But with the division of Númenor and the emigration of the Faithful to Middle-earth, a profound and radical change in settlement patterns must have emerged. Now whole families and households were sailing over Sea to the mortal lands, and most of them were going to Pelargir.

They needed land but they also needed to know they would not be harassed, either by Sauron, the wild men of the Dales, or the Kings Men. Pelargir was a visible source of Númenorean power. There was really no equivalent to it in the north. A strong garrison there, loyal to the Kings of Númenor but nonetheless friendly to the Eldar, would ensure that the political strife didn't spill over into the colonies.

The ultimate result of the gradual shift in settlement patterns, favoring the southern colonization over the northern, would have been a fundamental division in philosophical outlooks. The northern Dunedain must have been more stable and therefore more conservative in outlook than the Dunedain of Pelargir and its dependent settlements. Dunedain in the south would have been more prone to open new lands. Dunedain in the north would have been more likely to live in peace with their neighbors. Hence, a Bree could rise up in the heart of Dunadan territory, where the majority of the people were Gwathuirim, but the people of the southern lands were mostly of Dunadan or mixed descent because they were constantly at war with the Gwathuirim, who had been driven back to the mountains.

The arrival of Elendil's ships in Middle-earth did not alter these fundamental differences. Elendil reached Lindon with four ships of Númenoreans. At most they could have founded one small city by themselves. More likely they spread out across Eriador. Probably a majority of these "New Númenoreans" settled with Elendil by Lake Evendim at Annúminas, and some would have led the colonists who garrisoned Fornost Erain in the North Downs. But these cities must have been populated mostly by people recruited from the local populations, which had been established two thousand years before and had been recolonizing Eriador for more than fifteen hundred years since the War of the Elves and Sauron.

Isildur and Anarion reached Anduin with five ships. Again, they had too few people to build more than one city, and they appear to have settled at Osgiliath early on. Pelargir may have welcomed the sons of Elendil but there was either no room for five shiploads of refugees there or else the tradition of opening new lands prevailed and Isildur and Anarion led a new wave of conquest and colonization north along the river's shores.

Of Osgiliath and Annúminas, Osgiliath was probably the larger city. Not only did Isildur and Anarion arrive with one more ship than their father, Pelargir had probably been the haven most sought after by the Faithful Númenoreans who fled Númenor in the years of Ar-Pharazôn's rule. He had driven many of them to leave Númenor before Elendil rounded up the last handful of families. So there must also have been a large population of recent immigrants to swell the numbers of people sympathetic to Isildur and Anarion. They would have been familiar with the family of Amandil.

One can almost picture Isildur arriving in Middle-earth on his storm-driven ship. The coastlines have been ravaged, doubtless many people have died or are homeless, and they are wondering what the heck is going on. As word of the arrival of the refugees spreads through the lands, colonists would descend upon Pelargir. They would be curious for a glimpse of the last Númenoreans to arrive in Middle-earth, but there must also be many people looking for guidance and reassurance. Perhaps Isildur and Anarion stand upon the quays of Pelargir, or in some great public square, and in Fëanorian fashion address their people and move them to rebuild their homes and establish a new realm. Out of fear and despair arise hope and ambition.

Whole families, clans, communities must have made the decision to move deeper inland. Osgiliath was founded, and Minas Anor, and Minas Ithil (possibly in 3320, possibly later, between 3339 and 3379, when Isildur's second son was born in Osgiliath and his third son was born in Minas Ithil respectively -- see "The Heirs of Elendil" in *The Peoples of Middle-earth* for dates). The colonists spread throughout Ithilien and Anorien, and they entered Calenardhon. Isildur reached some sort of settlement with the King of the Mountains, not incorporating that Gwathuirim realm into Gondor. Nonetheless, fortresses were built at Orthanc and Aglarond, doubtless to control the Gap of Calenardhon and the passage of the Angren river (which was later called the Isen by the Rohirrim).

It's doubtful Elendil's people broke many new lands or felt the desire to. If the Dunedain of Gondor took Isildur and Anarion as their lords because they were brave and ambitious, the people of Arnor must have accepted Elendil because he was noble and represented the last of a great heritage from Númenor. There should have been few if any Elrosians in Middle-earth. If the recent immigrants fleeing persecution had mostly settled near Pelargir, the northern Dunedain may have retained a greater reverence for Númenor, and Elendil and his companions would be their only link with the past. They would, furthermore, be reminders of what was great about Númenor, and not what had become dark and forbidding.

Great changes must have been wrought upon the northern lands as well as in the south. Lond Daer Ened seems to have been abandoned, and Tharbad became the chief port of the north. How many people were displaced along the coast and driven inland? These may have constituted the bulk of Elendil's colonists, and if they came from Lond Daer Ened they probably were mostly of Númenorean descent.

The conservative values of the north survived long into the Third Age. Although Arnor may have fought one or more wars under the High Kings, it did not embark upon wars of conquest and was generally safe from invasion. Gondor, on the other hand, remained in many ways a frontier society, or at least retained the vigor of a frontier society which enabled it to continue expanding for a thousand years. The Gondorians moved west and north along the coasts, and they clashed with Umbar and the Haradrim, pushing the borders of the Gondor south into enemy territories.

The difference in outlooks and military advances between the two kingdoms may stem from initial differences in colonization patterns, which in turn were influenced by the events occurring in Númenor. A bolder, more arrogant people may have arisen in Gondor because its history reflected a greater degree of instability, arising from Númenor's restlessness. Arnor's people seem to have forgotten the restlessness, and to have become less ambitious. They were Númenoreans living peacefully beside other Men.

It may be worthwhile to ask if, during the violent storm which drove the ships of the Faithful eastward, whether a moment of choice came upon the captains, and if the more conservative captains steered closer to Elendil's ship and the more adventurous captains stayed with Isildur and Anarion. Perhaps the older generations sailed away northward toward Lindon and a life much like that which their ancestors had known. The younger generations forged a path toward the frontier around Pelargir, and a grander destiny than the old families could conceive of.

In the end both kingdoms declined. Arnor descended into a sort of brilliant decadence, ending in the squabbles of three princes who could not live together as their ancestors had been able to live beside Men of strange kin. Gondor eventually turned its aggression inward, embroiling itself in a civil war born out of pride and arrogance and nearly bleeding itself dry in the process. In both situations the final legacy of Númenor made its appearance: the darker nature of the Dunedain, their tendency toward division and self-destruction. Neither kingdom, born out of the ashes of the older realm, could quite shed itself of the Númenorean heritage which had brought an end to Númenor.

So the founding of the realms in exile seems more a respite than a resolution or reward. The Faithful could not escape their doom. Númenor didn't fail so much as proceed through a process of winnowing, and when the wheat was separated from the chaff, Arnor and Gondor started the process over again. They were, like the seedling of the White Tree which Isildur brought to Middle-earth, seedlings which replanted the Númenorean culture in fertile ground. But they were also a step in transition in which the Dunedain were moving back toward their roots. Eventually, they would no longer be Dunedain, but would again be Men of Middle-earth.

And that is where Arnor and Gondor belong in the legendarium. They are the gateways by which Tolkien brought his Atlanteans home, and removed them from legend and restored them to the path of history. All or nearly all was forgotten of the Númenor which had been, both great and humble, because it was never really a part of Middle-earth, greatly though it had contributed toward the construction of that world, both literarily and historically.

Chapter 16:
Shhh! It's a secret ring!

I get asked a lot of questions about Tolkien's world, and sometimes I just file the really interesting ones away for future reference. But the other day someone asked me something I don't believe I've ever come across before. Who knew about the Rings? A very astute reader pointed out to me that Boromir recognized the Ring immediately, Faramir figured out there was a Ring which concerned Gandalf, Denethor seemed to know all about it....When it comes right down to it, everyone who comes into contact with Frodo seems to know about "the precious Ring" (as Bombadil called it).

If I may borrow from one of the comparisons Tolkien so detested, it's almost equivalent to every gas station attendant along Route 66 asking J. Robert Oppenheimer if they can have a look at Fat Man and Little Boy as he is driving to Los Alamos. Sauron's Ring was supposed to be a big secret, yet so many people whom Frodo encountered seemed to know about it. Gildor Inglorion figured out what was going on (and how he knew Frodo was "bearing a great burden without guidance", as Glorfindel put it, is *never* explained anywhere).

How would it come about that so many people should know something about the One Ring at the end of the Third Age, especially considering that it had been lost to the knowledge of those who were most concerned with it for three thousand years?

The answer must lie in the days of Elendil and Gil-galad, when they first put together their great alliance. Tolkien wrote very little about what actually happened, but we know that Sauron attacked Gondor and took Minas Ithil. Isildur escaped with his wife and sons. Anarion fortified Anduin and held off Sauron's forces while Isildur sailed to Arnor. There Isildur consulted with Elendil and Elendil in turn consulted with Gil-galad (Cf. "Of the Rings of Power and the Third Age", *The Silmarillion*).

Up until this time, we can be sure, the fullest knowledge of the Rings of Power was limited to only the Elves. But how much did they know in general? Did just any old Elf know there were Rings of Power, or was the knowledge confined only to a select group? Well, there are no facts to answer these questions. That is, no Tolkien essay or note has yet been published which explains how the knowledge of the Rings spread. Elrond told the people at his council the full history of the Rings. "A part of his tale was known to some there, but the full tale to none," Tolkien writes in "The Council of Elrond".

That seems remarkable. Didn't even Gandalf know the full history of the Rings? Well, Gandalf didn't go in for Ring lore until Bilbo came along, so maybe he was still playing catch-up. But one gets the impression that Elrond's story was labeled "Top Secret, Need To Know, and YOU don't need to know!" except for him, Galadriel, and Cirdan (and maybe Celeborn, but everyone knows he was an outsider).

When Sauron first approached the Elves in the Second Age, many of them were suspicious of him, according to one discarded history of Celeborn and Galadriel published in *Unfinished Tales*. Galadriel didn't recognize Sauron (who called himself Aulendil in this account, although elsewhere he is said to have taken the name of Annatar). She mistrusted a Maia who suddenly appeared and claimed to be acting in the interests of the Valar. It's interesting that no attempt was made to confirm his story with Valinor. The Númenoreans returned to Middle-earth in SA 600 and Sauron began looking for a few good suckers centuries later. Heck, for that matter, the Eldar should have been able to pray to the Valar for some sort of guidance.

So it seems strange to begin with that Aulendil/Annatar's credentials were never checked. Perhaps someone did try to poke around his resume, but maybe there were just so many Maiar that the older Noldor scratched their heads and said, "Well, maybe...." I can't help but think of the mayor in "The Music Man" sending the four town councilmen to find out what the Professor's credentials are, and he turns them into a barbershop quartet. Maybe Sauron was a lot like Robert Preston, especially given the Elves' propensity for song.

Maybe Maglor was sent to get the credentials and Sauron asked him why he seemed so depressed and ....

The point is, Sauron wiggled his way into Eregion at a time when there were a lot of Elves running around Middle-earth. Gil-galad's kingdom extended from the seashores of Lindon to the Baranduin river. Nandor, Sindar, and Noldor were apparently wandering around the rest of Eriador. Plenty of Noldor and Sindar were living happily in Eregion, trading with the Dwarves, building cities, and doing whatever it is that Elves do. Across the Misty Mountains the Sindar had established two or more kingdoms among the Silvan Elves. And Edhellond was a quiet little corner hideaway south of the Ered Nimrais. It was, all in all, a very Elvish world. Men just happened to be hanging around, but aside from the Númenoreans, Men weren't really doing much.

Sauron supposedly visited more than one Elvish land in his quest for susceptible Elvish minds. Presumably the Silvan Elves would have had little interest in *preserving* Middle-earth. And fading? What is fading? Maybe Eönwë had mentioned the prospect of the Elves' fading to them when he traveled around summoning them all to Valinor for a second time, maybe not.

In Lindon, Elrond and Gil-galad refused to treat with Sauron. They wouldn't even admit him to the realm. Sauron must have sent a letter or messenger offering to tutor the Eldar in high and lofty matters. Perhaps it was a bit arrogant of Sauron to make such an offer, but Gil-galad's reaction may have seemed surprising. He was just a young fellow when Beleriand was trampled into the sea by the Valar. What did he know of Valinor and its bliss?

So it may be that Gil-galad's people were indeed mostly younger Elves. Few of the original Exiles actually survived the Wars of Beleriand. Of those, many apparently returned to the West after the Ban of the Valar was lifted. So only a handful of the truly ancient Elves must have remained in Middle-earth. Of these, the highest and most well-known was Galadriel, and for some reason, she didn't hang around Lindon for too long. So Galadriel may have been in Eregion when Sauron came sniffing around. Actually, that's what the discarded history says, since she and Celeborn were (according to this account) the original rulers of Eregion.

Sauron devoted his attention to "Celebrimbor and his fellow-smiths, who had formed a society or brotherhood, very powerful in Eregion, the Gwaith-i-Mirdain; but he worked in secret, unknown to Galadriel and Celeborn". In this account, Christopher Tolkien's summary of an outline which was itself never fully published, Celebrimbor and the Gwaith-i-Mirdain had many professional secrets. They didn't share their knowledge freely with other Noldor.

The Noldor, the Fëanorians in particular, were very secretive even in Valinor. They were a factious lot who couldn't seem to get along with each other. Even their Avari cousins, the Tatyar, seem to have been more divided than the Nelyarin Avari (who were related to the Teleri, the Eldar from whom came the Sindar). Fëanor never revealed many of his secrets to other Elves. So when he died a lot of his lore died with him. Of course, a lot of the ancient lore was lost in the Wars of Beleriand anyway. Celebrimbor and the boys may have been the last heirs of the great secrets of the First Age. Or they may have been a group of revivalists, borrowing as much as they could from the Dwarves and figuring out things on their own.

The end result was that the Rings of Power were originally a secret project. Most Elves didn't know anything about them. Sauron's early overtures must have seemed rather vague, playing on doubts and concerns of a very general nature. It would not be until he could have a long heart-to-heart talk with Celebrimbor about the Elves' future that Sauron would be able to spring the Big Plan on the Elven lord. And it's not like Celebrimbor should have been stupid. In fact, he was probably one of the most intelligent Elves of the early Second Age. His keen knowledge and insight, coupled with his brilliance, would have made him a crucial target for Sauron's deception.

And that deception seems to have required centuries to work. Sauron must have very patiently taught the Gwaith-i-Mirdain many secrets about the making of things before he won their full trust. Tolkien offers us only a glimpse of the kind of artifacts the Elves were capable of making: the boats of Lórien, the ropes and cloaks of the Silvan Elves, Galadriel's basin. These were most likely humble, everyday enchantments, things of little interest to the master smiths. The Palantiri, created in Valinor, might have been the sort of artifacts the Gwaith-i-Mirdain would have pursued. Or perhaps they endeavored to recreate the Silmarils, even though the Light of the Two Trees was preserved only in the light of the Sun, Moon, and the Star of Ëarendil.

Elrond's explanation of the motives of the Ring-makers implies they were very noble in their goals: "those who made [the rings] did not desire strength or domination or hoarded wealth, but understanding, making, and healing, to preserve all things unstained." We understand the desire "to preserve all things unstained". The Elves wanted to create a little bit of Valinor in Middle-earth by holding back the effects of Time. But "understanding, making, and healing" seem a bit out of place. What needed to be understood, what needed healing, that all the natural talents of the Elves weren't sufficient to understand or heal?

Tolkien implies in one essay that it was Middle-earth itself which required healing. It was tainted, stained by Melkor, and damaged by the War of Wrath. Perhaps the Gwaith-i-Mirdain hoped to devise something which would cleanse the Melkor-element from Middle-earth. How tragically ironic it was that they relied upon that very element to create the Rings.

There is another story concerning Galadriel and Celebrimbor. This is the tale of the Elessar, the green stone which Galadriel gave to Aragorn on behalf of Arwen. The story is, of course, unfinished, and Tolkien changed his mind about many details. Ultimately, Celebrimbor was to become a smith of Gondolin (but the story was composed before Celebrimbor was incorporated into the family of Fëanor) who made two Elessars. One was borne into the West by Ëarendil and the second one replaced the first and came to Aragorn (Cf. "The Elessar" in "The History of Galadriel and Celeborn", *Unfinished Tales*).

The Elessars' power was concerned with healing and preservation, and the second Elessar is said to be Celebrimbor's greatest creation after the Rings of Power. It must have been a very potent device, and Aragorn's ability to heal many people in Gondor must therefore be attributed in some measure to his possession of the Elessar.

Thus it seems that the Gwaith-i-Mirdain spent a lot of their time constructing magical items which the Elves used to heal or preserve small parts of Middle-earth, or otherwise to enhance their native talents. Sauron's help would have enhanced the effectiveness of their devices. For a while they may have turned out the lesser rings, mere "essays in the craft before it was full-grown", as Gandalf put it. He describes them as being "of various kinds, some more potent and some less". The "various kinds" phrase is curious. Perhaps it implies that the lesser rings only had very specific powers or properties, whereas the Great Rings, the Rings of Power, possessed many properties.

A preoccupation with preservation and healing would have given Sauron an inside line with the Elves. He could introduce them to more and more ideas, help them advance their goals in frustrating little leaps. And then, one day, he would be able to implant the idea of creating massively powerful artifacts. I don't think Sauron would have proposed the idea directly. The Elves seem to have been enthusiastic about the project, and therefore they may have believed it was their own idea. The deception would be more clever that way. But it would also seem less manipulative, on the surface, if Sauron were merely to support the Elves in their own endeavors, rather than give them explicit instruction in what should be done.

And so there must have been a fair amount of talking and planning. Scoping out the goals of the project alone could have taken months or years. Why? Because the Gwaith-i-Mirdain probably didn't want anyone to know what they were doing. The moral implications of what they hoped to attempt, to delay the effects of Time itself, would not have been wholly understood. The Rings of Power represented a new technology, whose impact upon society had not yet been measured -- a society which, at the time, was dominated by the Elves themselves.

Furthermore, the secret nature of the project must have demanded that as few people as possible be privy to it. It may be that no more than seventeen Elves knew about the Rings: Celebrimbor and sixteen other Gwaith-i-Mirdain, perhaps comprising the entire membership of the society. Many people say it's better to seek forgiveness than to ask permission. The Noldor in particular seemed to favor that philosophy. When the time came to decide whether to make the attempt, Celebrimbor and his companions may have had long discussions about the moral consequences of doing anything. Perhaps in the end they justified their final decision by weighing all the good they hoped to achieve against the possible harm they were risking. After all, no one even suspected that Sauron might betray them.

So, until the Rings were made, the Gwaith-i-Mirdain may have had good reason not to reveal what was going on to anyone outside their brotherhood. The Rings, as they were produced, would have seemed just like "normal" rings to other Elves, if they could be perceived at all. The veil of secrecy would have been burdened with shame and guilt once the Elves realized Sauron had betrayed them. Imagine how Celebrimbor must have felt, knowing he had forged the Rings in secret, upon learning that Sauron was Melkor's old servant, now arrayed with his own Master Ring. Whether Tolkien would have retained Celebrimbor's rebellion (which is recorded in the discarded history of Galadriel and Celeborn) or would have changed the story, Celebrimbor would have had to confront Galadriel with the truth. Something terrible had happened, but something much worse was about to befall the Elves.

So, once Galadriel knew about the Rings, she counseled Celebrimbor to hide them. The Elves couldn't find it in their hearts to destroy their own works. Two Rings were given to Gil-galad, who must have been told everything. Whatever his feelings might have been about Celebrimbor's foolishness, he, too, elected not to destroy the Rings. The fear of fading must have been pervasive in Noldorin society. So one must ask if Elrond was told at first, or Cirdan? On the one hand, Celebrimbor, Galadriel, and Gil-galad must have known there would be a war. Sauron had just attempted to enslave the greatest and most powerful of the Noldor. He had failed, his cover was blown, and the Elves knew that Middle-earth had a Dark Lord once again. It wasn't the sort of situation which required Sauron to lie low until the storm blew over.

For his part, Gil-galad asked the Númenoreans for help. But he didn't tell them about the Rings. Tolkien mentions this omission in Elf-Dunadan relations: "I do not think Ar-Pharazôn knew anything about the One Ring. The Elves kept the matter of the Rings very secret, as long as they could...." (*The Letters of J.R.R. Tolkien*, No. 211) So Gil-galad's plea to Númenor must have been very carefully worded. He had previously called upon Númenor for help while Sauron was fumbling around Middle-earth, stirring up evil creatures. Before Sauron decided to settle in Mordor, Gil-galad was only aware that some evil power was organizing men and Morgoth's old servants. But he couldn't find a source for his concerns. Sauron's unmasking as the maker of the One Ring confirmed Gil-galad's worst fears. At the very least, he had justification for starting a war with Sauron.

Númenor sent men and supplies to Middle-earth and, over the course of 100 years, the Númenoreans built up forts and stockpiles along the Lhun and Gwathlo rivers (Cf. "The History of Galadriel and Celeborn", *Unfinished Tales*). The overall strategy appears to have been a defensive one. The Elves knew a war was coming but they didn't know when. Sauron was powerful but he didn't control Middle-earth the way Morgoth had. And Númenor didn't yet command the huge armies and navies it would one day muster. A pre-emptive strike was apparently not considered. Perhaps Gil-galad didn't yet know where Sauron's domain lay. Mordor doesn't seem so far from Eriador when one looks at the map, but there was a great distance of 1000 miles between Barad-dur and Lindon. And Gil-galad may not yet have known in which direction even to start looking.

So the Elves said nothing to their allies about the Rings of Power, or what the war was really about. It may have suited their policy of secrecy to let Sauron strike first. They would then be justified in calling upon Númenor for even more help. The Elves would be the aggrieved party. They already were, considering that Sauron had tried to enslave the Gwaith-i-Mirdain. But the grievance was morally weak. What business did the Noldor have fooling around with Time anyway?

But more importantly, Gil-galad seems not to have shared the truth with his people. I doubt very many of his advisors would have known about the Rings. Some of the Noldor might have decided to just throw Celebrimbor and the Gwaith-i-Mirdain to the Wargs, rather than spend their blood in another insane war.

Of course, the more people who know a secret, the less of a secret it is. Gil-galad had several potential captains to send east to reinforce Eregion. Why did he choose Elrond? Cirdan was an ancient lord of the Eldar, experienced in the Wars of Beleriand (in fact, he was the only field commander to survive the wars). Glorfindel had returned to Middle-earth to help in the war, according to a brief essay Tolkien wrote late in his life (Cf. "Of Glorfindel", *The Peoples of Middle-earth*). He would also have been a good choice to send to Eregion. But it was Elrond whom Gil-galad sent. I would guess that Elrond must have been present when Celebrimbor told Gil-galad about the Rings. He was close to Gil-galad, and therefore would be the only captain Gil-galad could trust with the knowledge of the Rings. Not that Gil-galad's nobles would have been rebellious, but why burden them with guilt that wasn't theirs? And Elrond was a descendant of Finwë. Gil-galad may have been more willing to trust a close kinsman than most of his advisors.

But if even Gil-galad's silence was damning, what could or should Celebrimbor have told the Elves of Eregion? Many of them seem to have escaped, either through Moria or by fleeing overland. Yet, did they know what the war was all about? Did Celebrimbor ever tell his people what had happened? I don't think so. The tragedy of Celebrimbor's folly would be heightened if his shame forbade him to confess what he and the Gwaith-i-Mirdain had done. If they weren't telling the Dunedain anything for secrecy's sake, then it would be best not to tell the people of Eregion anything, either. And so that means the Dwarves of Moria couldn't have known what the war was about. All anyone would be told was that the big bad Dark Lord was coming.

And come he did. Sauron swept north and attacked everything in sight. He didn't just invade Eregion, he also moved up into the Vales of Anduin and the lands east of Greenwood the Great. The Northmen were driven into the woods and mountains. Their culture was virtually wiped out (Cf. "Dwarves and Men", *The Peoples of Middle-earth*). Many Elves must have perished as well. Eregion fell quickly and Sauron laid it waste. As many Elves as escaped, many more must have suffered horrible deaths as Sauron searched desperately for the Rings of Power. If he couldn't have the Elves as his slaves, he certainly wouldn't want them to have their Valinor-in-Middle-earth!

The defense of Ost-in-Edhil (Eregion's chief city) would have been particularly bitter. In one version of the history of these events, we are told that Celeborn led out a sortie (Cf. "The History of Galadriel and Celeborn", *Unfinished Tales*). The purpose of the sortie isn't really stated, but it might imply that Celebrimbor recognized the hopelessness of the situation. Celeborn could have been given command of the most innocent Elves, whereas the Gwaith-i-Mirdain and their followers would have stayed behind and held the city. Celebrimbor's last stand might have been an attempt to atone for what he had done. But instead of dying in battle and taking the secrets of the Rings with him, he was driven back to the steps of the House of the Mirdain (*Ibid.*). Sauron must have given orders that Celebrimbor be taken alive at all costs. Imagine the Orcs sacrificing themselves, much as their ancestors did in taking Hurin after the Nirnaeth.

The loss of Eregion most likely meant that all of the Gwaith-i-Mirdain perished, and their secret shame was preserved only by the few Eldarin lords who knew the full score. The Gwaith are never mentioned again, in any writing. It is interesting to note that another society, or "school", the Lambengolmor (Masters of Languages), survived the war. Their last member was Pengolod, who lived in Eregion. He escaped, and after the war he took ship and left Middle-earth. The destruction of Eregion seems to imply that many other ancient and scholarly groups also perished, or suffered so terribly that their survivors left when they could. At the beginning of the table for the Third Age in "The Tale of years" (Appendix B, *The Lord of the Rings*), Tolkien says that the Eldar attempted nothing new in the Third Age. It may simply be there was no one left who was accomplished enough in the ancient sub-creative arts to create new artifacts.

In the wake of the war, Gil-galad had to rebuild his realm. Lindon survived but undoubtedly suffered much loss. Elrond had also survived. He never succeeded in reinforcing Celebrimbor, but was instead driven north (perhaps with Celeborn). Elrond had rounded up as many Men and Elves as he could, and held out in Imladris. In that time many grieving people would have asked, "Why? Why did this war happen?" And Elrond would not have been able to answer them. Yet he had to know the truth. His defense was stalwart and brave, but it was perhaps strengthened by a resolution born of guilt and a desire to atone for the terrible decisions Celebrimbor -- his kinsman -- had made. In a way, the War of the Elves and Sauron marks a final loss of innocence for the Noldor. In the First Age, those Noldor who were born in Beleriand knew their history and heritage. In the Second Age, no one really knew the score. It was too dangerous to tell anyone. The Rings seem to have all had a very debilitating effect on the judgement of the people who knew of them. Neither Galadriel nor Gil-galad, who had nothing to do with the Rings' making, could find the strength to destroy the Three.

After the war, Gil-galad convened a council at Imladris. Perhaps there he finally revealed to other Elven lords what had actually happened. Tolkien doesn't tell us who attended, but it's possible that even the Númenoreans were excluded from the council. Númenor wasn't yet really concerned with Middle-earth. Gil-galad would have thanked and rewarded the Númenoreans profusely, to be sure, but he didn't tell them about the Rings of Power. It would have been assumed that Sauron had found the Nine and Seven, since none of the surviving Elves possessed them. It doesn't seem likely that the Elves could foresee what Sauron intended to do with the Rings. Why would they remain silent if they knew Men and Dwarves might be ensnared? And yet, Gil-galad and his advisors must have realized that Sauron could achieve terrible things with such potent devices. So they must have taken a "wait and see" posture.

But the Eldar's decision to tell no one about the Rings only compounded the errors of the Gwaith-i-Mirdain. For now Sauron was able to prey upon Dwarves and Men with impunity. Of course, many people ask how Sauron could still move around without being labeled public enemy number one. The answer is simple: He must have assumed a new guise. Tolkien wrote that his fair form was one of splendor, man-like, yet larger than that of a man. He seemed gigantic. Still, he could have taken the form of a dwarf or a humble Druadan. He could have approached virtually anyone in the perfect disguise, won their trust, and finally bestowed a Ring upon them. Or, worse, he might have enticed people into seeking lost Elven treasures. Both Men and Dwarves were willing to seek treasure. They had proven that before. So the sixteen captured Rings of Power could have been very cleverly left in secret places for a chosen handful of lords of Men and Dwarves to find. And they would not have told anyone of their discoveries.

The veil of secrecy thus worked toward Sauron's ends. He may have failed to enslave the Dwarven lords who took the Seven Rings, but he was still able to corrupt their hearts. The nine Men who took Rings of Power turned into wraiths and became Sauron's most terrible servants. Men scattered across Middle-earth wouldn't have known what to make of these Ringwraiths, but the Númenoreans would have remembered that Sauron of old was a master of phantoms and sorcery. The Dark Servants would not necessarily have been called Ringwraiths. They might have been perceived as wraiths, or demons, or something else.

As the Second Age rushed on, the Númenoreans became more powerful, but then they became divided over the consequences of Elros' choice to remain a mortal man. Many Númenoreans longed for the immortality of the Elven race, and they eventually turned away from the Elves in bitter envy and jealousy. So, even if Gil-galad might have contemplated revealing the secret of the Rings to his allies, the growing antipathy toward Elves among the Kings and their followers would have discouraged such a policy. Why throw wood on a growing fire? The Númenoreans could just as easily have blamed the Elves for their troubles as not.

And yet the Faithful Númenoreans stood by the Elves. They even colonized lands near Gil-galad's kingdom so they could continue to enjoy the companionship of the Elves. How often could Gil-galad and Elrond have looked into the eyes of Men who greeted them with full trust and friendship, who knew nothing about the Rings? Centuries of such friendship must have proven to be a great burden to them.

At last, after Númenor was destroyed and everyone hoped Sauron might be dead for all time, he reappeared with an army and attacked Gondor. Isildur carried word of the assault to Arnor, and there Elendil consulted with Gil-galad. Obviously Sauron wasn't going to be easy to kill, but the Dunedain knew their history. There was apparently no record of any Maia returning to life in the First Age. Death for them was a very potent experience, too. How could Sauron have survived? Imagine the guilty faces which must have confronted Elendil and Isildur if they posed these questions to Gil-galad and his counselors. Hey, guys, you're not telling us everything, are you?

So the Last Alliance of Elves and Men had to be formed on the basis of absolution. That is, Gil-galad had to tell Elendil and Isildur what was going on. And for their part, Elendil and Isildur had to forgive Gil-galad. Not just for themselves, but for countless generations of Men who couldn't speak for themselves. In addition, they had to figure out what became of the missing Rings of Power. The Nazgul had been known of for nearly a thousand years. In that time, the Eldarin lords who knew about the Rings of Power must have wondered if there was a connection. In fact, when the nine Men who became wraiths were still alive, Tolkien says they were great kings and sorcerors. If they were famous, did the Elves hear about their strange powers? Was there any curiosity about them?

It would have been difficult for Gil-galad to learn much about the Rings of Power. If he and Galadriel couldn't find the knowledge they required through some sort of spying (as she did with her mirror in Lórien in the Third Age), they would either have to tell their spies and scouts what to look for, or they'd have to just wait and piece together bits and pieces of information through the centuries.

Some readers are of the opinion that the Ring-rhyme in *The Lord of the Rings* must have been composed soon after the War of the Elves and Sauron. But whomever composed the rhyme would have to know what the fates of the Seven and the Nine were. So far, there is no way to show that the Elves knew anything about the Seven before they were free to talk to the Dwarves. The Dwarves certainly weren't running around telling people they had magic Rings. So the nine sorceror-kings who arose among Men would have been conspicuous only in their longevity and their approximate contemporary lifetimes. And yet, if the Elves were looking for signs of Rings of Power, they would have been looking for sixteen, not nine, or seven, Rings. The fact that Sauron perverted the Rings before he gave them out would further complicate matters for the Elves. Gil-galad may not have really understood what was going on until Durin IV was invited into the alliance.

We don't know for sure that Durin IV was the King of the Longbeards at the end of the Second Age, but there is a little evidence pointing to that being his name. And the manner of his entering the alliance isn't provided. It seems that Gil-galad and Elendil formed their alliance and then marched to Imladris. From there, they seem to have sent out messengers to Greenwood, Lórien, Khazad-dum, and perhaps a few other regions. I would say it's most likely that Gil-galad had a second "white council" at Imladris. It would have been as momentous as the Council of Elrond three thousand years later, perhaps more so. For there would have been kings in attendance, and many lords and princes. And it would have to be the first time ever that the Elves spoke openly about the Rings of Power to all their allies.

It would be natural for the attendees to want to know why they should join the alliance. Sauron had been terrorizing Middle-earth for a long time. But his death in Númenor and reappearance 100 years later implied that he wasn't just going to go away. And because the problem with the Rings originated in Middle-earth, it may be that any appeals to Valinor would have fallen on deaf ears. The Elves created the problem and they needed to resolve it. But they couldn't do that alone. And it would serve no purpose for the various non-Eldarin kings to deliver recrimination after recrimination. Especially since Celebrimbor and the Ringmakers were all dead. The people truly responsible for the problem had already paid with their lives, and their legacy was becoming an equal burden on everyone.

But if the Elves could stand forth and admit what they had done, perhaps the Dwarves were moved to confess that their ancestors had been given Rings. It may be that Gil-galad was able, with Durin's help, to bring all seven Dwarf lords to Imladris. And hearing that the Elves had betrayed everyone not once, but twice, most of the Dwarves may have elected to stand aside. They would keep their Rings, which obviously didn't prolong their lives, or turn them into wraiths. And they would let the world decide its own affairs. That seems a very Dwarvish attitude. Only the Longbeards developed any real affinity for the Eldar. Durin's folk had been joined by the Belegostians, who had also been friendly with the Eldar, but the Nogrodians had an ancient grudge against the Eldar. The four eastern groups may have been in the minority, but they certainly had little if any connection to the Elves and Dunedain.

So, it must be that the Ring-rhyme was devised during the early years of the Last Alliance. Most likely it was composed at Imladris, soon after (if not during) whatever council Gil-galad held with the other rulers of Middle-earth. The Nazgul's nature and possession of the missing Nine Rings would have to be inferred, but it was by this time certain who had the Rings. And Middle-earth's best-kept secret was no longer really a secret. Yet Gil-galad would not have divulged who possessed the Three Rings. For safe-keeping he gave his two Rings to Elrond and Cirdan. Yet the Ring-rhyme says that the Three were bestowed upon Elven-kings. The rhyme-composer therefore could not have known where the Three were. He (or she) must have believed that Gil-galad, Oropher, and Amdir had the Three. Conveniently, all three died in the war, and no one claimed the Three from their bodies. So the Elves and their allies must have been thrown into doubt about who had the Three soon after Gil-galad's death. And that doubt would have been reflected in the Ring-rhyme if it had been composed after Gil-galad's death.

And this brings us to the Third Age. The Last Alliance was victorious, and the victors always write the histories of wars. Scholars in Arnor, Gondor, Khazad-dum, and other lands must have recorded many things about the war. Arnor's libraries were eventually lost or destroyed. Gondor's wisdom declined, and most of its people forgot the greater part of their history. Khazad-dum was taken over by a Balrog, and most of Durin's Folk were scattered or slain. Yet a few people preserved a knowledge of ancient events here and there. If most of the Men of Arnor and Gondor at one time understood what the War of the Last Alliance was about, they would have passed on the knowledge. For there were still Rings of Power out there, and they were perilous things.

At the end of the Third Age, Gandalf had few resources to consult on matters of Ring-lore, but Saruman had been the specialist. He could have found many archives to which Gandalf didn't have access during the two thousand years he was in Middle-earth. And Elrond must have had many conversations with Saruman about the Rings and those who made them. He undoubtedly knew Celebrimbor personally, and may have known some of the other Ring-smiths. Other members of Elrond's household, or perhaps nearby Elven lords, such as Gildor Inglorion, may have been able to tell Saruman things about Sauron's sojourn in Eregion. Something Tolkien doesn't tell us is whether Saruman accumulated his own library in Orthanc, after he settled there, with copies of books and scrolls preserving Ring-lore.

It would have been useful to study Ring-lore to be able to figure out who the next bad guys might be. Saruman (and the Eldar) couldn't have known whether Sauron had taken back the Rings of Power from the Nazgul, not until Gandalf discovered that Sauron was gathering all the Rings in 2851. But the Dwarven Rings were vanishing. Were they being consumed by dragons, or falling into the hands of adventurers? And what were the full capabilities of the Rings? Saruman's knowledge would have been very useful to the Eldar and the Istari, for they needed to understand what Sauron had done to the Rings. And they needed to know who could wield them, as well.

Ultimately, knowledge of the Rings would have receded into the musty corners of the elite. Middle-earth's scholars tended to come from the wealthier families. And matters of ancient lore, which might one day affect the welfare of nations, would be carefully hoarded and cultivated by the lords of those nations. Denethor was master of many secrets, and he seemed to be fully aware of what the Ring was. The exchange Gandalf reports at Elrond's council gives one the impression that Denethor didn't know about the scroll of Isildur, but I'm not convinced. Gandalf wasn't exactly sharing his concerns with Denethor, so why should Denethor have shared what he knew about the Rings? Denethor had no reason to volunteer information which he didn't know Gandalf was seeking.

Faramir, of course, was devoted to Gandalf, and may very well have been with Gandalf as the wizard was scrambling through the ancient records. If Gandalf trusted Faramir to be discreet, then the prince may very well have seen the scroll Gandalf was most interested in, and therefore he may have studied it. So, when Faramir met Frodo and Sam, he was able to talk knowledgeably about the One Ring. He didn't necessarily divulge all he knew at first, but Faramir seems to have very readily agreed to Gandalf's plan. Why so? Unless he had been taught the full history of the War of the Last Alliance, Faramir should have been pretty clueless. Boromir reveals he knew about the Ring at Elrond's council, but he is surprised to learn that Isildur took it. It is his statement that "if ever such a tale was told in the South, it has long been forgotten" which leads us to believe that no one in Gondor remembers the One Ring.

The answer must be that Boromir only paid attention to the facts of the case. That is, he was probably only interested in the neato gizmos of power, and not the motivations which led to their creation, nor the events which surrounded them. Boromir was a warrior at heart and not really much of a scholar. So Boromir makes a poor first impression on the reader insofar as the scholarship of Gondor is concerned. Faramir tells Frodo and Sam that he and his brother were taught the story of their city and sires, and that the Stewards preserved much ancient lore which only a few people ever accessed.

The fact of the One Ring's existence, (and of the existence of a general group of magic "Rings of Power") was thus, if not common knowledge, then still well-known to the rulers and elite classes of Middle-earth at one time. Even Gloin seems to know something of the Rings when he speaks at Elrond's council, though he knows less about the Elven Rings than he implies. It may be that Dain opened up

Erebor's library and gave Gloin a briefing, but Gloin was Dain's cousin, a member of the royal family. It seems unlikely that he would have been completely excluded from the family's records. He probably knew as much about the general history of the Rings of Power as most scholarly nobles of his day.

Knowledge of the Rings of Power would not have been available among the "younger" peoples and nations. The Northmen were ancient, but their cultures had evolved and diverged through the long years of the Third Age. The Rohirrim didn't keep written records, and they weren't interested in ancient matters except where their ancestors figured as the heroes of songs. The Men of Dale and the Woodmen of Mirkwood, even if they did keep a few records, didn't really have the ancient history to sustain a full account of the Rings of Power. Arnor and its successor realms, Arthedain, Rhudaur, and Cardolan, had fallen. All that remained were the Breelanders, the Hobbits of the Shire, and Aragorn's people. And the Hobbits weren't very concerned with history at all, let alone ancient history.

And as the centuries passed, the Rings became less and less important to the peoples of Middle-earth. Sauron wanted them, and the White Council knew they still posed a threat to the Free Peoples. But there were no new quests to find them, as the people who knew of the Rings understood that such things were perilous. Or at least they should have known that great and terrible wars had been fought over the Rings in the past. The full history was probably known only to Elrond, Galadriel, and Cirdan, and most likely to Saruman and Gandalf. Maybe a few other members of the White Council knew the full account as well. For everyone else, there were bits and pieces of lore handed on generation after generation.

Hence, when Mordor's first assault upon Gondor had been defeated, and Aragorn and Gandalf met with Eomer and the lords of Gondor and Rohan, they were able to speak freely about the One Ring. Gandalf even seems to have confided to Theoden a little something about the Ringbearer's quest when he took the aged king aside and spoke to him. It was enough to mention the One Ring. The lords knew what Gandalf was speaking of. They understood that a great and powerful talisman was being risked. They understood, essentially, that the entire war was really being fought over the Ring.

One could say that generations of nobles must have passed on the barest knowledge of the Rings of Power in an almost religious devotion. When all other lore of ancient days was lost or forgotten amid unreadable scrolls, men remembered to tell their sons that, at one time, there was a Dark Lord who had a very terrible Ring. And that Ring was unlike all other magical things in Middle-earth. The knowledge persisted where it was needed most, so that when the time came, it served to strengthen the resolve of the men who had to stand up to the Dark Lord and laugh in his face, while a couple of Hobbits scampered up the side of Orodruin. No one really needed to understand the history of the Rings to remember that they existed. People were aware of them in a vague, general way. But the long years and the devastations wreaked upon Men, Elves, and Dwarves had served to make secret again the ancient shame of the Eldar.

Chapter 17:
Make room for dragons

People sometimes ask why there are no dragon stories from the Second Age. In the development of Middle-earth, the Second Age was almost an after-thought, and it didn't really call for dragons, although we have to assume for the sake of the pseudo-history that they were always there, in the background, waiting for an opportunity to make their appearance.

Dragons, like so many other literary devices, appear only rarely in the pages of Tolkien's fiction. Only two dragons are featured prominently in the tales: Glaurung and Smaug. Glaurung had a high purpose. He was one of the prime characters in the tragic story of the children of Hurin. Smaug, on the other hand, was just an adventure. A goal for the Hobbit and Dwarves to reach. In the earliest versions of *The Hobbit*, all which came after Smaug's death was quickly summarized. The dragon was the capstone of the story.

There are two more named dragons in Tolkien's Middle-earth tales: Ancalagon the Black and Scatha the Worm. Ancalagon has no real story attached to him. Or, rather, he is barely more than a footnote in a much longer tale, *The Silmarillion*. He appears briefly in a final assault upon the Host of Valinor before Ëarendil slays him in the sky, culminating a night-long battle. Scatha is the core of a story told only as an anecdote about the Northman hero Fram, who slays the dragon and recovers a hoard taken from the Dwarves. Scatha's death does not end Fram's tale, however, for the Dwarves demand that he return their hoard and he refuses, so they kill him (or arrange for his death).

Fram's story is unique. Túrin mortally wounds Glaurung in the early hours of the morning and then kills himself soon afterward; Ëarendil slays Ancalagon in the dawn skies and then retreats into legend; Bard the Bowman slays Smaug in the night and goes on to become King of Dale. We know nothing about Fram's encounter with Scatha, and he does not end either tragically, mythologically, or gloriously like his fellow dragon-slayers. He simply meets his death and the history of his people continues.

There is, however, a certain symmetry in these four dragon stories. Both Glaurung and Ancalagon served Morgoth, whereas Scatha and Smaug were at the very least semi-independent, if not completely independent of Sauron. Tolkien provides only one comment, in "The Quest of Erebor", where Gandalf tells Frodo and other members of the Fellowship of the Ring that "the Dragon Sauron might use with terrible effect". The clear implication is that Sauron either possessed or could have achieved some measure of control over Smaug, when he was ready to launch his final war against the northern world.

Nonetheless, one may entertain the strong impression that dragons were drifting away from the Dark Lords and assuming their own priorities by the end of the Third Age. In fact, after the Downfall of Sauron in the War of the Ring, dragons had to assume their own priorities.

But what happened with the beasties in the Second Age? There are no dragons in Númenor, and they are not mentioned in the brief accounts of the War of the Elves and Sauron or the War of the Last Alliance of Elves and Men. If there were dragon stories for the Second Age, what would be their purpose, and who would be their heroes?

In 1949 Tolkien wrote to Naomi Mitcheson, "I find 'dragons' a fascinating product of imagination. But I don't think the Beowulf one is frightfully good. But the whole problem of the 'intrusion' of the dragon into northern imagination and its transformation there is one I do not know enough about. Fafnir in the late Norse versions of the Sigurd story is better; and Smaug and his conversation obviously is in debt here." (*The Letters of J.R.R. Tolkien*, No. 122)

He didn't view dragons as an innate part of northern myth, and it's true that dragons occur in the earlier Greek mythologies which probably had some influence on northern mythology. Dragons were old when men were young, so to speak. And the men of Middle-earth became young again in the Second Age. The western Edain, wizened by their brush with Angband in the First Age, sailed over Sea to become the Númenoreans, High Men. Edainic peoples who stayed behind in Middle-earth enjoyed a millennium of peace and prosperity, in which they neither achieved anything great nor fell into darkness. They would have forgotten all they once knew about the darkness of the world, unless their Elven and Dwarven friends reminded them of the great wars of old.

So, is there room for dragons in the Second Age? The question beckons the imagination a bit hesitantly, because dragons are not only intrusive, they are disruptive. Glaurung led the way in turning the tide against the Eldar of Beleriand, and he destroyed Nargothrond. Smaug took out the Kingdom under the Mountain and Dale. When a dragon appears, heroes need to be close by and handy, or else all the world tumbles into darkness.

Dragonkind could not have troubled the northern world of the Eldar and the Edain prior to the War of the Elves and Sauron, but if we hear little about Lindon, Eriador, and Rhovanion in the Second Age, we hear virtually nothing about the far eastern lands of Middle-earth. We know only that the dragons fled east from the ruin of Angband, and did not trouble the world for many years after.

But if dragons settled in the Withered Heath and nursed their wounds, why did they not recover quickly? The tales of Glaurung and Smaug show these creatures were powerful and cunning. It may be that the early dragons depended upon Morgoth's evil will, and much like Sauron's Ring of Power their apparent autonomy of will was more a disassociated act of their master's malice. That is, the early dragons could have been reduced to an almost mindless state once Morgoth was gone.

Such creatures would be able to breed true, and having the capacity for intelligence would eventually have recovered it or developed it. But would that process have required 5,000 years? Or, can those of us who long for tales of courage and daring-do in the Second Age rationalize an adventure among the scaly beasts before Sauron could make full use of them?

Dragons could have migrated further east in the early part of the Second Age, spreading their primitive beastly terror among the distant and darkened lands where the Eldar and Dunedain had no contacts and all records perished. There dragons could have become fearsome demigods, through no wit of their own, among primitive men who would know no better than to think that Morgoth had sent them.

Sauron indeed began to organize the evil creatures which had once served Morgoth after about the fifth century of the Second Age. He stayed far away from Lindon and Eriador, but not so far that Gil-galad didn't hear rumor of someone or something moving in the shadows. When Gil-galad shared his concerns with Tar-Meneldur, the Elvenking wrote: "A new shadow rises in the East. It is no tyranny of evil Men, as your son believes; but a servant of Morgoth is stirring, and evil things wake again. Each year it gains in strength, for most Men are ripe to its purpose. Not far off is the day, I judge, when it will become too great for the Eldar unaided to withstand."

However, Gil-galad's letter reached Tar-Meneldur in the year 882, and Sauron did not even begin establishing Mordor as a stronghold until around the year 1000. "The Tale of Years" in *The Lord of the Rings* says that it was Sauron's alarm at the growing power of the Númenoreans which led him to make Mordor as his new home. The Númenoreans had not, by that time, established any permanent havens in Middle-earth. But Sauron must have foreseen the time was not far off when they would do just that.

It's all very vague and mysterious, and one wonders what the heck was going on in the wastelands of eastern Middle-earth. Aldarion, while he was still sailing to Middle-earth and scouting out the lands for Gil-galad, doesn't seem to have met any dragons. Tolkien surely would have mentioned such an encounter. And Aldarion doesn't seem to have strayed far from water anyway. His role was chiefly as an ambassador on behalf of Gil-galad, who sought out Men deliberately, to either forge alliances with them, or to gain knowledge about them and perhaps to forestall their succumbing to the influence of the dark power he had perceived as stirring in the east.

So if dragons were part of Sauron's scheme, they must not have been very effective for him in those early years. Why else did they not scrape the Elves off the scorched earth of Eriador? Dragons would have to be some sort of disappointment to Sauron, at least by the middle of the Second Age, or else they should have served him as a powerful weapon in his wars with the Elves.

On the other hand, we are led to believe that many tribes of Edainic Men and perhaps several Elven nations vanished from the lands east of the Misty Mountains in the War of the Elves and Sauron. Sauron did not simply march against Eregion. He launched a campaign against the Longbeard Dwarves and their Edainic allies which all but destroyed the northern peoples. The essay "Dwarves and Men" (*The Peoples of Middle-earth*) describes the war so:

> Very great changes came to pass as the Second Age proceeded. The first ships of the Númenoreans appeared off the coasts of Middle-earth about Second Age 600, no rumour of this portent reached the distant north. At the same time, however, Sauron came out of hiding and revealed himself in fair form. For long he paid little heed to the Dwarves or Men and endeavoured to win the friendship and trust of the Eldar. But slowly he reverted again to the allegiance of Morgoth and began to seek power by force, marshalling and directing the Orks and other evil things of the First Age, and secretly building his great fortress in the mountain-girt land in the South that was afterwards known as Mordor. The Second Age had reached only the middle of its course (c. Second Age 1695) when he invaded Eriador and destroyed Eregion, a small realm established by the Eldar migrating from the ruin of Beleriand that had formed an alliance also with the Longbeards of Moria. This marked the end of the Alliance of the Longbeards with Men of the North. For though Moria remained impregnable for many centuries, the Orks reinforced and commanded by servants of Sauron invaded the mountains again. Gundabad was re-taken, the Ered Mithrin infested and the communication between Moria and the Iron Hills for a time cut off. The Men of the Alliance were involved in war not only with Orks but with alien Men of evil sort. For Sauron had acquired dominion over many savage tribes in the East (of old corrupted by Morgoth), and he now urged them to seek land and booty in the West. When the storm passed, the Men of the old Alliance were diminished and scattered, and those that lingered on in their old regions were impoverished, and lived mostly in caves or in the borders of the Forest.

Who were these "servants of Sauron" who reinforced and commanded the Orks? They could not be Nazgul, for the Nazgul had not yet come to be. They might be lesser Maiar, but the War of Wrath seems to have depleted their ranks tremendously. Gil-galad's identification of the power in the East as a servant of Morgoth indicates that he, at least, believed one or more of Morgoth's former lieutenants had survived the war. Such a servant could only be immortal, and therefore had to be a lesser Maia. But Morgoth had once been served by multitudes of Maiar, and though few are named or described, their numbers were sufficient that the Valar seldom took direct action against them.

Some people speculate that the dragons might be incarnations of lesser Maiar, who also seem to have taken shape as were-wolves and vampires and Orcs. But dragons were powerful, and Morgoth bred them. Tolkien implied strongly that reproducing biologically weakened the Maiar, at least to the point where they lost the ability to change their shape (this point, discussed in a couple of Tolkien's late essays, including the "Osanwë-kenta", is not canonically established -- that is, it is not made in any of the primary texts). If the principle of diminishment through biological reproduction were true, then dragons could not be bred from lesser Maiar, for they seem to have increased in power in the Third Age.

It may be, therefore, that dragons could have fallen to a more primitive state in the Second Age, deprived of the will of Morgoth, and that Sauron made use of them in the East to establish his control over Men and Orcs. But though he would have used the power of the One Ring to control his servants by the time of the War of the Elves and Sauron, he may not have had sufficient time to raise dragons back to their primal state. If he utilized them in the war, then brave deeds by Elves, Dwarves, and Men against dragons could have reset the clock. That is, while still little more than great beasts, powerful and terrifying in their native state, dragons would not have possessed the cunning and malice of a Glaurung or Smaug.

Sauron could have miscalculated and simply used up his dragon-stock too soon, depriving himself of potential great servants and captains. Hence, if the dragons were reduced to weak and simple-minded creatures without Morgoth's will, the loss of great numbers of dragons in the War of the Elves and Sauron could have forced Sauron to turn his attention to other means of extending his power. By the end of the Second Age, when Sauron was moving against Gondor, dragons may no longer have fit into his plans.

So, one can easily surmise there must have been battles with dragons in the Second Age, perhaps even grand battles where the dragons served as powerful war beasts much like elephants in the classical world (or the Oliphaunts of the Southrons in *The War of the Ring*). But these dragons lacked the great intellect of the more powerful creatures of legend. They would eventually recover that malice and cunning, and breed true to their kind. But it would be thousands of years before they could achieve their comeback.

And so there should be no stories of great dragon-slayers from the Second Age. The dragons could not threaten the Eldar and the Dunedain, who were steeped in the lore of ages, great warriors, and capable of taking on the most dread of all Morgoth's servants. Dragons worked best for the dark lords when they had large numbers, and the Elves feared them, and Men could not withstand them. Without the guidance of Morgoth and Sauron, dragons must have learned to fend for themselves, much as the Orcs did. But whereas the Orcs could breed quickly and replenish their numbers, dragons may not have produced the numbers Sauron would have required to use them effectively.

Dragon-hunting should never have become a popular pastime among Elves and Men, but there had to be a reason dragons returned to or stayed in the far north for so long. Permitting a young warrior to kill a dragon as a rite of passage would belittle the power and terror of these marvelous monsters. Tolkien would never have written a story about a Man killing a weak and mindless dragon. Better to let the dragons sleep quietly in the shadows until they were ready to burst upon the world once again.

And perhaps that is what really happened to dragons. Like the Balrog under Moria, maybe they fled to holes in the far north and laid themselves down to sleep, and so passed through the Second Age unscathed, unused, and only began to rouse from their ancient slumber in the Third Age when Men and Dwarves accidentally woke them. Instead of declining into a primitive bestial state, the dragons waited until a time came when they could once again make their mark upon the world.

Chapter 18:
A History of the Last Alliance
of Elves and Men

The legend of Gil-galad and Elendil's war against Sauron at the end of the Second Age of Middle-earth has been the subject of much research and speculation among Tolkien's fans. As with all aspects of his mythology, the few mentions of this great struggle imply a depth which draws the imagination toward a fuller account which surely must have existed in the author's mind, if not in any of his extant writings. Most of us are familiar with the outline of the war, and many can sketch out the events in a general progression from the first assault on Minas Ithil to the final combat on Orodruin.

Yet so many questions remain that one must wonder if Tolkien himself did not ask them of himself. Who were the great princes and captains the memory of whose banners made Elrond pause and sigh at his council an Age later? Where did these armies come from, and what were their reasons for joining the Alliance? If we do not know their numbers, do we know anything at all of their battle order and progressions?

Perhaps.

Some of what follows is necessarily speculative. It cannot be otherwise for there are gaps in the record. Yet Tolkien sprinkled here and there pieces of information concerning this great war in which "all living things were divided...save the Elves only" (*The Silmarillion*, p. 294).

The final war of the Second Age brought together many peoples on both sides for a cataclysmic engagement which rivaled the great War of Wrath at the end of the First Age of the Sun. Although the Valar did not participate in this war, the conflict culminated a long and pendulous series of disputes between Sauron and the Elves and the

Men of Númenor. The war represented Sauron's last desperate grasp for power in Middle-earth in his ancient campaign to gain control over the Elves and Men.

The seeds of the war were laid down millennia before when Sauron, in the guise of "Aulendil" ("Annatar"), began approaching the Elves in an effort to seduce them[1]. Galadriel did not trust him, claiming to have known no such Maia in Valinor[2], and Gil-galad mistrusted him, having long sensed that some evil power had arisen in Middle-earth[3]. In fact, most of the Elven lords refused to treat with Sauron, except for the smith Celebrimbor, whose reasons for rejecting the counsel of Gil-galad are not given. But perhaps he had inherited the great pride of his house, and as the last surviving heir of Fëanor he rejected Gil-galad's advice in an act of rebellion.

Celebrimbor did not live to see the fruition of the seeds he helped Sauron plant and nurture in the Rings of Power. Although he came to understand his folly before the War of the Elves and Sauron, Celebrimbor perished when Sauron took Ost-in-Edhil[4]. Like Fëanor before him, Celebrimbor led the Noldor down a path the end of which he never saw, and their tragic history was both enriched and diminished because of the choices he made.

Because they aided Gil-galad during the War of the Elves and Sauron, the Dunedain became irrevocably enmeshed in the affairs of Middle-earth, earning Sauron's undying enmity. Within 100 years of the war the Dunedain began making permanent havens in Middle-earth: Lond Daer Ened, Pelargir, Umbar, and others now forgotten[5]. From these havens came at least three of the Nazgul, the Ringwraiths who by the year 2251 revealed themselves for the first time, leading Sauron's armies against his enemies[6].

The conflicts between the Dunedain and Sauron eventually dwarfed the ongoing struggle between Sauron and the Elves. While many of the Eldar fled Middle-earth, more and more Dunedain settled there, coming from both factions in Númenor: the King's Men and the Faithful. The Dunedain pursued conquests of their own, clashing with Sauron's lieutenants and earning his greater hatred[7]. Sauron's rivalry with the Dunedain led to his voluntary imprisonment in Númenor where he seduced the greater part of the Dunedain to his cause. Their fortresses in Middle-earth southward of Pelargir thus extended Sauron's true power, where before they had contested it.

Surviving the destruction of Númenor, Sauron returned to a Middle-earth much changed. Gil-galad had recovered his ancient power and extended his sway to new lands[8]. All the Elves were now apparently united in purpose and strengthened by the long peaceful respite his absence had given them. The Dunedain who survived the Downfall of Númenor were still divided into two groups, but the Faithful now established two kingdoms which though nurtured by Gil-galad's power provided Lindon with a stronger buffer against invasion than either Eregion or Imladris ever had.

Elendil's realm in Arnor was greater in size and strength than his sons' kingdom of Gondor. The Dunedain and the peoples they settled amongst dwelt between the Lhun and the Gwathlo rivers[9]. Elendil's people dwelt mostly between the Lhun and the Baranduin rivers, and between the Hills of Evendim and the North Downs[10]. Some also settled in Tyrn Gorthad and the South Downs. Tharbad, an ancient Dunadan outpost and port on the river Gwathlo, became a link between the two kingdoms with a fortress on either side of Gwathlo and a bridge spanning the river[11].

Other Men lived in Eriador besides the Dunedain. The Men of Bree, most northerly representatives of their race, were akin to most of the peoples of Minhiriath and Enedwaith as well as to the wild tribes of Ered Nimrais and Calenardhon who lived on Gondor's western frontier[12]. The hill-tribes who lived between Bruinen and Mitheithel may have been friendly to the Elves, but appear not to have acknowledged Elendil's authority. Nor did the tribes living in the north, members of the Forodwaith who later gave rise to the Lossoth and perhaps the Men of Carn Dum[13]. However, Elendil's people probably also included descendants of clans related to the Folk of Bor and Ulfang in the First Age[14].

Gondor's people came mostly from the Dunedain and their kin living in and near Pelargir, as well as along the coast of Belfalas. They built the new cities of Osgiliath, Minas Anor, and Minas Ithil, thinking that Sauron was no longer a threat[15]. Elendil's sons extended their sway northward into Calenardhon as well.

But the choice of location for their new cities implies the Black Númenoreans of the south were a cause for concern[16]. And though the ancient Elvish haven of Edhellond lay west of Gondor's heart, the dales of Ered Nimrais from Lamedon to the sources of the rivers Lefnui and Adorn were home to a race of men who had served Sauron in previous centuries[17]. When it became evident that Sauron had survived the Downfall of Númenor, Isildur formed an alliance with at least one group of these men, but their king feared Sauron too much to fulfill his oath.

There were other men in Enedwaith, akin to the mountain-folk of Ered Nimrais and the Men of Bree, who had long opposed Númenorean incursions. Their antipathy forced Gondor to construct the twin fortresses of Angrenost and Aglarond, which guarded the pass of Calenardhon against the west, rather than the east[18]. Thus the need for a strong garrison at Tharbad was underscored by the need for a strong guard over Enedwaith itself.

Although Sauron was a Maia of great power and wisdom, he seems to have underestimated the resolve and skill of his foes. Gil-galad, born in Beleriand in the First Age[19], was a native son of Middle-earth, ruling his people in the last remnant of Beleriand itself, now called Lindon. He may have seemed weak to Sauron, having taken no action against Morgoth in the First Age, and unable or unwilling to defeat Sauron's own armies in Eriador without the aid the Dunedain. But the strategy the Eldar had used in their war with Sauron was Gil-galad's, who led the victorious army of Lindon and Númenor in sweeping Sauron's forces from the north. As High King of the Elves of the West, he sent Elrond against Sauron in the early years of the War of the Elves and Sauron[20].

Beside Gil-galad stood Cirdan, most ancient of the Elven lords and wise with the bitter lessons learned in the long war against Morgoth. Cirdan had been the only Sindarin lord to ally himself with the Noldor against Morgoth in the War of the Jewels[21]. Since Gil-galad had dwelt with Cirdan from an early age, the Noldorin king must have been greatly influenced by Cirdan, who was as brave and valiant as any Elven king. In the Second Age he befriended the Dunedain, teaching them how to build and sail ships, and how to manage the harbors they made in Middle-earth[22]. Cirdan, too, saw deep into the hearts of others, and he never refrained from the necessity of opposing either Morgoth or Sauron. Cirdan must have seemed a formidable opponent to Sauron.

Elrond, being half-Elven, did not forget his ties to the Dunedain. He had marched with their fathers against Thangorodrim in the War of Wrath[23], and he was in Lindon when Vëantur first sailed to Middle-earth. He would have known Aldarion in his youth, the great mariner King of Númenor. Although he failed to break through Sauron's forces to relieve Eregion, Elrond had preserved many Elves and Men from death or capture in the War of the Elves and Sauron, and he withstood a lengthy siege. Descended of a powerful Maia and of both Sindarin and Noldorin kings, Elrond had been fostered by a son of Fëanor, had stood with the Host of Valinor at the breaking of Thangorodrim, and had been enhanced by Eönwë in wisdom and skill upon choosing to be of Elven-kind. As he was Gil-galad's vice-regent in Eriador[24], so Elrond may have represented the High King of the Elves of the West in his dealings with other Elven lords.

Oropher was probably the greatest of the other Elven lords. Proud and independent, a survivor of Doriath, his realm dominated southern Greenwood the Great beyond Anduin. Although unfriendly to both the Noldor and the Dwarves[25], he may have revered Elrond's Sindarin ancestry, and clearly saw the need for joining in the alliance against Sauron. Oropher was strong-willed and proud, however, and he refused to march under Gil-galad's banner, but held himself an equal[26].

Amdir, known also as Malgalad[27], was probably the least powerful of the Elven kings of the Second Age. He ruled fewer people than

Oropher yet was friendly toward the Noldor, taking many refugees from Eregion into his kingdom. He must also have been on friendly terms with the Dwarves of Khazad-dum, his neighbors and perhaps sometimes allies[28].

Isildur was the most rash of the Dunadan kings. He was proud and brave, renowned for his rescue of a sapling of Nimloth, the White Tree of Númenor, despite Sauron's precautions against such an attempt[29]. He boldly planted himself (and the sapling) in the Ephel Duath on Sauron's border. But Isildur may have been less a captain in war than his father and brother, and perhaps was not the leader of Men that Elendil was. Yet it was Isildur's city which Sauron singled out for the first assault, perhaps seeking revenge against the Dunadan lord for his deeds in Númenor.

Elendil the Tall was a mighty sea-captain, a master of lore, and as High King of the Dunedain-in-Exile assembled a great host of Men in Arnor. He seems to have had no disputes with subject peoples and allies, unlike Isildur, though the distance between Sauron and the peoples of Eriador surely made his influence there quite weak. Elendil was deeply affected by the destruction of Númenor, and by the loss of his father, Amandil.

After Isildur departed for Arnor, Anarion ruled Gondor alone, defending it against Sauron's forces[30]. Anarion seems to have commanded the entire southern campaign for the Alliance. He not only drove Sauron's armies back into Mordor, he eventually passed over the mountains himself.

Durin IV of Khazad-dum joined the Alliance as well[31]. Since his realm lay so close to Lorinand he must have mustered his army close to Amdir's. And yet, Oropher's reputed dislike for Dwarves may have forced Durin to march beside Gil-galad's army, perhaps even to stand as a fourth equal among the leaders of the full alliance: Gil-galad as lord of the Elves of the West, Elendil as lord of the Men of the West, Oropher as lord of the Elves of the East, and Durin as lord of the Dwarves of Khazad-dum (encompassing two or three Dwarven kindreds). Because the Dwarves of Nogrod and Belegost had long before swelled Khazad-dum's numbers, Durin's army may have been the largest Dwarf-host assembled to that time or any time since.

The actual war began with the assault upon Minas Ithil in SA 3429[32]. When the city was lost, Isildur and his family escaped to Osgiliath[33]. From there they sailed away, leaving Anarion to defend the realm. It may be that at this time Isildur stopped at Edhellond, and passed northward to Erech to call upon the King of the Mountains to fulfill the oath his predecessors had sworn; or, it may be at this time Isildur extracted the oath from the King, to be fulfilled later when the West was ready to march against Sauron[34].

In any event, Anarion apparently was not troubled by the men of Ered Nimrais, though he may have prudently mounted a watch against betrayal from the west. The presence of the Elven haven at Edhellond may have been a comfort to the Dunedain, however. Also, since Sauron had gathered his allies in Mordor, the armies of Herumor and Fuinur did not attack from the south. They must have passed north into Mordor through the Nargil Pass[35], or else they marched northward along the Ephel Duath to assist in the assault on Osgiliath.

Elendil and Gil-galad held a council in SA 3430 where the Alliance was formally created[36]. The council must have been quite a large gathering of lords from Arnor, Gondor, Lindon, and other lands. Besides Gil-galad and Elendil we can guess that Isildur and Cirdan were in attendance, and perhaps also Elrond, Celeborn, Galadriel, Gildor Inglorion, and Glorfindel[37]. Isildur's sons Elendur, Aratan, and Ciryon might also have been in attendance; at the very least Elendur was probably there.

There may also have been emissaries from the Vales of Anduin (if not Durin IV, Oropher, and Amdir themselves). Possible emissaries from the Elves would include Thranduil and Amroth. However, it may be that the Alliance originally included only Lindon, Arnor, Gondor, and Imladris.

The Alliance could only have had one military purpose: march upon Mordor and achieve a complete and total victory against Sauron. They knew they could beat him in the field, as this had been accomplished on more than one occasion in past wars. The real question must have been what they would do once they breached Sauron's defenses. How long could he hold out against the Alliance, and what would he be able to contrive against his enemies while besieged in Barad-dur? Sauron's forces were considerable, for he commanded not only the Orcs and Trolls, but also many Men, and his chief servants were the Nazgul.

Gil-galad and Cirdan marched east from Lindon in 3431[38]. Elendil had already mustered his army at Amon Sul and he waited there for the Elvish host[39]. But they stopped in Imladris for three years, apparently to train and equip their armies, and perhaps also to persuade Oropher, Amdir, and Durin to join the Alliance, if they had not yet done so[40]. In that time, Sauron must have established an army in the lands between Greenwood and Mordor[41]. Such a development certainly would have been persuasive with Oropher. It may be that during this time Elendil sent an army to Gondor to reinforce Anarion[42].

There were two probable lines of march for the Alliance armies when they finally began to move in 3434. It may be that Oropher and Amdir advanced down the eastern shore of Anduin, while Gil-galad, Elendil, and Durin passed west of Lorinand toward Parth Celebrant. Or perhaps Gil-galad and Elendil crossed the river by the Men-I-Naugrim, using the ford where there had once been an ancient bridge. Oropher could have preceded or followed them on their road south, and Amdir and Durin would have crossed Anduin via boats (much as Celeborn several thousand years later when he assaulted Dol Guldur).

Sauron probably met the Alliance forces somewhere near the Undeeps, but seeing that he was outnumbered he fell back, destroying the ancient Entish domain north of the Emyn Muil (later known as "The Brown Lands") in an attempt to slow the advance of the Alliance[43]. The retreat to Mordor must have been rapid, yet the Alliance was able to overtake Sauron's army on the Dagorlad. It may be that a cavalry force from Lindon[44] forced Sauron's army to halt and dig in north of Udun, and that the two forces arrayed themselves for battle over the course of one or more following days.

Although we have no record of the Battle of Dagorlad itself, we can infer some probable alignments. Gil-galad, being the leader of the Alliance (or, more likely, the most senior of the four "equals"), probably commanded the center. Since Elrond was Gil-galad's herald in this campaign, it may be that Gil-galad's flanks were commanded by Celeborn and Cirdan (or Glorfindel or Gildor Inglorion may have commanded a "Noldorin" flank).

We know that in the course of the battle Amdir's army was cut off from the main host and cut to pieces in the marshes[45]. Therefore we may suppose that Oropher took the right side of the field with Amdir holding the outer flank. In this way the "independent-minded" Silvan Elves would be in a position to support Gil-galad without being hemmed in by his own forces. Elendil and Durin may therefore have stood upon the left (east) side of the field.

What we cannot infer is whether Anarion, with the host of Gondor, was present at the Battle of Dagorlad. Had Sauron divided his forces during the preceding years to keep Anarion occupied? The only possible allies Anarion could have called upon would have been the Elves of Edhellond, said to be mostly of Nandorin or Sindarin origin[46]. They would not have constituted a large force at all and may have been only a contingent of Anarion's host.

Sauron's forces would have been drawn from the Orcs and Trolls, probably dwelling mostly in Mordor at that time; the Easterlings, perhaps quite primitive; the Haradrim, ruled by Black Númenoreans and including large numbers of such; and whatever Men may have lived in Mordor itself (if any). A few Dwarves are said to have fought for him as well, though nothing is mentioned of their home or kindred[47].

If Anarion was prevented from immediately joining Gil-galad by an army in the south, Sauron may have had only a few Haradrim at the Battle of Dagorlad. Thus, he may only have had two armies: the Easterlings and his own forces from Mordor and Harad. Sauron's left flank may have been the strongest part of his army, since he was able to drive in on Amdir's Silvan Elves, pushing them into the marshes[48].

It may be that the Easterlings did not stand on Sauron's right, but perhaps came against the eastern flank of the Alliance host (where may have stood the hosts of Arnor and Khazad-dum). This strategy would at least have afforded the left flank an opportunity to crush the Silvan Elves while the main host held Gil-galad's attention in the center.

Gil-galad may have played a cautious strategy, holding back from assaulting Sauron's line. Perhaps Sauron either drew Amdir out with a sortie or perhaps even launched the attack himself. The advantage in launching the attack would lie in Sauron's chance to split the Elven host and destroy the Silvan Elves. Since Amdir and more than half his army were killed, Sauron's forces in this area were quite effective. But since Sauron ultimately gave up the field[49], his right flank must have collapsed under the assault of the other Alliance armies. It may be that the entire force which engaged Amdir in the marshes was abandoned by Sauron in the retreat.

Although we don't know whether parts of Sauron's army survived the Battle of Dagorlad, we can be certain that his forces were greatly diminished. Yet he apparently was able to make one more stand outside the Barad-dur, for Oropher led a premature assault on Mordor[50]. The Silvan Elves may have been enraged by the slaughter that occurred in the marshes, and perhaps Oropher thought Sauron's forces were weaker than they were.

But though the Silvan Elves again suffered grievous losses[51], Gil-galad and the Alliance broke into Mordor, pushing Sauron all the way out of Udun and into Barad-dur, where they took up the seven-year siege. By this time Anarion must have brought Gondor's army into Mordor, perhaps passing through Ephel Duath to ensure Sauron could not escape to the south.

Sauron's defense of the Barad-dur was not passive. He sent out many sorties[52]. The fortress itself used missile weapons to inflict great losses on the armies of the Alliance, including the taking of Anarion's life in 3440[53].

Elrond's brief description of the last struggle between Sauron and his foes implies that Gil-galad had taken up a position on Orodruin. This seems to be quite a distance from Barad-dur, but it may be that during the years of the siege Gil-galad had to contend with forces outside the Barad-dur in the lands to the east and south. If so, then Orodruin would have made an excellent command post, but this would also imply that the armies of the Alliance (weakened by the battles in the north) must have been spread thin.

It thus seems that Sauron was either able to take Gil-galad by surprise or he led a last, massive charge against Orodruin. Once Sauron reached the slopes of the fiery mountain, only Elendil stood close enough to directly aid the Elf-king, though Elrond, Cirdan, and Isildur were closer than others. How did Sauron manage to get so close to Gil-galad? Did the Elven-king perhaps offer Sauron a challenge to single combat (like his grandfather Fingolfin had challenged Morgoth)? Did Sauron hope to murder Gil-galad and thus discourage his enemies?

In the event, Gil-galad fell before Sauron's assault and it was Elendil who struck the "mortal" blow that felled the Dark Lord. Sauron must nonetheless have retained enough strength and presence of mind to throw himself upon Elendil, since it was the heat of his body which killed the Dunadan king. Isildur then charged up the slope to cut the Ring from Sauron's hand, but did he do this knowing that Sauron's spirit would flee or was he immediately drawn to the Ring's power?

The final combat must have resulted in a near complete loss of will among the surviving Orcs and Trolls[54]. If any Easterlings or Haradrim continued to exist outside Barad-dur, they either fled or fought until they were destroyed, as happened among Sauron's forces at the end of the Third Age[55]. But the Barad-dur itself had to be razed, and fortresses were built in the Ephel Duath and Udun to maintain a watch on Mordor[56].

Most of the original leaders of the Alliance never saw the end they worked so hard to achieve: Gil-galad, Elendil, Oropher, Amdir, and Anarion all perished. The Elvish forces suffered grievous losses, as apparently did Arnor's host, too. Nothing is said of what happened to Khazad-dum's army and king.

One of the probable benefits of the war to the Free Peoples was a diminishment of the Black Númenoreans who, though not destroyed, were unable to establish a great kingdom like Gondor or Arnor (unless it were Umbar, which eventually was conquered). But one of the great costs of the war would have been the virtual ruin of the ancient Beleriandic civilization in Lindon. Cirdan's folk absorbed a remnant of Gil-galad's people into Mithlond and some may have settled in or near Imladris, but most of the survivors abandoned Middle-earth[57].

Arnor emerged from the struggle greatly weakened. Gondor, however, grew in power from that time onward, and for more than 1600 years maintained a watch upon Mordor against Sauron's eventual return. The Alliance failed to achieve a lasting victory over Sauron, largely because in the end Isildur failed to destroy the One Ring when he had the chance. And yet, had he followed the advice of Cirdan and Elrond, what would have become of the Elves in Middle-earth? Isildur's folly was the Alliance's triumph, for the Eldar were thus able to use their three remaining Rings of Power for more than 3000 years to enhance their world.

Tolkien wrote that the Third Age was "the fading years of the Eldar. For long they were at peace, wielding the Three Rings while Sauron slept and the One Ring was lost; but they attempted nothing new, living in memory of past." (*The Return Of The King*, p. 365). Perhaps they established no new kingdoms, but the Elvish songs relating the tragic stories of Nimrodel and the Ents' search for the Ent-wives show that the Elves continued to flourish and interact with other peoples around them long after the war was over.

Notes

1. *The Silmarillion*, p. 287. "Men he found the easiest to sway of all the peoples of the Earth; but long he sought to persuade the Elves to his service, for he knew that the Firstborn had the greater power; and he went far and wide among them, and his hue was still that of one both fair and wise."

2. *Unfinished Tales*, p. 254. "...The note goes on to say that Galadriel was not deceived, saying that this Aulendil was not in the train of Aulë in Valinor...." This and all subsequent references to Galadriel and Celeborn make use of the essay "Concerning Galadriel and Celeborn", provided in Unfinished Tales, which most closely fits with the events detailed in Tolkien's other writings. However, this narrative stipulates that Amroth was their son, an idea Tolkien later abandoned, which decision is accepted by and incorporated into this work.

3. Ibid., pp. 199-200. "A new shadow rises in the East...." The letter Gil-galad wrote to Tar-Meneldil was composed in SA 882. Since Tolkien elsewhere states that Sauron began stirring again around SA 500, it may be that Gil-galad was aware of some growing evil well before the end of the 9th Century.

4. Ibid., p. 238. "...At last the attackers broke into Eregion with ruin and devastation, and captured the chief object of Sauron's assault...Then Celebrimbor was put to torment...Concerning the Three Rings Sauron could learn nothing from Celebrimbor; and he had him put to death."

   Although other parts of this history conflict with some of the sources, this much agrees with "Of The Rings Of Power And The Third Age" in *The Silmarillion* (p. 288), which implies that Celebrimbor died there.

5. *The Return Of The King*, p. 364. "The Tale Of Years" states only that the Númenoreans began making permanent havens around the year SA 1800. Unfinished Tales reveals something of Lond Daer (Vinyalondë) in the sections concerning Númenor and the History of Galadriel and Celeborn. Umbar and Pelargir are attested in various sources, and other, unnamed havens are said to have been built far to the south and east.

6. *The Silmarillion*, p. 267. "Yet Sauron was ever guileful, and it is said that three were great lords of Númenorean race." Since Sauron did not

visit Númenor prior to his "imprisonment" there, he would have had to seduce the three Númenoreans in Middle-earth. It is interesting that he was able to do this relatively soon after the War of the Elves and Sauron. Perhaps they were already quite old for their race when they accepted the Rings.

Unfinished Tales (p. 221) indicates that the Shadow first fell on Númenor in the days of Tar-Atanamir, but his father Tar-Ciryatan was the first "willful" king, and his entry in "The Line Of Elros" suggests the Shadow may have fallen on Númenor in his time. So, it may be that the Númenoreans were becoming uncomfortable with their mortality by the time of the War of the Elves and Sauron, and so three aging Númenorean lords could be easily seduced by Sauron.

7. *The Silmarillion*, pp. 269-70. "...For Pharazôn son of Gimilkhad...had fared often abroad, as a leader in the wars that the Númenoreans made then in the coastlands of Middle-earth...For he had learned in Middle-earth of the strength of the realm of Sauron, and of his hatred of Westernesse. And now there came to him the masters of ships and captains returning out of the East, and they reported that Sauron was putting forth his might, since Ar-Pharazôn had gone back from Middle-earth, and he was pressing down upon the cities by the coasts...."

8. Ibid., p. 290. "...There [Sauron] found that the power of Gil-galad had grown great in the years of his absence, and it was spread now over wide regions of the north and west, and had passed beyond the Misty Mountains and the Great River even to the borders of Greenwood the Great, and was drawing nigh to the strong places where once he had dwelt secure."

9. *Unfinished Tales*, p. 264. "...Later [the Glanduin], with the Gwathlo formed by its confluence with the Mitheithel, formed the southern boundary of the North Kingdom."

10. *The Silmarillion* says that Elendil's "people dwelt in many places in Eriador about the courses of the Lhun and the Baranduin; but his chief city was at Annúminas beside the water of Lake Nenuial. At Fornost upon the North Downs also the Númenoreans dwelt, and in Cardolan, and in the hills of Rhudaur..." (pp. 290-1).

11. *Unfinished Tales*, p. 264. "...Before the decay of the North Kingdom...both kingdoms shared an interest in [Enedwaith], and together built and maintained the Bridge of Tharbad and the long causeways that carried the road to it on either side of the Gwathlo and Mitheithel across the fens in the plains of Minhiriath and Enedwaith...."

12. *The Return Of The King*, pp. 407-8. "...Alien, too, or only remotely akin, was the language of the Dunlendings. These were a remnant of the peoples that had dwelt in the vales of the White Mountains in ages past. The Dead Men of Dunharrow were of their kin. But in the Dark Years others had removed to the southern dales of the Misty Mountains; and thence some had passed into the empty lands as far north as the Barrow-downs. From them came the Men of Bree...."

13. Ibid., p. 321. "These [Lossoth] are a strange, unfriendly people, remnant of the Forodwaith." Where the Forodwaith actually dwelt at the end of the Second Age is a matter of speculation, as Tolkien really tells us nothing of their history. Cf. note 14 below.

14. *The War Of The Jewels*, pp. 60-1. "It was after thought that the people of Ulfang were already secretly in the service of Morgoth ere they came to Beleriand. Not so the people of Bor, who were worthy folk and tillers of the earth. Of them, it is said, came the most ancient of the Men that dwelt in the north of Eriador in the Second Age and [? read in] after-days."

The connection between the Folk of Bor (and Ulfang) and the northernmost men of Eriador in the Second Age implies that the Lossoth (and, hence, the Forodwaith, of whom the Lossoth were a "remnant") were in fact the descendants of these clans.

15. *The Return Of The King*, p. 317. "...Elendil was the High King and dwelt in the North at Annúminas; and the rule in the South was committed to his sons, Isildur and Anarion. They founded there Osgiliath, between Minas Ithil and Minas Anor, not far from the confines of Mordor. For this good at least they believed had come out of ruin, that Sauron also had perished."

16. *The Silmarillion*, p. 291. "...The chief city of this southern realm was Osgiliath, through the midst of which the Great River flowed...." In fact, the narrative makes no such connection. But why would Isildur and

Anarion build their cities north of Pelargir and Emyn Arnen? That the narrative makes mention of Herumor and Fuinur implies that they were significant in some way to the historians of Gondor.

17. Ibid., p. 291. "...and to the westward Minas Anor...as a shield against the wild men of the dales...."

Tolkien says very little about the constituent "tribes" of this race. The group who broke their vow to Isildur swore their oath at Erech but haunted Dunharrow on the northern side of the mountains. There probably was another tribe in what became Lamedon, one dwelling in the upper vales by the source of the Lefnui, another dwelling near the Adorn, another to the north of the Isen, and another tribe dwelling in Calenardhon itself. Obviously other groups lived north of that region as far as Bree.

18. *The Silmarillion* says "other works marvellous and strong [the Númenoreans] built in the days of their power, at the Argonath, and at Aglarond, and at Erech; and in the circle of Angrenost..." (p. 291). No specific date is given for when these works were erected, though the context implies the early years of Gondor's history.

However, *The Return Of The King* says that Minalcar "built the pillars of the Argonath at the entrance to Nen Hithoel" (p. 326), whereas Isildur is said to have erected the stone at Erech (p. 55). We also know that one of the Palantiri, given to Amandil by the Eldar of Tol Eressëa and taken to Middle-earth by Elendil and his sons, was placed at Orthanc in Angrenost, so the fortress must have been constructed no later than the beginning of the realm of Gondor.

If Angrenost and Aglarond were older than Gondor then perhaps they were constructed as a defense against Mordor; but if Isildur and Anarion built the fortresses, they would have used them to guard Calenardhon against the Dunlendings, who had long been unfriendly to the Dunedain, since the Dunedain thought Sauron had perished in Númenor's Downfall.

19. *The Silmarillion*, p. 154. Tolkien says here only that (after Fingolfin's death) "his young son Ereinion (who was after named Gil-galad) [Fingon] sent to the Havens." "Young" implies that Ereinion was not yet a fully adult Elf. Morgoth's Ring states that Elves required about fifty years (of the Sun) to achieve full maturity (p. 210). Hence, Ereinion was

probably born sometime after the year FA 405 (given that the Dagor Bragollach and Fingolfin's death occurred in FA 455).

20. *The Return Of The King*, p. 364. This entry in "The Tale Of Years" agrees with the account given in Unfinished Tales in "Concerning Galadriel And Celeborn", which describes the war in the fullest detail published to date.

21. *The Silmarillion*, p. 113. At Mereth Aderthad, Tolkien writes, the Elves swore oaths of alliance. Cirdan was one of the lords who attended the feast. He subsequently aided the Noldor on several occasions (pp. 154, 160, & 190).

22. *Unfinished Tales*, pp. 171, 175. "...But there were shipwrights among them who had been instructed by the Eldar..." and "...It is said that [Aldarion's] delay was due to the eagerness he had to learn all that he could of Cirdan, both in the making and management of ships, and in the building of walls to withstand the hunger of the sea."

23. *The Fellowship Of The Ring*, p. 256. "'...It recalled to me the glory of the Elder Days and the hosts of Beleriand, so many great princes and captains were assembled. And yet not so many, nor so fair, as when Thangorodrim was broken....'"

24. *Unfinished Tales*, p. 239. As with Celebrimbor's fate, it seems reasonable to use "Concerning Galadriel and Celeborn" as a source concerning other individuals such as Elrond. The founding of Imladris is certainly confirmed in "The Tale Of Years". Cf. note 20 above.

25. Ibid, p. 258. "...Oropher...had withdrawn northward beyond the Gladden Fields. This he did to be free from the power and encroachments of the Dwarves of Moria...and also he resented the intrusions of Celeborn and Galadriel into Lórien." Oropher's motives and history, like those of Galadriel and Celeborn, contain some inconsistencies. Cf. also pp. 280-281.

26. Ibid. In fact the passage states that "the Silvan Elves were hardy and valiant, but ill-equipped with armour or weapons in comparison with the Eldar of the West; also they were independent, and not disposed to place themselves under the supreme command of Gil-galad."

27. The name of this Elf-king is in doubt. In one narrative he is called Amdir and in another Malgalad (*Unfinished Tales*, pp. 240, 243-4, 258). Christopher Tolkien is unable to establish which name his father preferred for this character; hence, I have adopted the convention of referring to him as Amdir Malgalad, or simply Amdir, which is used more frequently and matches the style of Amroth, his son's name.

28. *The Silmarillion*, p. 288-90. "From that time war never ceased between Sauron and the Elves...." Being closest of all Elven realms to Mordor, Amdir's kingdom in Lorinand must have borne the brunt of this extended period of conflict, and the influx of Noldor and Sindar from Eregion after the fall of that Elven realm would have provided impetus to a friendship between Amdir's people and the Dwarves, though certainly not one as close as had existed between Eregion and Khazad-dum.

29. Ibid, p. 273. "...For [Isildur] passed in disguise to Armenelos and to the courts of the King, which were now forbidden to the Faithful; and he came to the place of the Tree, which was forbidden to all by the orders of Sauron, and the Tree was watched day and night by guards in his service...and Isildur passed through the guards and took from the Tree a fruit that hung upon it...."

30. Ibid, p. 293. "When therefore Sauron saw his time he came with great force against the new realm of Gondor, and he took Minas Ithil...But Isildur escaped...and they sailed from the mouths of Anduin seeking Elendil. Meanwhile Anarion held Osgiliath against the Enemy, and for that time drove him back to the mountains...."

31. Ibid, p. 294. Claiming that this king was actually named Durin may be erroneous. The passage says only: "Of the Dwarves few fought upon either side; but the kindred of Durin of Moria fought against Sauron." If he was named Durin, then he could not have been Durin III, because that was the Durin who opposed Sauron in the War of the Elves and Sauron (*Unfinished Tales*, p. 238). So, he was either Durin IV or Durin V. I have elected to call him Durin IV for lack of any information concerning either.

It is also strange that Tolkien says "...the kindred of Durin..." in referring to these Dwarves. Elsewhere he writes that most of the Dwarves of Nogrod and Belegost migrated to Khazad-dum early in the Second Age. They seem to have retained their distinctive lineages until the end of the

Third Age as the Appendix to The Return Of The King says "Bifur, Bofur, and Bombur were descended from Dwarves of Moria but were not of Durin's line" (p. 361).

32. *The Silmarillion*, p. 293. Also, *The Return Of The King*, p. 365.

33. *The Silmarillion*, p. 293. Cf. note 30 above.

34. *The Return Of The King*, p. 55. "'...For at Erech there stands yet a black stone...and it was set upon a hill, and upon it the King of the Mountains swore allegiance to [Isildur] in the beginning of the realm of Gondor. But when Sauron returned and grew in might again, Isildur summoned the Men of the Mountains to fulfill their oath, and they would not: for they had worshiped Sauron in the Dark Years.'"

35. *The Treason Of Isengard*, p. 310. This pass was the source of the river Harnen in the southern mountains of Mordor.

36. *The Silmarillion*, p. 293. The existence of such a council is speculative. The passage says only "now Elendil and Gil-galad took counsel together...." However, it's unlikely so grave a decision would have been made by these two alone.

37. I have inferred that Gildor and Glorfindel may have been involved in the Last Alliance. Gildor's history is attested only from the Third Age year 3001, when Bilbo said farewell to Gildor's folk in the Shire (*The Fellowship Of The Ring*, p. 92). However, he was the lord of a company of Noldor and his surname, Inglorion, means "scion of Inglor". Inglor was the original name of Finrod Felagund. Gildor also said he was "of the House of Finrod", and Finrod was the original name of Finarfin. It seems Tolkien originally intended a connection between Gildor and Galadriel's family, but this connection was not maintained when revisions were made to The Lord Of The Rings. So Gildor is enigmatic, but given that he is weary of the mortal lands by the end of the story, I have concluded he must have been quite ancient at the end of the Third Age.

Glorfindel is more probably a participant in the war. According to Christopher Tolkien, his father "came to the conclusion that Glorfindel of Gondolin, who fell to his death in combat with a Balrog after the sack of the city (II.192-4, IV.145), and Glorfindel of Rivendell were one and the same; he was released from Mandos and returned to Middle-earth in the Second Age" (*The Return Of The Shadow*, pp. 214-5). The profound implication of this conclusion is that Glorfindel played some role in the War of the Last Alliance, though perhaps not one so great as is hereafter postulated.

38. *The Silmarillion*, p. 293. "...Therefore they made that League which is called the Last Alliance, and they marched east into Middle-earth gathering a great host of Elves and Men...."

39. *The Fellowship Of The Ring*, p. 197. "'...It is told that Elendil stood [upon the tower of Amon Sul] watching for the coming of Gil-galad out of the West, in the days of the Last Alliance.'"

40. *The Return Of The King*, p. 353. "The Tale Of Years" only indicates the length of the stay in Imladris. There is really no text which tells how Gil-galad persuaded Oropher and Amdir to join the Alliance.

41. Sauron indeed sent troops north, for the Orcs who ambushed Isildur several years later were one such group. However, the army postulated here is assumed to be whatever force was driven south and engaged in the Battle of Dagorlad.

42. At some point during the war Isildur sent his sons Aratan and Ciryon to hold Minas Ithil against Sauron's flight: "All three [of Isildur's sons] had fought in the War of the Alliance, but Aratan and Ciryon had not been in the invasion of Mordor and the siege of Barad-dur, for Isildur had sent them to man his fortress of Minas Ithil, lest Sauron escape Gil-galad and Elendil and seek to force a way through Cirith Duath..." (*Unfinished Tales*, pp. 279-80).

43. *The Letters Of J.R.R. Tolkien*, p. 179. "I think that the Entwives had disappeared for good, being destroyed with their gardens in the War of the Last Alliance...when Sauron pursued a scorched earth policy and burned their land against the advance of the Allies down the Anduin...."

44. The Dunedain appear not to have used cavalry at this time. *Unfinished Tales* (pp. 278-9, Cf. note 7) says that most of the horses used by the Dunedain in the war were killed, but whether the animals were used for couriers or to move lighter archers, the Dunedain probably did not have an effective cavalry force.

Lindon, on the other hand, represented the last great Noldorin country in Middle-earth and Gil-galad probably still had many Elven horses. It is possible the Elves living in and near Imladris also contributed to such a force.

In *The Hobbit* the Elven-king rides out to hunt several times, but he does not uses horses in The Battle Of Five Armies, so it seems unlikely that Oropher possessed a cavalry. Amdir's army was small but contained Noldor and Sindar from Eregion. Nonetheless, the few published facts about the war do not imply Lorinand had cavalry.

45. *Unfinished Tales*, p. 258. "...Malgalad and more than half his following perished in the great battle of the Dagorlad, being cut off from the main host and driven into the Dead Marshes." The survivors may subsequently have been absorbed into Oropher's army, but perhaps were held back in reserve in the following battles.

46. Ibid., p. 247. The inference of Edhellond's participation in the war is supported only by one passage in "Of The Rings Of Power And The Third Age": "All living things were divided in that day, and some of every kind, even of beasts and birds, were found in either host, save the Elves only. They alone were undivided and followed Gil-galad" (*The Silmarillion*, p. 294).

The implication that yet other Elven realms (i.e., Avari) were involved is vaguely supported by an earlier passage describing how Sauron eventually seduced the Elves of Eregion (Cf. note 1 above).

47. *The Silmarillion*, p. 294. "Of the Dwarves few fought upon either side...." Tolkien offers no explanation of who these Dwarves were or why they fought for Sauron. It may be that he was able to influence one or two of their kings through a Ring of Power despite his inability to dominate them completely as he had dominated the Nazgul. Or it may be there was a rogue group of Dwarves who chose to side with the Dark Lord.

48. *The Two Towers*, p. 235. Sam, Frodo, and Gollum saw the faces of dead Men, Orcs, and Elves in the marshes. The Orcs obviously served Sauron, but perhaps the Men did as well. Cf. note 45 above.

49. *The Fellowship Of The Ring*, p. 256. "'...I was at the Battle of Dagorlad before the Black Gate, where we had the mastery: for the Spear of Gil-galad and the Sword of Elendil, Aiglos and Narsil, none could withstand....'"

50. *Unfinished Tales*, p. 258. "...Oropher was slain in the first assault upon Mordor, rushing forward at the head of his most doughty warriors before Gil-galad had given the signal for the advance."

51. Ibid. "Thranduil his son survived, but when the war ended...he led back home barely a third of the army that had marched to war."

52. *The Silmarillion*, p. 294. "Then Gil-galad and Elendil passed into Mordor and encompassed the stronghold of Sauron; and they laid siege to it for seven years, and suffered grievous loss by fire and by the darts and bolts of the Enemy, and Sauron sent many sorties against them."

53. Ibid. "...There in the valley of Gorgoroth Anarion son of Elendil was slain, and many others."

54. *Morgoth's Ring*, p. 420. "Nonetheless Sauron in time managed to unite [all the Orcs] in unreasoning hatred of the Elves and of Men who associated with them; while the Orcs of his own trained armies were so completely under his will that they would sacrifice themselves without hesitation at his command."

The Return Of The King, p. 227. "...As when death smites the swollen brooding thing that inhabits their crawling hill and holds them all in sway, ants will wander witless and purposeless and then feebly die, so the creatures of Sauron, Orc or troll or beast spell-enslaved, ran hither and thither mindless; and some slew themselves, or cast themselves in pits, or fled waiting back to hide in holes and dark lightless places far from hope."

55. Ibid., "...But the Men of Rhun and Harad, Easterling and Southron, saw the ruin of their war and the great majesty and glory of the Captains of the West. And those that were deepest and longest in evil servitude, hating the West, and yet were men proud and bold, in their turn now gathered themselves for a last stand of desperate battle."

56. *The Silmarillion*, p. 294. "The Dark Tower was leveled to the ground, yet its foundations remained, and it was not forgotten. The Númenoreans indeed set a guard upon the land of Mordor...."

57. Ibid., p. 298. "In Eriador Imladris was the chief dwelling of the High Elves; but at the Grey Havens of Lindon there abode also a remnant of the people of Gil-galad the Elvenking." Cirdan did in fact retain enough Elves, or their numbers recovered enough, to assist the Dunedain of Arnor on at least three occasions in the Third Age, but he was never able to raise an army like Gil-galad's.

Literature

Carpenter, Humphrey.
--The Letters Of J.R.R. Tolkien, Houghton Mifflin Company, 1981.

Tolkien, Christopher, ed.
--Morgoth's Ring, Houghton Mifflin Company, 1993.
--The Return Of The Shadow, Houghton Mifflin Company, 1988.
--The Treason Of Isengard, Houghton Mifflin Company, 1990.
--The War Of The Jewels, Houghton Mifflin Company, 1994.
--Unfinished Tales, Houghton Mifflin Company, 1980.

SECTION III:
THE MYTHOLOGY
OF MIDDLE-EARTH

MICHAEL MARTINEZ

Chapter 19:
Have you been to Valinor lately?

Traditionally we assign the Valinorean mythology to *The Hobbit*, *The Lord of the Rings*, *The Silmarillion*, *The Road Goes Ever On*, and *The Adventures of Tom Bombadil* (although the only real aspect of it in the latter is the poem "The Last Ship", about a mortal woman who is invited to sail over sea by some Elves). The Valinor mythology, or myth, is the cycle of half-told tales which tells the "Biblical" portion of Tolkien's grand mythology. But Valinor in some ways stands on its own.

The realm of the Valinor is a magical land, far beyond the western seas, where Elves and angels dwell. It is not heaven, not for humankind, and really not for Elven kind. It is simply a paradise which has been denied to Men (although another paradise was set up for Men). Heaven is where God dwells, Ilúvatar, Eru, the One, the All-father. In the end we may all meet up there, Elves, Men, Dwarves, and Angels. Or we may not. We don't really know for sure.

While part of the physical world we call Ambar (or Imbar), Valinor was merely another continent out of several. It could be reached by mortal Men, and was, but it was forbidden to them. As for the Elves, Valinor lay beyond the reach of many of them, too, except by death. The mythology of Valinor therefore includes the story of where Elves go when they die. It is not so much an Elf heaven as the final abode for Elven spirits (while Time lasts, that is). That they may be re-embodied there is insubstantial. If an Elf of Middle-earth dies, his or her spirit may pass westward to the Halls of Mandos.

Valinor, however, is also the abode of the rightful guardians of the world, the spiritual powers who are charged with watching over it. Ilúvatar may intervene in the world's affairs, as he does more than once, but it is the responsibility of the guardians to at least know what is going on in the world. So even after Ilúvatar took Valinor away from this physical world (and that is not to say he didn't make it a separate physical world -- it clearly remained a physical place where living beings could travel to, even if only Elves), the Valar were deeply concerned with events which occurred in the remaining world.

Middle-earth is thus a matter of grave concern to Valinor. Valinor is the "home" of the Valar but the Valar, and their servants the Maiar, must still watch and perhaps occasionally take action (at Ilúvatar's direction) in Middle-earth. The mythology thus includes a purpose for Valinor beyond its own existence and the fate of the Elves. Middle-earth has a purpose beyond its own existence, but that purpose is of a different nature: it is the home of Men (and of those Elves who have elected to remain in Middle-earth).

But if Valinor is concerned with Middle-earth, it is not permitted to interact directly with Middle-earth. The Valar represent primordial powers, the very essence of Nature's strength. When they undertake action mountains move, seas heave, and lands are crushed and broken, or rise up. It's a very delicate task to work with Middle-earth's history and not disrupt it, derailing Ilúvatar's plans. So as Time progresses the Valar become more a part of distant memory and eventually mythology and less a part of the affairs of Middle-earth.

We can glimpse the mythical Valinor in stories like *Smith of Wootton Major*, where Smith wanders into Faery:

> In Faery at first he walked for the most part quietly among the lesser folk and the gentler creatures in the woods and meads of fair valleys, and by the bright waters in which at night strange stars shone and at dawn the gleaming peaks of far mountains were mirrored.

The stars of Faery are not the stars of Earth, Middle-earth. Faery has been far removed from that part of the universe we have come to know. Smith discovers that Faery itself is just a small part of a larger world:

> When he first began to walk far without a guide he thought he would discover the further bounds of the land; but great mountains rose before him, and going by long ways round about them he came at last to a desolate shore. He stood beside the Sea of Windless Storm where the blue

waves like snowclad hills roll silently out of Unlight to the long strand, bearing the white ships that return from Battles on the Dark Marches of which men know nothing. He saw a great ship cast high upon the land, and the waters fell back in foam without a sound. The elven mariners were tall and terrible; their swords shone and their spears glinted and a piercing light was in their eyes. Suddenly they lifted up their voices in a song of triumph and his heart was shaken with fear, and he fell upon his face, and they passed over him and went away into the echoing hills.

What should the Dark Marches be that the Elves of Faery must venture out in their white ships upon the Sea of Windless Storm? The battles they wage there are unknown to men, undocumented and uncelebrated, except in brief glimpses in stories like "Smith".

Smith wanders through Faery and has encounter after encounter. The land is enchanted but it is natural and not so much mysterious as simply different. He finds the Inner Mountains and eventually the Vale of Evermorn, the heart of Faery, where the land is richer and more vibrant than anything in mortal experience. There he dances with the Queen of Faery, who years later tells him, when he recalls the little figure on the cake for the Feast of Twenty-four which was meant to represent her, "Better a little doll, maybe, than no memory of Faery at all."

That is the way Faery, or Valinor, is remembered. As Frodo sails toward Tol Eressëa he sees "white shores and beyond them a far green country under a swift sunrise". Resembling the dream he had had in Bombadil's house, the vision is the only glimpse of far Aman, the Blessed Land, in *The Lord of the Rings*. But it's not the only glimpse for readers of Tolkien.

Besides *Smith of Wootton Major* there is also *Roverandom*. Roverandom is a small metal dog who is given life by a wizard. The story is based on a toy one of Tolkien's sons lost, but it follows the author's purest flights of fancy as he wanders to the moon and back in a fashion that even the Elves would envy. In his merry (and some not-so-merry) adventures, the enchanted dog finds himself visiting the Mer-folk under the sea. Roverandom is befriended by another enchanted dog, Rover, and together they go traveling with an ancient whale, old Uin. One day, Uin takes them farther than ever before:

> Another time he took them to the other side (or as near as he dared), and that was a still longer and more exciting journey, the most marvellous of all Roverandom's travels, as he realised later, when he was grown to be an older and a wiser dog. It would take the whole of another story, at least, to tell you of all their adventures in Uncharted Waters and of their glimpses of lands unknown to geography, before they passed the Shadowy Seas and reached the great Bay of Fairyland (as we call it) beyond the Magic Isles; and saw far off in the last West the Mountains of Elvenhome and the light of Faery upon the waves. Roverandom thought he caught a glimpse of the city of the Elves on the green hill beneath the Mountains, a glint of white far away; but Uin dived again so suddenly that he could not be sure. If he was right, he was one of very few creatures, on two legs or four, who can walk about our own lands and say they have glimpsed that other land, however far away.

Roverandom is, unfortunately, an undeveloped text. Written and completed in 1925, it was set aside for many years and Tolkien never returned to it. Had he done so he undoubtedly would have written more about the ill-tempered wizards, the man in the moon, the Mer-folk, and perhaps even the Elves of Elvenhome (whose city on the hill in the mountains still stands after millennia, though Tirion upon Tuna is said to have been destroyed in "Akallabeth").

The mythology of Valinor is glimpsed when old Uin turns away. He has dared the forbidden, bringing creatures from the Outer Lands to view the enchanted shores of the forbidden realm. Valinor is a land of which we may dream, but we may never live there. Nor should we think of visiting there.

It is the myth of Valinor itself which persuades men to seek for it. An immortal land where immortals dwell, can a man perhaps himself find immortality there? Or, if not immortality, will he at least find a memory which lives within him brighter than all other memories? The myth is a dangerous one best forgotten, or only remembered in the form of a small doll, which poses no threat, wakes no imagination, rouses no desire.

In *The Road to Middle-earth* Professor Tom Shippey, like so many critics, dwells upon the odious literary qualities of the stories. Rather than appreciate the tales for tales in themselves, he absolves himself of guilt by pointing out for the reader that he was once warned by Professor Tolkien not to look too deeply beneath the covers of the book, and being so warned he is well able to avoid the pitfalls inherently bound up with seeking sources...or so he hopes.

But the pitfalls of seeking sources cannot be avoided, because in order to seek the sources of a story one must dissect the story, and "he that breaks a thing to find out what it is has left the path of wisdom". The "path of wisdom" is itself a treacherous thing. The Wise often fall from the path, or stumble. The wise Eldar rebelled against the Valar and left Valinor, and in Middle-earth they found a terrible doom, even one much worse than the inevitable defeat at the hands of Melkor. For if Valinor is denied to Men, Middle-earth is ultimately denied to Elves, who must fade and be forgotten, except perhaps as dolls atop special cakes.

Shippey finds clear semblance between the characters of *Smith* and Tolkien's own profession of philology, identifying even Smith himself with Tolkien:

> If the old Cook is a philologist-figure, and Nokes a critic-figure, the suspicion must be that Smith is a Tolkien-figure. Smith himself never becomes Cook, never bakes a Great Cake. It is perhaps fair to remark that Tolkien never produced a major full-length work on medieval literature. Against that Smith's life is one of useful activity: pots, pans, bars, bolts, hinges, fire-dogs -- or, one might say, lectures, tutorials, scripts, pupils. Furthermore Smith has the ability to pass into Fairie, and the mark of his strangeness is not only on his brow but in his song: he brings back visions for others. These visions furthermore expand. The doll 'on one foot like a snow-maiden dancing', the maiden 'with flowing hair and kilted skirt' who drags Smith into the dance, the Queen 'in her majesty and her glory' -- all three are avatars of the Queen of Faerie, representing successively the tawdry images of former fantasy which are all the modern world has left, Tolkien's own first attempts to produce something truer and better, his final awareness that what he had attempted had grown under his hand, from *Hobbit* to *Silmarillion*. The

image of Smith apologising for his people, and being forgiven -- 'Better a little doll, maybe, than no memory of Faery at all. For some the only glimpse. For some the awaking' -- might be taken without too much strain as Tolkien forgiving himself for 'Goblin Feet'. But still one is left with Alf.

Well, Alf is not so important as the fact that literary criticism, even the extraordinary kind which whips back the covers and reveals all the pages as Shippey's is able to do in one fashion or another, misses the enchantment of Valinor. The Valinor myth is not an allegory or an expression of wistfulness. It's the fulfillment of Tolkien's search for an explanation of what men have sought before him. That is, it's the land to which magic fled, the world where all the faeries and angels settled to watch us from afar, knowing more of our destiny than we do, but forbidden to share that knowledge with us. If we visit the forbidden land we cannot stay and we must quickly hide our memories in little cherished trinkets which have greater symbolic value than anything else.

The Valinor myth is the stumbling stone in the path of everyone who seeks to explain Tolkien's world. He had more than one world, he possessed a universe and was a dweller amid many worlds. But all those worlds were touched by the same myth. Tolkien never produced a great work on medieval literature because he was too busy producing a great work on something more important, something only he could define. Valinor is hinted at in medieval literature, and perhaps in more ancient traditions. But the literary criticism fails to see it, and the unfolding pages are always too quickly flipped back, leaving two or more swept together.

Leave it to a literary critic, one might say, to miss the whole point of a story. The story is meant to entertain and to elucidate. It may also illuminate, but illumination is a gift from afar that an author may not even be aware of, and the reader doesn't fully taste. It is the star within the cake, the gift of Faerie to mortal lands.

In the twilight of our dreams we glimpse afar a place where Tolkien walked and danced and watched immortal warriors march to and from ancient wars no one here remembers. If another author were to set pen to paper, Valinor would become a dry and dusty place, filled with modern fears and shadows, bereft of magic and distilled from glittery explanations of every detail. The Outer Mountains would be named, the Inner Mountains would be geographically mapped, the distance from Here to There would be calculated, the Uncharted Waters would be charted, and the singing would fail (or, worse, be silenced by a multitude of devices much like CD players and tape recorders).

The savage burdens of the Elves would become subsumed by petty mortal angst and ambition. Every motive would rival the source of cheap thrillers. Every action would become a reflection of trite and formulaic fiction. Why? Because Tolkien didn't dwell on what the thing should represent, he dwelt on the thing itself. He didn't wonder after the sources of the myth but cherished the myth and passed it on.

The Valinor myth is not a statement on our own failures and desires. It is simply an explanation of what we have sought through the long ages, and have come close to grasping. A few of us have glimpsed it, but either out of fear -- or a realization that we didn't belong -- those favored few did not settle there. Instead they returned to us and passed on the star, and every now and then some old Nokes comes along and tries to figure out what the star is.

He doesn't realize that Alf is sitting there, the King of Faery, watching, smiling, and waiting for the next generation to grow up. The cake is there for us to eat it. The star is there for us to wear on our brows. But we'll lose the magic if we try to define it, if we peek beneath the covers. If we break the thing to see what it is, we'll leave the path of wisdom, and we'll miss out on Valinor.

MICHAEL MARTINEZ

Chapter 20:
The manly men of myth
and Middle-earth

I was first introduced to the Beowulf legend in the fourth grade. My classmates and I were assembled along with a few hundred other lucky kids in an experimental school, the likes of which I have never seen again. We were given the usual lessons and textbooks, but there was a particular emphasis on sparking the children's imaginations. We were literally inundated with audio-visual aids and tools. We watched movies, played our own film strips, interrupted classes to follow the space missions, and made things in our cone's art room.

I remember vividly reading stories about Thor and his goat-drawn chariot. He was said to have killed the goats each night and eaten them, only to bring them back to life the next day. I followed the Mighty One on his dangerous adventures against the giants. And there was the story of Beowulf, with his ship-full of brave Geats, come to rescue King Hrothgar from the deadly menace of Grendel and his mother. I didn't know then, however, that the interest in Beowulf had been rekindled by a man in England named Tolkien. In fact, at the time, I knew nothing of Tolkien and Hobbits and Elves and Dragons. For some reason, he wasn't included in our unusual curriculum. It was a different world from today. My friends and I all wanted Richard Nixon to be President because our families believed he would keep us young lads out of the Vietnam War. I suppose the country had other things than Hobbits to think about at the time.

"Beowulf" the poem is an appropriate symbol for the generation of Americans who had to live through the Vietnam War. We grew weary of it. Hrothgar's people were weary of the terror which Grendel wreaked upon their lives. His warriors were brave men, but they had reached a point where they refused to go up against the monster. "Sore is my soul to say to any of the race of man what ruth for me in Heorot Grendel with hate hath wrought, what sudden harryings," Hrothgar tells Beowulf when the Geats first arrive in Heorot. "Hall-folk fail me, my warriors wane; for Wyrd hath swept them into Grendel's grasp."

Except for the preamble which informs the audience of Beowulf's mission, one would not know from the coastal warden's speech that his people are so oppressed. He is a brave man, who confronts Beowulf's company alone, while his men wait behind him. And he judges Beowulf to be trustworthy and sets his own men to guard Beowulf's ship, while he himself leads the hero and his company to Heorot. If Hrothgar is still served by such men, what sort of men served him before?

Beowulf is an unusual man. He has the grip of thirty men, and he vows to fight the monster without weapons and armor. Unferth, one of Hrothgar's men, challenges Beowulf and accuses him of having lost a contest of strength and endurance to a man named Breca. Beowulf scoffs at the accusation, "What a deal hast uttered, dear my Unferth, drunken with beer, of Breca now, told of his triumph!" He goes on to tell how he and Breca, as mere boys, swam through the sea in full armor (chain shirts), carrying swords with which to defend themselves against whales. They swam for five days and nights, and Beowulf ended up fighting one of the whales.

The best athletes in the world today can't wear a heavy chain shirt, carry a sword, and swim for five days, let alone fight a whale (and kill it). Clearly, Beowulf is a highly unusual man, a hero of epic proportions. He is to the northern world what Samson was to Israel and Judah, what Herakles was to Greece. Beowulf performs impossible feats and men sing his praises. To say he had great P/R is an understatement.

Many people claim (with some justification) that Tolkien was strongly influenced by "Beowulf". The poem's stylistic boasting doesn't carry over to Middle-earth, but something of the imagery does. And yet, there is a distinct difference between the world of Beowulf and the world of Middle-earth. Beowulf, like people today, cannot help but talk about himself. It is not that he is self-absorbed. If anything, he is extremely polite and quite self-sacrificing. But he does ask Hrothgar for a special favor: Beowulf wants to be the man who kills Grendel. No one else may have that honor. And Beowulf establishes his claim by reminding all present -- thanks to an opportunity provided by Unferth -- that he is a man capable of achieving great deeds.

Beowulf's boasts are not born of pride so much as of custom. The Roman historian Tacitus (circa 56 CE - 116 CE) notes with some scorn that the ancient Germans loved to boast about their deeds and valor. Tacitus and other Roman writers considered such boasting to be immodest; a man's bravery is best celebrated by others. But Beowulf's tales of valor are his resume. A resume is, in fact, the modern world's version of the old barbaric boasts. In a resume, anyone who has written a "Hello, world" program becomes a systems engineer. Anyone who has held the door open for customers is a customer service manager. Anyone who has used a hammer is a certified technician for a manually operated high impact delivery system.

We embellish what we've done, pretty it up, and make it look good. Someone once told me, "It's not lying. It's telling prospective employers what they want to hear." Maybe, but if you lay it on too thickly, all the layers of deception will come dripping off under pressure, and suddenly you're unable to deliver the goods. Still, the resume tells anyone who would hire us what we are capable of doing. If you really have been a data processing manager, then you can tell people that.

Beowulf responds to Unferth by accusing him of cowardice. In short, he lays his life on the line in challenging a mere man before he goes up against the monster. Were Unferth not a coward, were his accusation true, he would stand up to Beowulf and challenge him to a duel to defend his honor. Of course, Unferth has no honor, and the poem establishes Beowulf's credibility by allowing him to put Unferth to shame.

Tolkien's heroes come from a different culture. Call it an Elven culture. Even the Rohirrim are not given to boasting about themselves. There is a subtle understanding among the heroic characters of Middle-earth that you just don't prattle on about how good you are. A man is judged by his deeds, not by his willingness to endure challenger after challenger, duel after duel. When a great hero, like Túrin, puts a companion to shame (as he did Gwindor in the councils of Nargothrond), the deed is not remembered kindly.

The restraint we see in Aragorn, Eomer, and others is undoubtedly due to the fact that they have grown up in the shadow of the Elves. Elven culture undoubtedly imparted a set of values to the Edain and other peoples under their influence. But the Edain and their relatives (the Northmen) valued bravery and action. And, despite their reticence, the Elves could be brave and active. Even though Eomer had probably never seen an Elf, he knew of them, had heard tales of them, and feared them or at least respected them. When Eomer threatens Gimli, Legolas quickly draws an arrow, fits it to his bow, and aims it at Eomer. No one doubts the Elf can and will kill Eomer if he gives the order to his men to kill Gimli. And Legolas is never rebuked.

The Elves were not the manliest of men in Middle-earth. Hurin was probably the strongest hero on record. He slew seventy trolls and countless Orcs, yelling out "Aure entuluva! (Day shall come again!)" before he was finally overborne and taken prisoner. His son Túrin survived disaster after disaster, walking away from more battles than many long-lived Elven lords had. And Beren faced the depths of Angband, robbing the Dark Lord Morgoth himself.

These names mean little to the first-time reader of *The Lord of the Rings* but they mean a great deal to Aragorn. And Eomer undoubtedly knows something of the ancient heroes, too, since his grandmother came from Gondor. The deeds of the great heroes cast a long shadow in Middle-earth, and it's difficult for succeeding generations to match them. Isildur, for example, broke into the well-guarded royal palace of Númenor to steal a sapling of the White Tree. That's a pretty significant accomplishment, but does it rival Hurin's stand at the fens of Serech, or Túrin's slaying of Glaurung, or Ëarendil's defeat of Ancalagon (not to mention his years of voyaging to find Valinor)?

Gil-galad was the only Elven king ever to defeat a Dark Lord. Fëanor, Fingolfin, Maedhros, and Fingon had briefer reigns, but they figure prominently in the ancient legends. Gil-galad's long, cautious reign over northwestern Middle-earth is nonetheless shrouded in mystery. Until we get to the final combat with Sauron on the slopes of Orodruin, there really isn't much in Gil-galad's resume that compares with the accomplishments of his predecessors. One could have stood upon a peak of the Misty Mountains, looked down upon the assembled hosts of the Last Alliance of Elves and Men, and said, "They just don't make Elven kings like they used to. Fëanor would have gone in with only the vanguard."

Of course, Fëanor and his vanguard were all killed, so there is something to be said for Gil-galad's strategy of building up massive, overwhelming, superior force. In fact, it was such a good strategy, Sauron borrowed it for the next rematch. But Gil-galad didn't just have the biggest army on the map. He was accompanied by some legendary warriors. And a few fools, I suppose. Oropher's ill-fated assault against Mordor doesn't seem to have been too bright. But then, he wasn't enthusiastic about joining the Last Alliance in the first place. Common sense must have won Oropher over to the cause, but he apparently lost it after seeing his friend (and perhaps relative) Amdir get blistered in the Dead Marshes.

Rash actions are probably the one great failing of the Elves. They are brave, strong, and intelligent. But when they lose control, they lose control. So Fëanor rushes ahead of his army, and his company is wiped out. Gwindor succumbs to the provocation of seeing his brother chopped to pieces, and prematurely launches the Nirnaeth Arnoediad. Turgon loses all common sense and decides to go down with the tower in Gondolin. Why? What is so heroic about throwing one's life away in a lost cause?

Well, except for Turgon, the Elves who made rash decisions and lost their lives (and battles) didn't really have reason to believe their causes were lost. Maybe Orodreth, watching his army wither away before Glaurung's fire, uttered a final "oops!" before donning his helm for the last time. Perhaps Thingol, pursuing the Dwarves in anger for their theft of the Silmaril (well, that's sort of what Tolkien wanted to happen), suddenly found himself surrounded with few friends by his side, and briefly wondered what he ever saw in the stupid gem anyway.

Middle-earth's heroism is not for the brave and foolish, unless your name is Túrin. Túrin had a lot going against him, but he managed to pull through every situation anyway. It was only when he came face to face with his own despair that he took his own life. But by then, he had slain Glaurung and removed a terrible evil from the world. There were still dragons left, but Túrin couldn't have killed them all. Quite probably, had he lived (with or without Nienor), Túrin would never have met another dragon anyway. Morgoth had other plans for them.

It does seem a bit odd, however, that with all the heroic Elves in Gondolin (Ecthelion, Glorfindel, Turgon, et. al.), they didn't wipe the floor with the dragons. It's not like they hadn't been in a fierce battle before. Turgon led ten thousand warriors to the Nirnaeth, and he actually retreated with some remnants of Fingon's army. So how is it that the mighty Elven warriors couldn't do the job? Or maybe they did. The conquest of Gondolin was the last major action Morgoth initiated. He apparently didn't feel threatened by the re-established Doriath, or by Gil-galad's refuge on Balar, or by Arvernien's small population. Or maybe he just didn't have the forces left to go up against any more Elves.

The Noldor of the First Age were tough, fierce, determined, valiant, and just downright hard to kill. They may not have had a chance to defeat Morgoth, but they certainly forced him to go back to the drawing board more than once. Sauron's strategies of the Third Age -- coupling a long, slow buildup of forces with arranging the estrangement of his enemies -- wouldn't have worked had the Noldor of the First Age hung around until the Third Age. They'd have brought together their armies and taken out Angmar rather than let it hang around for 700 years. Dol Guldur would have been surrounded and besieged.

The Noldorin strategists may not have had a plan for destroying Angband, but they certainly weren't afraid of it. The arrogance they displayed in laying siege to Morgoth was only surpassed by the creation of the Rings of Power and Ar-Pharazôn's assault on Valinor. But Morgoth eventually beat them down. Legolas said that of all Elf-banes, the Balrogs were the most deadly. And yet, it wasn't until Morgoth had a large force of dragons (well, at least several of them) that he was able to crush the Noldor. He needed the help of treacherous men to win the Nirnaeth, but Glaurung took out Nargothrond, and the dragons made the difference at Gondolin.

In the aftermath of these losses, the fight had been taken out of the Elves. Orodreth's defeat signaled the end of Eldarin initiatives against Morgoth, and Orodreth really wasn't a strategist. Túrin was the real mover and shaker in Nargothrond, but he didn't have the power and presence of, say, a Maedhros or Fingon to carry the day against Glaurung. Maybe if Túrin hadn't carried Gwindor out of the battle, he could have faced Glaurung and at least given Orodreth's people a chance to escape. But Túrin's chief flaw was his incomparable ability to choose his personal priorities over everyone else's.

Maedhros lost his charisma. He slowly settled into petty malice, consumed by the Oath of Fëanor. His deeds of valor were among the greatest ever achieved by the Noldor. His suffering on the peaks of Thangorodrim was a much greater endurance test than any faced by Beowulf or Samson. Maedhros was hanging in the wind for a couple of years. That's rough. A lesser Elf might have died. A man probably would have died. Relinquishing his claim to the kingship over the Noldor was a gallant act, and not the last one Maedhros would make. But after the Nirnaeth, he no longer dreamed of defeating Angband. He was willing to settle for one Silmaril, and to get that Silmaril he destroyed the Kingdom of Doriath and the people of Arvernien.

Something of the special heroism which Maedhros helped to forge died in the last century of the First Age. It's not like the Eldar and Edain had lost their spirit. The Edain, when given the chance, turned against Morgoth, and in so doing earned a special reward from the Valar. But tales of individual heroism became few and far between after the First Age. The occasional dragonslayer -- Fram, Bard -- might have been renowned for a time, but they didn't really achieve anything lasting in the fight against the Dark Lord. The sacrifices of Fingolfin, Fingon, Turgon, Hurin, and others were also only briefly celebrated.

The Greeks looked back to Herakles and noted that despite all his flaws, he had changed their world. Beowulf, too, changed the world. Both heroes removed monsters which had terrorized mankind. They reduced the amount of overwhelmingly powerful evil in the world a great deal. They couldn't remove the evil from men's hearts, but the normal evils we face we can deal with ourselves.

The Elvish and Edainic heroes, however, engaged in superhuman efforts which often proved fruitless, or the results of which were undone by subsequent foolish decisions. The Noldor didn't defeat Morgoth, but they did force him to concentrate his thought on the northwestern regions of Middle-earth. The rest of the world consequently benefited from a relative withdrawal of evil, as Morgoth concentrated his forces in and around Angband. That made the Valar's task in overthrowing Morgoth much easier. But more than a thousand years later, the Noldor of Eregion unwittingly paved the way for Sauron's ascendancy.

Gil-galad, Elendil, and many of their allies made the ultimate sacrifice to defeat Sauron. His forces were destroyed or scattered, his kingdom conquered, and Sauron himself was overthrown. But Isildur succumbed to the lure of the One Ring and took it. Thus, Middle-earth was given a respite which only lasted about 1,000 years. And then Sauron returned, and things started looking evil again.

Given that the greatest heroes of Middle-earth seemed to accomplish so little, it seems little wonder that men like Aragorn and Eomer seldom if ever boasted of their deeds. In the long history of wars and quests, great deeds might amount to little. Individual men, like Baldor son of Brego, might squander their valor on ridiculous quests. Or they might establish great nations. But each generation inherited the consequences of the previous generation's mistakes. That is the true difference between heroes like Beowulf and heroes like Aragorn. We don't remember Beowulf because of his boasting. We remember him because of his accomplishments and the love his people bore him.

Aragorn was remembered for his accomplishments and the love his people bore him as well. But when Aragorn was challenged, he did not roll out his resume to prove his credentials. He took action, and let his valor speak for itself.

In so much, the manly men of Middle-earth were a bit humbler than the manly men of myth and folklore. We model our heroes on ourselves, and we still engage in boasting. But Tolkien's heroes were nobler and more 'Elvish' than are men today. They understood that words are free and easy, but lasting deeds are hard to come by.

[Citations from "Beowulf" were taken from the translation available at Medieval Sourcebook: Beowulf (http://www.fordham.edu/halsall/basis/beowulf.html).]

Chapter 21:
Tolkien's time machine:
when literary worlds collide

Although it may seem obvious that Middle-earth is "the world in which J.R.R. Tolkien sets his Elf and Hobbit stories", that is not precisely the case. There are Elf stories which are not part of the world of *The Lord of the Rings*, *The Hobbit*, and *The Silmarillion*. I speak of the Elves in *The Father Christmas Letters* and *Smith of Wootton Major*. Of course, there are similarities between these worlds. Like a run on bad puns, Tolkien kept resurrecting old ideas and giving them new form. Hence, the Elves help Father Christmas fight off the goblins, and Smith sees Elven warriors returning from strange and foreign wars when he is visiting Faerie. Middle-earth, which Tolkien said is our world in some imaginary time in the past, is distinct from the other worlds.

But Middle-earth itself is a hodge-podge of literary worlds, borrowing extensively from the original *Hobbit* (which Tolkien drew into the Middle-earth canon by proposing a second edition for the book in 1947) and a bit from the 1937 "Silmarillion" text, which itself was a rewrite of an earlier "Silmarillion" which in turn was a complete rewrite of the themes Tolkien had used for *The Book of Lost Tales*. Númenor came straight out of a science fiction time travel story, "The Drowning of Anadune". And then *The Lord of the Rings* itself produced new terrain and peoples: Rohan and the Ents, Gondor and Arnor, and the mysterious Eregion whose Elven people only the stones could recall.

And, of course, behind these stories lay the older, non-Tolkienien myths and folklore which inspired him to create his own myths and folklore in the first place. Tolkien grew up on stories of Greek gods and heroes, and he discovered the primal beauty of Gothic and Anglo-Saxon verse and poetry. His devotion to Catholicism and Christianity ensured he would absorb Biblical traditions, and his curiosity led him to explore the traditions and sciences of Finland, Egypt, Babylon, and other sources of western civilization.

A recurring theme in Tolkien seems to be the clash between civilization and barbarism. The Elves' civilization collides with the barbarous Mannish tribes, and the tribes eventually replace the Elves. The Númenoreans' civilization returns to Middle-earth, where it becomes mingled with the barbarism of the Númenoreans' Edainic cousins. And in the end, the high civilization of Arnor descends into a semi-barbarism which reaches out to the remnants of high civilization in Gondor far to the south.

What stands between civilization and barbarism is the power of choice. Those who choose to improve their lives, to study the world and its ways, and to learn from their mistakes, raise up the new civilizations. These civilizations are always born of a sense of wonder, a newness which evokes the symbology of a young world, freshly awakened from a long sleep. Those who have freedom of choice stripped from them live in darkness, and at best roam the world as wild folk (Men or Elves, or Dwarves), outcasts and outlaws, or simply untamed barbarians. The rest become slaves or willing servants and allies of personified evil, the Dark Lords who oppose civilization.

But when Tolkien set out to write his stories, he did not necessarily choose the theme of civilization versus barbarism. Rather, the theme he constantly pursued, and never fully realized, was the collision between ideals from two different worlds. Civilization and barbarism are the past and present (or future) aspect of the same world. All civilizations arise from barbarism. All civilizations eventually meet new barbarians. But Tolkien's theme was a more wistful look at a past we never had.

His quest began with the attempt to create a mythology for England, to devise an Anglo-Saxon mythos which explained (from his point of view), many curious elements left behind in the wake of the Norman invasion of 1066. There must once have been people who knew (or thought they knew) what a wood-wose was, for example. Well, that is the official version of the story, as propounded by Tom Shippey and others. The problem is that the mythology for England, *The Book of Lost Tales*, lacks any such references. Instead, it tosses around terms like "gnomes" (from French), "pixies" (admittedly from Old English "Puck"), "fays" (from French by way of Old English), and "sprites" (also from French).

The Anglo-Saxon angle is not so much in the fairies as in the lost wanderer (Eriol, Aelfwine) who discovers that they really exist and that once they were a part of the world of men. The fairies once lived in what has now become England, and there they fought a long and harsh war with men, eventually losing it or fleeing as more and more men arrived. In a sense, Tolkien's English mythology was really a Celtic mythology, because the men who drove the fairies from England were Anglo-Saxons, although Eriol's descendants remained in rapport with them for an unspecified number of generations. But those descendants became the Kings of Kent, which was traditionally a Jutish kingdom, and quickly became overshadowed by the Anglo and Saxon kings in Mercia, Wessex, and Northummbria. The name "Kent" is believed to derive from the earlier name of a Celtic tribe anyway (the Cantiaci or Cantii).

When *The Silmarillion* was rejected by a reader at Allen & Unwin for being very "Celtic", Tolkien objected to such a description. By then he had eliminated most of the Celticisms, and Eriol himself was no longer a part of the mythology. England, too, had been dropped from the tales. The whole thing was no longer English, but there remained the "Geste of Beren and Lúthien" and the "Lay of the Children of Hurin". Like Arthurian Romance, Tolkien Romance was still borrowing heavily from French roots.

Which is not to say it all came from French traditions. Hurin Thalion owes something to the tragic figure of Heracles in Greek mythology, or perhaps to Samson in the Bible. All three men possessed great strength, and they were champions of their people who fought against powerful enemies. And all three experienced tragedy. Heracles and Hurin both lost their families. And Heracles and Hurin also both had brothers whose sons founded dynasties (Iolaus was the son of Heracles' brother Iphicles, and Iolaus founded a kingdom on Sardinia with the sons of Heracles; Tuor was the son of Hurin's brother Huor, and Tuor was the grandfather of Elros, first king of Númenor). And Gondolin owes something to the story of Troy (also called Ilion).

Although *The Hobbit* was little more than a light-hearted romp through fairy-tale clichés, Tolkien blended elements from Anglo-Saxon and Norse literature which revealed his love for the northern world's old traditions. Hence, Bilbo and the dragon Smaug lift a cup-theft from "Beowulf", the Hobbit's conversation with Smaug recalls Fafnir's exchange with Sigurd, and Gandalf and the Dwarves peek out from the name lists of the Elder Edda. And yet, Bard the Bowman's lake-town is still influenced by a French Celtic lake village. Even while honing his ability to utilize Anglo-Saxon literature and imagery, Tolkien still found himself looking beyond England to France. But he wasn't out of the woods yet, so to speak.

When the name "Rohiroth" first appeared on a sketch-map for the lands south of the *Hobbit's* Misty Mountains (as Tolkien worked on the narrative for *The Lord of the Rings*), alternative names for them included Anaxippians and Hippanaletians. Years later, in a letter to publisher Milton Waldman at Collins, Tolkien wrote "the better and nobler sort of Men are in fact the kin of those that had departed to Númenor, but remain in a simple 'Homeric' state of patriarchal and tribal life" (*The Letters of J.R.R. Tolkien*, No. 131). Further on he writes, "*The Lord of the Rings*...concludes the whole business -- an attempt is made to include in it...elves, dwarves, the Kings of Men, heroic 'homeric' horsemen,...."

Among Tolkien scholars and researchers, it is almost regarded as axiomatic that Tolkien drew strictly upon northern resources in fashioning his mythologies. So then why should Tolkien refer to Homer twice when describing the (then as-yet unpublished) cycle if everything, as people like Tom Shippey seem to argue, is cleanly derived from Anglo-Saxon, Norse, and Finnish sources? The best answer to that unanswerable question may lie in the 1991 paper by Jonathan Glenn, titled 'To translate a hero: *The Hobbit* as *Beowulf* retold'. Although Glenn stresses the importance of "Beowulf" in the Tolkien tradition, he takes the unusual position of disagreeing with classical Tolkien analysis. That is, he doesn't think Tolkien was lifting his ideas quite so cleanly from "Beowulf".

> ...studies of these issues are with few exceptions flawed in three dangerous ways," Glenn writes in his introduction. "By the general critical sin of Sloppy Statements, by a tendency to simple-minded and profligate Parallel-Hunting, and by the Voilà Syndrome, whereby the critic impressively points to something but fails to ask that first of all critical questions, 'So what?'

He proceeds to rip into Bonniejean Christensen's treatment of Tolkien and "Beowulf" and then offers an argument in favor of a completely different reading: that Bilbo and Beorn are not following the models others have proposed for Tolkien. Rather, Glenn believes that Tolkien was devising "an alternative hierarchy" to the northern world's traditional hierarchy, one in which Tolkien substitutes the Adventurer for the Warrior and the Leader for the Hero. Such a substitution is easily recognizable in many analyses of Aragorn's character, who is indeed more of an adventurer and leader than warrior and hero. But Aragorn is not equated with Beowulf, whereas Bilbo has been so identified in critical literature.

To support his thesis, Glenn more than once draws upon Biblical examples which would easily have been available to Tolkien, the devout Catholic. Now, Tolkien admitted freely that "Beowulf is among my most valued sources" to *The Observer* in 1937 after *The Hobbit* was published, although he pointed out that "it was not consciously present to the mind in the process of writing, in which the episode of the theft [of the cup from Smaug's hoard] arose naturally (and almost inevitably) from the circumstances."

If Tolkien was not consciously borrowing from "Beowulf" when he wrote about the cup-theft, then it must be equally true that he did not keep a copy of his essay, "On Fairy-Stories", in front of him as he wrote either *The Hobbit* (impossible, since the essay was first composed and presented as a lecture in 1938) or *The Lord of the Rings*. Tolkien never mentions the essay or the theory of story construction which he explains in it in any of his notes or letters from the period

1938-52, when he worked on *The Lord of the Rings*. Some people seem to believe he felt completely bound by the principles he set forth. But by the time Tolkien began to write *The Lord of the Rings*, he was bound by other material which had appeared in print, and which he had been working on or had worked on throughout the previous twenty-two years.

In fact, in the essay, Tolkien admonishes, "Let us not divide the human race into Eloi and Morlocks: pretty children -- 'elves' as the eighteenth century often idiotically called them -- with their fairy-tales (carefully pruned), and dark Morlocks tending their machines. If fairy-story as a kind is worth reading at all it is worthy to be written for and read by adults." He had already violated this cardinal rule by writing *The Hobbit* for his children, and it was not the only such fairy-story to leave Tolkien's hand in that style. And there are other cardinal rules in the essay which Tolkien proceeded to violate with *The Lord of the Rings*, such as the requirement for a happy ending. He almost had one with the Epilogue, in which Sam, Rosie, and the kids anticipated Aragorn's visit to the Shire. But Tolkien was persuaded to drop the Epilogue in favor of Sam's unforgettable and bittersweet, "Well, I'm back."

Although whole volumes of analysis have been published which correctly point to various Anglo-Saxonisms in *The Lord of the Rings*, particularly with respect to nomenclature in The Shire and Rohan, a world of Greek influences has been overlooked in an apparently zealous attempt to convert *The Lord of the Rings* into a modern Anglo-Saxon anthem. Tolkien studied other languages, other stories. He made reference to them. He buried their elements in his own stories.

For example, you won't find mention of a staff in "Beowulf", but Theoden and Gandalf both lean on staves, which are symbols of their authority: Gandalf the self-acclaimed steward and Theoden the king of the Homeric Rohirrim. But where would Tolkien find inspiration to use a staff as the symbol of authority, especially royal authority among the Rohirrim?

How about "The Iliad"?

> King Agamemnon stood up, holding his staff,
> one fashioned by Hephaestus' careful craftsmanship.
> That god had given it to lord Zeus, son of Cronos.
> Later Zeus had presented it to Hermes,
> the guide, killer of Argus. Hermes, in his turn,
> gave it to King Pelops, the chariot racer,
> who passed the staff to Atreus, the people's leader.
> This man, as he lay dying, left it for Thyestes,
> who owned many flocks. Thyestes, in his turn,
> passed it on to Agamemnon, who held it
> as ruler of all Argos and many islands.
> With this staff as his support, Agamemnon spoke:

Source: Homer, The Iliad: a new translation by Ian Johnston
(http://www.mala.bc.ca/~johnstoi/homer/iliad_title.htm).

Homer doesn't just put a staff into Agamemnon's hand; he glorifies the staff, bestowed upon the king from the hands of the gods (through his family). When Agamemnon raised his staff, the Achaean kings listened to him in such as way as they would not listen to any other person. The speeches that Agamemnon and others make in "The Iliad" provide a template for the speeches in "The Wanderings of Hurin" (*The War of the Jewels*). Agamemnon orders his heralds to sound their trumpets, and thousands of Achaeans come to a vast assembly to hear him speak. Hardang, Halad of Brethil, is forced to call an assembly of the Folk of Brethil (a Folkmoot), in which the chieftains of the people come by the hundreds. A trumpet is sounded there, too. In both stories, men get up and address the assemblies, and they win the support of the assemblies by appealing to the peoples' strong sense of morality and law.

In the tradition of Rohan, two early leaders stand out from the rest: Eorl and Helm Hammerhand. When Tolkien wrote *The Lord of the Rings*, only a handful of people knew about the as-yet unpublished *Silmarillion*, so he may have borrowed lightly from himself by modeling Helm on Hurin and Eorl on Hador Lorindol. Helm was a man of great strength and temper, and because of his ungracious handling of Freca, Helm launched a war which nearly destroyed Rohan. Helm's son Haleth fell defending Meduseld against the army led by Freca's son Wulf. Helm himself died later on, somewhere out in the miserable cold, alone. Túrin killed himself after defeating the dragon Glaurung in defense of Brethil, and Hurin eventually wandered off to die somewhere in the south, perhaps alone. Eorl, like Hador, was already the leader of his people when he became their king (Hador became the first Lord of Dor-lomin). Both men were tall and golden-haired, and they were celebrated in song. Both men also fell in battle with their traditional enemies and were avenged by their sons. Both men led their people to new lands within the borders of great kingdoms.

Tolkien's protagonists, for large stories and small, seem to fit the mold that Glenn proposes: they are either Adventurers (such as Túrin, Beren, and Aragorn) or Leaders (such as Hador, Hurin, Eorl, Helm, Theoden, and Aragorn), or both (such as Aragorn and Isildur). The traditional northern hero, brave and arrogant, or tragic and foolhardy, a bit dim-witted, doesn't really serve Tolkien's purpose. He looks beyond the northern tradition for a more suitable hero archetype, and associated symbology. The merging of mythical worlds thus results in the most unique of mythical worlds, and one which reasonably echoes traces of all classical western literature.

If Tolkien continuously explores the motif of cultural conflicts, he nonetheless invigorates the art by mingling his narrative sources. However, he chooses the elements carefully, selecting archetypes and symbols which go well together. His Rohirrim, depicting all that is best of the Northmen, thus demand representation in a northern language, and therefore why not Tolkien's beloved Anglo-Saxon? But the choice of Anglo-Saxon, Old English, as the language of Rohan forced Tolkien to lead the reader into making associations which he later felt compelled to deny. Hence, the Rohirrim may be too much of a good thing for their own sake.

In *The Road to Middle-earth*, Shippey concedes that "Tolkien did not approve of the academic search for 'sources'. He thought it tended to distract attention from the work of art itself, and to undervalue the

artist by the suggestion that he had 'got it all' from somewhere else."
The pursuit of identifying and justifying the Anglo-Saxon connections
consumes the reader, especially the well-read reader like Shippey. He
feels compelled to defend Tolkien against what he himself might
regard as "Sloppy Statements" and "simple-minded and profligate
Parallel-Hunting". There is certainly nothing simple-minded in
Shippey's own parallel-hunting, but he barely mentions the Bible and
perhaps once mentions Greek tragedy at all during the process of
convincing the world that Tolkien's literature nearly begins and ends
with the Anglo-Saxon language. Finnish and the Kalevala are accorded
some respect, since Tolkien himself pointed out the connections, but
The Lord of the Rings owes a great deal more to the classics than most
commentators have conceded.

However, though the Anglo-Saxonists seek something specifically
English in Tolkien's work, Tolkien himself may have been working
toward a pseudo-English literature. That is, just as it is undeniable that
he used Anglo-Saxon nomenclature in *The Lord of the Rings*, and just
as Shippey argues convincingly that there are strong parallels between
snippets of Tolkien's story and numerous medieval sources, it remains
nonetheless that Tolkien abandoned the mythology for England. He
abandoned it long before he wrote *The Lord of the Rings*. But it may
be that he did so because he realized there was a more desirable, and
much more easily achieved, goal. Or perhaps a more necessary one.

Tolkien wrote "I have very little interest in serial literary history, and
no interest at all in the history of present situation of the English
'novel'. My work is *not* a 'novel', but an 'heroic romance' a much
older and quite different variety of literature." (*The Letters of J.R.R.
Tolkien*, No. 329) Elsewhere he wrote, "Certainly I have not been
nourished by English literature, in which I do not suppose that I am
better read than you; for the simple reason that I have never found
much there in which to rest my heart (or heart and head together). I
was brought up in the Classics, and first discovered the sensation of
literary pleasure in Homer." (Ibid., No. 142)

And yet, Tolkien also pointed out, in response to a request for help
with a translation of *The Lord of the Rings* into Polish, that "as [the

translator] perceives, this is an English book and its Englishry should not be eradicated." (Ibid., No. 217) Well, that's a rather peculiar thing to say, coming from a person who on more than one occasion denied any particular fondness for English literature. Heroic romances, in Tolkien's opinion, go all the way back to Homer, and realized their most widespread popularity in Medieval literature. So Tolkien may only have been denying himself a place in both modern English and Medieval literature. He didn't say the book was Medieval, or Anglo-Saxon. In fact, it's not either. A Medieval or Anglo-Saxon reader probably would not understand most of what was going on in the story.

But a modern Anglo-Saxon reader might. Not simply an Englishman, but an Anglo-Saxon Englishman. Tolkien was certainly no stranger to "what if" literature. His time traveling story-tellers, and his numerous essays pondering the philosophical aspects of Middle-earth, make it clear that Tolkien enjoyed wandering through the halls of What Might Have Been or What Could Be. *The Lord of the Rings* may be the culmination of a theory of literature which had been slowly brewing under his care and consideration for more than twenty years.

The Lord of the Rings may be Tolkien's attempt define the modern English heroic romance as it might have evolved from an uninterrupted Anglo-Saxon literary tradition. Such a tradition could not have helped avoid importing influences from abroad. Anglo-Saxon authors would eventually have been introduced and reintroduced to the classics as the centuries unfolded. As Tolkien devised alternative plural forms for words such as "dwarf" ("dwarrows" and "dwarves" instead of the traditional "dwarfs"), so he may have sought to devise an alternative model for English literature. Eschewing the 'novel', he brought the heroic romance forward and gave it the framework that a rich literary tradition would have to provide. He could pick and choose from the best traditions that western literature has to offer. Why not? Anglo-Saxon authors throughout the past 1,000 years would not have ignored so many important steps in the evolution. Especially not when England became the dominant power in the world, and the English provoked their thought with ideas from around the globe.

UNDERSTANDING MIDDLE-EARTH

Just as *The Lord of the Rings* is set in an imaginary time in our past, so it purports to be a translation of an ancient work, *The Red Book of Westmarch*. In fact, it may be a fictitious work on another level, an example of how the English might have carried forward their heroic traditions, and adopted models from other traditions, had there been no 1066 invasion. In "On the Cold Hill's Side", chapter 8 of *The Road to Middle-earth*, Tom Shippey writes "Tolkien liked to bring 'philologist-figures' into his fiction" and he provides several examples. Shippey discerns double-entendre throughout Tolkien's works, and perhaps rightly so. Whether by intent or applicability, Tolkien's characters often speak on two levels.

Faramir's words to Frodo may be another example of that double intent or applicability. As Tolkien's fictitious literary tradition became more like modern literature, modern literature (through *The Lord of the Rings*) became more like his fictitious literary tradition. In other words, Tolkien's imaginary Anglo-Saxon literature evolved into an imaginary English literature. In Tolkien's imaginary past, Shakespeare's English literature might not have been so disappointing. *The Lord of the Rings* is therefore what a philologist might recognize as an "asterisk-book". Shippey devotes many pages to explaining philology and its historical roots, but let it suffice to say that philology is the study of language and history. The philologist, at least one like Tolkien, cannot understand a word without understanding its history, and in understanding a word he understands the history with which the word is associated.

One example of this outlook is Tolkien's reaction to a lecture his son Christopher gave. Shippey quotes Tolkien's excited comment about the apparent derivation of the name "Attila" from the Gothic word "atta" (father). "Attila" means "Little Father", and apparently implies that his Gothic warriors were very devoted to him. Many Goths did indeed serve in Attila's army. Historians have never fully agreed upon why, and the Tolkien explanation seems as good as any: Attila delivered the goods to his soldiers, and they didn't care who was a Hun and who was a Goth.

In reconstructing the languages of our past, and therefore providing some insights into our past, philologists devise what are referred to as "asterisk-words". These are words which the philologists conclude must have existed at some time, and perhaps have evolved into new words. They are denoted in word-lists and dictionaries with an asterisk (*) placed at the front. Anyone who has read Tolkien's "Etymologies" knows he scattered many asterisk-words throughout his invented languages. He didn't presume to know everything possible about Elvish languages, but left it for others to see what he had discovered and to follow in his footsteps. At least, in an imaginary tradition of philology it must be so.

So, *The Lord of the Rings* is an asterisk-book. It is Tolkien's example of how the Anglo-Saxon literary tradition might have evolved. Although they are usually devised in an attempt to look further back, asterisk-words may be devised from known or postulated roots in an effort to extend our knowledge about poorly documented languages. In the same way, Tolkien brought Old English literature forward, leap-frogging across a thousand years by looking at the evolution of literary motifs and drawing upon sources from across the ages.

Tolkien's imaginary modern Anglo-Saxons would therefore be a diverse people, and they would be Catholic, and they would be great story-tellers. This is my long-winded way of saying the Anglo-Saxonists may have been on to something without realizing it. But though I take great joy in finding some common ground with them, the sad fact is that we now may know why there will never be another book like *The Lord of the Rings*. It would take a philologist of J.R.R. Tolkien's calibre (sharing his personal preferences and background) to add another title to that imaginary literary tradition he created, and a man of his genius and insight may come along only once in a thousand years.

Chapter 22:
The other way round

When *The Lord of the Rings* was first published, some reviewers apparently decided that "all the good [peoples were] just good, and the bad just bad." In indirect response to such complaints, Tolkien noted to one reader: "...the Elves were *not* wholly good or in the right" (*The Letters of J.R.R. Tolkien*, No. 154). Indeed, none of his characters were wholly "good" or "evil"; and Elrond acknowledged as much, telling the members of his council that "nothing is evil in the beginning. Even Sauron was not so."

The Rohirrim are another example of a group who seem good but do evil (on occasion). The treason of Grima Wormtongue is foreshadowed by the rebellion of Freca and his son Wulf, who overthrows King Helm Hammerhand with the aid of Dunlendings, Easterlings, and Corsairs. But the Rohirrim engage in questionable behavior even as a people. When Theoden offers a great reward to Ghan-Buri-Ghan for leading his army to Minas Tirith, Ghan-Buri-Ghan only asks that the Rohirrim stop hunting his people like animals. The Rohirrim are thus not perfect, and sometimes readers have to be shown so. All too many people through the years have mistaken the Rohirrim for a pro-Fascist Nordic purity stereotype (completely unaware of Tolkien's opposition to the German Fascists and their racist views).

Yet readers also focus on the Rohirrim for another reason: except for Eowyn, many people note, Tolkien put no strong women characters in his stories. Inevitably, people point to Galadriel and Lúthien as counter-examples. Now, Galadriel does not play much of a role in *The Lord of the Rings*, and Lúthien is barely mentioned. Even Eowyn's role is covered in the space of a few chapters (none of which are devoted exclusively to her). On the other hand, *The Silmarillion* provides more active roles for women. And *Unfinished Tales* offers tantalizing glimpses into the lives of several women (most notably, Galadriel).

But in *The Lord of the Rings*, Eowyn is introduced as little more than throne-dressing for Theoden. She graduates to a promised reward for Grima Wormtongue, and then proceeds to fall hopelessly in love with Aragorn, who (of course) rejects her for the noblest of reasons (his love is already given to another). Eowyn's long empty life fills her with despair, which leads her to seek a glorious death on the battlefield, and thus Tolkien's shield-maiden comes to life. Many an argument has swirled over the value Eowyn brings to what is mostly a "boy story". She is, in some ways, the one redeeming quality about the Rohirrim, and in other ways their most damning attribute.

The Rohirrim inspire debate and division among Tolkien readers more than any other group, except perhaps the Elves. The Rohirrim are often compared to the Anglo-Saxons, and there are people who argue that the Rohirrim *must* be modeled on the Anglo-Saxons because Tolkien used Old English (Anglo-Saxon) to represent their language. It's merely a silly fiction, after all, that he was translating a lost book into modern English, and needed to represent forgotten languages with documented languages. The fallacy in this line of thought is twofold: first, it contradicts Tolkien's own admonition not to confuse the Rohirrim with Anglo-Saxons; and secondly, perhaps more importantly, it assumes that the Rohirrim make some sort of statement about Anglo-Saxon culture.

In effect, if the Rohirrim are based on the Anglo-Saxons, they are an allegory (and a thinly disguised one). Such an identification thus makes Tolkien a liar twice over, because he noted on more than one occasion (including in the book's Foreword) that "I cordially dislike allegory in all its manifestations, and have always done so...." And yet, he acknowledges that there is an 'applicability' factor, noting that "many confuse 'applicability' with 'allegory'; but the one resides in the freedom of the reader, and the other in the purposed domination of the author."

He most certainly chose those final words carefully: "the purposed domination of the author." The peril of the One Ring, for the world at large, is its ability to confer upon its wielder (who must first control it) the ability to dominate the wills of others. It was for this reason that

Sauron made the Ring. The domination of the author eliminates all purposeful study by the reader, and Tolkien really cannot have been pretending he would prefer something so stringent and restricting. The chief beauty of *The Lord of the Rings* lies outside the story itself: it has become many things to many people.

And, in Eowyn, some of Tolkien's readers have found an iconography of the ideal woman of action. She is both stern and enduring, yet forceful and decisive when need demands she be so. But Eowyn is also tragic; in fact, her original storyline resulted in her death. In revising the book (prior to its initial publication), Tolkien softened Eowyn's part, and allowed her not only to live, but to find love and healing with Faramir. Her choices represent a combination of ideas which Tolkien synthesized only through multiple drafts. Eowyn became a refraction of several models blended into one unique character.

Eowyn is a complex character because she seems to require some justification. Tolkien received a letter from a reader in the 1960s who apparently objected to the speed with which Eowyn fell in love with Faramir. In reply, Tolkien said: "...In my experience feelings and decisions ripen very quickly (as measured by mere 'clock-time', which is actually not justly applicable) in periods of great stress, and especially under the expectation of imminent death. And I do *not* think that persons of high estate and breeding need all the petty fencing and approaches in matters of 'love'. This tale does not deal with a period of 'Courtly Love' and its pretences; but with a culture more primitive (sc. less corrupt) and nobler." (Ibid., No. 244)

Well. Tolkien might as well say the Rohirrim are not medieval. But wait. He did say that, in Letter 211: "...The Rohirrim were not 'mediaeval', in our sense." Yadda, yadda, yadda. That citation gets dragged out at the drop of a chain mail reference, and is used on both sides of the fence. But if the Rohirrim were not medieval "in our sense", what were they? Setting aside all comparisons to medieval sources for a moment (which are perfectly applicable in many cases), one can easily find other sources of inspiration Tolkien drew upon.

And Eowyn is a perfect example of how Tolkien synthesized elements from both classical and medieval sources.

In fact, Eowyn owes far more to Greek mythology than to the virtually non-existent Anglo-Saxon literary tradition. She is certainly comparable in her rebellious state to some women from Middle English literature. Eowyn seems to challenge the social fabric of Rohan in her dialogue with Aragorn, in which she complains there is no place for women in the coming war. But Eowyn is acknowledged as a shield-maiden by the narrative (and thus, through implication, by her people), a term familiar to the historical Germanic world. And yet her swift passage to glory reflects a much older tradition, a classical one. Eowyn is not concerned with either piety or sexuality, two themes frequently associated with women in medieval English literature. Medieval writers unfortunately decided that women were somehow responsible for sin (even though the Bible claimed that Adam was the source of all our woes). Classical writers gave women more faults than that.

Quintus of Smyrna was a late Classical writer. He lived in the 4th century CE, more than 1,000 years after Homer and the other poets who created the Epic Cycle of Greece. Homer and his fellow Cyclic Poets composed their verses in commemoration of the Trojan War. To them, perhaps, the war was very real, and they were preserving traditions which had been handed down for generations. Homer's "Iliad" covers a period of only 50 days, but the whole ten-year war is supposed to have been recorded in the Cycle's epic poetry. The Cyclic Poets established a Poetic Renaissance in Greece, which had only recently emerged from a centuries-long dark age that had begun soon after Troy fell to its enemies. (Archaeology has revealed that Troy was sacked several times, but Homeric Troy was destroyed just prior to the onset of the Greek Dark Age, circa 1200 BCE.)

Quintus is believed to have rewritten the work of Arctinus (who composed "The Coming of Memnon", AKA "Aethiopis", and "The Destruction of Troy", AKA "Iliupersus", around 776 BCE) and Lesches (who composed "Little Iliad" around 700 BCE). Our image of late Homeric Trojan (pseudo) history derives much from "The Fall of Troy", which was Quintus' epic, composed in the Homeric tradition. He is credited as having been so familiar with Homer's work that he came very close to duplicating Homer's style, although there are criticisms leveled against Quintus -- he too often failed to match Homer's details on specific events, or built up toward a Homeric climax which was never realized.

In 1916, while recovering from Trench Fever (contracted in the war in France), Tolkien began writing the first of his own mythological stories. In title, "The Fall of Troy" sounds very much like "The Fall of Gondolin" (the first of Tolkien's mythic compositions). Indeed, like Troy, Gondolin was a city built on a hill-top, whose enemies struck at it through treachery (and despite a prophetic warning of impending disaster). Cassandra warned the Trojans not to accept the gift of the wooden horse from the Greeks, and her people ignored her. Tuor warned Turgon that it was time to leave Gondolin, and Turgon ignored him. And just as Greek warriors emerged from the wooden horse to open the gates to the city, the original Gondolin story included metal dragons who carried Orc soldiers inside them.

"The Fall of Gondolin" is firmly rooted in Greek mythological precedents, from the catalogues of Elvish lords and their houses, to sack of the city itself; and the story thus laid the groundwork for Tolkien's mythology for England. "The Fall of Gondolin" was a shameless retelling of the Trojan myth in an Anglo-Saxon mode (or, what Tolkien felt might pass for one in 1916/7). Like Quintus before him, Tolkien looked back to the Epic Cycle for inspiration. But though Tolkien was not striving to create an epic poem in Homeric style, he *was* seeking to achieve something Homeric: the creation of an epic cycle for England, just as Homer (and others) had created an epic cycle for Greece. Tolkien wanted to translate Greek mythological achievements into Anglo-Saxon mythological possibilities.

Tolkien loved Greek mythology. It had a profound influence upon him. In fact, Middle-earth undoubtedly owes a great deal more to Greek mythology than shall ever be acknowledged by all the dusty, cobweb-laden artifices of higher scholarship which weigh down the library shelves of Tolkien research. Greek mythology is the uttermost foundation of Middle-earth, because Tolkien saw in Greek mythology that which he could not find in the scraps of Anglo-Saxon literature which he eventually taught about. Without Greek mythology, it is highly unlikely Tolkien would ever have dreamed of an Anglo-Saxon (or modern English) mythology.

In a draft for a letter to one of his readers, Tolkien wrote in January 1956: "It was just as the 1914 War burst upon me that I made the discovery that 'legends' depend upon the language to which they belong; but a living language depends equally on the 'legends' which it conveys by tradition. (For example, that the Greek mythology depends far more on the marvellous aesthetic of its language and so of its nomenclature of persons and places and less on its content than people realize, though of course it depends on both. And *vice versa*...)." (Ibid., No. 180)

Middle-earth still lay decades ahead of Tolkien, a distant glimmer on the horizon of his future, when he made his innocent discovery in 1914. There were stories which would soon burst from his hand, imaginative tales he hoped might one day constitute a mythology for England. In 1951, Tolkien confessed to the publisher Milton Waldman (of Collins, to whom he was hoping to sell the as-yet unpublished *Lord of the Rings* and *Silmarillion* books):

> But an equally basic passion of mine *ab initio* [tr: from the beginning] was for myth (not allegory!) and for fairy-story, and above all for heroic legend on the brink of fairy-tale and history, of which there is far too little in the world (accessible to me) for my appetite. I was an undergraduate before thought and experience revealed to me that these were not divergent interests -- opposite poles of science and romance -- but integrally related. I am *not* 'learned' [Footnote: Though I have thought *about* them a good deal.] in the matters of myth and fairy-story, however, for in such things (as far as is known to me) I have always been seeking material, things of a certain tone and air, and not simple knowledge. Also -- and here I hope I shall not sound absurd -- I was from early days grieved by the poverty of my own beloved country: it had no stories of its own (bound up with its tongue and soil), not of the quality that I sought, and found (as ingredient) in legends of other lands. There

was Greek, and Celtic, and Romance, Germanic, Scandinavian, and Finnish (which greatly affected me); but nothing English, save impoverished chap-book stuff....(Ibid., No. 131)

In December 1953, Tolkien noted to his friend Father Robert Murray: "Certainly I have not been nurtured by English Literature....I was bought up on the Classics, and first discovered the sensation of literary pleasure in Homer. Also being a philologist, getting a large part of any aesthetic pleasure that I am capable of from the *form* of words (and especially from the *fresh* association of word-form with word-sense), I have always best enjoyed things in a foreign language, or one so remote as to feel like it (such as Anglo-Saxon)...." (Ibid., No. 142)

Tolkien's introduction to Greek language and literature began while he was still quite young, in Sixth Class at King Edward's School (First Class was the senior-most level in the school). In time, Tolkien studied the New Testament in Greek as well, and Humphrey Carpenter quotes Tolkien as saying: "The fluidity of Greek, punctuated by hardness, and with its surface glitter captivated me. But part of the attraction was antiquity and alien remoteness (from me): it did not touch home."

Yet though Greek played an important role in Tolkien's education, and ultimately assumed a permanent place in his imagination, his love of *philology* (the study of linguistic change) was sparked by a teacher at King Edward's who introduced Tolkien and his classmates to Chaucer and Middle English. Carpenter observes that the teacher's recitation of Chaucer in the original Middle English "was a revelation, and [Tolkien] determined to learn more about the history of the [English] language." King Edward's curriculum focused on the study of Latin and Greek, and therefore it prepared Tolkien for a lifetime of study in other languages. He never forgot the Classics, though he is seldom associated with them any more.

Tolkien's transition from the study of Greek and Latin Classics to the study of Gothic, Anglo-Saxon, Finnish, and other languages really began when he attended Oxford University. There he was introduced to new influences and he committed himself to the Philological field.

But Tolkien credited the nearly two years he spent working on the Oxford English Dictionary in 1919 and 1920 with honing his linguistic skills more than any other phase in his life. The OED is famous for taking English words back as far as they can go. Modern English, like all European languages, extends back several thousand years through many periods of change. The earliest language common to all the European peoples is Indo-European (and it's also common to non-European peoples, including Iranians, Indians, and a few other groups). Many of the OED entries include (postulated) Indo-European and intermediate (ex.: proto-Germanic) roots.

While "The Fall of Gondolin" proved to be the first of Tolkien's Greek-inspired myths, Carpenter tells us that at the time Tolkien was working on the Oxford English Dictionary, he "began (on New Year's Day 1919) to keep a diary in which he recorded principal events and his thoughts on them. After starting it in ordinary handwriting he began instead to use a remarkable alphabet that he had just invented, which looked like a mixture of Hebrew, Greek, and Pitman's shorthand. He soon decided to involve it with his mythology, and he named it 'The Alphabet of Rumil' after an elvish sage in his stories."

That alphabet evolved into the Tengwar of *The Lord of the Rings*, and it represents the first in a series of departures from the pseudo Anglo-Saxon tradition which Tolkien eventually abandoned. Officially, he did not abandon the *Book of Lost Tales* until about 1925 or 1926. Tolkien continued to write stories and devise notes concerning his mythological lost age for England up until that time. As Homer and his contemporaries memorialized Amazons, gods, sirens, Cyclopes, and other mythological creatures and peoples, so Tolkien memorialized imaginary prehistoric inhabitants of England. He did not neglect the Anglo-Saxon element, but his stories were really about fantastic creatures who retreated before the encroachment of the Anglo-Saxon peoples.

Anglo-Saxon, of course, continued to influence Tolkien's thought and fiction in many ways. In June, 1925, Tolkien applied for the Rawlinson and Bosworth Professorship of Anglo-Saxon at Oxford. Tolkien dutifully noted that he had specialized in Greek philology for his Classical Moderations, but he added Old Icelandic, Gothic, Old and Middle English, and Medieval Welsh to the category of languages in which he was expert. And it has oft been noted that Old Icelandic provided Tolkien with several sources for the new mythologies he developed. For while he worked on the new Silmarillion mythology (which began to emerge in 1925), Tolkien also began writing the story which eventually became *The Hobbit*. It shimmered across his thought briefly in 1925, when he wrote, "In a hole in the ground there lived a Hobbit" on the back of a blank exam paper, and by 1930 Tolkien was entertaining his children with the adventures of Mr. Baggins. From *The Hobbit* there emerged the Norse/Icelandic names of Tolkien's Dwarves, and the tantalizing history of Dale, the first of his Northman kingdoms, as well as the dark and perilous Mirkwood Forest. In fact, much of *The Hobbit* reads like a light excursion into Norse mythology, with giants, shape-changers, wizards, dwarves, and dragons.

From 1918 (or 1921) through 1925, Tolkien worked on "Lay of the Children of Hurin" (Urin). This poem was composed in alliterative verse, following Old English styles. But when Tolkien began working on "Lay of Leithian" (the story of Beren and Lúthien) in 1925, he changed modes, preferring instead the octosyllabic couplets (pairs of rhyming lines with eight syllables each) which originated in French Romance (around the 12th century and introduced into Middle English in the 13th century). The transition represented another departure for Tolkien from the Anglo-Saxon tradition. But Romance afforded him a much friendlier (if more difficult) mode in which to work.

Homer worked with hexameter (six syllables per line), which doesn't occur in any of Tolkien's major poems (perhaps none of them). The octosyllabic form took root under Tolkien's hand and flourished in his stories; he transformed it in some of his poems, such as Bilbo's song of Ëarendil and Legolas' song of Nimrodel. "Ëarendil" used the very difficult trisyllabic assonance form (the last three syllables of every other line rhyme). "Nimrodel" was more standardized, rhyming in every other line. Gimli, on the other hand, retained the older octosyllabic couplets for his song about Moria in Durin's time. In *The Lord of the Rings*, therefore, Tolkien favored the Romance verse style, but he occasionally broke with the form and became experimental.

And as Tolkien well knew, experimentation was a hallmark of Greek poetry, which had so profound an effect on Western literature and lyric that we still describe our poetic forms in Greek terminology today. Therefore, it should come as no surprise that Tolkien eschewed rigid adherence to Franco-English medieval poetic forms in all cases. In contrast to "Ëarendil" and "Nimrodel", Galadriel's "Namárië" seems to be composed in a ten-syllable blank verse (but some of the lines have eleven or twelve syllables -- Tolkien may have used a Welsh form, or perhaps a Finnish form, and I am unfamiliar with both). Tolkien therefore experimented liberally with the verse forms in *The Lord of the Rings*.

Each poem sheds a little light on Middle-earth's mythology. In true Greek fashion, Tolkien tells a story which is bound up with a name or word. For example, when the Fellowship comes to the river Nimrodel, Legolas tells his companions about the ancient Elf-maiden who gave her name to the river, and he sings the song about her ill-fated love for Amroth. The poetry is not simply window-dressing. It is part of a larger composite element, consisting of the name (Nimrodel) and the story (an Elf-maiden flees her land, is separated from her lover, and is ultimately lost), and the poem commemorating her story. Greek mythology follows the same pattern. Homer took the name of a city (Ilion, Ilium) and used it for the name of a poem which told part of the story of the destruction of that city. Troy passed into the canon of Greek myth which survives today through Homer's poem. In his time, and for many centuries afterward, the events in the "Iliad" were regarded as historical.

In Letter 156, Tolkien said that the Númenoreans "were still living on the borders of myth". His story "exhibits 'myth' passing into History or the Dominion of Men". He was seeking "heroic legend on the brink of fairy-tale and history" (Ibid., No. 131). He strove to provide a Homeric link between his contemporary audience and an imaginary past which seems as real as the legendary past Homer and the Cyclic Poets immortalized.

The Cyclic Epic, of course, does not concern itself with the battle between an incarnate evil being and free peoples. Instead, it details the moral struggles of the Achaeans and Trojans (and their allies) to come to terms with the choices they have made. Homer's warriors are both noble and petty, gallant and petulant. Glaucus and Diomedes exchange armor and vow not to attack each other in battle; Achilles sulks in his tent over the loss of a slave-girl while the Trojans run down the other Achaeans. The Epic Cycle balances the struggles of men with the struggles of the Olympian gods. They know that Troy must eventually fall, but some of the Olympians sneak around and help the Achaeans, and Zeus waffles back and forth between favors owed to followers and family.

In much the same way, Tolkien's Rohirrim are engaged in a struggle with other men, the Dunlendings, which has become swept up in the greater battle with Sauron (and Saruman, who is Sauron's surrogate). The Rohirrim fight Orcs and live close to Ents, all creatures of fantasy, but they are mythologically equivalent to men. That is, the Ents and Orcs are what Tolkien would call "aspects of the humane", and they represent human interests (isolationist communities and barbaric ravaging hordes). The Rohan-Dunland conflict only briefly rises to the surface in *The Lord of the Rings*, but it is the underlying reason for the peril which threatens Rohan. The Rohirrim, for their part, are ambivalent toward the Dunlendings; sometimes they intermarry with the Dunlendings, and sometimes they exchange brutal raids with the Dunlendings.

Tolkien introduces the reader to the Rohirrim through a heroic procession as Eomer and 114 Riders pass by Aragorn, Gimli, and Legolas. Protected by Elvish cloaks, Aragorn and his companions are nearly invisible to the Rohirrim, just as Achaeans and Trojans are occasionally hidden in clouds and whisked past each other by their meddling gods. When Aragorn and Eomer meet face to face, they nearly come to blows, but Aragorn reminds Eomer that they have a common foe, and he acknowledges a past relationship with Eomer's father, just as Diomedes acknowledges a family connection with Glaucus' family. The two do not exchange armor, but Eomer lends Aragorn and his companions two horses, a risky act which evokes the one-sided exchange between Glaucus and Diomedes: Glaucus' golden armor was worth ten times Diomedes' bronze armor.

But Tolkien also looks to the Anglo-Saxon poem "Beowulf" for inspiration, as some are quick to point out. The approach of Aragorn, Gandalf, Gimli, and Legolas to Edoras has been compared to Beowulf's arrival in Denmark. Guardsmen at the gate of Edoras challenge the four travelers, and a coastguardsman challenges Beowulf and his fourteen men. Both groups are accompanied to the halls of the local lords, and both guardsmen depart. Heorot, the golden hall of Hrothgar, serves as a convenient model for Meduseld, Theoden's golden-roofed (but otherwise humble and mundane) hall.

Curiously, both Beowulf's Danes and Geats and Homer's Achaeans travel by ship, and they live on islands or on a peninsula jutting out into a small sea. Beowulf and his Geats, and Menelaus and his Achaeans, have crossed their local seas seeking war. Menelaus goes to retrieve his estranged wife, Helen, and Beowulf goes to help Hrothgar defeat a monster. The enemies in "Beowulf" are all monsters, whereas the Achaeans are fighting other men (though half-gods abound on either side, as Zeus and his family have been busily consorting with local families for generations).

There are no monsters threatening Rohan, although the wolf-riders and Orcs are certainly terrifying creatures. But they do not steal into Theoden's hall at night and kill his warriors. Theoden, in fact, commands a very capable army, just as Priam of Troy and Menelaus command very capable armies. The war between Rohan and Isengard depends as much on morale as it does on strategy. Battles rage across the landscape and armies retreat as the fortunes of war scramble from side to side. And just as the Trojans mount an assault on the Achaeans' camp, breaching the walls, so Saruman's army mounts an assault on the Hornburg, in which the walls are breached. Patroclus, Achilles' friend, helps to route the Trojans by donning Achilles' armor and leading the Myrmidons in a counter-attack. But Patroclus is eventually slain, forcing Achilles to make peace with the other chieftains. Theoden and Eomer are estranged over Eomer's breach of orders. But after word arrives of the death of Theodred, the king's son, and Gandalf helps to heal Theoden of his despair, Theoden is reconciled with Eomer.

The striking similarities between the Rohirrim and Homer's heroes are numerous. And Tolkien seems to have added more Homeric elements to the story of the Rohirrim after *The Lord of the Rings* was published. "The Battles of the Fords of Isen" (published in *Unfinished Tales*), for example, recounts how Theodred was slain, and the Rohirrim defended his body where it fell much as the Achaeans defended the body of Patroclus.

In his letter to Milton Waldman, Tolkien notes: "The sequel [to *The Hobbit*], *The Lord of the Rings*, much the largest, and I hope also in proportion the best, of the entire cycle, concludes the whole business -- an attempt is made to include in it, and wind up, all the elements and motives of what has preceded: elves, dwarves, the Kings of Men, heroic 'Homeric' horsemen, orcs and demons, the terrors of the Ring-servants and Necromancy, and the vast horror of the Dark Throne, even in style it is to include the colloquialism and vulgarity of Hobbits, poetry and the highest style of prose." (*The Letters of J.R.R. Tolkien*, No. 131) "The cycle", as he calls it, extends from *The Silmarillion* (then still unpublished) through *The Hobbit* to *The Lord of the Rings*. Tolkien would eventually add *The Adventures of Tom Bombadil* and *The Road Goes Ever On*. It would fall to his son Christopher to add a *Silmarillion* and *Unfinished Tales*.

Unlike the Beowulf poet, Tolkien wasn't simply telling a rollicking good story. He was creating a mythology. The Beowulf poet was codifying a popular tale, perhaps Christianizing it along the way, and quite possibly was introducing a few classical elements of his own. But the Danes and Geats of "Beowulf" bear little resemblance to the Rohirrim in style. The Rohirrim do not boast about their own deeds, whereas Beowulf proudly corrects the conniving Unferth by telling how he engaged in a contest of strength and endurance with Breca years before. The heroes of Beowulf live in a Germanic world which looks and feels like the Northman culture of Rohan: kings sit in halls, noble women serve drinking cups, warriors stand beside their lords, men value courage and trust in their convictions. The boasting is, in fact, a trait which "Beowulf" shares with the "Iliad". Both Achaeans and Trojans often break into long-winded accounts of their genealogies and deeds. Poetically, the story-tellers must remind their audiences of who was whom, and how they were all related to each other.

It is the poetic form where Tolkien borrows extensively from Anglo-Saxons for the Rohirrim, though. He uses the Anglo-Saxon (Old English) language as a model for the Rohirrim's mode of speech. He depicts the Rohirrim as a more primitive, less sophisticated people in comparison to the rural Hobbits and Cosmopolitan Dunedain and Elves, who speak colloquial modern English or an affected archaic modern English. The Rohirrim play the role that an Anglo-Saxon tribe, living beside modern Englishmen, might be allotted. But whereas the Anglo-Saxons learned to write, and bequeathed to their descendants documents such as "Beowulf", Bede's *Ecclesiastical History of the English People*, and *The Anglo-Saxon Chronicle*, the Rohirrim did not write down their legends and laws. So, song and poetry are the hallmark of Rohirric culture.

Aragorn breaks out into song when he and his companions approach Edoras, passing by the mounds where Rohan's kings are buried. When Legolas concludes that the song is in Rohirric, and is "laden with the sadness of Mortal Men", Aragorn translates it for his companions. He starts out in an alliterative form but quickly loses meter and all sense of order. The song just sort of sputters out, indecisive regarding what form it wants to follow. Somewhat later, the rejuvenated Theoden summons his warriors: "Arise now, arise, Riders of Theoden! Dire deeds awake, dark is it eastward. Let horse be bridled, horn be sounded! Forth Eorlingas!" This verse does a pretty good job of preserving the simplistic Anglo-Saxon alliterative-stress meter.

Tolkien doesn't simply park the Rohirrim in a 4-beat Anglo-Saxon poetic mode. He lets them wallow a bit in pentameter and other measures. But they retain the distinctive alliterative form. He is declaring in an unspoken way that the Rohirric poets are not hemmed in by poetic tradition. They are changing and experimenting with verse forms. They are "a culture more primitive" than the high medieval culture of Anglo-Saxon England. And yet, Anglo-Saxon poetry serves as Tolkien's model for all the Rohirric experiments.

There is something playful in Tolkien's approach, a free spirited "what if" exercise.

And "what if" leads us to the most distinctive representative of the Rohirrim: Eowyn. She is unique not only because she is a woman warrior (the only one named in any of the stories); she also achieves more personally than any of her contemporaries. She even overshadows Eomer, her brother. It is Eowyn who strikes down the Lord of the Nazgul in an encounter of almost Beowulfian proportion. Whereas the Rohirrim do not confront monsters in their own land, they do have to contend with them in Gondor and Mordor. If the Rohirrim are truly an homage to the Anglo-Saxons of poetry, as Tom Shippey argues in *The Road to Middle-earth*, the highest tribute is paid to Anglo-Saxon women, not their men, through Eowyn.

There is little precedent for Eowyn in Anglo-Saxon England. Little, but not quite none. While Anglo-Saxon laws don't mention women-warriors, how they are to be trained, and who is to equip or lead them, there is one outstanding woman in Anglo-Saxon history: Aethelflaed. The daughter of King Alfred, she married Aethelred of East Mercia. After the death of her husband, Aethelflaed ruled the Mercians by herself. She and her brother eventually defeated the Danes, and only Aethelflaed's sudden death due to illness prevented her from seeing the culmination of their efforts. The only other warrior princess among the Anglo-Saxons was a dubious, unnamed woman whom the Byzantine writer Procopius claimed had led an army of 100,000 of her countrymen against the Varni after their king, Radigis, refused to marry her.

But though Tolkien had no Anglo-Saxon models for Eowyn, he would have found one in Quintus' "The Fall of Troy". Quintus, in Tolkien-like fashion, drew upon ancient Homeric sources as a model and inspiration. And he introduced (or preserved) the heroic Amazon queen Penthesileia for future generations to admire. Penthesileia accidentally killed her sister, Queen Hippolyte, and she fled the Amazon city of Thermodon with twelve companions. Quintus names all twelve, calling one "dark-eyed Harmothoe" and another "Thermodosa glorying with the spear."

Penthesileia and her companions arrive in Troy soon after the funeral of Hector, which event ends Homer's "Iliad". Penthesileia has been driven mad by the Greek Furies as a punishment for the accidental murder of her sister, and she is seeking solace in war. Having heard about the prowess of Achilles, she decides that she is the one who will strike him down.

> So peerless amid all the Amazons
> Unto Troy-town Penthesileia came.
> To right, to left, from all sides hurrying thronged
> The Trojans, greatly marvelling, when they saw
> The tireless War-god's child, the mailed maid,
> Like to the Blessed Gods; for in her face
> Glowed beauty glorious and terrible.
> Her smile was ravishing: beneath her brows
> Her love-enkindling eyes shone like to stars,
> And with the crimson rose of shamefastness
> Bright were her cheeks, and mantled over them
> Unearthly grace with battle-prowess clad.
> (Translation by A.S. Way,
> http://sunsite.berkeley.edu/OMACL/Troy/)

Quintus includes an anachronistic reference to mail (an armor type which first appeared only about 6-700 years before he lived, long after Homer and the Cyclic Poets had died). Nonetheless, the image fits Eowyn well enough: "Very fair was her face, and her long hair was like a river of gold. Slender and tall she was in her white robe girt with silver; but strong she seemed and stern as steel, a daughter of kings." ("The King of the Golden Hall", *The Lord of the Rings*)

Penthesileia is welcomed by the grieving king Priam:

> Into his halls he led the Maid,
> And with glad welcome honoured her, as one
> Who greets a daughter to her home returned
> From a far country in the twentieth year;
> And set a feast before her, sumptuous
> As battle-glorious kings, who have brought low
> Nations of foes, array in splendour of pomp,
> With hearts in pride of victory triumphing.

And gifts he gave her costly and fair to see,
And pledged him to give many more, so she
Would save the Trojans from the imminent doom.
And she such deeds she promised as no man
Had hoped for, even to lay Achilles low,
To smite the wide host of the Argive men,
And cast the brands red-flaming on the ships.
Ah fool! -- but little knew she him, the lord
Of ashen spears, how far Achilles' might
In warrior-wasting strife o'erpassed her own!

The Amazons' arrival is very similar to that of Beowulf and his men. They arrive unlooked-for and seek out the king, promising to rid him of his greatest foe. As Hrothgar bestows gifts and praise upon Beowulf, so Priam showers Penthesileia with favor, and both hero and heroine are treated to a royal feast. Eowyn is given short shrift in the catalogue of heroic introductions. She stands silently beside Theoden and is then dismissed when Gandalf and the boys arrive at Meduseld. In fact, the only time she is treated with distinction is when Theoden leaves her in charge of Edoras. Then he gives her a mail shirt and sword.

Nonetheless, the procession of Penthesileia sleeps in Priam's hall on the eve of battle, just as Beowulf sleeps in Hrothgar's hall to await Grendel's nightly attack. But whereas Beowulf seeks out Grendel in order to help Hrothgar's beleaguered people, Penthesileia acquires her ambition to slay Achilles from a dream. And Eowyn only seeks death in battle, because she has become so filled with despair she has lost her will to live. At this point, Beowulfian foreshadowings vanish from Quintus' poem, but Tolkien continues to walk in Quintus' and Homer's footsteps. As Homer's Achaeans don helms with horse-hair plumes, so Quintus has Penthesileia take up a helmet with a golden-haired plume. And Eomer, when he greets Aragorn for the first time, rides forward wearing a helm adorned with a white horsetail crest.

The "horse-taming Trojans" also wear horse-hair plumes in Homer's "Iliad". Horses are important to both the Achaeans and Trojans, for the great beasts draw the war-chariots of both armies. Yet Penthesileia merely rides her horse into battle (a classical trait of the Amazons, according to centuries of Greek artwork).

> ...Swiftly all
> Hearkened her gathering-ery, and thronging came,
> Champions, yea, even such as theretofore
> Shrank back from standing in the ranks of war
> Against Achilles the all-ravager.
> But she in pride of triumph on she rode
> Throned on a goodly steed and fleet, the gift
> Of Oreithyia, the wild North-wind's bride,
> Given to her guest the warrior-maid, what time
> She came to Thrace, a steed whose flying feet
> Could match the Harpies' wings. Riding thereon
> Penthesileia in her goodlihead
> Left the tall palaces of Troy behind.

Penthesileia rides through the Achaean forces like an unstoppable force. Even as her Amazonian companions are struck down, one by one, she decimates the Achaean warriors, so that they fall back before her in terror. Seeing his men dispersed and their morale broken, Achilles turns his attention upon the Amazon. The confrontation between Achilles and Penthesileia is both long and thrilling, and quite sad. She is the daughter of Ares, but Achilles is invulnerable to all her weapons. As the Amazon attempts to ride him down, Achilles pierces both horse and rider with a spear, and Penthesileia takes a mortal wound. Her fall disheartens the Trojans, who to this point have all but routed the Achaeans and are (once again, as happens in the "Iliad") on the verge of burning the Achaeans' ships. The Trojans thus flee back to their city, and Achilles gloats over his kill. But he does not enjoy his victory for long. For Achilles removes Penthesileia's helmet, and seeing her beauty, he falls in love with her, even as she lays dead before him:

> So spake he, and his ashen spear the son
> Of Peleus drew from that swift horse, and from
> Penthesileia in death's agony.
> Then steed and rider gasped their lives away
> Slain by one spear. Now from her head he plucked

The helmet splendour-flashing like the beams
Of the great sun, or Zeus' own glory-light.
Then, there as fallen in dust and blood she lay,
Rose, like the breaking of the dawn, to view
'Neath dainty-pencilled brows a lovely face,
Lovely in death. The Argives thronged around,
And all they saw and marvelled, for she seemed
Like an Immortal. In her armour there
Upon the earth she lay, and seemed the
Child Of Zeus, the tireless Huntress Artemis
Sleeping, what time her feet forwearied are
With following lions with her flying shafts
Over the hills far-stretching. She was made
A wonder of beauty even in her death
By Aphrodite glorious-crowned, the
Bride Of the strong War-god, to the end that he,
The son of noble Peleus, might be pierced
With the sharp arrow of repentant love.
The warriors gazed, and in their hearts they prayed
That fair and sweet like her their wives might seem,
Laid on the bed of love, when home they won.
Yea, and Achilles' very heart was wrung
With love's remorse to have slain a thing so sweet,
Who might have borne her home, his queenly bride,
To chariot-glorious Phthia; for she was
Flawless, a very daughter of the Gods,
Divinely tall, and most divinely fair.

Achilles' bittersweet vengeance leaves him wracked with love and
loss. It is an eerie scene, disturbing and deeply tragic. Tolkien seems
almost determined to set right this ancient wrong when, as Prince
Imrahil rides out from Minas Tirith to support the Rohirrim on the
Pelennor Fields, he comes upon the carnage where Theoden and his
knights have fallen before the Lord of the Nazgul:

Then the prince went from his horse, and knelt by the bier in honour
of the king and his great onset; and he wept. And rising he looked
then on Éowyn and was amazed. 'Surely, here is a woman?' he said.
'Have even the women of the Rohirrim come to war in our need?'

'Nay! One only,' they answered. 'The Lady Éowyn is she, sister of Éomer; and we knew naught of her riding until this hour, and greatly we rue it.'

Then the prince seeing her beauty, though her face was pale and cold, touched her hand as he bent to look more closely on her. 'Men of Rohan!' he cried. 'Are there no leeches among you? She is hurt to the death maybe, but I deem that she yet lives.' And he held the bright-burnished vambrace that was upon his arm before her cold tips, and behold! a little mist was laid on it hardly to be seen.

'Haste now is needed,' he said, and he sent one riding back swiftly to the City to bring aid. But he bowing low to the fallen, bade them farewell, and mounting rode away into battle. ("The Battle of the Pelennor Fields", *The Lord of the Rings*)

There are other images Tolkien probably lifted from the Greek poets: the omens and portents represented by eagles, as when an eagle drops a snake over the Trojan army in the "Iliad", and Legolas sees an eagle (Gwaihir) flying far off over the fields of Rohan. The Greek gods assume mortal forms and join Achaeans and Trojans in combat, and their presence immediately restores the morale of warriors; Gandalf, an angelic Maia, has come to Middle-earth in the form of a Man, and when he and Prince Imrahil make their rounds in the besieged city of Minas Tirith, men take heart and sometimes break out into song. And Tolkien delights in describing siege after siege: Helm's Deep, Minas Tirith, and Aragorn's last stand around the two knolls just north of Mordor.

But though some will undoubtedly argue that applicability says far more about Tolkien's connection with Greek mythology than Tolkien himself, Tolkien spoke passionately about Greek history and literature on numerous occasions, as in a letter he sent to his son Christopher during the Second World War:

Mr. Eden in the house the other day expressed pain at the occurrences in Greece 'the home of democracy'. Is he ignorant, or insincere? [Greek word for 'democracy'] was not in Greek a word of approval but was nearly equivalent to 'mob-rule'; and he neglected to note that Greek Philosophers -- and far more is Greece the home of philosophy -- did *not* approve of it. And the great Greek states, esp. Athens at the time of its high art and power, were rather Dictatorships, if they were not military monarchies like Sparta! And modern Greece has as little connexion with ancient Hellas as we have with Britain before Julius Agricola....(*The Letters of J.R.R. Tolkien*, No. 94)

Well, perhaps the modern Greeks would take exception to Tolkien's last comment, but it is completely ironic and somewhat tragic that modern Anglo-Saxonists might take exception to any attempt to document his extensive connections to ancient Greek literature, language, and myth. Even in *The Book of Lost Tales*, the "mythology for England", Tolkien could not help but rely upon the Greek word "Gnomos" (thought, intelligence) as the root for his "Gnomes", the precursors of the Noldor of Middle-earth (Ibid., No. 239).

There is certainly no denying the strong connection between Tolkien's work and the Anglo-Saxon language, poetry, and literature. He also drew extensively upon Middle English poetry and literature. But, as Tolkien might put it, the Anglo-Saxonists are not wholly correct or in the *right* because, to their great detriment and the diminishment of those who seek to learn from them, Tolkien owed a great debt to Greek language, myth, and literature. Nothing is Anglo-Saxon in the beginning, not even Middle-earth.

If the reader perceives only an echo of Aethelflaed or, worse, no more than a shadow of Brunhilde in Eowyn, and fails to note the tragic beauty and strength of Penthesileia in the fair maiden lying amid the carnage of battle, did Tolkien succeed in creating his mythology, or has his work only been mythologized?

...The other way round seems rather like describing a place (or stage in a journey) in terms of the different routes by which people have arrived there, though the place has a location and existence quite independent of these routes, direct or more circuitous.(Ibid., No. 209)

Chapter 23:
Et tu, Faramir?

The one thing even J.R.R. Tolkien could not provide his readers (or himself) was a large corpus of Middle-earth literature, stories and narratives written by the inhabitants of Middle-earth. We have a few poems and songs, enough to tantalize the more avid hunters of esoteric snippets among us, but there is really no attempt to construct a literary tradition for Middle-earth. *The Silmarillion* source texts are mostly written as Tolkien's own retellings of the older stories.

In a few places, such as the appendices to *The Lord of the Rings*, Tolkien provides brief translated citations from the imaginary older texts. One example occurs in the section on Arnor (Appendix A), where the chieftains of the Dunedain are discussed:

> There were fourteen Chieftains, before the fifteenth and last was born, Aragorn II, who became again King of born Gondor and Arnor. 'Our King, we call him; and when he comes north to his house in Ann minas restored and stays for a while by Lake Evendim, then everyone in the Shire is glad. But he does not enter this land and binds himself by the law that he has made, that none of the Big People shall pass its borders. But he rides often with many fair people to the Great Bridge, and there he welcomes his friends, and any others who wish to see him; and some ride away with him and stay in his house as long as they have a mind. Thain Peregrin has been there many times; and so has Master Samwise the Mayor. His daughter Elanor the Fair is one of the maids of Queen Evenstar.'

Everything within the single-quoted material is supposed to be a translation from the *Red Book of Westmarch*. *The Lord of the Rings* is therefore a modern retelling of an ancient (forgotten) story, and not strictly a translation, as many have characterized it. Tolkien tells it in his own words and style, so he is not so much acting as a translator as merely a story-teller.

In presenting the legends this way, Tolkien frees the reader's imagination to devise ancient texts of virtually any style and length. But he also irrevocably denies us the most complete look through his mind's eye at what became Middle-earth. It's a bit silly to argue over who "actually" wrote a certain text. We don't really have enough texts to evaluate the styles and voices.

And yet, I feel as though I can almost tell who wrote what. The above citation, for example, is written from a Hobbit's perspective, and I feel as though it has Merry's "voice". Why? Perhaps because both Thain Peregrin and Master Samwise are mentioned in the third person. Merry might write about his companions but not himself in a formal language. On the other hand, it might just as well be a Took's voice. The apparent respect in the brief mention of both, and the distance the writer places between himself (herself?) and the King's friends, imply that the writer felt some reverence for Pippin and Samwise (and possibly Merry).

The passage can be reasonably dated to sometime between Shire Year 1436 and S.Y. 1442. Elanor became one of the queen's handmaids in 1436, and in 1442 her family rode to Gondor on a visit. She was probably not in Arwen's service for more than a year or two. Sam was Mayor in these years, and Merry had become Master of Buckland in 1432. Pippin became Thain in 1434.

Another citation, much longer than that given above, occurs in the section on Gondor's kings. It begins in the midst of the summary of the career of Romendacil II with "'For the high men of Gondor already looked askance at the Northmen among them; and it was a thing unheard of before that the heir to the crown, or any son of the King, should wed one of lesser and alien race....'"

This just does not sound like something a Hobbit, even Master Meriadoc of the Buckland, would write. Furthermore, the citation concludes with "'...Umbar remained at war with Gondor for many lives of men, a threat to its coastlands and to all traffic on the sea. It was never again completely subdued until the days of Elessar; and the region of South Gondor became a debatable land between the Corsairs and the Kings.'"

Another citation follows immediately upon this one, but the closing sentence implies that this particular citation was written after Elessar's (Aragorn's) death. We know that the last Gondorian to have written any of the Red Book's material was Findegil, the King's Writer in Fourth Age 172, more than 50 years after Aragorn died. The language is formal and stylized, as a royal writer's should be.

But not all the late citations are derived strictly from Gondor (if any). "The Tale of Aragorn and Arwen", for example, is offered completely as a citation, but it concludes with "Here ends this tale, as it has come to us from the South; and with the passing of Evenstar no more is said in this book of the days of old."

One must ask if the entire story, up to but not including this final sentence, represents a Gondorian style, or if some Hobbit writer of the late Second Century (Fourth Age) rewrote the story, which Tolkien then translated for his readers.

"The Tale of Aragorn and Arwen" may be the longest citation Tolkien included in his Middle-earth works. Of course, some people might argue that "Aldarion and Erendis: The Mariner's wife" is another translated story, but the presentation is wholly different. And Tolkien never finished the tale, so we have no obvious clues about whose voice the narration conveys, Tolkien's or some imaginary ancient writer's. Even "The Disaster of the Gladden Fields" fails that test because it is accompanied by Author's Notes which clearly show that Tolkien was interweaving texts to fill out the history provided in *The Lord of the Rings* (including "Cirion and Eorl").

Tolkien's fiction isn't *about* forgotten stories so much as it is pretending to *be* forgotten stories. He is acting not so much like a translator as a revivalist, resurrecting the old campfire tradition Aragorn practices when he tells Frodo and the boys a story about Beren and Lúthien. The stories in Middle-earth's history were told and retold, seldom written down, and the *Red Book of Westmarch* preserves those stories in a state which conveys an artificiality. That is, we are led to believe (or to assume) that the stories must have been told only a certain way.

In fact, the trail of translation and retelling is quite lengthy. The *Red Book* which Tolkien claims to have possessed is not the original book which Bilbo and Frodo wrote. It is a copy, "written in Gondor, probably at the request of the great-grandson of Peregrin, and completed in S.R. 1592 (F.A. 172). Its southern scribe appended this note: Findegil, King's Writer, finished this work in IV 172. It is an exact copy in all details of the Thain's Book in Minas Tirith. That book was a copy, made at the request of King Elessar, of the Red Book of the Perriannath, and was brought to him by the Thain Peregrin when he retired to Gondor in IV 64."

So, Tolkien's *Red Book* was a copy of a copy. The original book was actually four volumes: the diary of Bilbo and Frodo, completed by Sam, and Bilbo's three volumes titled *Translations from the Elvish*. The *Translations* are presumably the sources for the Silmarillion material. And who wrote those stories? Elrond was born only 58 years before the end of the First Age. Most of the exciting stuff had already occurred. So even if he himself had written all of Bilbo's source material, it would have included many second-hand stories.

In fact, in *The War of the Jewels*, we are told that "Narn i Chin Hurin" (published as "Narn i Hin Hurin" in *Unfinished Tales*) was written by Dirhavel, an Adan who interviewed survivors in Arvernien and composed his Narn. Dirhavel's account must have been memorized or written down before the Fëanorians destroyed Arvernien. Elrond might have been given a copy of it by Maglor, or it may be that he would have had to wait until he joined Gil-galad's kingdom in the Second Age to learn about the Narn. If it was until that time only preserved orally, then whomever wrote it down for Bilbo's research was providing him with a third-hand account.

With each retelling of the story, one must assume there would have been lost details and new embellishments. In attempting to rationalize the obviously unscientific history of the Two Trees and the creation of the Sun and Moon as recounted in the Silmarillion legends, Tolkien at one point in his life concluded that the original stories had become confused and misunderstood through serial retellings.

As a linguist who knew the relationship between Indo-European *dyeu-* and its descendants *Tyr* (a Norse god of war), *Zeus* (the king of the Greek gods), and Latin *Deus*, Tolkien understood very well how words and the traditions bound up with them could change through the centuries. Tyr, Zeus, Jove, and other derivatives were associated with the sky, but Tyr went on to become a warrior-god of secondary importance (his most notable adventure consisting of his sacrificing his right hand in the capture of the Fenris wolf, which undoubtedly inspired Beren's confrontation with Carcharoth).

Hence, Tolkien would have had no problem with all these stories-behind-stories. Somewhere in each he preserved enough of the true legend that the reader can understand Tolkien is sharing a memory of what really happened. But he is not sharing the literature which originally preserved that memory. To be faithful to the concept, Tolkien would have had to write fairly simple verses and narratives.

For example, "The Epic of Gilgamesh" is often cited as the first great adventure story, but modern English translations of it -- were they presented as original works -- would hardly win any readers because of sheer textual boredom:

> He who saw everything in the broad-boned earth,
> and knew what was to be known
> Who had experienced what there was,
> and had become familiar with all things
> He, to whom wisdom clung like cloak,
> and who dwelt together with Existence in Harmony
> He knew the secret of things and laid them bare.
> And told of those times before the Flood
> In his city, Uruk, he made the walls,
> which formed a rampart stretching on
> And the temple called Eanna, which was the house of An, the Sky God
> And also of Inanna, Goddess of Love and Battle

Source: 'He who saw everything'
(http://www.angelfire.com/tx/gatestobabylon/temple1.html).

Admittedly, a modern translation sinks or swims largely on the talent
of the translator, but modern readers have the luxury of buying concise
paperback books, whereas the original readers of the Gilgamesh epic
had to handle clay tablets. The tale was preserved from a true oral
tradition, too, and most audiences would not have been able to wallow
in a story the way we can follow Hobbits from book to book, night
after night, week after week. The really great stories were probably
told at festivals, weddings, and on holidays celebrating special events.

The ancients loved to swap stories, and it has been suggested by more
than one scholar that many classical mythologies borrow from older
mythologies. All of Zeus' infidelities, for example, may represent
attempts to merge various legends about an ancient sky god into a
coherent mythology.

As the centuries passed by, story-tellers accumulated greater
sophistication. Technology slowly caught up with the audience's
ability to absorb more information, too. Eventually, Herodotus would
be able to compose the first extended diary. His *Histories* record his
thoughts about the traditions he had learned from several peoples with
whom the Greeks had contact. He was not analyzing traditions so
much as preserving them. But his writing was sophisticated even by
modern standards, in that he was able to revisit themes many chapters
(or books) after their introduction.

Some of the Roman writers attempted to write lengthy histories, too,
but they also developed the art of writing encapsulated histories, a skill
which was passed on to the Roman Catholic Church. History itself
became less important as story-telling returned to prominence. Early
medieval literature offers us Bede's *Ecclesiastical History of England*,
which modern historians may both praise and curse. Bede mostly
wanted to tell a few good stories and lecture some contemporary kings
about their failings. In doing so, he alluded to things which have long
since been forgotten. It would have been nice if he had offered a few
footnotes explaining what the heck he was referring to.

Tolkien does provide footnotes...and end notes...and notes within notes, asides, anecdotes, essays, outlines, and everything else including scraps of paper and scribbles on morning newspapers. He wanted to document as much as he could about Middle-earth, but he had too little time to devote to the project, and creating a literature to support the stories was not a priority. The stories were more important than the literature, just as Bede's stories were more important than his history, just as Herodotus' anecdotes were more important than simply relating the facts as they were then known.

Herodotus' anecdotes are often derided as amateurish mishmash which should not have been included in the first attempt to write a formal history. But if Herodotus had not told us about the Egyptian brothers who tried to rob a tomb, leading to the tragic sacrifice of one brother to save the other, would his history have been half as interesting to read as it is? There was so much Herodotus needed to preserve, and he had to choose between folktales and myths. He understood well enough what seemed incredible to even his contemporary audience. He also understood that subsequent generations might not believe everything he had to say.

Nonetheless, Herodotus' hand is quite evident in Tolkien's Middle-earth stories. Tolkien, like Herodotus, was trying to preserve *something*. Like St. John viewing the apocalypse, Tolkien was granted a vision and he hastened to write down whatever he saw. But Tolkien saw so much he couldn't describe it all, he couldn't record it all. He became sidetracked time and time again. For Tolkien, history only became interesting when it was tied to a word. A word is such a simple thing, and yet it has a long history. Words seldom just *appear*, although we seem to *coin* them all the time. They mostly come down to us from other people, and often the subtle changes we make in the uses and meanings of words compress volumes of history which will be forgotten.

Tolkien often stopped to explain where a word came from, and that of course entailed relating the history of the thing the word described, which in turn led to other words. As a formal historian, Tolkien was worse than Herodotus. Herodotus at least followed some plan. Tolkien would start a book and leave it unfinished, abandoning the work near the end, halfway through, or near the beginning, as whimsy or real life led him. Maybe somewhere in all the never-realized plans, Tolkien did indeed intend to create a literature for Middle-earth.

He certainly didn't lack for basic plots: the children of Hurin, Beren and Lúthien, Aldarion and Erendis, Fëanor, and at least a half dozen other stories actually made it through the process in coherent enough shape that Christopher Tolkien really did not need to do much work on them.

One such experiment may have been the "Athrabeth Finrod ah Andreth". Tolkien says the purpose of the "Athrabeth" is "dramatic: to exhibit the generosity of Finrod's mind, his love and pity for Andreth, and the tragic situations which must arise in the meeting of Elves and Men". Tolkien's commentary on the "Athrabeth" makes it clear the narrative is simply a modernist perspective on the cultural differences between Eldar and Edain. But it would not have taken much work, since the narrative consists mostly of dialogue, to present the "Athrabeth" as a translation of an ancient text. However, Tolkien seems to have abandoned the motif of feigned translation for most of his post-LoTR writing.

The only significant corpus of feigned translations was published in *The Adventures of Tom Bombadil*, but that collection of poems is unsatisfactory, as most of them were written independently of *The Lord of the Rings* and *The Silmarillion*, and they do not reflect much of Tolkien's thought about the styles and voices of the ancient narrators whose traditions he was passing on.

For legitimacy, one must fall back upon the Quenya and Sindarin texts, which are insufficient to represent a "literature". Galadriel's lament does not tell a story. It relates no history. Rather, it implies much which has passed, and some things which may yet be. Like Bede's allusions to contemporary kings, Galadriel's lament really requires that the reader possess a considerable knowledge about Galadriel's life and history in order to understand what she is talking about. Otherwise, her song is just a pretty poem with a distinct sadness attached to it.

But though archaeology may one day prevail and give us insight into Bede's obscurities, we are left staring at Tolkien's world through his distant, half-closed eyes as he wanders across a mindscape of confused priorities. Our knowledge of Middle-earth's history and literature is as filtered as would be that of the students of Shakespeare, were his words the only source we had for traditions concerning Hamlet, Richard III, King John, Henry V, and Julius Caesar.

Shakespeare wrote about real people and imaginary people, and his most famous lines have been quoted time and time again. "Et tu, Brute" may be one of the most oft-quoted lines from Shakespeare, and some people say he may only have borrowed those words from tradition. If so, Tolkien (who disliked Shakespeare) appointed himself the task of playing Shakespeare to Middle-earth. He rewrote the stories which were never written, retold the untold tales, and invented traditions which he passed on to be cherished for generations.

The pretense Tolkien made, of lifting these stories from an older literature, was not really original. Some people claim Plato's account of Atlantis is nothing more than a fabrication, a pseudo-history he never took seriously. The Atlantis story has excited the imagination for over 2,000 years. And, in fact, it found a place in Middle-earth, for Tolkien admitted more than once that the tale of Númenor was derived from the story of Atlantis.

Even Faramir's dream, of the overpowering wave welling up in the ocean, owes something to a real experience. Tolkien himself confessed to having had the dream. Like every writer before him, and every writer since, Tolkien put something of himself into his creation. And, of course, Tolkien did borrow from ancient traditions to contrive his own imaginary traditions. From Beren's sacrificing a hand to the wolf, to Faramir's dream of the oncoming wave, Tolkien felt no compunction about making the real traditions of literature the sources for his lost literature.

The new stories are certainly interesting enough on their own terms. They are not merely the same old stories. Tolkien explored a new angle in the theme of death and the search for deathlessness. We'll be unraveling his anecdotes for generations to come, and arguing about which of his heroes had the most impact on their imaginary world. And only Time will tell if Tolkien has given us the equivalent of "et tu, Faramir".

Chapter 24:
Middle-earth revised, again

Sometime around April 1956, 20 months after *The Fellowship of the Ring* was published in August 1954, J.R.R. Tolkien wrote to H. Cotton Minchin, saying, "as 'research students' always discover, however long they are allowed, and careful their work and notes, there is always a rush at the end, when the last date suddenly approaches on which their thesis must be presented. So it was with this book, and the maps...." (*The Letters of J.R.R. Tolkien*, No. 187)

He was speaking, of course, about *The Lord of the Rings*, and the maps associated with the text. In the course of the letter, Tolkien described parts of the project which had to be abandoned:

I am, however, primarily a philologist and to some extent a calligrapher .... And my son after me. To us far and away the most absorbing interest is the Elvish tongues, and the nomenclature based on them; and the alphabets. My plans for the 'specialist volume' were largely linguistic. An index of names was to be produced, which by etymological interpretation would also provide quite a large Elvish vocabulary; this is of course a first requirement. I worked at it for months, and indexed the first two vols. (it was the chief cause of the delay of Vol iii) until it became clear that size and cost were ruinous. Reluctantly also I had to abandon, under pressure from the 'production department', the 'facsimiles' of the three pages of the *Book of Mazarbul*, burned tattered and blood-stained, which I had spent much time on producing or forging. Without them the opening of Book Two, ch. 5 (which was meant to have the facsimiles and a transcript alongside) is defective, and the Runes of the Appendices unnecessary.

Well, two of the facsimile pages (nos. 1 and 3) have now been published in *J.R.R. Tolkien: Artist & Illustrator*. I have yet to see the second page reproduced. And much material which JRRT had worked on through the years has also been brought forth since 1980, the year in which Christopher Tolkien first published *Unfinished Tales*. There is now far more information available about Middle-earth, in the form of paintings and doodles, essays and notes, maps, and linguistic analysis, than Tolkien ever dreamed could be possibly published.

But what do we have to show for all that? We can research Middle-earth to our hearts' content, but do all these things bring us any closer to realizing what Tolkien had in mind other than just *The Lord of the Rings* itself? A question that has been posed to me before but is seldom asked any more is: "Which books *are* considered unimpeachable resources?"

That is not an easy question to answer. The answer depends on who is doing the considering and what the scope of the research is concerned with. The question above was posed to me after I had said, "People just don't seem to understand that there are clear and definite divisions between the various mythologies."

Well, anyone who wants to take exception with *that* statement will certainly find plenty of support for doing so. And that just underscores the first point I made: "People just don't seem to understand". Which, by implication, means I think I *do* understand...something. Of course I think that. And so everyone who disagrees with me thinks of their own knowledge. It's the rest of the readership out *there*, vaguely wraithlike in their undefined demographic, who self-admittedly don't have a clue and are earnestly seeking good solid information.

The problem is that there really is no good solid information. Not on Middle-earth. Or darned little of it.

What exactly *is* Middle-earth anyway? If you were to have asked Tolkien, he would have told you that "Middle-earth is just archaic English for *oikumene* the inhabited world of men. It lay then as it does. In fact, just as it does, round and inescapable." (*The Letters of J.R.R. Tolkien*, No. 152), or "the inhabited lands of men 'between the seas'" (Ibid., No 165), "the abiding place of Men, the objectively real world, in use specifically opposed to imaginary worlds (Fairyland) or unseen worlds (as Heaven and Hell)" (Ibid., No. 183).

And as useful as those explanations are, they provide no real help in understanding or visualizing Middle-earth the way Tolkien understood and saw it. You can't really see it the way he did. In any event, Middle-earth proved to be an extremely fluid vision for Tolkien, unfolding more quickly than he could describe it. He heard the Music from afar and beheld the Vision, but he could not Create what he perceived. He could only sub-create a description of it, and in that he achieved far less than he desired.

If we accept, as a starting point, that Middle-earth is defined only by the books Tolkien himself published in his lifetime, we find ourselves concerned only with four titles: *The Hobbit* (Second Edition of 1950), *The Lord of the Rings* (First Edition of 1954-5), *The Adventures of Tom Bombadil*, and *The Road Goes Ever On*. In 1969, Pauline Baynes published a map of Middle-earth for which Tolkien provided her special information. It was the Baynes map which marked the first appearance of Lond Daer Ened, for example.

And if these works are the authoritative resources, life should be fairly simple, if incomplete. But thanks to Donald Wolheim (then with Ace Books in the United States), in 1965 Tolkien had to recreate Middle-earth so that he could properly secure a copyright for it. Wolheim shrewdly guessed that the American university market was ripe for a mass market edition of *The Lord of the Rings*. So he took advantage of a loop-hole in copyright law to publish unauthorized editions of the book.

After the brouhaha had died down, we were left with the Third Edition of *The Hobbit* and the Second Edition of *The Lord of the Rings*. In order to qualify for new copyright status, the books had to be substantively altered. Now, a copyright applies only to the expression of an idea, not to the idea of itself. But in literature the expression of an idea can be radically bumped from its normal course as a result of only a minor change in text.

So it was with Tolkien's work, and he did not confine himself to merely minor changes. The plot and characterizations remained the same. Tolkien tightened up the writing in a few places but he mostly altered the backdrop for the story, perhaps so as to preserve as much of the beloved tale as possible, but also (I think) to take advantage of the situation and correct a few flaws in the picture he had painted.

The Hobbit proved to be more of a challenge than *The Lord of the Rings*. About the latter, Tolkien wrote to Rayner Unwin in May 1965:

> I am not relishing the task of 're-editing' *The Lord of the Rings*. I think it will prove very difficult if not impossible to make any substantial changes in the general text. Volume I has now been gone through and the number of necessary or desirable corrections is very small. I am bound to say that my admiration for the tightness of the author's construction is somewhat increased. The poor fellow (who now seems to me only a remote friend) must have put a lot of work into it. I am hoping that alteration of the introductions, considerable modifications of the appendices and the inclusion of an index may prove sufficient for the purpose....

Indeed, they did. But he found *The Hobbit* to be "very poor" (according to Humphrey Carpenter's biography). There are glimpses of Tolkien's dissatisfaction with *The Hobbit* in some of his letters. He felt he was too condescending to children in the early part of the book, and he would have preferred to rewrite it completely, had there been time to do so.

But 1965 is probably the high mark of post-LoTR era Middle-earthian contemplation for Tolkien. Although he would not produce any more books on the subject, he had been quite active behind the scenes, working on material which would eventually be placed in the hands of his son Christopher.

One of the most recent stories Tolkien had worked on at this point was "Aldarion and Erendis: The Mariner's Wife" (begun around 1960, but a typed version was made in early 1965). Christopher Tolkien says that, of all the texts included in *Unfinished Tales*, this one was the most incomplete (and presumably he was not thinking of the various scraps and notes he assembled for the chapter on the Istari). An accompanying text, "A description of Númenor", is dated to the same period, as is "The Line of Elros", which contains "several minor chronological puzzles, but also allows clarification of some apparent errors in the Appendices to *The Lord of the Rings*" (Christopher Tolkien, "Introduction" to *Unfinished Tales*).

Tolkien did not stop there, however. Ninni M. Pettersson, a member of Mellonath Daeron, the Language Guild of Forodrim (the Tolkien Society of Sweden), has assembled a chronology for Tolkien's various books and essays. Although one must speculate on certain dates, Pettersson's work is about as good as you're going to get outside the Christopher Tolkien household (http://www.forodrim.org/daeron/ md_hmco.html).

The only other *Lord of the Rings*-compatible text JRRT worked on in the 1965-6 years was the collection of writings that Christopher assembled into the essay on the *Palantiri* (for *Unfinished Tales*). Although he did not find much to change in *The Fellowship of the Ring*, Christopher points out that his father "made substantial emendations to a passage in *The Two Towers*, [Book] III [Chapter] II 'The Palantir' ... and some others in the same connection in *The Return of the King*, V 7 'The Pyre of Denethor' ... though these emendations were not incorporated into the text until the second impression of the revised edition (1967)."

Tolkien returned to Middle-earth in 1968, but it would not be until early 1969 when he would produce the last substantial body of work associated with *The Lord of the Rings*. Although I have not mentioned his post-*Lord of the Rings* work on *The Silmarillion* thus far, it did consume a great deal of his time. Most of the work Tolkien did in the 1950s, after *The Lord of the Rings* was published, was concerned with *The Silmarillion*. And in this last phase of his life, *The Silmarillion* competed with *The Lord of the Rings* for his time.

But the canonical Middle-earth did not include *The Silmarillion*. That is, in 1969, Middle-earth was only canonically, or authoritatively, defined by the books which had been published to that time. The essays Tolkien wrote from 1969 through 1972 about matters in *The Lord of the Rings* (and, by association, *The Hobbit*) were largely anchored by the 1965 editions. It is difficult to find incompatibilities between these texts and the published works, although the linguistic essays gouge the canon at almost every opportunity.

In the introduction to *Unfinished Tales*, Christopher writes:

> I judge these fragments [the 'Cirion and Eorl' essays] to belong to the same period as 'The Disaster of the Gladden Fields', when my father was greatly interested in the earlier history of Gondor and Rohan; they were doubtless intended to form parts of a substantial history, developing in detail the summary accounts given in Appendix A to *The Lord of the Rings*. The material is in the first stage of composition, very disordered, full of variants, breaking off into rapid jottings that are part illegible.

It is much to suppose that J.R.R. Tolkien intended to create, at the end of his life, a companion volume to *The Lord of the Rings*. And yet, one easily gets the impression that is what he was working toward, with or without clear intention. The works Christopher associates with this project were "Cirion and Eorl", "The Disaster of the Gladden Fields", the essay on the Druedain (a fragment, published in *Unfinished Tales*, of the larger essay "Dwarves and Men", the rest of which was published in *The Peoples of Middle-earth*), "and the philological essays excerpted in 'The History of Galadriel and Celeborn'".

Those philological essays form the basis of the appendices to the History of Galadriel and Celeborn: "The Silvan Elves and their Speech", "The Sindarin Princes of the Silvan Elves", "The Boundaries of Lórien", "The Port of Lond Daer", and possibly the writings behind the final appendix concerning the names of Galadriel and Celeborn. There is, however, another essay from the same period which has received only limited attention: "The Rivers and Beacon-hills of Gondor", published in Vinyar Tengwar 42 (http://www.elvish.org/VT/, the original title is given as "Nomenclature", so the current title is taken from Christopher's description of the text in *The Peoples of Middle-earth*).

But though these essays and fragments constitute all that is presently published of the secondary canon for (Second and Third Age) Middle-earth, there is, in fact, still more material. Virtually any reply that

Tolkien made in his letters to questions about Middle-earth contains information which is seldom if ever actually contradicted by later material. There are some points where Tolkien contradicts himself, either because he did not have the texts available to consult or because he was reporting on transitions.

Another text which has intrigued readers is *The New Shadow*, published in *The Peoples of Middle-earth*. Set early in the Fourth Age, but near the end of King Eldarion's reign, the book would have followed a plot to overthrow the rightful king. But Tolkien concluded it would have been nothing more than a thriller, a type of story in which he had no interest, and he ceased to work on it.

And then there are the interviews Tolkien gave concerning his work. While the average commercial newspaper was hardly likely to entice serious comment from Tolkien on Middle-earth's underpinnings, he treated the fan magazines and other small publications with greater respect. Or, perhaps, they simply had sense enough to ask him the really meaty questions.

There are assuredly older Tolkien fans who collected these interviews in the 1960s and 1970s, and it would be interesting to see them brought together in some publishable form. Regrettably, I only have a partial citation from one, but I will share it here. It can still be found in a few places on the Internet. This fragment was provided to me by Chris Seeman, the editor and publisher of *Other Hands* (no longer in publication, thanks to Tolkien Enterprises). Chris included this citation in an article he wrote titled: "A Journey in the Dark: Reflections on the identity of Queen Beruthiel".

Chris' source was Daphne Castell's article, "The Realms of Tolkien", published in *New Worlds* in November 1966 and reprinted in *Carandaith* in 1969:

> ...Most of the allusions to older legends scattered about the tale, or summarized in Appendix A are to things which really have an existence as some kind in the history of which 'The Lord of the Rings' is part. There's one exception that puzzles me: Beruthiel. I really don't know

anything of her -- you remember Aragorn's allusion in Book I (page 325) to the cats of Queen Beruthiel, that could find their way home on a blind night? She just popped up, and obviously called for attention, but I don't really know anything certain about her; though, oddly enough, I have a notion that she was the wife of one of the ship-kings of Pelargir. She loathed the smell of the sea, and fish, and the gulls. Rather like Skadi, the giantess, who came to the gods in Valhalla, demanding a recompense for the accidental death of her father. She wanted a husband. The gods all lined up behind a curtain, and she selected the pair of feet that appealed to her most. She thought she'd got Baldur, the beautiful god, but it turned out to be Njord the sea-god, and after she'd married him, she got absolutely fed up with the seaside life, and the gulls kept her awake, and finally she went back to live in Jotunheim.

Well, Beruthiel went back to live in the inland city, and went to the bad (or returned to it -- she was a Black Númenorean in origin, I guess). She was one of these people who loathe cats, but cats will jump on them and follow them about -- you know how sometimes they pursue people who hate them? I have a friend like that. I'm afraid she took to torturing them for amusement, but she kept some and used them: trained them to go on evil errands by night, to spy on her enemies or terrify them.

Christopher Tolkien, of course, covered the history of Beruthiel in a note appended to the section on the Istari in *Unfinished Tales*:

In a letter written in 1956 my father said that 'There is hardly any reference in *The Lord of the Rings* to things that do not actually *exist*, on its own plane (of secondary or sub-creational reality)', and added in a footnote to this: 'The cats of Queen Beruthiel and the names of the other two wizards (five minus Saruman, Gandalf, Radagast) are all that I recollect.' (In Moria Aragorn said of Gandalf that 'He is surer of finding the way home in a blind night than the cats of Queen Beruthiel' (*The Fellowship of the Ring* II 4).

Even the story of Queen Beruthiel does exist, however, if only in a very 'primitive' outline, in one part illegible. She was the nefarious, solitary, and loveless wife of Tarannon, twelfth King of Gondor (Third Age 830-913) and the first of the 'Ship-kings', who took the crown in the name of Falastur 'Lord of the Coasts', and was the first childless king (*The Lord of the Rings*, Appendix A, I, ii and iv). Beruthiel lived in the King's House in Osgiliath, hating the sounds and smells of the sea and the house that Tarannon built below Pelargir 'upon arches whose feet stood deep in the wide waters of Ethir Anduin'; she hated all making, all colours and elaborate adornment, wearing only black and silver and living in bare chambers, and the gardens of the house in Osgiliath were filled with tormented sculptures beneath cypresses and yews. She had nine black cats and one white, her slaves, with whom she conversed, or read their memories, setting them to discover all the dark secrets of Gondor, so that she knew those things 'that men wish most to keep hidden', setting the white cat to spy upon the black, and tormenting them. No man in Gondor dared touch them; all were afraid of them, and cursed when they saw them pass. What follows is almost wholly illegible in the unique manuscript, except for the ending, which states that her name was erased from the Book of the Kings ('but the memory of men is not wholly shut in books, and the cats of Queen Beruthiel never passed wholly out of men's speech'), and that King Tarannon had her set on a ship alone with her cats and set adrift on the sea before a north wind. The ship was last seen flying pas Umbar under a sickle moon, with a cat at the masthead and another as a figure-head on the prow.

Beruthiel's history foreshadows the explosive effort J.R.R. Tolkien put forth only a few years later in an attempt to flesh out the history of the Third Age. The essays from 1969-71 were "the rush at the end". It was almost as if Tolkien sensed that time was finally running out for him, and he felt compelled to jot down everything possible. But he left just enough to both tantalize and almost sate the average reader who wants to know more.

Typical reviews of Tolkien's career note with appropriate solemnity that it fell upon his son Christopher's shoulders to bear the burden of bringing a *Silmarillion* to publication. And that book, while a worthy text in itself, only approximates what might have been, had J.R.R. Tolkien only lived another few years (or however long it would have taken him to finish it).

But few people seem to have noticed that he never actually finished working on the first part of the mythology, the sequel to *The Hobbit* which his publisher was so impatient to receive. Who is to say that, had he lived longer, Tolkien would not have divulged a full history of the events of the Kingdom of Arnor? It might only have required a few questions from interested readers to prompt Tolkien into explaining the history of Bree, who the kings of Cardolan and Rhudaur were, and why their dynasties failed so quickly.

And who knows? Maybe one day he would have returned to *The New Shadow* with a fresh outlook, and might have produced something heroic, if not entirely mythological, beyond the scope of a mere thriller.

SECTION IV:
THE REST
OF MIDDLE-EARTH

MICHAEL MARTINEZ

Chapter 25:
Middle-earth Connections:
Lore of the Rings

Point 1: Time stands still for Rings of Power

> 'How long do you think I shall have here?' said Frodo to Bilbo when Gandalf had gone.

> 'Oh, I don't know. I can't count days in Rivendell,' said Bilbo....

This exchange, recorded in "The Ring Goes South", is the first indication that Frodo Baggins and his friends have come into the presence of a Ring of Power other than the One Ring which Frodo has carried for many years (since Bilbo left the Shire). The Rings of Power were created to hold back Time, or to delay its effects. But what was the range of their power? Was there some sort of absolute limit to each Ring's chrono-inhibition? Would the effects extend *this far* and no farther?

The curious matter is that the One Ring, the most powerful of all the artifacts so contrived as to hold back Time, only inhibited the effects of Time upon its keeper. The Shire didn't become timeless because Bilbo had brought the Ring there. Bilbo in effect became timeless, and Frodo after him. How is it, then, that no one else was affected, whereas in Rivendell and Lórien the entire lands (but apparently not the non-Elvish inhabitants) were preserved?

Studying the effects of the Rings of Power reveals many apparent inconsistencies in how they worked, and it may be no wonder that Saruman went mad with desire for possessing one (or all) of them.

When Elrond described the powers of the Elven Rings he said "they were not made as weapons of war or conquest: that is not their power. Those who made them did not desire strength or domination or hoarded wealth, but understanding, making, and healing." His description is quite different from Tolkien's description of the Rings' powers:

> The chief power (of all the rings alike) was the prevention or slowing of *decay* (i.e., 'change' viewed as a regrettable thing), the preservation of what is desired or loved, or its semblance -- this is more or less an Elvish motive. But also they enhanced the natural powers of a possessor -- thus approaching 'magic', a motive easily corruptible into evil, a lust for domination. And finally they had other powers, more directly derived from Sauron ('the Necromancer': so he is called as he casts a fleeting shadow and presage on the pages of *The Hobbit*): such as rendering invisible the material body, and making things of the invisible world visible.

> The Elves of Eregion made Three supremely beautiful and powerful rings, almost solely of their own imagination, and directed to the preservation of beauty: they did not confer invisibility....(*The Letters of J.R.R. Tolkien*, No. 131).

It is possible to infer that Elrond's description of the Rings' powers is intended to deflect further inquiry by presenting only examples of their powers. The true nature of the Rings, to hold back the effects of Time, is reflected only in Elrond's brief statement: "So much only in this hour of doubt I may now say. They are not idle."

Indeed, Elrond and Galadriel (unwisely) used their Rings of Power throughout the Third Age to preserve Elven realms. Galadriel's history is unclear, but she probably did not live in Lórien throughout the Third Age. Rather, when it became clear that Amroth's people would all depart from Lórien if nothing were done, she and Celeborn went to live among the Silvan Elves who had not yet departed.

Galadriel took with her Nenya, the Ring of Adamant, and she may have used its power to induce the Silvan Elves to stay in Lórien. We don't know if she actually used the Ring before then (1981 or shortly thereafter). Tolkien says only that "the [One] Ring is lost [at the beginning of the Third Age], for ever it is hoped; and the Three Rings of the Elves, wielded by secret guardians, are operative in preserving the memory of the beauty of old, maintaining enchanted enclaves of peace where Time seems to stand still and decay is restrained, a semblance of the bliss of the True West." (Ibid.)   However, the introduction to the Third Age in "The Tale of Years" (Appendix B, *The Lord of the Rings*) states that "These were the fading years for the Eldar. For long they were at peace, wielding the Three Rings while Sauron slept and the One Ring was lost..."

Elsewhere, Tolkien notes that the Three Rings worked even during the Second Age, for they did not have to be worn in order to delay the effects of Time. Hence, the departure of Amroth, who had been a stalwart defender of the West throughout the second millennium of the Third Age, may have spurred the Elves into action unlike any they had taken before. It may indeed be that Elrond and Galadriel at last decided to actively *use* their Rings of Power to forestall a mass exodus of Elves from Middle-earth. If so, they were only delaying the inevitable, which was the purpose intended for the Rings anyway.

Point 2: The Elves cannot stay in Middle-earth

The Elves had been leaving Middle-earth for ages. The catastrophe for them in the Third Age was quite different from those of the previous ages. When the Eldar originally sailed over Sea it was at the invitation of the Valar, who had found the Elves in their homeland of Cuiviënen. But the Elves were troubled by Melkor, who was then de facto ruler of the majority of Arda. The Valar waged a terrible war against Melkor and his Maiaric servants and bred creatures, and they took him prisoner and brought an end to his terrible reign. But desiring to be in the company of the Elves (whose arrival they had anticipated throughout innumerable ages), and to provide them with a safe haven beyond the reach of Melkor's servants, the Valar summoned the Elves to live with them in Aman, the Uttermost West.

Not all the Elves were willing to leave Middle-earth, which was their homeland and the only place they knew. And of those Elves who accepted the summons, many never made it (alive) over Sea. Still, the first waves of migration out of Middle-earth were "healthy", or made when the Elves were young and strong and not yet weary of the world. Neither were they as deeply entrenched in Middle-earth.

When Fëanor rebelled against the Valar, he led most of the Noldor back to Middle-earth (or, rather, led most of them out of Eldamar, and then abandoned the greater part of his people, most of whom chose to follow Fingolfin to Middle-earth). Of these Exiles, the vast majority (and their descendants) were slain or enslaved by Melkor, now returned to Middle-earth as a Dark Lord. The spirits of these slain Elves returned to Aman where they awaited a "rebirth" or "re-embodiment", if such a reward could be earned by their deeds in life.

For the remainder, a terrible curse was imposed. Not the Doom of the Noldor, which was the curse that the Valar lay upon them to fail in their war with Melkor. Rather, they were told that "those that endure in Middle-earth shall grow weary of the world as with a great burden, and shall wane, and become as shadows of regret before the younger race that cometh after." ("Of the Flight of the Noldor", *The Silmarillion*)

This doom was applied, really, to all the Elves, and was perhaps a warning more than a judgement. In describing the events of the Second Age for Milton Waldman, JRRT wrote "the three main themes are thus The Delaying Elves that lingered in Middle-earth; Sauron's growth to a new Dark Lord, master and god of Men; and Númenor-Atlantis." (*The Letters of J.R.R. Tolkien*, No. 131)

After the final overthrow of Morgoth in the War of Wrath, Eönwë (herald of Manwë and leader of the Host of Valinor) traveled throughout Middle-earth, summoning all Elves once again to sail over Sea. The invitation which previously had been withdrawn to include only the Eldar (the original Elves who had actually accepted the summons the first time) was now extended to ALL Elves. Many of the surviving Noldor and Sindar of Beleriand responded and left Middle-earth. But the remaining Noldor and Sindar joined the Nandor and Avari in Middle-earth. They "lingered".

Tolkien notes that:

> in the first [Second Age theme] we see a sort of second fall or at least 'error' of the Elves. There was nothing wrong essentially in their

lingering against counsel, still sadly with the mortal lands of their old heroic deeds. But they wanted to have their cake without eating it. They wanted the peace and bliss and perfect memory of 'The West', and yet to remain on ordinary earth where their prestige as the highest people, above wild Elves, dwarves, and Men, was greater than at the bottom of the hierarchy of Valinor. They thus became obsessed with 'fading', the mode in which the changes of time (the law of the world under the sun) was perceived by them. They became sad, and their art (shall we say) antiquarian, and their efforts all really a kind of embalming -- even though they also retained the old motive of their kind, the adornment of earth, and the healing of its hurts....

(Ibid.)

Elsewhere Tolkien reiterated this situation by saying:

the Elves are *not* wholly good or in the right. Not so much because they had flirted with Sauron; as because with or without his assistance they were 'embalmers'. They wanted to have their cake and eat it: to live in the mortal historical Middle-earth because they had become fond of it (and perhaps because they there had the advantages of a superior caste), and so tried to stop its change and history, stop its growth, keep it as a pleasaunce, even largely a desert, where they could be 'artists' -- and they were overburdened with sadness and nostalgic regret....

(*The Letters of J.R.R. Tolkien*, No. 154)

Sauron had also lingered in Middle-earth. Having seen the complete overthrow of Morgoth, he actually repented (according to Tolkien). Seeing that the powers of Light had indeed overcome the power of Darkness, he realized that maybe his earlier choices were not the right ones for him. But when Eönwë summoned him to Valinor to be judged by the Valar, Sauron refused, and he fled away to hide himself in exile. Either he feared he might suffer the same fate as Melkor (who was executed and forced to leave Ea, the universe, in a terribly weakened state) or that he might be imprisoned for some interminably long time.

The "reformed" Sauron at first wanted only to help heal the earth he had originally help to damage. Tolkien notes that "his motives and those of the Elves seemed to go partly together: the healing of the desolate lands." (Letters, No. 131) But Sauron's intentions changed, and in time he decided that he could best "heal" the lands by directing the Elves' efforts, and this ultimately evolved into a desire for domination over the Elves (and through them, Middle-earth).

And so Sauron:

> found [the Elves'] weak point in suggesting that, helping one another, they could make Western Middle-earth as beautiful as Valinor. It was really a veiled attack on the gods, an incitement to try and make a separate independent paradise. Gilgalad [sic] repulsed all such overtures, as also did Elrond. But at Eregion great work began -- and the Elves came their nearest to falling to 'magic' and machinery. With the aid of Sauron's lore they made *Rings of Power*....

(Ibid.)

In essence, Sauron was saying, "You don't have to fade. You don't have to sail over Sea. You can recreate Valinor here in Middle-earth and enjoy all the benefits it has to offer you." The offer was too tempting to some of the Elves, the Noldor of Eregion. Sauron (disguised as Annatar, or Aulendil, a Maia from Aulë's own people in Valinor) was offering the Eldar a chance to forestall the inevitable doom which had been decreed for them.

But what does Tolkien mean when he says "the Elves came their nearest to falling to 'magic' and machinery"?

Point 3: Art versus Magic

Tolkien tried to explain his use of "magic" on more than one occasion, and he didn't always succeed. "I am afraid I have been far too casual about 'magic' and especially the use of the word," he wrote in a draft for an extension to a letter which was never sent (Ibid., No. 155). "Though Galadriel and others show by the criticism of the 'mortal' use of the word, that the thought about it is not altogether casual."

In his letter to Milton Waldman, Tolkien tried to explain Art and the Machine by speaking of "Fall, Mortality, and the Machine." The story was concerned with:

Fall inevitably, and that motive occurs in several modes. With Mortality, especially as it affects art and the creative (I should say, the sub-creative) desire which seems to have no biological function, and to be apart from the satisfactions of plain ordinary biological life, with which, in our world, it is indeed usually at strife. This desire is at once wedded to a passionate love of the real primary world, and hence filled with the sense of mortality, and yet unsatisfied by it. It has various opportunities of 'Fall'. It may become possessive, clinging to the things made as 'its own', the sub-creator wishes to be the Lord and God of his private creation. He will rebel against the laws of the Creator -- especially against mortality. Both of these (alone or together) will lead to the desire for Power, for making the will more quickly effective -- and so to the Machine (or Magic). By the last I intend all use of external plans or devices (apparatus) instead of development of the inherent powers or talents -- of even the use of those talents with the corrupted motive of dominating: bulldozing the real world, or coercing other wills. The Machine is our more obvious modern form though more closely related to Magic than is usually recognized.

Tolkien goes on to concede again (or, in fact, prior to his concession above) that:

I have not used 'magic' consistently, and indeed the Elven-queen Galadriel is obliged to remonstrate with the Hobbits on their confused use of the word both for the devices and operations of the Enemy, and for those of the Elves. I have not, because there is not a word for the latter (since all human stories have suffered the same confusion). But the Elves are there (in my tales) to demonstrate the difference. Their 'magic' is Art, delivered from many of its human limitations: more effortless, more quick, more complete (product, and vision in unflawed correspondence). And its object is Art not Power, sub-creation not domination and tyrannous re-forming of Creation. The 'Elves' are 'immortal', at least as far as this world goes: and hence are concerned rather with the griefs and burdens of deathlessness in time and change, than with death. The Enemy in successive forms is always 'naturally' concerned with sheer Domination, and so the Lord of magic of machines; but the problem: that this frightful evil can and does arise from an apparently good root the desire to benefit the world and others -- speedily and according to the benefactor's own plans -- is a recurrent motive.

Art therefore makes use of the natural world, and develops its natural tendencies, whereas the Machine imposes an external (unnatural) will upon the world, or other wills. Tolkien notes that the Elves of Eregion "came their nearest to falling to 'magic' and machinery." In creating the Rings of Power, they used their Art to create a Machine, but it was a Machine which they intended to be used only for preservation, not alteration. Nonetheless, the restraint of Time is a very serious action, contrary to the laws of nature. It is an act of rebellion "against the laws of the Creator."

The Rings of Power are thus a paradox: they provide for healing and restoration, but also for an unnatural preservation. The very motive behind the Rings, to delay or prevent the inevitable fading the Elves must suffer, is a rebellious motive. The devices are external to the environments they control, and the (Eregion) Elves do not at first realize the wrong they were doing. They pay a terrible price for their folly. Sauron destroys their realm and takes most of their Rings for himself, when he finds that his plan to control them through the Rings will not work. It must be emphasized that most of the aspects of the Machine present in the Rings derive from Sauron, because the intention to use them to control other beings is strictly his own. In fact, Sauron seduced the Elves by holding out the prospect of their creating a Valinorean bliss in Middle-earth under his direction.

The combination of Art and Magic is at once both powerful and destructive for the Elves. They achieve a small measure of their ultimate goal, but things never really work out as they intend.

Point 4: The Product of Art and Machine

When Sauron took the Seven and the Nine, Tolkien writes in "Of the Rings of Power and the Third Age" (*The Silmarillion*), he returned to Mordor (in fact, he was eventually driven back to Mordor by the Eldar of Lindon and their Númenorean allies, who at the time had no idea of what the war was all about). There Sauron "perverted" the Rings, and he gave them out to Dwarves and Men in a new scheme intended to extend Sauron's sway over those races much as he had intended to use them to control the Elves.

Tolkien doesn't say exactly how Sauron perverted the Rings, but his ultimate goal was to create powerful lords who would be his slaves. The Nine worked perfectly, and the nine men who accepted the Rings used them to become great lords, but eventually they lost their free will and their bodies. They became wraiths, forever invisible and unable to interact directly with the world except through some sort of procedure whereby they could take shape when given clothing. Was it natural clothing or magical? We don't know.

But as the Nine and the Seven were imbued with the abilities to render the wearers invisible or to allow them to see normally invisible things (presumably, wraiths, the spirits of other beings), it follows that Sauron used these abilities to grant powers of necromancy (the practice of communing with or controlling the dead or other disembodied spirits) to the keepers of the Rings. Tolkien doesn't say that any Dwarf ever practiced necromancy. In fact, the Rings could not render the Dwarves invisible. It would seem therefore that the Rings offered nothing of value to the Dwarves in terms of dealing with the dead. Their spirits must not have lingered in Middle-earth when they died.

The Elves, on the other hand, didn't always go immediately to Mandos in Aman when they died (or faded). They could refuse the summons, forsaking any hope of regaining a physical body. It thus makes sense that Sauron would induce the Elves of Eregion to include Necromantic powers in their Rings. In Aman, the Elves were accustomed to living alongside the Valar and Maiar, who might appear to them in a physical form or in "spirit" form (and the Valar and Maiar could control whether they were perceived by the Elves when in spirit form).

Elvish spirits might not be equivalent to the Valar and Maiar, but presumably the Elves hoped to talk to Mom and Dad on occasion, provided they had not gone swiftly to Aman upon the deaths of their bodies. Or it may be that the process of fading had already set in, or that the Elves were anticipating a quick transition to the Fading Years.

Who would be most likely to fade? An ancient Elf, presumably. And the more ancient the Elf, the more likely he or she was to have lived in Valinor (if among the Noldor) or to have lived at Cuiviénen. He or she might also be the head of a family. So the Rings of Power were probably created for various Elven lords, princes and kings. The younger Elves, born in Middle-earth -- even in the Second Age -- would either have to wait their turns or else would have to hope the Rings could help them, too.

When Gandalf was discussing the confrontation with the Nazgul at the Ford of Bruinen with Frodo ("Many Meetings" in *The Lord of the Rings*), Frodo asked if the shining figure he saw was Glorfindel. "Yes," Gandalf replied. "You saw him for a moment as he is on the other side: one of the mighty of the First-born. He is an Elf-lord of a house of princes." A little earlier in the same conversation, Gandalf also noted that Rivendell was home to "the Elven-wise, lords of the Eldar from beyond the furthest seas. They do not fear the Ringwraiths, for those who have dwelt in the Blessed Realm live at once in both worlds, and against both the Seen and the Unseen they have great power."

So, perhaps the Rings were not necessarily intended for Elves who had actually lived in Aman. Rather, the Rings may have been intended for their younger cousins or children, Elves who had been born in Middle-earth, who had not learned to live "at once in both worlds."

It must have been important to the Elves to possess this ability, and perhaps it meant they would be less likely to fade, since they would be able to move between both realms, so to speak. Not move physically, but via their will. They should have been able to perceive and interact with disembodied spirits (wraiths) in Aman, and so they wished to do so in Middle-earth.

The interaction must have included "making things of the invisible world visible". Could the restorative powers of the Rings actually bring an Elf back to life? Could the Rings have been used to give the Elves new bodies? Or could they simply have been used to make Elf-wraiths visible to all? In "The Tale of Aragorn and Arwen", Aragorn briefly imagined that "he had strayed into a dream, or that he had received the gift of the Elf-minstrels, who can make things of which they sing appear before the eyes of those that listen."

Something of this ability is also gleaned in the account of Finrod's duel of sorcery with Sauron in the fortress upon Tol Sirion. Finrod sang of his life in Valinor, but his song turned against him as he was forced to sing about the Kinslaying, and Sauron was able to capitalize on Finrod's guilt and regret (though Finrod himself had not participated in the Kinslaying). The ability to render visible images with the power of song implies the Elves, with a greater effort leaning toward the Machine, could pervert their Art (or at least misuse it) to render visible things from the invisible world. Sauron may only have needed to provide a little guidance to them.

Celebrimbor made the Three Rings by himself, and these Rings did not confer invisibility upon their wearers. Presumably they didn't make invisible things visible, either. The Three are thus more compliant with Elrond's description of what the Rings of Power did.

But that still doesn't answer the question of how the Rings worked. Why didn't all the Hobbits of the Shire (or at least Hobbiton) enjoy the benefits of the One Ring?

Point 5: Using the Machine through Art

The answer seems to be a matter of will. Tolkien wrote that the Three Rings effectively held back Time even while they were not actively used. Thus, during the Second Age, the Elves of Lindon enjoyed the benefit intended for the Elves of Eregion even though no one dared put on one of the Rings. Celebrimbor must therefore have given the Three a natural ability to just extend their power over the countryside. The effect's range may not have been measured in miles, however, but rather in people and objects. That is to say, if someone were wearing one of the Three, he (or she) might be able to decide that all Mallorn trees and all Elves would be preserved. The effects would be somewhat random if the Rings were not worn.

In this way, Gandalf could intentionally restrain the Time-delaying effects of Narya, the Ring of Fire which Cirdan gave to him. Or Gandalf could have desired only to let the Ring affect Elves. Cirdan said the Ring was idle when he gave it to Gandalf, so it would seem he was not actually *wearing* the Ring and directing its benefits. Gandalf, therefore, need not have used Narya to delay the fading process for anyone (including himself, though he was in no danger of fading).

Elrond and Galadriel may have taken a cue from Cirdan. Gil-galad originally possessed both Vilya and Narya, and he gave these Rings to Elrond and Cirdan near the end of the Second Age (perhaps having a bit of foresight about his final battle with Sauron). Celebrimbor seems to have given Galadriel her Ring.

Since Elrond and Cirdan advised Isildur to destroy the One Ring when Isildur cut it from Sauron's hand, it seems strange they should just return home and start using their Rings of Power right away. Maybe they took up the Rings when they learned that Isildur and the One Ring had been lost. But it may also be that the three Keepers left their Rings idle for at least a thousand years.

Then Gandalf showed up, Cirdan gave him Narya, and the genie was let out of the bottle. Elrond might have been using Vilya sooner, since he gathered many High Elves (Noldor) in and around Rivendell. He might have had a lot of fading Elves on his hands. Tolkien doesn't say when the Elves figured out Elrond held one of the Rings, but they seem to have known it by the end of the Third Age. If word slowly spread that one wouldn't fade if one settled at or near Rivendell, that would be a sign that one of the Three was kept there.

Much the same could be true of Galadriel. She could have arrived in Lórien and offered to keep the Silvan Elves from fading. They must have known about the Rings of Power by then. They had lost one king, Amroth's father, in the war against Sauron at the end of the Second Age. And Amroth had helped Elrond more than once in the wars against Angmar. Haldir specifically referred to the "power of the Lady of the Galadrim" when Sam mentioned he felt as if he "was *inside* a song". Haldir seems to have known Galadriel was using a Ring. He would not have spoken of it openly, but both Elrond and Galadriel implied all the Elves were united in their belief that it would be better to lose the Three than to allow the One to continue to exist. Many Elves must therefore have had a pretty good idea of where Vilya and Nenya were hidden.

But if the Rings could be directed consciously, either to extend to certain limits or to work only on certain creatures and plants, then it makes sense that there was a physical limit to the power of the Three. At some point the Company of the Ring crossed into the realm of Galadriel's power, and that may or may not have coincided with the physical borders of Lórien (in fact, since the Elves withdrew to deep within the woods, it would seem the extent of Nenya's influence was considerably less than the boundaries of the forest).

Full Circle: The Rings, Time, and Wraiths

So why didn't the Shire benefit from the presence of the One Ring? Probably because only the Three acted on any geographical basis, and though the One possessed the powers of the other Rings, it may not have possessed the ranges of the Three Rings because Sauron was not present when Celebrimbor made them. Sauron himself had no real use for creating a Valinor in Middle-earth, so why use the One Ring to hold back decay around him? On the other hand, Smeagol, Bilbo, and Frodo all went without wearing the One Ring for long periods of time. So it, too, must have had a minimal geographical range that was, perhaps, more keyed to who possessed the Ring than anything else.

The Rings don't really hold back Time. They just slow the impact it has on a biological body. For something like a tree, which has no spirit (Ents and Huorns not considered), there is no real harm. An animal, though intelligent, might also benefit from the effect of the Rings because it didn't have a spirit. An Elf, whose spirit was intended to remain in Arda until the end of Time, would not feel stretched, as Bilbo put it.

The problem for "mortals" was that their spirits wanted to go elsewhere. After a certain length of time, mortal Men had to die. They had to give up their spirits. A Ring of Power obstructed this natural tendency. The body would keep on living, functioning the same as the day it came into possession of the Ring. But the spirit would be constantly striving to leave. Hence, the struggle between spirit and body (or spirit and Ring) must have produced the "stretched" feeling that Bilbo complained about. He wasn't physically stretched, but just torn between powerful forces.

Thus, when Sauron perverted the Seven and the Nine, he must have altered their natural tendency toward preservation to engage the opposite effect. The Nine keepers didn't become wraiths because they used the Rings, but because they possessed them. Using the Rings may have speeded the fading process, but probably any Elf who might have taken one of the altered Nine or Seven would have faded as well, and become just as enslaved as the nine Men eventually did.

People often ask if a man would fade were he in possession of one of the Three. I don't believe so. I think he would just continue, day after day, and eventually lose track of time. He would see the sun pass overhead, and perhaps note the phases of the moon (although the Company of the Ring didn't seem to when they were in Lórien). But for him time would eventually just become a trap. His body wouldn't grow old. It would just live and live and live, and life would become a constant torment to him, because he would always be in conflict with his own nature.

The world would sweep past such an unfortunate soul, who might ultimately feel nothing but a deep longing for release from the torment.

UNDERSTANDING MIDDLE-EARTH

Chapter 26:
The Middle-earth Mysteries

Part of the joy of reading about Middle-earth is finding out more about some obscure dude or tribe long after they show up somewhere else in the "canon". Take the Druedain, the Woses as they are called in *The Lord of the Rings*. When you read the book for the first time, they just sort of show up and lead the Rohirrim around an army of Orcs and Easterlings.

Do they have a point other than to move the story forward? Yes and no. They are there to give the Rohirrim a viable passage around the blocking force that the Lord of the Nazgul has placed on the road through Anorien, and the purpose of the blocking force is to show the reader that Sauron is so powerful he can lob armies all over the map. But the Druedain also serve to remind the reader that Middle-earth is filled with all sorts of strange and mysterious creatures.

Maybe Tolkien was thinking, "..and here it will be good to throw in another magical race of creatures" when he plotted that part of the story, but clearly he didn't stop there. Many years later he wrote a long essay which covered a great deal of history concerning Dwarves and Men, but it also covered the Druedain, and explained who they were, where they came from, and how they ended up in Druadan Forest. The choice of the name "Druadan" may have been convenient, or it may have been intentional.

Tolkien in fact started out calling Ghan-buri-Ghan's people the "dark men of Eilenach" and the wood was "Eilenach Forest". But then they became the Druedain of Druadan Forest, and in the published *Lord of the Rings*, they became the Woses but the wood remained Druadan Forest. The association of the word "adan" with a non-Edainic race is very peculiar, and had long puzzled many people. But in 1980 Christopher Tolkien published much of the Druadan material in *Unfinished Tales* and the mystery was cleared up.

These were a fourth tribe associated with the Edain, not numbered among the "houses" of the Edain, but nonetheless given access to Númenor as a reward for their service and suffering in Beleriand. And there is virtually no mention of them in *The Silmarillion*, because it was only in the late 1960s that Tolkien decided upon the origins and fate of the Druedain, long after most of *The Silmarillion* material had been brought up to the point where Christopher found it upon his father's death.

Tolkien liked the word "wose", by the way. He used it as one of Túrin's nicknames (Saeros called him a woodwose in "Narn i Chin Hurin") and "woodwose" is the modern form of the Anglo-Saxon "wudu-wasa", "wild man of the woods" (another of Túrin's nicknames). "Woses" is therefore intended to be a translation of the actual Rohirric word, "Rogin" (sing. Rog), with much the same meaning, "wild men of the woods". The Rohirrim were ignorant (as was Tolkien, when he wrote *Lord of the Rings*) of the Woses' ancient history.

There is much mystery bound up in the forests of Middle-earth. Tolkien loved trees, and he revered them in a special way. He always seemed to think they had gotten the bitter half of the bargain in sharing the world with men. He was upset with "the shabby use made in Shakespeare of the coming of 'Great Birnam wood to high Dunsinane hill'" (*The Letters of J.R.R. Tolkien*, No. 163). He wanted the trees to really march to war, and eventually this longing achieved fruition in the Ents.

One must ask how the Ents came to live in Fangorn Forest. Tolkien doesn't ever really say. Fangorn (Treebeard) himself speaks of having wandered freely in Beleriand, in lands largely untroubled by Morgoth even during the wars with the Elves. Clearly, if the Ents had survived the destruction of Beleriand at the end of the First Age, they must have wandered eastward, and in Eriador there was once an ancient forest where, Elrond said, "time was when a squirrel could go from tree to tree from what is now the Shire to Dunland west of Isengard. In those lands I journeyed once, and many things wild and strange I knew." ("The Council of Elrond", *The Lord of the Rings*)

Elrond's journeys aside, one must ask how the squirrels (and the Ents) crossed the mighty river Gwathlo. It was wide and deep enough that ocean-faring ships could navigate it as far inland as Tharbad, where, perhaps, the waters became shallow enough for the Ents to travel across.

But why should they do so? At what point in time did they leave the northern woods? Apparently they did so before the War of the Elves and Sauron, and in another text Tolkien notes that Fangorn himself met with the King of Lothlórien early in the Second Age and set a boundary between their realms. Did the eastward migration of Beleriandic Elves in the Second Age push the Ents eastward as well? Or did the Ents at one time become so numerous they had to spread out? There is much we'll never know about the Ents' history, alas.

Another woodland creature that has a mysterious past is the giant spider of Mirkwood. Where and when did these creatures show up? They are said to be the descendants of Ungoliant, and Mirkwood was Greenwood the Great until Sauron arose in the Third Age and established himself on Dol Guldur. He undoubtedly brought or induced some of Ungoliant's offspring to move north to the forest, but how did they get there? Why didn't anyone stop them? And where did Ungoliant live at the time? It doesn't seem likely Isildur would build a city right next to a monstrous spider which fed on Men and Elves.

Something that has always bothered me is who those mysterious Men were who traded with Laketown in *The Hobbit*. They lived south of the Long Lake and were apparently Northmen, but where did they live? The Old Forest Road, according to the book, "was overgrown and disused at its eastern end and led to impassable marshes where the paths had been long lost." The road was originally made by Dwarves. They used it to reach the Celduin and from there somehow passed northeast to the Iron Hills.

If there were men still living along Celduin (the Running River, which arose in Erebor), why didn't they settle at the point where the Old Forest Road met the river? Or perhaps they had at one time lived there but had been driven off. So, where did they eventually settle down?

Then there is the question of why Gandalf and Beorn decided to take Bilbo all the way around the northern skirts of Mirkwood when they returned to the west. There were, in fact, men living in those regions in ancient times, and probably still men living there at the end of the Third Age, but there is no indication of that on the Hobbit map or in the text. It just seems a very strange decision given that the Elvenking probably would have ensured their safe passage through the forest.

Turning south, we can look at Pelargir and ask what became of Gondor's fleet. Aragorn's raid on Umbar was the last time any Gondorian ships moved against an enemy in the Third Age. By the time of the War of the Ring the threat from Umbar and other southern havens was so great that Denethor was willing to leave 9/10ths of Gondor's forces near the coastlands to ward them against attack from the sea. Had he disbanded Gondor's fleet after becoming Steward, perhaps because it had been Thorongil, his rival, who had led the attack on the City of the Corsairs?

And why did no one attempt to recolonize Eriador after the destruction of Angmar? The presence of the Barrow-wights in Tyrn Gorthad, the Barrow-downs, explains why no one tried to settle there again. But were the plains south of Sarn Ford that uninhabitable? What about the South Downs? What prevented people from living there? What became of Tharbad's people when that town was finally deserted? Did they wander north to the Angle and join the Dunedain who lived there? It seems the Dunedain should have prospered, and either many of them left for other parts of the world (perhaps going south to Gondor), or many must have perished in the wilds of Eriador.

There are so many questions about Middle-earth that one can almost picture an "In Search Of..." going on year after year, proposing bizarre theories which attempt to resolve the various mysteries. These unanswerable questions lend a great deal to the perception of "depth" we often speak of in Middle-earth. They are like glimpses of mountains on the distant horizon which we'll never approach. The answers are there, beyond our reach, forever lost to us.

Chapter 27:
Where have all the dragons gone?

I always thought the movie "Dragonslayer" was a bit goofy and slow in some places, but there is one memorable scene that pretty much sells the movie, I think, to anyone who sees it. That's where the dragon's head rises up to dwarf the young magician who really has no clue about what he's up against.

I think whoever came up with that scene must have read Tolkien. In the story of Túrin Turambar in *The Silmarillion*, after Glaurung has destroyed Nargothrond and sent Túrin north to Dor-lomin on a hopeless quest, Morwen and Nienor leave the safety of Doriath. They are overtaken by Mablung and a company of Elven horsemen who are nonetheless persuaded to accompany the women to Nargothrond.

There by the river Narog Glaurung raises a mist and disperses Mablung's company. Morwen is carried off by her maddened horse and the Elves never hear of her again. But Nienor recovers her wits and returns to Amon Ethir, the Hill of Spies, which stands directly east of Nargothrond (across the river). "And looking westward," we are told in the story, "she stared straight into the eyes of Glaurung, whose head lay upon the hill-top."

Now, that is one big dragon.

I think most fans would say that dragons and Tolkien go hand in hand. Tolkien definitely likes to tell dragon tales. Yet, surprisingly, he only told us two full stories about dragons. In 1954 Naomi Mitcheson asked Tolkien some questions about Middle-earth after she looked over the galleys for *The Lord of the Rings*. He responded to a question about dragons with:

Some stray answers. *Dragons.* They had not stopped; since they were active in far later times, close to our own. Have I said anything to suggest the final ending of dragons? If so it should be altered. The only passage I can think of is Vol. I p. 70: 'there is not now any dragon left on earth in which the old fire is hot enough'. But that implies, I think, that there are still dragons, if not of full primeval stature....(*The Letters of J.R.R. Tolkien*, No. 144)

Tolkien's first dragon tale is long since lost, and probably wasn't very long anyway. Of that story he could only recall one detail, years later, when writing to W.H. Auden: "I first tried to write a story when I was about seven. It was about a dragon. I remember nothing about it except a philological fact. My mother said nothing about the dragon, but pointed out that one could not say 'a green great dragon', but had to say 'a great green dragon'. I wondered why, and still do." (Ibid., No. 163)

When the time came to tell the tale of a Hobbit, Tolkien needed a monster greater than all other monsters. He had goblins and wolves and spiders, but he wanted something more terrifying, more powerful. He wanted a dragon. Of all the creatures encountered in *The Hobbit*, only Smaug seems invincible except for the one bare patch on his chest. One could well imagine Beorn charging the dragon in his bear form only to end up burned to a crisp. As great a warrior and hero as Beorn was, he was no match for a dragon.

Bard the Bowman, on the other hand, was the descendant of ancient kings whose realm had been destroyed by Smaug. Fate was on his side, and he possessed the ability to speak with thrushes, too. But perhaps if Bard had not had the black arrow which passed down to him from his ancestors of old, even his skill and courage might not have been sufficient to bring down the great dragon (which was not green).

The black arrow was made by the Dwarves of Erebor before Smaug destroyed their kingdom. Why should it be a potent weapon against dragons? Dwarves had no love for dragons, and the dragons had certainly been a plague upon the Dwarves. But was the arrow really an "arrow of dragon-slaying", or was it just an arrow of exceptionally good quality?

Tolkien's Dwarf and Dragon conflicts extended all the way back to the First Age. The Dwarves of Nogrod and Belegost were allied with the Noldor against Morgoth. Telchar of Nogrod made a helm shaped in the image of Glaurung, father of dragons. This helm was given to Azaghal, lord of Belegost, who in turn gave it to Maedhros, who in turn gave it to Fingon, who in turn gave it to Hador, first Lord of Dor-lomin.

While Hador wore the Dragon-helm he was invincible in battle. Thus, he must not have worn the dragon-helm when he led a rearguard action for Fingolfin soon after the Dagor Bragollach. Hador and his younger son Gundor fell before the walls of Eithel Sirion, the mighty fortress which protected one of the chief passes over the Ered Wethrin into Hithlum. Galdor the Tall, Hador's elder son, inherited the dragon-helm with his father's lordship, but "Narn i Chin Hurin" (*Unfinished Tales*) says that "by ill-fortune Galdor did not wear it when he defended Eithel Sirion", seven years after his father's death, "for the assault was sudden, and he ran barehead to the walls, and an orc-arrow pierced his eye."

Hurin could wear the helm but because of his short stature he was uncomfortable with it, and he preferred to look his foes directly in the eye. So the helm stayed behind in Hithlum when Hurin rode off to fight in the Nirnaeth Arnoediad, and Morwen his wife sent the helm with their son Túrin to Doriath. When Túrin grew to manhood and left Doriath, Beleg brought him the dragon-helm, and with that heirloom of his house Túrin began to earn a name for himself. Unfortunately, because of Hurin's pride and defiance, Morgoth set his will against Hurin's children, and all of Túrin's endeavors turned to grief.

The day came when Túrin persuaded Orodreth to ride to open battle with Morgoth's armies, and Glaurung destroyed Orodreth and his people. When Túrin returned to Nargothrond, he wore the helm and Glaurung was afraid of him. But the dragon goaded Túrin into lifting the helm's visor and in so doing Túrin exposed himself to Glaurung's power.

The dragon-helm was thus a very powerful artifact, and with it Túrin might have had stood a chance of doing battle against Glaurung. Or would he? Even though Glaurung couldn't daunt him, would the dragon have been so vulnerable to Túrin?

Glaurung's first appearance two centuries before had resulted in a victory for Fingon and the Elven archers of Hithlum. They rode around the young dragon and pierced him with many arrows, driving him back to Angband. Glaurung fared better in the Dagor Bragollach and he undoubtedly wrought his vengeance against the Elves with glee. But barely a generation later he led a group of dragons against Maedhros' army in the Nirnaeth Arnoediad and this time they were opposed by the Dwarves.

Azaghal of Belegost went up against Glaurung and wounded him, though the deed cost Azaghal his life. Glaurung and his children retreated from the field of battle. When the dragon reappeared later he seems to have avoided trying to crush warriors with his belly, as he had tried to crush Azaghal, who fell beneath him.

In Túrin's final confrontation with Glaurung, he dealt the dragon a mortal wound in almost exactly the same fashion as Azaghal had wounded the beast, and the sword Túrin used had been made by Eöl, who learned a great deal about smithcraft from the Dwarves of Nogrod and Belegost. Glaurung was smart and wary, but when he crossed the ravine of the Teiglin, he had no idea that Túrin waited for him below.

Glaurung felt such pain that he leaped across the ravine and thrashed around on the far side, spewing flames until he became too weak to continue. The sight of the dying dragon would have been horrific to anyone nearby. Túrin simply strode back across the ravine and drew his sword out of the dragon's belly. And yet Glaurung was still living, and he had enough strength to stare at Túrin again and use what remained of his power to overcome Túrin's will and cause him to faint.

Killing the old dragon was just not an easy task, and there was no greater warrior than Túrin in his day. So could Túrin have done the deed without the element of surprise? I don't think so. Simply stabbing Glaurung in the belly wasn't sufficient. Azaghal had done that, but his blade was too short. The wound had to be deep and I doubt most weapons would have sunk that deep. The Noldor most likely didn't have dragons in mind when they made their weapons.

The Elves didn't do all that badly a few years later when dragons helped destroy the city of Gondolin. Turgon's people had learned much from Maeglin, Eol's son, about mining and smithing. That's not to say they actually killed any dragons. Rather, it took all night for the dragons, Orcs, and Balrogs to destroy most of Turgon's people. These dragons had probably not yet come to their full growth. But it may also be that Gondolin was simply better defended than Nargothrond, whose army had perished mostly in the open field.

Still, since the Dagor Bragollach, the score had become dragons 4, elves 0, dwarves ½. Túrin remained the only individual to actually kill a dragon until the end of the First Age. Then Morgoth unleashed the winged dragons against the Host of Valinor. If the ground-based dragons were formidable, the flying dragons were overwhelming, and the Host gave way before them until Ëarendil and the Eagles of Manwë arrived to do battle.

Tolkien doesn't tell us how long the battle lasted, but it was probably not a short one. Many Eagles must have perished but also many dragons, including Ancalagon himself. Ancalagon appears only briefly in *The Silmarillion*, but Gandalf mentions him knowledgeably when speaking with Frodo. I infer from Gandalf's remark that the great dragon must have terrorized the Host of Valinor for quite some time. He had not only been named, he was still remembered with a certain awe and dread nearly 7,000 years later.

Ëarendil must have done some fancy talking to get Manwë's permission to lead a counter-assault against the dragons. He had been forbidden to return to Middle-earth, and the will of the Valar wasn't something one easily turned aside. So the situation in Beleriand (or what remained of it) must have been desperate. And one must ask how Ëarendil could fight the dragons from a flying ship anyway? He had the Silmaril with him but was that all? Or did he, like Bard thousands of years later, wield a bow and arrow of great potency? Who would have made the bow, Aulë himself?

Ëarendil's battle with Ancalagon lasted a day and a night. The fighting must have covered a lot of territory, so that only the Valar and Maiar might have been able to see the final conflict. Ëarendil would have been a shining spot in the sky, but his opponent would have rained fire around him. The re-engineered Vingelot either had modulating multi-phasic shields or someone was looking out for Ëarendil. Nonetheless, the mariner in the sky must have been hard-pressed on occasion. It couldn't have been a simple case of dragon-hunting for him. He had to guide the ship and figure out where Ancalagon would be attacking from next.

Ëarendil's battle with Ancalagon had to be the mother of all dragon-hero fights, and words fail to describe adequately what can be glimpsed only by the imagination. But when Ancalagon fell and it became clear that all was lost, what happened to the remaining dragons? Did no more than two, a male and female, survive the final onslaught? And, if so, why didn't the dragons re-emerge in the Second Age?

For that matter, what the heck is a cold-drake? The only mention of a cold-drake is a brief anecdote in Appendix A to *The Lord of the Rings* where Tolkien says that a Dwarven king and one of his sons were slain by a cold-drake in front of their hall. People have wondered through the years what the difference between a cold-drake and a regular dragon might be. Gaming systems tell us the cold-drake must be a dragon which breathes cold air, using frost as a breath weapon rather than fire.

I'm not so sure Tolkien envisioned various breath weapons. The cold-drakes may simply have been dragons which didn't breathe fire. Although that may seem a bit of a let-down, dragons don't have to breathe fire in order to be terrifying and powerful. People have enough trouble rationalizing how Morgoth could have bred dragons and then winged dragons from non-winged dragons like Glaurung. Their massive size, their ability to just stare you in the eye and mesmerize you, their incredible strength -- these would be sufficient armaments for the typical hungry dragon. Tossing in frost-breathers, water dragons, and all the role-playing game variants trivializes Middle-earth's monsters. Tolkien's dragons were creatures you just didn't go messing around with. For example, no one ever seems to have killed the mysterious cold-drake.

The only two dragons to be named in the Third Age were Scatha and Smaug. Smaug, as noted, is featured prominently in *The Hobbit*. We can read lots about him. Scatha, on the other hand, merits barely more than a footnote in an appendix and one comment from Eowyn in the main text of *The Lord of the Rings*. What's up with that? Scatha didn't even enter the canon until Tolkien was reviewing the galley proofs for *The Lord of the Rings*. So, unfortunately, there just isn't much of a story to tell there.

But we know that Fram was the son of Frumgar, and it was Frumgar who led the Eotheod north in the year 1977 to claim the eastern lands of what had once been the realm of Angmar. The Eotheod must not have known there were dragons in the area, or else they just felt they had no choice but to get up there. If Frumgar was a man in full vigor in the year 1977 then he probably died sometime around the year 2000. But when did Fram die? My guess is probably sometime after the year 1981. That was the year the Dwarves fled Khazad-dum, and many of them settled in the Grey Mountains, which ran eastward from the Misty Mountains.

With Dwarves and Men moving into the region, and with the demise of Angmar, the handful of dragons in the north may have been stirred up. But why would there have been only a few dragons? One would think the Witch-king of Angmar would want to keep one or two broods on hand to help out in the wars. And yet there is no mention of dragons troubling the Dunedain in Eriador. There isn't even a dragon in the final war with Gondor and the Elves. Tolkien's love for the great monsters seems to have been tempered with caution. Like the Eagles, which he felt should not have been abused as literary devices, the author seems to have refrained from tossing a dragon into the mix every time a nasty old monster was required.

The dragons may have been to Melkor what the Eagles were to Manwë: special emissaries with a specific mission. But Melkor was removed from the world and his evil will diminished. Some aspect of Melkor (or Morgoth) remained in Arda, and Middle-earth in particular, because he had infused a part of his strength, his spirit, throughout the world and its creatures. Dragons, in particular, must have had a pretty large share of this evil spirit. It would make them both "magical" creatures and very powerful (as well as quite evil -- so there is no hope of finding a good dragon in Middle-earth). Tolkien does seem to imply as much in "Narn i Chin Hurin":

> Therefore walking at guess [Nienor] found the hill [of Amon Ethir], which was indeed close at hand, by the rising of the ground before her feet; and slowly she climbed the path that led up from the east. And as she climbed so the fog grew thinner, until she came at last out into the sunlight on the bare summit. Then she stepped forward and looked westward. And there right before her was the great head of Glaurung, who had even then crept up from the other side; and before she was aware her eyes looked in his eyes, and they were terrible, being filled with the fell spirit of Morgoth, his master.

When Túrin asked the Men of Brethil to help him fight the dragon, he said: "I know somewhat of him. His power is rather in the evil spirit that dwells within him than in the might of his body, great though that be." I have long wondered what these passages might mean. Did Morgoth imprison or embed some spirit within the body of the dragon? If so, where did it come from? Only Ilúvatar could create a spirit, and Tolkien was troubled by the idea that Ilúvatar might create something he knew would turn to evil, which must turn to evil. Of course, Ilúvatar must have known that Melkor would eventually become evil. So at some point it is reasonable to say that if there is a freedom of choice for the spirit, then Ilúvatar would create it. But is there a freedom of choice for such monsters as dragons?

An alternative explanation of these passages is a simpler one: the spirit referred to is literally the spirit of Morgoth. Not the primary will of

Morgoth, his awareness or consciousness, if you will. But simply a part of his power, his strength. The One Ring provides an example of how, when a great being's power is partially externalized, a thing can seem to take on a will and consciousness of its own. The One Ring strove to return to Sauron, and in many ways it tried to corrupt and master those who bore it, or anyone who could potentially take it and use it. Through the years many people have tried to rationalize how this Ring could act on its own accord if it wasn't a truly sentient thing. Analogies with computers have been devised, but I think such analogies miss the point.

The primal energy of an Ainurian spirit is an incorporeal force. Ilúvatar gave will to these forces, but the wills are only aspects. The spirit is a thing unto itself, but Melkor and Sauron showed that they could diffuse their spirits, divide their essence among multiple physical shells. Sauron put a great part of himself into the Ring, but he remained in his self-incarnated form, his body. It was the body where his will resided. And yet Sauron would have been able to perceive events and beings through his Ring, if only in a crude fashion. When Frodo put the Ring on and took the High Seat on Amon Hen, he looked upon Barad-dur in the vision which played before him and Sauron was aware of him instantly. Tolkien notes that Sauron was in rapport with the Ring while it existed, but he wasn't in communication with it. Being cut off from the Ring was like having one's arm go numb, perhaps, while still feeling a prickling in the fingers even though -- in the darkness of night -- one could not be sure of where the hand lay.

In "Myths Transformed" (*Morgoth's Ring*), Tolkien expounded upon this process further in an essay which explores the nature of the Valar and Ainur in general:

> Melkor 'incarnated' himself (as Morgoth) permanently. He did this so as to control the *hroa*, the 'flesh' or physical matter, of Arda. He attempted to identify himself with it. A vaster, and more perilous procedure, though of similar sort to the operations of Sauron with the Rings. Thus, outside the Blessed Realm, all 'matter' was likely to have a 'Melkor ingredient', and those who had bodies, nourished by the *hroa*

of Arda, had as it were a tendency, small or great, towards Melkor: they were none of them wholly free of him in their incarnate form, and their bodies had an effect upon their spirits.

Further on, he added:

...Moreover, the final eradication of Sauron (as a power directing evil) was achievable by the destruction of the Ring. No such eradication of Morgoth was possible, since this required the complete disintegration of the 'matter' of Arda. Sauron's power was not (for example) in gold as such, but in a particular form or shape made of a particular portion of total gold. Morgoth's power was disseminated throughout Gold, if nowhere absolute (for he did not create Gold) it was nowhere absent. (It was this Morgoth-element in matter, indeed, which was a prerequisite for such 'magic' and other evils as Sauron practised with it and upon it.)

Dragons have an affinity for gold. They like to gather it up in a huge mound and lay upon it. Tolkien's reasoning may be that they are thus nourished by the Morgoth-element which is present in gold, indeed which is stronger in gold than in other substances (such as silver and water). This could explain how dragons are able to go for long periods of time without actually eating anything. The gold sustains them, and is thus as important to them as food would be to a starving man on a desert island. It could also explain why the dragons experienced a period of decline. Their power would be diminished without Morgoth to control them, and until they could accumulate new hoards they would be very weak.

It may be that the dragons, when they fled from Beleriand, had to flee into the northern wastes because they were simply too weak to deal with the Dwarves, Elves, and Men any more. They had spent themselves on Morgoth's behalf and only barely survived. And a dependence upon gold and the spirit of Morgoth might explain why there seemed to be so few dragons until late in the Third Age. They might need gold to breed. Morgoth certainly wouldn't have lacked for it in Angband, where he could mine the depths of the earth for whatever minerals and metals he required. And as Elvish treasures were brought to him he would be able to breed yet more dragons, greater and more powerful than the earlier generations.

Dragons would thus essentially be living artifacts. People speculate on how Morgoth could breed dragons. That is, what creatures would he have brought together in a controlled breeding program to produce dragons? I don't think that is quite what Tolkien intended, either. Rather, it may be that he envisioned Morgoth starting out with a couple of creatures, say lizards or snakes, exerting his will upon their bodies. His goal would have been to produce offspring which would be dragons. Glaurung was therefore an experiment, a prototype, and Ancalagon was the final production model. Each brood of dragons thus produced would have been infused with part of Morgoth's power. They had "wills" but not necessarily independent wills. They were more than puppets but less than true sentient creatures.

Without the aid of Morgoth's direct intervention, breeding for dragons may have become a great and onerous task. In fact, left to themselves, the dragons seem to have been less efficient than when leading Morgoth's armies. Glaurung took a long time to make his way from Nargothrond to Brethil. He apparently blazed a path across the landscape, burning trees and everything else, but every now and then just laid down to sleep. The burning rampage would just be an expression of the dragon's malice, although it also probably ensured that no one stayed around to trouble him during the naps. But it must have represented an incredible expenditure of energy. In "Narn i Chin Hurin", Glaurung sent an army to attack Brethil and Túrin destroyed the army. The dragon waited several months before moving out against the woodmen himself. He may have been charging his batteries, so to speak, building up his energy reserves.

Such a limitation makes the dragons incapable of taking over the world without a greater power behind them. And it also makes it possible for people to live relatively close to the dragons (as the Men of the Long Lake and the Elves of Northern Mirkwood did) without having to find cover every other day. The dragons, so long as they weren't disturbed, would sustain themselves on their golden hoards until moved to action for some reason. They may have had little in the way of a mating instinct, and perhaps there was a conflict between their need to reproduce and their need simply to exist. A dragon which brought forth children might weaken itself, perhaps even die, unless it had a very, very large hoard of gold. Smaug seems to have been the largest and most successful of the dragons of his generation. But if the hoards of Erebor and Dale were vaster than anything his kind had accumulated since the end of the First Age, he may have become sort of drunk with power, too besotted to go find a mate.

A dependence upon gold and the strength to withstand all but the mightiest of wills would also explain why the Witch-king of Angmar was unable to control or breed dragons. He would simply have been too weak to accomplish the task. Sauron might have been able to exert his full will and gain control over the dragons. Gandalf certainly feared as much according to Tolkien, but Sauron appears to have nearly recovered all his strength by the end of the Third Age (minus the portion stored in the Ring). When Angmar arose around the year 1300 Sauron was still weak and hiding in Mirkwood. He may not have become capable of working with the dragons until much later.

But the re-emergence of dragons in the north in the 26th century may be an indication that Sauron was doing something with them. He returned to Dol Guldur in 2460 "with increased strength", according to the Tale of Years in Appendix B to *The Lord of the Rings*. The dragons reappeared in the north around the year 2570. Coincidence? Sauron could certainly have arranged for the dragons to get a few shipments of gold. In fact, he could have begun working on a dragon breeding program soon after leaving Dol Guldur in 2063 in preparation for his eventual return.

So it would seem that the story of Scatha was a bit of a fluke. The dragons would have been incapable of wreaking havoc among the northern peoples until the Dwarves started settling in the Grey Mountains in large numbers. Some Dwarf-colony may have awakened Scatha and he slew them, taking their hoard. A few survivors would have spread word that a dragon was living in the mountains. So what brought Fram into the picture? Would he really have set out to slay a dragon in the hope of getting treasure? That seems so unlike the heroic Rohirrim and their ancestors, the Eotheod who helped Gondor. Fram may have been a proud and arrogant man with little love for Dwarves, but I think it would be out of character for him to be greedy and pretentious enough to go dragon-hunting. Scatha must have seemed a real threat to the Eotheod.

If, fueled by a small Dwarven hoard, Scatha decided to seek his fortune in the wider world, he should have come into conflict with the Eotheod. As a lord Fram would have had to take action against the worm, much as Túrin had to take action against Glaurung in the First Age, and Bard would later have to take action against Smaug. Brave men just didn't go seeking dragons unless they were fools or desperate. Scatha was called "the great dragon of Ered Mithrin", so he must have been the most powerful dragon of his time. If he accumulated a hoard and grew strong from it, his malice could have led him to range farther and farther afield.

Fram's adventure might thus have played out similarly to Túrin's. He would recruit a few brave companions to help him hunt the dragon. Perhaps there was more than one encounter. It may have come down to only Fram and Scatha in the end, as Fram's companions may all have perished or fled in terror. Fram would have to devise some means of killing the dragon, most likely piercing him from below. The final struggle would be a valiant battle, with the outcome in doubt. The mountains might have echoed with the dragon's roars, and the night sky may have been lit up for miles around from the dragon's flames. The Eotheod would huddle in their homes and sing songs to calm their children. The Dwarves would put down their hammers and harps, and listen as the stone of their halls resounded with the sound of man clashing with dragon.

In the end Fram defeated the dragon, and he lived to boast of the deed. And Tolkien writes that the northern "land had peace from the long-worms afterwards". The dragons had been dealt a devastating blow with the loss of Scatha. As when Azaghal wounded Glaurung and the dragons retreated to Angband in dismay, so the long-worms may have fallen back to the Withered Heath beyond the mountains. Would fear be their only reason for avoiding Men? Or would it be that Scatha had possessed the greatest power, and with his death that power was lost to dragon-kind? Could it be they had to share strength among themselves to survive, and if a dragon died far from the others they were rendered weak?

Smaug's departure from the north might thus explain why the dragons became less of a threat, not more. While they were together they were strong. But when the strongest among them departed, their pool of strength would have been diminished. Their collective strength had been sustained and nourished by long centuries of hoarding gold and stealing it from the Dwarves. The Dwarves had been fleeing the mountains for generations anyway. What is the point in staying around a land where you're likely to be killed by a dragon? So if we assume that Sauron was behind the rise of the dragons, then he must have been pleased at first by Smaug's conquest of Dale and Erebor. And yet the consequence of Smaug's death would have been the loss of a great part of the dragon-power of the north.

It's said that when Augustus Caesar learned that Quintillius Varus had been defeated by the Germans in the Teutoberg Wald, and that three Roman legions had been massacred, Augustus rampaged through his palace and cried out, "Varus! Give me back my legions!" Sauron might have felt a similar rage and despair when he learned about the death of Smaug. He need not necessarily have infused the dragons with any of his own strength (which, in his Ringless state, was precious and spare). But he may have expended a great amount of resources in nourishing them. Such a setback might have radically altered Sauron's plans. His hope of sending armies rampaging across the northern world would be diminished.

The victory over Smaug thus heralds something more than a chance to restore the Longbeard Dwarves to their former glory. It signals the last time the dragons would be in alliance with an incarnate power greater than themselves. Sauron was overcome less than 100 years later, and though dragons survived without him they were utterly on their own. They would have to begin the long slow process of rebuilding their strength without help. But they would never again produce a Smaug or Scatha, or any worm capable of destroying an entire kingdom. At best they might terrorize the countryside or frighten off small tribes. And they would be without real purpose. Though something of Morgoth's will survived in them, there would be no outside direction from powers like Sauron and no harmony or real sense of community among them.

The days of the dragons would thus be numbered, as eventually it would become possible for men to hunt them down and seize their hoards. And being hoardless they would eventually fall asleep never to awaken, and the last of Morgoth's enchanted creatures would recede into distant memory, folklore, and legend.

Chapter 28:
Magic by Melkor, no returns accepted

Why gold? I've had that question put to me a few times now. Where on Earth did I get the idea that dragons might draw power from gold, or, more specifically, that there was something special about gold when it came to magic?

Well, I neglected to mention one crucial paragraph when I was citing Tolkien's essay (which, by the way, Christopher Tolkien called "Notes on motives in the Silmarillion" -- the Morgoth-element paragraphs were lifted from near the end of section ii).

When last we referred to Tolkien's view on how the magic worked for Sauron, he had said:

> ...Morgoth's power was disseminated throughout Gold, if nowhere absolute (for he did not create Gold) it was nowhere absent. (It was this Morgoth-element in matter, indeed, which was a prerequisite for such 'magic' and other evils as Sauron practised with it and upon it.)

But what follows explains my fascination with gold, and why I think dragons might have been able to sustain themselves upon it:

> It is quite possible, of course, that certain 'elements' of conditions of matter had attracted Morgoth's special attention (mainly, unless in the remote past, for reasons of his own plans). For example, all gold (in Middle-earth) seems to have had a specially 'evil' trend -- but not silver. Water is represented as being almost entirely free of Morgoth. (This, of course, does not mean that any particular sea, stream, river, well, or even vessel of water could not be poisoned or defiled -- as all things could.)

So, there is no specific dragon connection but Tolkien did at least give some thought to gold's peculiar place in the hierarchy of what we could call "magical substances" in Middle-earth. Gold is a fascinating element. It's the third most conductive metal we know of (only copper and silver being more effective). In it's purest form gold can be safely eaten (although gold bouillon is quite expensive, I'm told) though it has no real nutritive value for us. Dragons may or may not have benefited from soaking up some ounces.

Of course, it's been pointed out to me that a dragon's hoard included more than just gold. Smaug's belly, for example, was encrusted with jewels. That's true. But anyone who has seen the picture of Bilbo and Smaug which Tolkien painted for *The Hobbit* ("Conversation with Smaug", *J.R.R. Tolkien: Artist & Illustrator*, No.140) cannot fail to notice that the bulk of the dragon's bed is made of gold. Yes, there are all sorts of sparkly things scattered across the pile (including an Arkenstone atop the heap) but most of the treasure was gold.

Now, that's not to say jewels cannot be special in their own right. Recall how Ungoliant lusted after the gems Melkor stole from the Noldor at Formenos. She ate all but the Silmarils and grew more powerful as she did so. These gems could not possibly have contained what Tolkien referred to as the Morgoth-element, even though Melkor had been held in Aman for a very long time. So, the question arises of whether there was some other "magic" element that Ungoliant was feeding upon, or if she was simply feeding on the essence of the gemstones themselves.

When Ungoliant sucked the life from the Two Trees and then drank the liquid light from the Wells of Varda she grew to an immense size. She became so large and powerful that Melkor feared her. Light was Ungoliant's sustenance, but the light of the Two Trees was the product of what might be deemed "pure magic", the power of a Vala. Yavanna had brought the Two Trees to life by the power of her song, an act of sub-creation within the Halls of Ëa which was unequalled, and which she claimed she would never be able to repeat. Thus fed by the power of Yavanna's greatest enchantment, Ungoliant became huge and even more powerful than before.

Likewise the stolen gems of the Noldor were enchanted. Fëanor had learned how to make gem-stones which glowed under the starlight, or which glowed of their own accord. He had many years in which to build up a great treasury, and this treasury was moved to Formenos when Fëanor, Finwë, Fëanor's sons, and the Noldor who followed them settled there far in the north of Valinor during the period of Fëanor's banishment from Tirion. So Ungoliant was able to feed not only upon the essence of the Noldorin jewels but also the power Fëanor (and any other crafters) had put into them.

If the Noldor were able to create magical gems in Aman, they were no less able to create them in Middle-earth. And as the Noldor were taught by the Valar and Maiar, and especially by Aulë, so, too, were the Dwarves taught by Aulë himself. The Dwarves had their own skills and special powers. They may have been less powerful than the Eldar, or perhaps less ambitious (for they never made artifacts like the Rings of Power or the Silmarils). But the Dwarves may also have put their thought into the things they made, such as the dragon-helm of Dor-lomin, which warded its bearers against harm. And the Black Arrow of Erebor which Bard used to slay Smaug may have been the product of more than just expert fletching and smithing. Perhaps some Dwarven master, slain by the dragon so that all his lore was lost with him, had put a great effort into the shaft and it bore something of his power.

Elf- and Dwarf-power might not be the equal of Morgoth- or Yavanna-power, but it would still be a source of enchantment. A dragon sitting upon an Elf hoard (as in Nargothrond) or a Dwarf hoard (as in Erebor) might draw upon or simply bask in the energies of the makers of the enchanted items as much or nearly so as upon the Morgoth-element in gold. Which is not to say that dragons had to do this, but clearly the passing of power from a being to an object is a motif Tolkien used over and over again, and in turn he gave us an example of power passing from an object to a being. The immense energies Melkor dispersed throughout Arda in his efforts to identify it with himself would, collectively, overshadow those of the Elven and Dwarven makers of items. But a hoard of gold and gems no matter how large would still be a mere fraction of the essence of Arda. So every little bit would help.

A sense of scale develops when one weighs the great (evil) powers of the First Age against those of later ages. Melkor governed his realm from Angband, where he was surrounded by his servants: Sauron, the

Balrogs, Draugluin and the were-wolves, Orcs, Trolls, Thuringwethil and perhaps other bat-like creatures, and other monsters unnamed in the legends of the Elves and Edain. He bred the dragons there and nourished Carcharoth, the great Wolf. But his creatures also dwelt throughout Middle-earth. The siege of Angband was more a show than anything else, because Melkor's forces were able to come and go as they pleased by northern routes. And Melkor recruited many Men from the east.

In the Second Age Sauron started out with himself. He eventually gathered all evil creatures together again, but nearly all of Melkor's Maiaric servants had perished or hidden themselves. And if there were dragons in Sauron's service, they don't seem to have achieved much in Eriador (unless it were that when Sauron set the great forests of Minhiriath and Enedwaith aflame in the War of the Elves and Sauron he did so with the aid of dragons). By the end of the Age Sauron had enslaved the nine Nazgul. Since a vast army of Elves, Dwarves, and Men was able to defeat him, Sauron wasn't really as powerful (militarily) as Melkor had been at the end of the First Age. Part of that military strength no doubt arose from the number of sorcerors in Melkor's service, and their quality. Even in their fallen state the corrupted Maiar were very powerful.

In the third Age Sauron took shape very slowly, and he concentrated his efforts around Dol Guldur for a long time. He sent the Lord of the Nazgul north to found the Witch-realm of Angmar, and from Angmar Sauron struck out at the Dunedain of the North (and to a lesser extent at the Eldar, too). Part of Angmar's strategy seems to have been to corrupt the Hill-folk of Rhudaur, some of whom became sorcerors. But though perhaps feared by Men, these sorcerors don't seem to have made a lasting mark upon history. They were virtually wiped out during or after the war of 1409.

Though Tolkien doesn't speak of the sorceries performed by the Hill-folk he does reveal something of the kinds of sorcery used by the Lord of the Nazgul and by the Barrow-wights, which were sent by the Witch-king to inhabit the barrows of Tyrn Gorthad after the Great Plague destroyed most of Cardolan's people. The Nazgul and the

Wights seem to be adept at killing living beings, and the Nazgul especially (with their Morgul-blades) enslaved the spirits of those whom they had slain. The Barrow-wight which captured Frodo and the Hobbits was ready to sacrifice them, presumably to send their spirits to Sauron or the Lord of the Nazgul.

In *Morgoth's Ring*, the essay on "Death and the severance of the *fea* and *hrondo* (>*hroa*)", Tolkien speaks of how the spirits of slain Elves can linger in Middle-earth:

> But it would seem that in these after-days more and more of the Elves, be they of the Eldalië in origin or be they of other kinds, who linger in Middle-earth now refuse the summons of Mandos, and wander houseless in the world, unwilling to leave it and unable to inhabit it, haunting trees or springs or hidden places that once they knew. Not all of these are kindly or unstained by the Shadow. Indeed the refusal of the summons (of Namo to Mandos) is in itself a sign of taint.

> It is therefore a foolish and perilous thing, besides being a wrong deed forbidden justly by the appointed Rulers of Arda, if the Living seek to commune with the Unbodied, though the houseless may desire it, especially the most unworthy among them. For the Unbodied, wandering in the world, are those who at the least have refused the door of life and remain in regret and self-pity. Some are filled with bitterness, grievance, and envy. Some were enslaved by the Dark Lord and do his work still, though he himself is gone. They will not speak truth or wisdom. To call on them is folly. To attempt to master them and to make them servants of one's own will is wickedness. Such practices are of Morgoth; and the necromancers are of the host of Sauron his servant.

> Some say that the Houseless desire bodies, though they are not willing to seek them lawfully by submission to the judgement of Mandos. The wicked among them will take bodies, if they can, unlawfully. The peril of communing with them is, therefore, not only the peril of being deluded by fantasies or lies: there is peril also of destruction. For one of the hungry Houseless, if it is admitted to the friendship of the Living, may seek to eject the *fea* from its body; and in the contest for mastery the body may be gravely injured, even if it be not wrested from its rightful habitant. Or the Houseless may plead for shelter, and if it is admitted, then it will seek to enslave its host and use both his will and his body for

its own purposes. It is said that Sauron did these things, and taught his followers how to achieve them.

One must wonder what that last sentence means. Sauron was known as the Necromancer during the long years he dwelt on Dol Guldur. Did he work bodilessly to enslave others while he regained his strength? Did he at times forsake his body to work with sorcerors who thought they might enslave him? What would become of the slaves Sauron made this way, and who were his followers who could also practice such deceptions? Were the Nazgul taking possession of would-be sorcerors? Such perilous communions with Sauron might explain both how he was able to control so many leaders of men and why they would be drawn to him in the first place. The shamans and kings and chieftains wouldn't know, until it was too late, that their predecessors who had become powerful were in fact little more than avatars for Sauron. That is not to say that all of Sauron's servants would be so directly manipulated. But the most powerful leaders among his servants and allies may indeed have been sorcerous puppets.

Perhaps that also explains the heathen custom where kings would have themselves burned on a pyre. Denethor II chooses to die this way and Gandalf rebukes him for it, saying only the heathen kings are so treated. If Sauron decided he had no further use for one of these slaves it might be convenient to destroy all the evidence of his possession of it rather than let his followers learn the truth, or some portion of it. On the other hand, one might argue, if Sauron and the Nazgul could possess people, why didn't the Lord of the Nazgul use Eärnur's body to gain control over Gondor? It may be that, if he made the attempt, the Lord of the Nazgul didn't possess the power necessary. Eärnur would not have willingly communed with a Nazgul or even Sauron himself. His will might be broken but he would probably die, burned out by the struggle.

The fear some of the Rohirrim express, wondering if Aragorn and his companions may be Elvish wights when he takes the Paths of the Dead, may also be grounded in a suspicion that perhaps they have been possessed by Elven spirits. The speculation implies that the Rohirrim have had experience with men who have been possessed by

Elven spirits, or perhaps have heard enough tales of such men to believe they are true. At the very least we know that Tolkien wasn't completely back-tracking when he wrote the essay on death and the severance of spirit and body. He was filling in some of the gaps for the framework already established by *The Lord of the Rings*.

And thus we can safely deduce that, in the world of Aragorn and his companions, there were or had been men who had foolishly attempted to become powerful through unnatural means. Perhaps envious of, or inspired by, the Istari and the Elves, who possessed such abilities naturally, men were drawn toward the darkness. And the apparent increase in strength and sophistication of the enemies of Arnor and Gondor may also show that men were succumbing to the temptation to seek out alliances with malevolent spirits, though they might not have thought they were doing so.

Which brings us back to how men could begin such experimentation. Even Sauron would need a first volunteer to succeed with. Did he discover that men were already toying with the notion when he first took shape again? Had he perhaps sown the seeds of such practices in the Second Age? If so, the ancient lore might have receded into the distant east but would not have been completely lost. Perhaps the Nazgul kept alive the knowledge in anticipation of Sauron's eventual return. And men seeking power might seek for objects of power. Gold would be valuable, but gold worked by Elves and Dwarves would be more magical than whatever Men could gain for themselves.

Hence, would-be sorcerors might strike up trade bargains with Elves and Dwarves if they had wealth and resources the Elves and Dwarves desired. Otherwise, Men would prey upon Elves and Dwarves in the hope of gaining treasures. The animosity and estrangement which developed between Men and the other races in the Third Age might have many causes, but Tolkien notes that the Dwarves were often plundered by Men, probably more so than by dragons. And so generation upon generation of sorcerors and students of necromancy would fight and haggle over precious artifacts and gems, valuing them not for their beauty but for their enchantment.

Not that all practitioners of magic would have to be evil. The Númenoreans of Cardolan, at least, had the means to make enchanted swords. The barrow-blades Tom Bombadil gave to the Hobbits were "wound about with spells for the bane of Mordor" according to Aragorn ("The Departure of Boromir", *The Lord of the Rings*). Faramir told Frodo and Sam that even in Gondor some of his people continued to make elixirs in their desperate search for longer life, and some men continued to consort with the Elves. And in one letter to a reader, Tolkien said that Beorn was a Man, "though a skin-changer and a bit of a magician". Such men would not have sought to commune with the Elvish spirits, the Unbodied, or with Sauron and the Nazgul. They would have sought a less tainted lore.

And since Melkor's power was disseminated through the physical world there would be plenty of material to work with. One did not need to enchant material which was already enchanted. Gold made a poor source for weaponry but it could be traced upon the blades of iron swords (as the barrow-blades were so traced). The barrow-blades were also decorated with gems, and made of a strange metal the Hobbits did not recognize. And Denethor knew at once that Pippin's sword had been made by Dunedain of the north. Did he recognize the weapons by their design, their materials, or by something else?

The Númenoreans also constructed the vast tower of Orthanc, which was so smooth and so strong its stone could not be broken by the Ents. Was there magic involved there? Was the dark stone with which the Númenoreans worked filled with an unusually large amount of Melkor's essence, or was there simply enough that they could sing or chant their thought into it so that the tower became nearly impregnable? And what was the black stone of Erech made of? Why was it so important to the Dead Men of Dunharrow? Isildur had placed it there, and their king had sworn an oath upon it. Was the stone perhaps a repository of a greater portion of the Morgoth-element than, say, other stones of similar size and shape?

But then, would Isildur still be able to make use of the Morgoth-element to curse the Men of Dunharrow for breaking their oath? As a Man he lacked the power to confine an entire tribe's spirits to Middle-earth for thousands of years. Even the mightiest of sorcerors among Men don't seem to have achieved anything comparable. Hence, Isildur's curse must have been powered by something greater, something more pure. Even the Valar did not have the authority to keep Men in the Halls of Ëa forever. It would be an act of defiance and rebellion for Namo to keep a Mannish spirit very long at all. So the will and authority to enforce Isildur's curse must have come from a greater power, and that could only be Ilúvatar himself.

As a King of Gondor, Isildur was, in fact, a priest of Ilúvatar on behalf of his people. "It later appears," Tolkien noted for his friend Robert Murray, "that there had been a 'hallow' on Mindolluin, only approachable by the King,...

> ...where he had anciently offered thanks and praise on behalf of his people; but it had been forgotten. It was re-entered by Aragorn, and there he found a sapling of the White Tree, and replanted it in the Court of the Fountain. It is to be presumed that with the reemergence of the lineal priest kings (of whom Lúthien the Blessed Elf-maiden was a foremother) the worship of God would be renewed, and His Name (or title) be again more often heard. But there would be no *temple* of the True God while Númenorean influence lasted. (*The Letters of J.R.R. Tolkien*, No. 156)

The Gondorian kings (and, presumably, the Arnorian kings) were only continuing or reviving the ancient worship their people had practiced in Númenor.

> The Númenoreans thus began a great new good, and as monotheists; but like the Jews (only more so) with only one physical centre of 'worship': the summit of the mountain Meneltarma 'Pillar of Heaven' -- literally, for they did not conceive of the sky as a divine residence -- in the centre of Númenor; but it had no building and no temple, as all such things had evil associations....(Ibid.)

Ilúvatar did not imbue Arda with his personal essence as Melkor had, but then there would be no need. Ilúvatar created Ëa with the Flame Imperishable, and he set the Flame at its heart. The Halls of Ëa are indisputably identifiable with the will of Ilúvatar, and Melkor's petty machinations could only bestow a veneer of identification upon Arda.

Hence, Ilúvatar is free to act within his own creation when he desires. And Gandalf points out to Frodo that there is some guiding purpose at work in Arda, when he says, "There was more than one power at work, Frodo. The Ring was trying to get back to its master....Behind that there was something else at work, beyond any design of the Ring-maker. I can put it no plainer than by saying that Bilbo was *meant* to find the Ring, and *not* by its maker...."

And we can be sure Gandalf was speaking of Ilúvatar because Tolkien says so in his letter to Robert Murray, "So God and the 'angelic' gods, the Lords or Powers of the West, only peep through in such places as Gandalf's conversation with Frodo". Whether the Valar had some part in the decision that Bilbo should find the Ring or not, Tolkien was clearly including Ilúvatar in the decision.

The infusion of a divine element into the "magic" of Middle-earth thus raises a question of applicability. Is the word being used too much? But there Tolkien expressed regret at using the word at all, which described both the sub-creational works of the Elves and "the deceits of the Enemy". Although he defined two aspects of magic, *magia* (physical effects) and *goiteia* (effects on the mind or spirit), he insisted that either type could be good or bad depending on the motive of the user, and that both the good actors (Elves, Valar) and bad actors (Melkor, Sauron) used both kinds of magic. And yet all "magic" or power ultimately came from the will or thought of Ilúvatar, who created the beings which practiced magic. So if the power of Melkor, or Ulmo, is the product of Ilúvatar's thought, does it differ in nature from Ilúvatar's own direct interventions?

In one respect, Melkor's power was his own: given to him irrevocably by Ilúvatar. Only Ilúvatar or Melkor could alter his natural strength. Other beings, like Manwë and Namo, might be able to capture and execute Melkor, and thus weaken him as a result of his being forcibly evicted from his physical incarnation. But such eviction was the result of the physical laws of Creation. That is, Ilúvatar made the rules by which even Melkor had to abide. He couldn't just refuse to be killed. His physical incarnation was subject to the consequences of physicality. Hence, there was a very real, if minimal, chance that

Fingolfin could have slain Melkor. And that is why Gil-galad and Elendil (or Isildur, as some hold) were able to slay Sauron. Sauron died in Númenor but the destruction of Númenor was achieved by Ilúvatar. Sauron's death on the slopes of Orodruin was achieved by a being or beings of far less power and stature than Manwë.

The divine aspect of "magic" is therefore identifiable with the laws of nature. That is, the will of Ilúvatar cannot be distinguished from an aspect of itself or its creation. If Creation must behave in a certain fashion, and Creation is itself achieved by Ilúvatar's power, then all things within Creation are by extension exhibiting Ilúvatar's power, though portions of that power have been given irrevocably to them.

There may, therefore, be an aspect of Arda (and all the Halls of Ea, Creation) which is very like the Morgoth-element, though more pure and more consistent: an Ilúvatar-element. Not usable for the purposes of conducting "magic", perhaps, but irrevocably imprinted with his will. Things exist because Ilúvatar says they should, and they work according to the Laws of Creation which he defined. Hence, all the power of the Ainur and the Elves and the Dwarves, whether they retain it or infuse other items with it, must exist and function according to Ilúvatar's natural laws. And Ilúvatar himself would thus not need to contravene his own natural laws in order to achieve his will within the world. The world will achieve his will for him because the laws of nature stem from his will.

That is to say, there is really no distinction between the "magic" of Ilúvatar and the "magic" of Melkor, except in scale and purity of purpose. Melkor's power is incomparably small beside Ilúvatar's, but Melkor's perversion has also corrupted or tainted his power so that it is impure. All power is cut from the same mold, and flows from the same source. But Ilúvatar bestows power irrevocably in some measure upon the creatures of his thought. Melkor's efforts to identify himself with Arda by disseminating his strength throughout the world are thus an act of defiance. And largely fruitless. Ilúvatar won't rescind his gift to Melkor, but neither is he barred by Melkor's will.

On the other hand, having made the Halls of Ëa and populated them with Ainur and other creatures of similar but lesser stature, Ilúvatar doesn't need to continually infuse Ëa with his power. So there is a finite aspect to magic. Only so much of it came into the universe, only so much has been added through the births of beings with the ability to enchant things. The separation of Aman from Middle-earth in a way limits or even diminishes the magic which can be "tapped" by Men or other beings. What Melkor left behind is about *it*. New Elves and Dwarves may be born, but their power is incomparably small next to Melkor's. As Elves leave or die, as Dwarves die, and as their artifacts vanish or are destroyed, the available reserve of usable, tractable magical energy diminishes.

That is, it should become more and more difficult through the passing millennia for Men to practice "true" magic because the sources of magic they require become fewer and fewer. One of the harshest criticisms leveled at Tolkien by modern fantasy writers is that there seems to be no limit to the magic in his world, and yet nothing could be farther from the truth. "Magic" is extremely difficult to define, but the expressions of power, the creation of "magical artifacts", diminish in scope and number as the ages pass because the power is leaving Middle-earth.

Hence Fëanor's Silmarils and the Rings of Power define an upper limit of the expression of power in Middle-earth. Undoubtedly other great works were achieved: the cities of Gondolin, Menegroth, and Khazad-dum were in many ways "magical". But they were the products of whole populations, the results of ages of labor. And yet nothing like them would be achieved again. Even in the Fourth Age, when Durin VII led his people back to Khazad-dum, it's unlikely they would revive the ancient glory of their city. Only an echo of the past would be achievable, in part because their numbers had been diminished, but also because they had lost so much ancient lore. Khazad-dum was the last relic of a span of ages when magical cities were possible. Now they are simply legends.

Galadriel's fear that her people would be diminished in the age of Men, doomed to become a rustic folk of cave and dell, is thus founded on a very real problem. Once the Rings of Power failed, the Elves (who had been sheltered from the effects of Time) had to leave Middle-earth. The Elves lost not just a great part of their pool of talent, but also of their "power reserve". That is, there were fewer Elves left to build new cities. Some of the High Elves remained in Imladris and Lindon but there would never again be a great Eldarin nation. There were no more artifacts, no more cities to be built in the lands of Men. And the Elves who understood that Arda still possessed the Morgoth-element might be reluctant to use it again on the scale of creating Rings of Power. They had learned through many bitter lessons what the price of working such magic would be.

Something might be said here of Mithril. If gold is highly magical, is Mithril even more so? I should think so. Unfortunately, it was extremely difficult to come by. Gold was much more plentiful. So were jewels, for that matter. And a lot of the Mithril which had been brought to light was lost. Tar-Telemmaite, fifteenth king of Númenor, gathered all he could find of Mithril. Sauron, too, collected all the Mithril he could. Although it's doubtful the Númenoreans were sorcerors, Sauron may indeed have found sorcerous uses for his Mithril. And when the Barad-dur was destroyed a great deal of Mithril may have been destroyed with it. Slowly Mithril vanished from Middle-earth.

There may be good reason for why the Balrog of Moria hid itself in or near a vein of Mithril. The Mithril in its raw state might have masked his power. And it may be that if dragons could in fact draw power from gold and jewels, they could draw it from Mithril, too. But then, if silver (normal silver) possessed less of the Morgoth-element than gold, would Mithril possess more than silver? Or, being "true silver", was Mithril nearly free of the Morgoth-element? We'll probably never know.

Chapter 29:
Beware that baker in the kitchen!

There's nothing like a good villain in Tolkien and, unfortunately, he has so few of them. Now, before people go hanging me, let me say that I think Tolkien intentionally kept the good villains to a minimum. The really evil folk were rare because they were corrupting and manipulating everyone else toward evil. Neither Melkor nor Sauron would have tolerated a rival Dark Lord. Almost all the other guys were just their minions. It's debatable whether the Balrog of Moria was really serving Sauron in the Third Age.

But Tolkien's evil is different from the evil in most stories. He is not focusing on evil in human beings. He is focusing on external evil, what he sometimes called Evil Incarnate. One would almost expect to hear those words reverberate when he spoke them. Thunder should peal from the heavens, and clouds should block the sun. Melkor and Sauron may have been good to begin with, but they walked down that dark path ahead of everyone else. Heck, Melkor blazed the trail and Sauron widened it.

There is human evil in Middle-earth: greed, avarice, pride, and so on. Kings and heroes can easily run amok and leave the path of Goodness and Light. Tolkien derives his tragedy from these human characters. But neither Melkor nor Sauron is tragic, though they could be. That is, there is no regret over the fall of these two once truly great and magnificent beings. They were Ainur, angels, children of the thought of Ilúvatar before there was Time, before the Children of Ilúvatar were brought into being. They weren't always dark, but were once of the light. And yet the choices they made led them down into destruction. Their corruption wasn't a foregone conclusion.

On the other hand, there is nothing of petty evil in Tolkien. No one gets mad at the village and poisons their bread, so to speak, in a petty act of revenge over cheap shots and insults. All acts of evil are universally despised. People have a sense of what is right and wrong, and they generally try to live by it. Except for "those other guys", the enemy. In every war, the victors are the good guys in their own sight. So Sauron's followers undoubtedly enjoyed the successes they experienced because they were on the right side. It was the evil Elves and the domineering Dunedain who needed to be destroyed.

On the other hand, one might be quick to point out, who would think the Orcs are "good" people? Even the Orcs seemed to despise themselves. Yes and no. We define good and evil by the values we are taught or learn while growing up. The Orcs were corrupted. What they might deem to be good wouldn't necessarily make sense to us, but it would make sense to them. "What is best in life?" "Crush your enemies. See them driven before you. Hear the lamentations of their women." Not exactly classic Tolkien dialogue, but it reflects the values of warriors in some people's imaginations.

Good, in the sense of what is best for the community, also existed among the Orcs. Aragorn pointed out that they would travel a long way to avenge a fallen captain. Why? The Orc was dead, after all, right? What was in it for the living Orcs to risk their lives trying to pay back someone who had killed a captain they probably hated? Pride. But not just pride. There had to be a pack sense, a tribal feeling which underlay all the inevitable abuse. The growling and fighting and snarling was part of the social pecking system. Chickens determine a social hierarchy and so do Orcs. That's just the way things are. So what if the head Orc probably killed five other Orc chiefs to take over the tribe?

The Orcs were loyal to their masters. They fought and died by the thousands for Melkor, Sauron, and Saruman. Many of them may have lost their free will, but even Melkor (Tolkien argues in one of his essays) couldn't directly control them all. They hated their masters but feared them. And yet, some of the Orcs seemed to take pride in their service. Shagrat, for example, was fiercely determined to see to it that Frodo was delivered to Barad-dur. Why? Gorbag and his boys didn't seem to feel compelled to stay on the path. Even when Shagrat was told an Elven warrior had breached his defenses, he insisted on sending the prisoner to Lugbúrz (though in the end only Frodo's mithril coat was taken). Shagrat was a "good Orc". He would be the kind of Orc you'd want working for you if you controlled Orcs. Gorbag wasn't all that good.

But that isn't to say that the Orcs' values should have been on a par with those of the Elves and Dunedain. The Orcs lived their lives according to the will of their masters. They could not know there was an absolute standard of good and evil, ultimately derived from the values of Ilúvatar. It would be His values which prevailed over all, and they might not necessarily match those of the Elves and Men. Ilúvatar, for example, permitted evil to exist. Why? That same question has been asked of the Judeo-Christian community for a long time. Why does God permit evil to exist?

The New Testament answer is that, if God were to end evil today, then nearly everyone would perish. He delays his judgement to give people as much time as He deems reasonable to reflect upon their sins and turn away from them. Ilúvatar's purposes are not so clearly explained. In fact, Tolkien was troubled by the implications of extending that principle to Ilúvatar. He recognized that if the Orcs were rational incarnates, like Men and Elves, then Ilúvatar was creating spirits which were doomed to live lives of evil. Why would Ilúvatar do that? It wasn't predestination which would doom the Orcs so much as their circumstances.

The answer eluded Tolkien. He could only decide that Ilúvatar knew what he was doing, but that if the Orcs were rational incarnates, this somehow served Ilúvatar's purpose. One might just as easily ask, however, why Ilúvatar would allow a child to be born who would grow up to become Ar-Pharazôn. What is the difference between a King of Númenor who turns to evil and the Orcs who are raised in evil, except that the Orcs are denied free choice? Gandalf seemed to speak of the Orcs when he told Denethor, "And for me, I pity even [Sauron's] slaves".

Evil exists on both sides of the war, then. So evil is not really about "us" and "them". It's about the choices one makes within the bounds of one's life. An Orc's choice to waylay and rob people is evil. Sauron probably didn't allow highway robbery in his realm. All the goods belonged to him and served his needs. Pity the Orc who robbed one of his supply trains!

But if evil is to be found everywhere, can good be found everywhere? This question is more difficult to answer. The Orcs would have abided by Sauron's laws for the most part. They feared him and they feared the consequences of disobedience. But was a law-abiding Orc being "good"? Put another way, if a Man were to live under Sauron's rule (and many did), and he acted no differently from the Orcs, was he any less evil for being a Man, or any more good? I don't think so. He had the advantage of caste, perhaps, but only if Men in general were treated better by Sauron than the Orcs. It may be that the Orcs got better treatment (but probably everyone was treated equally badly).

Saruman tried to set himself up as a dark lord, and he represents what Sauron might have achieved very early on, before the War of the Elves and Sauron. Sauron had to start out as a lonely Maia at some point in the Second Age. It would have taken him time to accumulate followers and slaves. And until he settled in Mordor, long before he made the One Ring, how effective was his control of other creatures? How many other creatures was he capable of imposing his will upon?

When Sauron began to dominate Melkor's former servants, he may have been only a little worse than an angry village baker. That is, his sins in the First Age were no doubt legion, but he had recanted for a time. A long time. It would be centuries before Sauron returned to his evil ways. Was there simply a moment of anger somewhere which triggered the return to darkness and evil? Was that how Saruman began to walk the path?

The quest for evil in Middle-earth is almost as long as the quest for redemption, it seems. Melkor was disruptive during the Ainulindalë and he apparently angered Ilúvatar, but was he really *evil*? When Melkor entered Ëa with the other Valar, he seems to have worked long to help them give shape and substance to the universe. There was no real strife until they were making that region which came to be known as Arda. And then he claimed it for his own, which he had no right to do. How long were the countless ages of the stars in which Melkor (and Sauron, and all the other nameless Maiar who eventually followed Melkor into evil) had not yet become evil?

On a smaller scale, how long was it before the Noldor fell into evil? They weren't evil when they reached Aman. They hadn't yet succumbed to the sins of pride that Melkor capitalized upon after his release from captivity. Weren't they still essentially a good people on the day Melkor was released from Mandos? What would that day have been like? And if only Fëanor, who had set himself aside from his father's household, were already succumbing to the pride which would be his downfall, did Melkor sense the taint of another evil in Valinor?

It was a long time before Melkor really achieved much of anything in the way of corrupting the Noldor. And though Fëanor rejected Melkor, the Valar believed that Melkor was somehow responsible for Fëanor's eventual dark mood. Had Melkor not slain the Two Trees, and Finwë besides, Fëanor might have been a bit rude, but he may not have gone over the edge. Yet it's clear that, when he ascended the hill of Tuna in defiance of the Valar and spoke to his people, Fëanor had finally crossed the line, and the Noldor would soon follow him.

It's hard to imagine how the Noldor slowly fell to the sin of pride. They became arrogant and openly distrustful of one another. There must have been arguments and disputes, but apparently nothing came to blows or crossing of swords. Did the bakers occasionally spike each others' cakes? What was the mindset of a people who could so easily (it seems) turn upon their neighbors (the Teleri of Alqualondë)? How did it come to pass that, when Fëanor ordered his people to steal the Telerin ships, no one stood forth and asked why God should need a starship (or, more appropriately, why Fëanor thought he had the right to take the ships)?

Was it too late for dissension in the ranks? Even the good-hearted Fingon went charging into the fray without knowing the just and unjust causes of the combatants, or seeking for them. His irresponsible and headlong charge, born of loyalty, seems to have doomed all of his people. What would have happened if Fingon had asked first what was going on? What if he had refused to support Fëanor's theft of the ships? Would the Noldor still have launched themselves into exile, or would only a small fraction of the nation have been doomed?

The road into darkness seems to have many pitfalls, but there are also pit stops. There are points where one may assess what one has done and turn back. Boromir's redemption is an example of how someone could set out upon the dark path, and yet not make the full journey. He still paid with his life for trying to take the Ring, but his death was a noble one. He sacrificed himself trying to save two companions.

Even Ar-Pharazôn is said to have hesitated when Sauron urged him to cut down the White Tree of Númenor. It was Isildur's valiant effort to save a fruit before the Tree was destroyed that finally pushed Ar-Pharazôn over the edge. It might be argued that, had Isildur done nothing, the king would still eventually have agreed to Sauron's suggestion. Sauron wasn't about to relent in his efforts to corrupt and destroy the Númenoreans. Nonetheless, Isildur's action prompted Ar-Pharazôn to reaction, and Ar-Pharazôn resumed the journey into darkness.

Eärnur, the last King of Gondor from the Line of Anarion, didn't exactly turn to evil, but he succumbed to pride. And yet his downfall was also delayed. The first time the Lord of the Nazgul issued a challenge to the king, the Steward Mardil was able to restrain Eärnur. Eärnur had a respite, but in time he resumed his self-destructive course. He responded to the second challenge.

It's not really easy for anyone to become evil in Middle-earth. The Orcs weren't always evil. Somewhere back in their beginnings they were good, as good as anyone else. They weren't really Orcs. There eventually came a day when they could be called Orcs, but what was the transitional process like? And were they so far gone down the path they couldn't return, if the desire entered their hearts? The question of the redeemability of the Orcs troubled Tolkien and has disturbed many of his readers. Many people assume the Orcs were all destroyed in the War of the Ring, but that is not the case. The Epilogue (which Tolkien was persuaded not to publish) indicates the Orcs were still around.

Sam even speculates that they won't ever be completely destroyed, and during World War II Tolkien often made reference to the "Orcs" in the British army in letters to his son.

Orcs, therefore, were not so utterly evil that they could always be distinguished from Men. Or perhaps Men were not always so good that they could be distinguished from Orcs. The Elves' disobedience wasn't universal, as was the disobedience of Men. The Elves were able to learn the errors of their ways, and to reject the path of darkness. Men had to wait for another form of redemption.

Yet we see the good and evil in Middle-earth mostly through the eyes of the Hobbits. There were some mean Hobbits, and Hobbits who willingly served Saruman. But, in general, the Hobbits possessed an innocence, a faithfulness to good, which all Men and Elves must have once shared. That is not to say the Hobbits hadn't shared in the Fall of Man. They must have, being (as Tolkien said) a branch of the Human race. But they had turned aside from the darkness and never wholly gone back toward it. A few, like Smeagol and Lotho Sackville-Baggins, stole down the path and vanished into oblivion.

To Hobbits, the Elves were good and the Orcs were bad. Such thinking was at once right (because the Hobbits judged the Elves and Orcs on the basis of their actions) and wrong (because the Hobbits didn't look deeper than their own experience). What did Sam think of Fëanor's rebellion? Well, it was all in the past for him, no doubt. It was a matter long set right. But did he understand that the Orcs weren't really to blame for their nature? Did he understand that Gandalf pitied even Sauron's slaves, or why?

On the other hand, Hobbits were generally of a gentle nature. They didn't beat their children, didn't (apparently) suffer from alcoholism, and seem not to have had much of a problem with bank robbers, murderers, and kidnappers. What would a Hobbit kidnapper demand for ransom, anyway? A cartload of pipeweed? The pride and anger which brought down other peoples really doesn't well up much in the Hobbits. They are long-suffering and long-enduring people, but they also lack ambition. And all the troubles of Elves and Men seem to come from ambition. Or desire.

About the most ambitious act any Hobbit, outside the Sackville-Baggins family, seemed to express was to steal mushrooms or cover as many taverns as possible. Lotho's ambition to become the Boss brought him to a sad and pathetic end. Paladin II, Pippin's father, was outraged that anyone should try to set himself up as ruler of the Shire, but he didn't do anything to contest Lotho. The Tooks simply waited out the storm in their own land, rather than marching to war against the Ruffians. It wasn't important enough for Paladin to start a war which might result in the deaths of many Hobbits.

As villains go, Lotho really doesn't accomplish much. By the time the reader even learns about what he has done to the Shire, betraying it into the hands of Saruman, he is already dead. He is even extended the excuse of being recognized as a fool who got in over his head. In some ways, Grima Wormtongue is also excused. His evil is more readily diagnosed by Gandalf. Grima wants Eowyn. But he also hopes to share in Saruman's power. And when Saruman is brought down so, too, is Grima, who scurries along like a faithful dog, but a bitter one.

There is an entire hierarchy of bad guys who each prey upon the lesser ranks in some ways. Sauron stands at the top, powerful and vain, immutable. Beneath him stand various lieutenants such as Saruman and the Lord of the Nazgul, powerful in their own right, but too weak to prevail over Men. Beneath Saruman stand servants like Grima and Lotho, petty but ambitious creatures with little real power. And yet both cause great harm to their people. And beneath Lotho are ruffians like Bill Ferny, brutal thugs with no real ambition except to be mean and petty.

There are many faces of evil in *The Lord of the Rings*, and degrees of evil and pettiness. There is little true redemption. Boromir could have been much worse than Lotho and Grima. He could have rivaled Saruman, perhaps, for he was already a prince of a great nation. But nearly everyone who falls stays fallen. Even wise old Denethor, who almost stumbles back from the brink in the end, suffers the fate his madness has decreed for him. He gives in to despair.

The only character whom Tolkien really excuses completely is Frodo himself. Frodo gives in to the Ring at last, but it has taken months of demonic torment to drive Frodo to claim the Ring for his own. The claim is not born of pride and arrogance, nor of ambition to become a great and powerful lord. It's essentially an act of insanity, an insanity brought about by the breaking of his mind. Frodo is in many ways reduced to the stature of an Orc. Not a mean, petty, vicious, murderous Orc. But rather an Orc who has had his free will stripped from him, his choices denied him. He is no better than the Orc slaves who first succumbed to Melkor's and Sauron's wills.

And if there is redemption for Frodo, and forgiveness, then should there be redemption and forgiveness for the Orcs?

Chapter 30:
Count, count, weigh, divide

Mene, mene, tekel, upharsin. Count, count, weigh, divide. Those words are familiar to anyone who has studied the Biblical book of Daniel. Belshazzar, son of Nebuchadnezzar, King of Babylon, was having a party when a mysterious finger appeared and traced those words on the wall. When the drunken Babylonians could not decipher the cryptic message, they sent for the aged Daniel, and he told them that their kingdom had been numbered, weighed in the balance, found wanting, and divided between the Medes and the Persians. That night, so the story goes, the Medes and Persians did indeed take the city of Babylon.

History hasn't been the same ever since. The Romans, especially, loved to decipher omens which appeared just prior to special events. Angelic armies have appeared in the skies prior to extended wars or massive battles. Reportedly, as the Nazi and Soviet representatives signed a non-aggression pact in Russia, Adolph Hitler and several guests were standing on the balcony of his private retreat. The sky turned dark red and thunder rumbled. One of the guests, a woman with psychic abilities, told her host that the phenomenon portended "blood, blood, and more blood." Hitler supposedly replied, "Good. Let it begin."

Although Tolkien's stories are filled with omens and portents, few characters ever make much fuss over them. For example, Aragorn warns Gandalf not to enter Moria, and then says little as they wander through the underground passages of the ancient Dwarven kingdom. Only after eight of the nine Walkers escape from Moria does Aragorn remember he had warned Gandalf not to enter the lost realm.

There is never any writing on the wall. Prophets do not wander in from foreign lands, warning the righteous to fear the fury of the Lord. Hedge priests don't crop up across the landscape, preaching about salvation and victory for the faithful in the next crusade. There are no visions on the road to Damascus. Middle-earth is devoid of all the trappings of religious prophecy and psychic phenomena.

Omens are almost always ill in *The Lord of the Rings*. When Merry says, "I will be ready, even if you bid me ride with you on the Paths of the Dead," Theoden replies, "Speak not words of omen! For there may be more roads than one that could bear that name."

The word "omen" occurs less than ten times in *The Lord of the Rings*, and it is never used of events such as birds taking flight, clouds moving in certain ways, or blood curling about entrails. Boromir says that Moria "is a name of ill omen". Eomer tells Aragorn that Saruman's "spies slip through every net, and his birds of ill omen are abroad in the sky".

Eomer does not mean that the sudden flight of birds is an omen, but rather that the birds, because of the purpose they serve, are themselves an ill omen. Their presence in the skies over Rohan portends of the war to come. But then, Eomer had plenty of similar omens to judge by: the marshaling of forces at Isengard, Saruman's sending of Orcs across Rohan, and the influence Grima wielded at Edoras. Men like Eomer did not need supernatural warnings to tell them something was wrong.

Faramir says it would be an ill omen if black squirrels from Mirkwood were to enter Ithilien. His ill omen is only an acknowledgement that the world would indeed be out of balance if Mirkwood's creatures were to cross hundreds of miles to reach Ithilien. It's doubtful the old wives of Gondor had pleasant rhymes foretelling doom and gloom when the black squirrels chewed the nuts of Ithil.

In the entire story, there are only a few events which may be safely deemed as supernatural omens. The first is the dream which is sent to Faramir and Boromir (presumably by the Valar, possibly by Ilúvatar himself), although we don't actually hear about the dream until after another omen occurs. The second omen is Frodo's dream in Bombadil's house. He seems to dream about faraway Valinor, which in time he will visit, although it's not very clear at the time that that is to be his fate.

Some people accept Frodo's dream about Gandalf as an omen, but it doesn't really portend anything. Rather, it seems to be a message, almost as if to say, "Gandalf has been detained, but he is alive and well."

The final supernatural omen seems to be the change in the wind which comes on the morning of the Battle of the Pelennor Fields. But is that so much an omen as the breath of Manwë, pushing back the clouds of Mordor so that the Men of Gondor and Rohan can fight their enemies without the horror of Sauron hanging over them? On the one hand, the western wind gives hope to Men. But it is a little late in foretelling the end of Sauron's power in Middle-earth. That is, we've already seen the means of defeating Sauron is a viable plan.

On the other hand, the omen may have been intended for Sauron, almost as if to say, "Your time is at an end, and you have been found wanting. Your realm has been given to the Men of the West." Is that reaching too far? Perhaps, perhaps not. Gandalf advises Aragorn and the Lords of Gondor and Rohan, after the victory of the Pelennor Fields, that Sauron "studies the signs: the Sword that robbed him of his treasure re-made; the winds of fortune turning in our favour, and the defeat unlooked-for of his first assault; the fall of his great Captain."

In the struggle with Sauron, every action portends some further action to come. Aragorn revealed himself to Sauron, hoping to draw Sauron's attention away from the borders of Mordor, thus opening a path for Frodo. But Aragorn had to challenge Sauron, reminding him of his past defeat, and threatening another defeat. Sauron did not have to interpret the songs of birds chirping at his window. He need only analyze practical strategic information.

Yet, as an angelic being himself who had "fallen to Earth", as it were, Sauron was himself capable of playing the omen game. He understood that there were greater powers than Men and Elves, and that these powers knew something of the future. He, too, knew something of the future. The future must have looked pretty good to him. Why else continue on with his plans for world domination? Who would want to play out a game where they knew they were doomed not only to failure, but to a defeat so crushing they would be reduced to near-complete impotence?

Tolkien mentions in one of his letters that Ilúvatar tipped the scales in the favor of the Valar. The Valar had sent emissaries to Middle-earth with the intention of guiding Men and Elves to a victory without actually directly intervening. The defeat of Sauron could not be brought about by the marshaling of an army. And, Tolkien suggests in an essay in *Morgoth's Ring*, there was no need for such an invasion. Elves and Men indeed had the power to defeat Sauron. Only when the Valar's plan backfired, however, and Saruman betrayed their trust, did Ilúvatar decide to enter the fray.

Unlike the Valar, he could effect a precision timing and introduce exactly the right amount of new strength at the right point. The Valar had sort of aimed a shotgun at Middle-earth and fired blindly into the mists of Time, hoping they were on the right track. After all, they had a feeling this was sort of how Sauron could be defeated. That feeling would have come from their knowledge of the Music and their recollection of the Vision. Perhaps Manwë even communed with Ilúvatar, asking advice.

Ilúvatar alone would have known just how perilous the Valar's plan was. Sauron, on the other hand, would have just been awakening within Middle-earth after a long sleep. It should have been a nightmarish sleep, filled with dreams of anger and impotence. The unnatural death of the body which a self-incarnated Ainu sometimes suffered was such a traumatizing experience that they normally could not restore their composure sufficiently to continue interacting with Ea. Sauron beat that game by placing the greater part of his native strength in the One Ring. The Ring anchored him to Middle-earth. But it also made him vulnerable.

Ilúvatar apparently did little or nothing in the War of the Last Alliance. We know so little of the war that we cannot say anything conclusively, but Sauron was only temporarily defeated. The Last Alliance failed to act responsibly with the Ring, and it fell to the Valar to inspire Elves and Men to work together again. Responsibility for defeating Sauron thus escalated: first it passed from Elves to the Last Alliance, then to the Valar, and finally to Ilúvatar.

But if Ilúvatar took a direct hand in events to ensure that Sauron would not be victorious, did he truly do so without warning Sauron? Even Melkor was warned about the consequences of giving into his arrogance and pride when Ilúvatar grew angry with Melkor's discord in the Ainulindalë. And should Sauron have received any warning, or was his status as fallen angel an exclusionary badge? That is, would Ilúvatar have a reason to warn Men but not rebellious Maiar?

Omens played an important part in the psychology of the ancient world. They relieved men of responsibility for the dreadful acts which they were capable of performing. An ill omen which portended the doom of an army seldom if ever persuaded leaders to stop and think about making peace with their enemies. Instead, they either ignored the omens and went down into infamy (their chroniclers always seem to find good omens which portended victory for them if they won), or else they withdrew from the conflict for a time, waiting for a better omen which promised victory. But either way, the outcome of the conflict was really in the hands of the gods.

Throughout history men have found inventive ways to shift the burdens of their moral responsibilities onto others. If the sky turns red portending blood, blood, and more blood, then is it really the fault of the people who witness the event if they issue the orders that bring about the bloodshed? Of course, asking the purpose of omens inevitably leads to asking whether man has free will. If God knows what we are about to do is so horrible that he sends warnings in the sky, is he not shifting the responsibility back to the men who do the deeds? Or is he merely telling everyone else, "Look out, here it comes again?"

Free will, however, does not exist in God's despite. That is, if he gave us free will he need not struggle with the consequences of that gift. Instead, he can turn the consequences of our choices to his own ends. Not by taking away free will, but by "hardening the heart of the Pharaoh". If a man makes a choice and follows through on it, the resolve he shores himself up with may not be entirely his own. He has made his choice, but now he has become a tool in God's greater plan.

Middle-earth doesn't require a meddlesome God, except in that he will ensure his plan is the one which plays out. That is to say, Tolkien's omens don't have to come from God because they do not relieve men of responsibility. Aragorn's warning to Gandalf was not an ill omen such as might be extended to a leader about to lead his army into disaster. Aragorn's warning was a personal message to Gandalf: 'Beware! You will pay a price for that passage greater than you expect.'

The ill omens associated with Saruman's flocks of birds are not omens born from the will of a god, but rather are the portents which are inherent in the actions taken by Saruman. Anyone who parks an army on your border probably intends to invade, or at least to stir up some sort of trouble. It's a bad sign when the neighbors' troops begin taking lessons in Basic Rohirric. But it's not a sign from God.

And yet, it is not men who are acting irresponsibly in Middle-earth. There are men who diverge from the right path. In fact, many do so, including Bill Ferny, Grima Wormtongue, Denethor, Boromir, and others. They choose to behave in a morally irresponsible fashion, and only Boromir is missed, because in his case his fall was driven by the lure of the One Ring. Who mourns for the servants of Denethor whom Beregond slays or wounds? Instead of doing the right thing, they elect to continue serving their obviously insane lord. Nonetheless, there are no prophets to call these wayward children back to Ilúvatar.

The signs, such as are given at all, are given to Saruman and Sauron, and to Gandalf. It is necessary in the mythic time of Middle-earth to assert the greatest prerogatives to the angelic beings who are gradually withdrawing from Middle-earth, either through death or departure. Hence, when Gandalf and the Balrog confront each other in Moria, Gandalf warns the Balrog that he is no mere man: "I am a servant of the Secret Fire", he says. *The Silmarillion* tells us that the Secret Fire is the Flame Imperishable, which is with Ilúvatar. Gandalf serves the

Holy Spirit of God himself. The Balrog should know from past experience that opposing the good guys is not in its best interests.

Gandalf was the Balrog's writing on the wall. In a way, Aragorn's prescient feeling that something might happen to Gandalf was Gandalf's writing the wall. And it's not that Gandalf was weighed in the balance and found wanting, so much, as that he was being asked to make a hard choice. And Gandalf made the correct choice, but in doing so he had to abandon the Valar's plan. It was the Valar's plan which was flawed, not Gandalf, and Ilúvatar needed to make some changes. Gandalf therefore went willingly to the sacrifice, as he had been forewarned.

The warnings for Sauron may not have been quite so direct. In fact, he may not have received any warnings. He is more like the drunken king of Babylon, confident in his power and secure behind the walls of his fortress. But while he revels in his wealth and power, his enemies are burrowing under his fortress.

It is left to Aragorn to warn Sauron that, mene mene tekel upharsin, your kingdom (on Middle-earth) has been numbered (reached the end of its days) and weighed in the balance (has no further worth in the overall scheme of things) and has been divided (between your slaves and your enemies). Gandalf implies as much to the lords of the west when he says that Sauron is studying the signs.

The signs are very real signs. Can it be anything other than an act of divine providence that Merry just happens to be in the right place at the right time to help Eowyn defeat the Lord of the Nazgul? Now, that may raise the question of whether Bombadil was Ilúvatar. In fact, Tolkien says that Ilúvatar did not manifest himself in Ëa (Time and Space). But as Ilúvatar could make his will known to some servants (such as Manwë) and through others (such as Aragorn), it follows that he could give Tom (whatever he is) a helping hand in choosing swords for the Hobbits.

In a way, the incident with the Barrow-wight is a portent. The Hobbits are captured by one of Sauron's creatures and are almost dispatched according to his purpose, but instead an outside power intervenes and provides the Hobbits with the means of destroying Sauron's chief captain, the Lord of the Nazgul. Why, exactly, did Frodo awaken in time to summon Bombadil? Was it the Ring which wished to preserve him, or was a higher power acting to ensure that the Ring did not fall into Sauron's hands again?

The incident at Weathertop could serve as another portent. Frodo foolishly put on the One Ring, and that act was a result of the influence of both the Ring and the Nazgul who were present. But somewhere Frodo found the strength to lunge out at the Lord of the Nazgul, as well as the presence of mind (if one may call it that) to yell out the name of Elbereth. "More deadly to him was the name of Elbereth," Aragorn tells Frodo's companions soon after the encounter. How could Frodo have known that? He could not have.

By the time Frodo eludes Sauron at Amon Hen, it should be clear to Sauron that some power is working against him. The Wicked Witch of the West would have said, "Curses! Someone always helps that Hobbit!" Someone helped him in the Barrow-downs, someone helped him at Weathertop, someone helped him at Rivendell, and someone helped him at Amon Hen. In fact, in all four cases, Frodo was helped either directly or indirectly by powerful beings who may very well have been acting at Ilúvatar's behest.

Tolkien says that Bombadil had taken a moral vow of poverty. He had impoverished himself with respect to control. That is, Bombadil elected not to impose his will on other creatures. Both Sauron and the Elves pursued control, though of a different fashion. Bombadil was a pacifist, in Tolkien's estimation. But pacifism, or a pursuit of knowledge for its own sake, does not eliminate Bombadil from Ilúvatar's plans and purposes.

Bombadil's knowledge of the world is incomplete, but he seems to understand what is at stake and why it's important not to let the Ring fall into Sauron's hands. In terms of role-playing game moral alignments, Bombadil would seem to be a lawful good creature, although many people seem to feel he is a neutral or neutral good.

Why should Bombadil be lawful good? Because he does what is right, and he does not impose his own will upon evil creatures. That is, he doesn't enslave them, but he does restrict or prevent them from increasing their power.

In support of that thesis, I can point to the fact that Bombadil agreed to help Frodo before he met the Hobbits. Gildor's Elvenfolk had asked Bombadil to watch out for Frodo and his friends, and to help them on their way. Although Bombadil was unwilling to leave his land and take direct action against Sauron -- indeed, was unlikely to understand the need to hide the Ring in Gandalf's estimation -- he understood that there was good reason to help Frodo. That is, in the struggle, he could give non-violent help to the side which had the moral high ground. He just didn't necessarily share all their priorities.

Some people might argue this makes Bombadil more of a chaotic good personality. That is, his choices would seem random to a casual observer, unstructured and intuitive. But Bombadil acts with purpose in everything he does. He restricts the movement of evil creatures which dwell in his country but he does not take away their independence unless they step over some moral boundary he sees more clearly than others. A lawful good being sees the right and wrong more easily than a chaotic good being.

Like Gandalf, Bombadil serves a purpose in Ilúvatar's plan. But unlike Gandalf, Bombadil is not charged by a higher authority with taking a more direct action against Sauron. Gandalf cannot use his power to overthrow Sauron, but he is obligated to work toward Sauron's defeat. Bombadil seems only obligated to preserve an enclave or two. That is, his function in Eriador seems to be that of a special guardian for the Shire and Bree. Gandalf suggests at the Council of Elrond that Bombadil had "withdrawn to a little land, within bounds that he has set, though none can see them, waiting perhaps for a change of days, and he will not step beyond them."

Gandalf doesn't speculate on why Bombadil has withdrawn to that land, though Bombadil himself hints at the reason when he bids farewell to the Hobbits: "I've got things to do, my making and my singing, my talking and my walking, and my watching of the country. Tom can't be always near to open doors and willow-cracks. Tom has his house to mind, and Goldberry is waiting."

In a very Ent-like fashion, Tom explains that he has responsibilities. His singing, talking, and walking may serve more purpose than to amuse the local water-lilies and critters. Maybe he is keeping the evil forces which have permeated the land in check. Maybe he is helping preserve something of Eriador's ancient civilization by holding back the anger of the Old Forest from overwhelming the Shire. When Gildor promises Frodo that he'll ask others to help the Hobbits, he names "the Wandering Companies...and those that have power for good". Bombadil is clearly one of "those that have power for good", for all he does is good, and he opposes evil in his own way.

Bombadil's function in the story thus serves to show that all the world opposes Sauron, not just his philosophical opposites among the leaders of the West. Bombadil's intervention legitimizes Frodo's task and paves the way for clearer signs of warning to Sauron. He might not have been able to win pardon from either the Valar or Ilúvatar before the end, but he might have been able to avoid the inevitable. Or perhaps he could simply have accepted his fate and not inflicted so much harm and suffering upon the lesser creatures of the world.

At every step, Sauron was given some sign of warning, but instead of acknowledging that he was in trouble, he reclined in the comfort of his arrogance and proceeded with his own designs. He ignored the writing on the wall and when the end came it was really his own fault and not because he had been outwitted. Sauron went up against a greater power than an alliance of Men, Elves, Hobbits, and Valar. He went up against Ilúvatar, and there was never really any hope of victory for him.

So, by the time the west wind blew at the Battle of the Pelennor Fields, Sauron's fate was sealed. Frodo and Sam still had to cross much of Mordor to reach their destination, and they had perils yet to face. But wherever they needed help, there they found it. Sauron decided he could win the war by crushing his enemies before they learned how to use the One Ring against him. And he thereby lost everything, because he didn't stop to consider just exactly who might be helping the Hobbit slip through his fingers at every turn.

MICHAEL MARTINEZ

Chapter 31:
Pasta la feasta, baby

How much attention did J.R.R. Tolkien pay to food in Middle-earth? That question comes up fairly often, usually with respect to the Elves. Most people think the Elves were vegetarians, although nothing could be farther from the truth. Well, it's true that the Green-elves of Ossiriand didn't eat meat, but they're about the only ones.

As with so many other aspects of Middle-earth, Tolkien didn't limit himself in the kinds of dishes enjoyed by his characters. The hobbits snuck in a few distinctly "English" plates (such as the fish and chips Sam offered to cook for Gollum). But there were some exotic dishes on the menu. For example, the honey-cakes that Beorn gave to Thorin and Company have elicited a lot of curiosity from fans. What's the recipe?

I doubt Tolkien had a specific recipe in mind, to be honest. But he probably knew that honey is a pretty good food (for most people, but only a few ancient civilizations would have been concerned about diabetes). Honey even has medicinal properties, although I doubt Tolkien would have had his characters smear honey on their wounds (it's a natural antiseptic, used in ancient Egypt for that purpose).

In fact, honey cakes are a historical food, having been invented or improved upon by many cultures. Beorn's honey cakes have long intrigued Tolkien fans, who would love to try them, but I've never come across *the* Beorning honey cake recipe. I don't believe there was one, unless Tolkien had sampled a honey cake and decided to include it in his story about Bilbo Baggins.

Another food item Tolkien fans have wanted to know more about, of course, is *lembas*, the Elven waybread. Once again Tolkien failed to provide a specific recipe, but he did actually write something about the history of *lembas*. It was a sort of holy bread, baked from a meal produced from a special corn given to the Eldar on the Great Journey by the Valar. The corn only grew in secret gardens attended by Elven women called Yavannildi, or Ivonwin, "the maidens of Yavanna".

So, we Tolkien researchers are off the hook as far as *lembas* is concerned. Without access to the special corn, there is no way we can try to make it. However, Tolkien's description of the white corn implies strongly that it was similar to maize, so anyone who has eaten good, old-fashioned cornbread may have appreciated something as close to *lembas* as we can get.

Food is the most basic necessity for living organisms. We have to have it. And, according to some researchers, mankind has been cooking its food for 500,000 years. That's a long time. That's a lot of boiled meat and vegetables. And there is a serious proposal that Neanderthals invented soup.

The best estimates suggest we've been baking bread for 12,000 years or thereabouts. One retired farmer has even reportedly bred einkorn wheat, similar to the original strain used by Neolithic peoples. He apparently did this so that people who didn't want to eat processed breads could return to a more primitive, natural bread. I suppose it won't be long before we see loaves of Neolithic Meal (tm) on the shelves in specialty food stores.

Tea has graced our tables since 2737 BCE. People started eating mushrooms soon afterward, and potatoes hit the New World diet around 2500 BCE. Cheese and grapes go back about 6,000 years.

All these foods are mentioned by Tolkien. Did he check out some books on the history of cooking before writing his stories? I doubt it. But being a philologist who loved to base stories and elements of stories around words, I wouldn't be surprised to learn that he knew the histories of these words. And if he knew there were ancient names for modern foods, then he knew those foods could be safely included in an imaginary time in our past.

Of course, Tolkien did let tomatoes, potatoes, and tobacco slip into Europe a few thousand years too soon, but he knew he was being a bit loose with the timeline. At the time he wrote *The Lord of the Rings* he was being fairly meticulous, but he didn't catch everything. He didn't really make food an important part of the story, although in the Prologue to LOTR, Tolkien said of Hobbits that "growing food and eating it occupied most of their time".

Readers should be forgiven for not knowing what kinds of foods are actually mentioned by Tolkien. For all the eating the hobbits seem to do in the story, the actual foods consumed are seldom named. But we do get an inventory of Barliman's menu on the night that Frodo and company arrived in Bree: "hot soup, cold meats, a blackberry tart, new loaves, slabs of butter, and half a ripe cheese: good plain food, as good as the Shire could grow". (For what it's worth, tarts and pastries seem to date from the medieval or post-medieval period.)

As for what the Shire actually grew, well, Tolkien gave a small category of farm crops when Gandalf departed from Bag End "The Shire had seldom seen so fair a summer, or so rich an autumn the trees were laden with apples, honey was dripping in the combs, and the corn was tall and full." Okay, maybe Tolkien slipped up on the maize, too. But the word "corn" itself is pretty ancient and was actually used of other grain crops. Caesar spent a fair amount of time in Gaul trying to secure his corn supply, but he wasn't importing maize from the Americas.

Apples seemed to be popular with the Elves as much as with the Hobbits. When Gildor Inglorion and his folk hosted Frodo, Sam, and Pippin for a night in Woody End, they served the Hobbits apples, "bread, surpassing the flavor of a fair white loaf to one who is starving; and fruits sweet as wildberries and richer than the tended fruits of gardens." Fruits are actually good traveling food. Although they will eventually ripen, they don't need to be cooked or refrigerated. And you can sun-dry fruits so they last longer, but I don't think Gildor's people were serving dried fruit that night.

At Rivendell, Bilbo compared Hobbits and Men to peas and apples. Peas are another Neolithic food. Grishnakh seems to have read his Bible, since he tells Ugluk that the Nazgul are the "apple of the Great

Eye". The Entwives liked apples, too, along with sloes (wild plums), cherries, and green herbs. These were among the kinds of plants the Entwives cultivated. And they also raised corn, teaching Men how to grow it.

Bombadil and Goldberry kept a pretty good larder, too. They served the Hobbits "yellow cream and honeycomb, white bread, and butter, milk, and cheese, and green herbs and ripe berries gathered." There is a distinct lack of meat in their diet, and I suspect Tom and Goldberry might have been vegetarians. The butter and cream had to come from one or more cows. Or maybe goats.

In Gondor, Pippin was treated to white cakes by Denethor, and to bread, butter, cheese, and apples by Beregond and Targon. The presence of butter and cheese implies that the Gondorians raised cattle and/or goats. But they were a pretty advanced civilization. When Frodo and Sam were fed at Henneth Annun, Faramir's men treated them to "pale yellow wine" and "bread and butter, and salted meats, and dried fruits, and good red cheese." Faramir later gave them "dried fruits, and salted meats, enough for many days; and bread enough to last while it was still fresh" for their journey into Mordor.

Butchers developed the technique of salting meats to preserve their unsold meats over weekends. The ancient civilizations of China and the Mediterranean basin developed salting techniques for tanning hides and preserving fish, as well as smoking techniques for preserving meats through the winter months.

We know a little bit more about Faramir's meats prepared for travelers. Sam pulls out "a small slip of cured meat" for Frodo and himself in Mordor (along with dried fruit). The "small slip" sounds vaguely like some sort of beef jerky.

The production of foods in Middle-earth seems to be very carefully thought out. There is even a little salt-box that Sam carried with him (mentioned in "The Ring Goes South" as the Company prepares to leave Rivendell). Merry and Pippin found "first-rate salted pork" and "rashers of bacon" in Saruman's stores. The food most likely came from the Shire, since Saruman seems not to have been doing business with Gondor. But where would the Hobbits get their salt?

The answer must be the Dwarves, who in turn had to bring it in from the coastlands. It's doubtful the Dwarves would have concerned themselves with working salt mines, but the Elves probably produced the commodity. If nothing else, it would give them something to trade to the Dwarves, although they probably needed it, too.

Salt production is a tricky thing in coastal areas. It requires a stable environment with plenty of sunshine and warm breezes; Britain was able to produce its own salt during Roman times (in part because sea levels were ideal for that sort of thing). Salt production in Europe dropped off during the Middle Ages because the sea levels began rising, ruining the old salt beds. Tolkien's use of salt is a tribute to the attention he paid to creating a historically credible world.

Middle-earth's economics are difficult to fathom, but it's plain that there must have been quite an export business in the Shire at the end of the Third Age. Saruman had to feed an army, and the Hobbits no doubt would have been glad to sell their surplus crops. But the production and distribution of food also implies that agriculture and food preparation were altogether different matters in Dunland and the Shire. That is, Saruman recruited many Dunlendings into his service, but how much did he rely upon Dunland for supplies? If he was willing to send as far away as the Shire, then he was verging on desperation.

Logistics is probably the one aspect of war that Tolkien really didn't deal with adequately. That is, we know that Saruman was importing food from the Shire, and that Henneth Annun was well-stocked with dried fruits and cured meats. But how was Aragorn's army supplied? His 7,000 men would have eaten the equivalent of about 3 pounds of food a day. That's 21,000 pounds of food every day from March 18 through May 1 (roughly speaking -- Aragorn was crowned before the gates of Minas Tirith on May 1).

All Sauron really had to do to defeat Aragorn was to cut his supply lines. Aragorn would have had to retreat or make a mad charge into

Mordor, looking for food. Theoden's army of about 6,000 Riders of Rohan could have carried enough food with them to get to Minas Tirith (5-6 days' worth, about 12-18 pounds per Rider), but the horses would have required a tremendous amount of forage.

Of course, Beowulf and Menelaus don't stop in the midst of their epic poems to discuss supply details with their sergeants. They summon their warriors and go, and the audience is expected to understand that the guys had food. Eating is only important to the characters when the story isn't being told. When the poet is singing of raging battles, marching armies, and proud kings and princes, he neglects to point out the mile-long baggage train bringing up the rear.

Middle-earth cuisine probably seems a bit sparse by modern western standards. We can dine out every night at a different style restaurant (finances permitting) in most major cities. Italian, French, American, Greek, Chinese, Mexican, and specialty restaurants are very common. Food doesn't have to be fast as long as it's prepared by someone else. In fact, the ancient Romans had a pretty good franchise on restaurants and fast food.

Rome supported a very large population, numbered in the hundreds of thousands. Feeding all those people required a lot of resources. But the Romans found early on during the Imperial period that letting everyone have their own kitchen was dangerous. Although the Romans were good at building with stone, the fact is that many of their houses were built on wood frames. All it took to start a major fire was one tilted brazier or one untended hearth. Rome had a very large and semi-professional fire fighting force (which, sadly, became corrupt and not only charged for putting out fires, but also started a few to help keep the money flowing).

After a major fire burned large parts of the city, the Romans stopped building apartments with hearths. Dining out became a daily ritual. Intrepid cooks set up shop along the streets, with little fast food restaurants where they would cook meals for passersby. The clientele sat on stools or stood at counters and ate the food prepared right before them. It would have been a very appealing lifestyle to many westerners, although the public toilet facilities seemed to consider modesty unimportant.

Middle-earth's larger cities would have had to sport similar dining arrangements. In fact, the infamous clichéd tavern one encounters in numerous fantasy novels is a nod toward the ancient custom. Taverns never quite went out of style because it was just too dangerous to have everyone cooking in their own homes. And, to be honest, how many families could afford to kill a whole cow and save the meat? Taverns and inns which served food along with beer, ale, and wine served a vital economic purpose.

Tolkien acknowledged the vitality of taverns by scattering them around the Shire. Gondor and Rohan most likely had plenty of taverns, too. But taverns fulfilled a social purpose beyond simply serving food and drink. They were gathering places for the local communities. Barliman's common hall in the Prancing Pony may in fact have served as the local post office, courthouse, and meeting room for the elders of Bree. But these matters were not important to Frodo's journey.

Armies don't gather at taverns, despite the fact that any role-playing gamer can probably recall having a character saunter into the local tavern and recruit a dozen or so men-at-arms for the task of taking out that dragon down the street. In all probability, though, places like the Prancing Pony were probably the chief source for provisions for travelers.

The business of food production and distribution had to be one of the most profitable in Middle-earth. If all other trades declined, people would still need to eat. Farmers would still need a place to sell or trade their food. Someone would still know of a town just beyond the horizon where families were hungry enough to pay for imports. The Bree-land had only four villages and though there must have been plenty of farms, Bree undoubtedly had to import products from the Shire. Especially salt (unless the Dwarves brought it directly to Bree).

Unfortunately (or fortunately), Frodo's journey after Bree never took him to another inn. He either roughed it in the wild or was treated to dinner by royalty (Elrond in Rivendell, Galadriel and Celeborn in Lothlórien, Aragorn in Minas Tirith). The layover at Henneth Annun was a fluke (though it could be said that Faramir, a prince of Gondor, was extending a similar courtesy to Frodo). Merry and Pippin got to enjoy the spoils of war, feasting on the remains of Saruman's stores. Clearly, it paid to have friends with powerful armies.

Hence, when Frodo leaves the familiarity and comfort of Bree behind, the reader says farewell to what could have been an endless array of inns and taverns with meaningless common room encounters (or avoidances). Instead, the journey was made largely in secret and as an extended camping trip. Middle-earth no doubt seems to be so *empty* because Gandalf and Aragorn insisted on avoiding as many people as possible.

Rivendell seems pretty innish, though, and I sometimes wonder if The Last Homely House East of the Sea wasn't, in fact, an Elvish inn. So what if Elrond had the blood of kings and angels running in his veins? An Elf has to make a living, too. And his days of leading armies were over. Everyone seems to have stopped by there: Dunedain, Elves, Dwarves, wizards. Heck, even Bilbo set up shop after a couple of layovers. He was clearly part of the local entertainment. Elrond may have had Bilbo on permanent retainer just so he'd maintain control over the Hobbit craze.

As far-fetched as that may seem, Elrond's chief economic function in Middle-earth does appear to have been to provide a specialized road-house or inn. Maybe only very important travelers stayed there, but he was a Half-elf with a mission to help defeat the Dark Lord. Ensuring that people running around the wild had a warm bed and a few good meals in the midst of their journeys was probably as good a contribution as he could make.

After all, armies travel on their stomachs. So do Hobbits, Dwarves, and Wizards. And Elrond seems to have been making a few silver pennies off his vineyards, or orchards. It's not clear what *miruvor* was made from, but Gandalf called it the "cordial of Imladris". A cordial is a liqueur (liquor). Elrond was supplying the goods, for sure.

That probably doesn't satisfy anyone's desire to find the recipe for *lembas*, but at least if someone asks you what people ate in Middle-earth you now have a better idea. They ate "good plain food". Just like us. Pass the peas, please. I'm getting hungry.

Chapter 32:
Trick or treat? Spooky Middle-earth

Most Tolkien fans will immediately recognize September 22 as the birthday of both Bilbo and Frodo Baggins, but their September 22 was not our September 22. Tolkien's offbeat calendar system for the Shire made the Hobbits' September 22 fall on our September 14 (September 13 in a Leap Year). So, for years, you've been toasting Bilbo and Frodo's good health 8 days too late.

Halloween is not an especially important date in the Tolkien calendars, either. Our October 31 (All Hallows' Eve) falls on the Hobbits' November 9. By that time, their harvest is way behind them. But Halloween did not really originate in a harvest festival, as some have told the tale. It began as the Celtic festival called Samhain in Irish Gaelic (pronounced SOW-en, despite the "m" in the middle of the word).

According to tradition, Samhain was the time of year when the Celts extinguished their hearth-fires, put on special costumes, and attended bonfires ignited by Druidic priests. The Celts believed this was the time of year, as Summer gave way to Autumn, when the spirits of the dead were most likely to return to the world of the living. These spirits were expected to help the living foretell each other's fortunes (and occasionally get into mischief). The Celts often dressed up in costumes as they celebrated their new year. When the festivities were over, so traditions say, the Druids would give an ember from the bonfire to each family in the community, and they would use that ember to relight their hearthfires for the coming year.

The Eldar of Imladris observed their New Year about the Shire's April 6, which would be about our March 29. The Shire's New Year fell on our December 23. And the poor Dwarves, living by a Lunar Calendar for part of their shadowy history, celebrated the last new moon of Autumn as their new year's day, calling it Durin's Day (perhaps commemorating the day Durin I awoke, or the day he died).

By some calculations, Durin's Day may have fallen around the 14th day of the 10th month in the year T.A. 2941 (the only year in which Durin's Day figures prominently in a story -- that story being *The Hobbit*). Well, our October 14 would be the Shire's October 22, which is as close as you can get a Middle-earth holiday to October 31.

Mid-October thus marks the Autumn period of the Shire and adjacent lands. And though the Shire-folk, who were largely farmers, put some emphasis on their harvests, they did not offer their first fruits to pagan gods, as the Celts did. Nor did the Hobbits engage in prophecy or dressing up in costume. They probably would have enjoyed the modern custom of trick-or-treating, which is believed to have arisen from a Church-sponsored practice of giving "soul-cakes" to poor people who begged for food on All Hallows' Eve. The poor people were expected to pray for the spirits of dead relatives (of the cake-givers).

It is possible that Frodo awoke in Rivendell around the time of Durin's Day. No one is really sure of when it would have occurred, although Tolkien used an Almanac for 1942 to calculate the phases of the moon for *The Lord of the Rings*. Frodo awoke on October 24 (Shire Reckoning, or October 14 in our reckoning).

Perhaps not coincidentally, Gandalf told Frodo that he had been on the brink of the wraith-world. Frodo's Morgul-wound had nearly made him a ghost, and Frodo had returned to the ranks of the fully living with Elrond's help. So Frodo began a period of introspection which lasted about two months. The highwater mark of this period was, of course, the Council of Elrond, at which various representatives of free peoples put together all the pieces of the large puzzle Tolkien had assembled. Gandalf even engaged in a little foretelling on the day Frodo awoke: he looked at Frodo and thought to himself that Frodo "may become like a glass filled with a clear light for eyes to see that can."

When Frodo awoke from his sleep, Elrond gave a feast for his honored guest, the Ring-bearer, and Frodo found himself sitting next to Gloin, a Dwarf. Afterward, the celebrants retired to the Hall of Fire, where

Frodo was reunited with Bilbo. The Elves sang many songs honoring Elbereth and probably other Valar. Strider was unmasked as *the Dunadan*, and Gandalf was compared (in Frodo's estimation, as he gazed upon the wizard at the feast) to "a wise king of ancient legend."

Another custom which was long associated with Halloween (and its predecessor holidays, including the ancient Roman holiday of Feralia, in which the passing of the dead was commemorated) was the telling of stories, especially about dead relatives and heroes. After Frodo was reunited with Bilbo, he began to drowse, but Bilbo's song of Ëarendil roused the younger Hobbit. Bilbo had the nerve (Aragorn felt) to sing about Ëarendil, the father of Elrond, in Elrond's house. In a Halloweenish way, Bilbo was honoring Elrond's "dead", although Ëarendil certainly had not died. He was lost to the mortal world, but Elrond could still expect to see his father some day. Life for the Eldar in Aman was therefore a bit like living in both this world and the next (and, indeed, Gandalf told Frodo that same day that those Elves who had dwelt in Aman lived at once in both the Seen and the Unseen worlds).

Although Durin's Day never again figured into any of the events of the War of the Ring, the Tale of Years says that the war officially ended in early November, which would have been close to our October 31. Saruman was slain at Bag End and his spirit passed away from the world of the living to the world of the dead (or the houseless). In one year, from Durin's Day 3018 to Durin's Day 3019, Middle-earth was changed forever. The powerful Maiar were overthrown or their purpose in Middle-earth brought to completion. The woeful spirits of dead Men (whether Nazgul, who weren't so much *dead* as faded, and the Dead Men of Dunharrow) were released from long bondage and allowed to seek their eternal rest.

Tolkien used to say that *The Lord of the Rings* was about death and the search for deathlessness. It is also, however, about life, and the search for purpose in living. A renewal. There is the passing of the old and the arrival of the new. Just as the Celts celebrated the passing of their old year and the arrival of their new year with a feast and celebration, so we still celebrate our change in year, although we do it at a historically oddball time of year (there is virtually no major religious significance in Christian or Celtic tradition to December 31/January 1).

The Rings of Power for the most part conferred upon their wearers the ability to see the Unseen, to interact with wraiths. These abilities were apparently sought by the Eldar of Eregion because they were afraid of *fading*. This fate, foretold to the Noldor by the Valar when the Noldor marched into rebellious exile, daunted even the mighty Noldor. Tolkien says the Elves wanted "to live in the mortal historical Middle-earth because they had become fond of it (and perhaps because they had there the advantages of a superior caste), and so tried to stop its change and history" (*The Letters of J.R.R. Tolkien*, No. 154).

By stopping change and history, the Elves hoped to forestall the inevitable fate that Ilúvatar had in store for them: death. Now, many people are quick to point out that the Elves were supposed to live with the life of Arda. That is, they would naturally endure in the world so long as the world itself endured. Men, on the other hand, grew weary of the world and sought elsewhere. In this sense, Tolkien seems to be speaking of a different kind of "death". Death in Tolkien usually refers to the death of the body. But the body is a physical shell, regarded as nothing more than raiment for the Valar, who were naturally disincarnate spirits.

For the Elves, physical death meant that their spirits would be summoned to the Halls of Mandos. If they elected to answer the summons, they had the hope of living a physical life again, although they would be expected to remain in Aman. If, however, they refused the summons, they could remain in Middle-earth, where they had dwelt. But they would remain as disembodied spirits. They were essentially wraiths, ghosts. The Elves would haunt their former lands.

Tolkien discussed the states of Elven spirits in "Laws and Customs among the Eldar", published in *Morgoth's Ring*. He called the dead Elves "houseless", and referred to their disembodied spirits as "houseless *fëa(r)*" (*fëa* was the Elvish word for "spirit"). The early Elves, who knew nothing or little of the Valar, frequently refused the Summons to Mandos. During Morgoth's tenure in Angband, he forced any Elvish spirits which refused the Summons into slavery. Such spirits would become truly tormented souls, and it is tempting to speculate on whether the Barrow-wights and other horrors might have been Elvish spirits, corrupted into the service of evil.

Elves were certainly capable of engaging in evil. The Noldor attacked other Elves in the three Kin-slayings, and the Eldar of Beleriand often strove with each other because of greed, jealousy, or even fear. Betrayal was apparently quite common, especially from Elves who had escaped from Angband. But after the fall of Morgoth, the Elves were freed from the peril of being forced into his service. Those Elves who loved Middle-earth need not, when they died, abandon it completely. In "Laws and Customs", Tolkien notes:

> ...in these after-days more and more of the Elves, be they of the Eldalië in origin or be they of other kinds, who linger in Middle-earth now refuse the summons of Mandos, and wander houseless in the world, unwilling to leave it and unable to inhabit it, haunting trees or springs or hidden places that once they knew. Not all of these are kindly or unstained by the Shadow. Indeed, the refusal of the summons is in itself a sign of taint.

Dead Elves still roam the world, and perhaps were plentiful in the Second Age. Would the former wraith-thralls of Morgoth have sought healing in Aman after his fall? Perhaps, perhaps not. It may be that the Noldor, in seeking to heal the hurts of the world (which was also one of their goals in making the Rings of Power), hoped to contact their dead brethren and perhaps commune with them or persuade them to seek comfort in the West. Such practices, however, would ultimately be forbidden, at least for men. Tolkien continued in the above essay with:

> It is therefore a foolish and perilous thing, besides being a wrong deed forbidden justly by the appointed Rulers of Arda, if the Living seek to commune with the Unbodied, though the houseless may desire it, especially the most unworthy among them. For the Unbodied, wandering in the world, are those who at the least have refused the door of life and remain in regret and self-pity. Some are filled with bitterness, grievance, and envy. Some were enslaved by the Dark Lord and do his work still, though he himself is gone. They will not speak truth or wisdom. To call

on them is folly. To attempt to master them and to make them servants of one's own will is wickedness. Such practices are of Morgoth; and the necromancers are of the host of Sauron his servant.

Eventually, Men who practice necromancy may find their bodies seized by the Houseless Elves, and themselves rendered houseless. What becomes of such Mannish spirits? The essay does not say, but it condemns necromancy in the strongest terms. The practice must therefore have been known among even the Elves, and it may be that their attempts to engage in necromancy led the Valar to decree that such communication was off-limits. But the damage had been done. People knew they could communicate with the dead, even if they couldn't be sure of whose dead with whom they communicated.

The War of the Ring thus represents a cleansing of the world, a restoration of the natural order. Although Elves might continue to remain in Middle-earth after death, the world has been granted a reprieve. With the Rings of Power destroyed, the Elves no longer need worry about the temptation of engaging in their own form of necromancy. And many of them, especially those who had come to depend upon the Time-stalling effects of the Three Rings, feel the onset of their world-weariness and they set sail over Sea to seek their own healing. In Aman they will continue to live physical lives, sustained by the Valar.

The Lord of the Rings is thus in some ways the ultimate Halloween tale, honoring fallen heroes and foretelling great deeds for those who stay the course and do what is right. The story recognizes the passage from the mythical world to the historic world. It acknowledges the heritage of forgotten peoples and struggles which have removed the physical incarnations of evil from the world, and helped to divide the world of the living from the world of the dead.

So, when the little Hobbits and Goblins come trick-or-treating to your front door, remember to give them soul-cakes and be sure to have a copy of Manhattan Transfer's "Soul Food to Go" in the CD-player. But, most of all, keep a copy of the best ghost story of the 20th century handy just in case someone starts up a bonfire and begins telling tall tales. I foretell you'll have a good time and perhaps will make a new friend or two. Just be sure those are really their own bodies....

Chapter 33:
Guess who's coming to the disaster

I'd been asked before if there was much appeal in Tolkien for female readers. Curiously, this came at a time when I'd found myself discussing *Visualizing Middle-earth* with a lot of women.

What is it about fantasy fiction that gives people the impression certain stories or authors only appeal to men or only to women? Take a C.J. Cherryh story, for example. She writes a pretty hard and fast science fiction story, but her fantasy can be both deep and moving, or sonorous as Tolkien might have put it. A good dip into Cherryh fantasy brings the reader into close quarters with women, men, love, hate, anger, and flashing swords. But I don't believe I've ever heard anyone say, "C.J. Cherryh -- there's a women's author if ever I've read one!"

For some reason, Tolkien has a reputation for leaving the ladies out of his books. But as nearly as I can tell, he puts a female character into most of the important sub-plots. There is Lobelia Sackville-Baggins and her quest for control over Bag End, Rosie Cotton has an undercurrent of wistful longing for Sam, Goldberry enchants the Hobbits while they visit Bombadil (and she foreshadows Galadriel and Eowyn in curious ways), Arwen graces the feast held in Frodo's honor and later sings a hymn of Valinor which captures Frodo's attention, the Balrog dances a jig with the serving girls in Moria.

Well, okay, Tolkien didn't actually say that about the Balrog.

The point is that, even in many scenes where no female characters are present, Tolkien manages to bring women and lost loves into the picture. Ask anyone what they remember most vividly about Merry and Pippin's encounter with Treebeard, and they will probably say something about the Entmoot or the storming of Isengard. But ask them what the most interesting question concerning the Ents is, and they'll probably say, "What happened to the Ent-wives?"

How is it that the Ent-wives merit so much curiosity when they aren't even in the story? They don't even have an impact on the story. It's not like Treebeard pulls out some ancient Ent-wife comb and says, "Here, lads. Take this comb and use it to ease your journey through the orchards of Rohan and Gondor, where the trees remember Fimbrethil and honor her name." The lonely old boy goes on at quite some length about his lost love and her little clique. But what do the Ent-wives add to the story, except a tinge of femininity? In a book that supposedly eschews women, Tolkien has one of the most powerful characters wistfully sing about the Ents and their lost mates.

Is this the sort of stuff the stereotypical fan-boy supposedly eats up in his sword-hacking fiction? I don't think so. The whole scene reminds me of those formulaic Hollywood war flicks, where the soldiers are sitting around the campfire talking about their girls back home. But instead of focusing on some assembly-line actor rattling off lines about how he's going to marry Becky Sue, settle down, and have a ton of kids (although he has no idea he'll be buying the farm in the minefield just over the hill), Tolkien gives us flashbacks of the tragic history of the Ents. These include Treebeard's account of how the Ents and Ent-wives grew apart, and the Elves' songs marking the poignance of their separation.

Treebeard knows he's not going to find Fimbrethil. He longs for her in the way that only a man who has realized his terrible mistake can. It's a bit of tenderness set amid a landscape of hardy adventurers doing the manly thing, whatever *the* manly thing may be. In Treebeard's case, he was sniffing around the edges of the forest, trying to figure out what was going on. He had a lot of thinking to do, and had been thinking a lot. Yet, in coming to the realization that the Ents were still strong, Treebeard was lollygagging about, reminiscing over lost loves and vanished girlfriends. Someone, please give me a hanky.

When it comes to displays of macho mentality, the Rohirrim aren't much better off than the Ents. Theoden is grieving over his lost son, of course, but Eowyn is steadfastly by his side, offering her support even when all she really wants to do is lop off Wormtongue's head. Eomer falls all over himself in a manly bout of political correctness when he meets up with Aragorn, Gimli, and Legolas. After a brief exchange of threats with the dwarf and elf, Eomer reveals that he could really use a hand back at Edoras. Whom does Eowyn ask for help?

As clichéd as the manly but sensitive hero may seem to be these days, Tolkien filled his book with them. There have been innumerable jokes about Sam and Frodo, including innuendo and fan fiction which put them together in ways the author never would have dreamed of. But there are also scenes where Sam comes on like a blood-thirsty thug. He kills an Orc in Moria, and he threatens Gollum more than once. In fact, Tolkien lays the blame for Gollum's final fall directly at Sam's insensitive feet. Had Sam paid closer attention to the changes in Gollum's personality, things might have turned out differently.

But Sam was focusing on the mission, and at the same time, he was concerned about Frodo. It was Sam who stood up to Faramir after Frodo blurted out his feelings concerning Boromir and the Ring. It was Sam who gushed and goggled at the Field of Cormallen when Aragorn and the boys were celebrating Frodo's gallantry and success. Frodo seems rather emotionless through thick and thin, but Sam rides the roller coaster of love, hate, and happiness. He gives nearly every emotion a double spin at some point in the book. There should be an old saying among Tolkien readers: don't rake with the gardener, dude!

Curiously, Gondor is about the only place where women are trivialized. That is, no Gondorian woman (in the main story) really achieves much. We get Ioreth and her babbling commentaries peppered with the lore of old wives. Of course, it's Celeborn who properly points out that old wives often remember things that were once needful for the wise to know. But not many people want to give Celeborn his due. He seems to sit in Galadriel's shadow, and she gets all the glory.

Lothlórien is a magical place, but most of the magic seems to be attributed to Galadriel, directly or indirectly. Until the Company is brought before the rulers of the land, the Elves speak of the Lord and Lady with equal reverence. But once Celeborn reneges on his greeting, and Galadriel gently rebukes him, readers drop away from Celeborn's banner in droves. It takes a strong man to accept his wife's rebuke in front of the kingdom, after he's just said he'd rather leave the eight wanderers to their deaths across the border. If Celeborn were really unsure of himself, he'd have tried to show his masculinity by putting Galadriel in her place. But he accords Galadriel a great deal of respect. He values her opinion enough that he doesn't cater to any conventions that "women should be seen and not heard".

I'm not sure if Celeborn strikes any women as sexy. He is the stern, quiet type of Elf. He's the sort of fellow you hope you meet while his wife has a positive influence on him. Celeborn, after all, leads armies of Elven warriors. It's not Galadriel who takes the offensive after Sauron is overthrown; Celeborn does the dirty work. In "The History of Galadriel and Celeborn" (*Unfinished Tales*), her name may come first in the title, but it's Celeborn who risks everything to lead a sortie against Sauron's army in the War of the Elves and Sauron. And despite the fact that she has a mirror which reveals all sorts of pretty pictures, Galadriel doesn't have a word to offer the Company concerning their journey south. Celeborn has to explain the deal to the travelers.

Not that traveling through perilous lands is the sole province of men in Tolkien. Arwen trots back and forth across the same mountains where her mother was taken by Orcs. People make a big fuss about how Elrond brought Arwen back to Rivendell in the year 3018 because the lands to the east were growing dangerous. Maybe so, but in Minas Tirith, Gandalf points out that if Smaug had not been killed decades before, there might have been no Queen for Aragorn (in "The Quest of Erebor", published in *Unfinished Tales*). When Frodo sits on the high seat at Amon Hen, he sees visions of Orcs pouring "out of a thousand holes" in the Misty Mountains. Tolkien doesn't say which way they were heading, but I don't get the impression it was only eastward (to the Vales of Anduin).

If Rivendell could be brought under siege during the years when Angmar was taking out the northern Dunadan kingdoms, it follows that Sauron's forces probably had an Elven enclave or two on their list of places to attack during the War of the Ring. Thranduil's kingdom in northern Mirkwood and Lothlórien were both attacked, so why should Rivendell be spared? Of course, there is no mention of attacks on Rivendell even in the appendices; so maybe the Orcs took a wrong turn at the High Pass and ended up in the land of the Beornings. So perhaps no merit badges were earned by the Orc Scouts that week.

Still, with all the sighing and longing going on, one might get the impression that Tolkien had included enough Romance clichés (or pseudo-clichés) to keep stereotypical female readers happy. Only that isn't the impression one gets. In fact, a lot of people seem to get the impression that almost no women are mentioned in the book. Who counted them all? If you go by Robert Foster's *Complete Guide To Middle-earth* you end up with almost as many female names as male names just in the "A" section.

Girls seem to be Tolkien's best-kept secret. Is that why so many women actually *like* Tolkien? Or are the stereotypes and clichés just getting in the way of everyone's criticism? If I had to sum up the complaints I've heard about Tolkien's supposed lack of appeal to women, and his stories' minimal inclusion of women, I would say people feel there aren't many details concerning relationships in Middle-earth.

In fact, except for *The Hobbit* (which only mentions one woman, Bilbo's mother, and offers a brief off-stage cameo by Lobelia at the end) and *The Lord of the Rings*, most of Tolkien's Middle-earth stories revolve around relationships between men and women: Beren and Lúthien (boy meets girl, falls in love, makes an idiot of himself, is repeatedly rescued by girl), Narn i Chin Hurin (the only characters with less sense than the women are the men), Tuor and Idril (she saves the day by digging an escape tunnel), Aldarion and Erendis (although she ends up embittered and diminished in the end), Ëarendil and Elwing (she saves the Silmaril and persuades the Teleri to man the ships, while all he does is get lost on the seas and fulfill a task long appointed him to by praying to Manwë). And most of these tales aren't just relationship stories; they involve adventure, life-threatening situations, commentaries on the folly of kings and princes, and emotional irony.

The briefer stories also seem to focus on how women have changed the lives or fates of Tolkien's men. Mithrellas introduces a strain of Elvish blood into Imrazôr's family. In fact, about the only memorable thing concerning Imrazôr is that he married an Elf. 'Oorah, old boy! On the other hand, we are told that Mithrellas lived in Lothlórien and was (apparently) one of Nimrodel's companions on the road. Somehow she survived in the mountains on her own. Mithrellas is a little more interesting than her husband. Perhaps that's why she left him in the night. Maybe she just needed a really good manicure, and by the time she got it, he had passed away. But Mithrellas had two children with Imrazôr; their son and his descendants were, of course, the Lords of Dol Amroth.

The House of Eorl was ennobled by Thengel's marriage to Morwen of Lossarnach (who just happened to be descended from the Lords of Dol Amroth, and therefore from Mithrellas). Morwen's legacy to her five children included the height and strength of the Dunedain, a thorough knowledge of Gondor's language and customs (mostly because Thengel didn't get along with his father and therefore lived in Gondor for a long time), and her popularity among the Rohirrim (when she finally became their queen), which no doubt enhanced her husband's reputation (and hence their children's reputations as the offspring of a beloved king and queen).

And Eowyn was Morwen's grand-daughter. Everyone seems to love Eowyn: faithful niece, shield-maiden, bearer of frustrated hobbits on arduous journeys, slayer of winged steeds of the Nazgul, and champion of mankind against the Lord of the Nazgul himself. When someone complained that Eowyn turned to Faramir all too easily in the story, Tolkien pointed out that "in my experience feelings and decisions ripen very quickly (as measured by mere 'clock-time', which is actually not justly applicable) in periods of great stress, and especially under the expectation of imminent death. And I do *not* think that persons of high estate and breeding need all the petty fencing and approaches in matters of 'love'. This tale does not deal with a period of 'Courtly Love' and its pretences; but with a culture more primitive (sc. less corrupt) and nobler." (*The Letters of J.R.R. Tolkien*, No. 244)

Well, so much for the medievalists' aspirations to prove that Courtly Love exists in Tolkien. Still, it's reasonable to point out that Eowyn, at least, had never been clued into the Main Plan. Faramir knew there was a chance, however remote, that Frodo might get through and win the day for everyone. Yet Eowyn had no real hope of survival. She believed that Aragorn, who had spurned her (from her point of view), had gone off to die in battle. After Sauron finished dealing with the little armies in the field, he would turn his attention back to Minas Tirith.

How often have we been entertained by war-time love stories, in which two people come together and feel something intensely in a matter of hours or days? Books and films have been using this idea for decades, if not centuries (as far as books are concerned, at least). Love isn't something which is predestined in Tolkien. It happens spontaneously and is as fierce as any emotion the human experience can digest. Why else would Aragorn wait so faithfully for a chance to woo Arwen, year in and year out? Most guys would have picked up other girlfriends along the way.

Faramir actually got to spend several days with Eowyn in a fairly secluded romantic setting. The Houses of Healing had their own gardens, and it appears that most of the sick and wounded people of the city were kept elsewhere, judging by Aragorn's long night abroad in Minas Tirith healing the casualties. And just as Aragorn seemed strong and authoritative to Eowyn, so, too, must Faramir have seemed to her. He was, technically, the Ruling Steward of Gondor. He even had to return to his duties as Steward after Sauron was defeated. It's not like she was scraping the bottom of the barrel. And when Faramir confessed his feelings for Eowyn, the two of them had spent far more time together than she had spent with Aragorn.

A man who could have been luckier in love than any other was Túrin. Two Elven babes fell for him. Nellas (a Sindarin Elf whom Thingol appointed to watch over Turin when he was a boy) seems to have fallen in love with Túrin, but he never knew of her feelings for him, and she didn't pursue him. Nellas was a strange Elf, a bit of a recluse, and perhaps as close to a manic-depressive as the Elves might have produced (unless Fëanor were a manic-depressive -- his moodiness is hard to decipher). Few people ask what became of Nellas. Was she slain when Doriath was destroyed? Did she survive its fall and live in the woods until Beleriand was ruined? Did she simply wander off and die of grief after the whole Túrin story played out?

Finduilas was the other Elven love of Túrin's life. Unlike Nellas, she tried to make her feelings known, but Túrin seems to have turned off his female radar or something. Tolkien tried to work out the details of their relationship, and it seems that Finduilas was torn between two loves. Yet her love for Túrin proved to be greater than her love for Gwindor (the Elven prince she had loved originally, and who befriended Turin in the wild). And it was all for nothing. Túrin acted like a dutiful servant, or maybe just a love-struck schoolboy who was too shy to admit he felt anything for Finduilas.

Although it's hard to guess what attracted Nellas to Túrin when he lived in Doriath, he was clearly a strong, brave, and forthright man who must have stood out among Orodreth's counselors in Nargothrond. Finduilas may have been attracted to the tall, handsome leader. Or it may be that his secretive nature made Túrin seem like just the sort of mystery which Finduilas would enjoy unraveling. Or it could be that Finduilas pierced his facade of bravado, and understood something of the deep sorrow and pain Túrin carried with him, even though she couldn't know the details of his life.

In classic tragic style, however, Túrin's romantic love was finally inspired by the one woman he shouldn't feel that way about: his sister. Túrin had never met Nienor before Glaurung took away her memory. Clearly, she would have seemed to him like just another forlorn victim of Morgoth's malice. And for her part, Nienor had no way of knowing she was being rescued and cared for by her brother. Deep down inside, something tried to warn her, but there was no way for Nienor or Túrin to realize what was going on. So their one chance for happiness doomed them to a cold hour of despair. There was never any real hope for either Túrin or Nienor to have a happy, fulfilling relationship.

Love may not be predestined in Tolkien, but tragedy does seem to be the most visible aspect of Morgoth's will. Cruel fate intervened even when marriages were supposedly solid. Aldarion and Erendis grew apart despite the great love they originally felt for one another. It becomes apparent only when Tar-Meneldur reads Gil-galad's letter that Gil-galad has been mostly responsible for Aldarion's inevitable delays in returning home. The weather is blamed here and there, but the truth is that Aldarion sacrificed his marriage because he felt he could achieve something against the return of the darkness.

And yet, the best which can be said of Aldarion's sacrifice is only that he delayed Sauron's rise for a short time. And the consequences of the failure of Aldarion's marriage were far-reaching. Had he and Erendis remained together, they might have had a son. And that son would have inherited the Sceptre instead of Tar-Ancalimë, for whose sake Tar-Aldarion had the inheritance laws changed.

A whole new royal line would have been forged within the Line of Elros. Ancalimë would have become like Silmarien of an earlier generation, a princess rather than a queen. And if Ancalimë (who seemed to marry only so she could become Queen) didn't have any children, then Ar-Pharazôn would not have been born. He would not have seized the throne and forced his cousin Miriel to marry him. Sauron would not have been taken to Númenor, and the Númenoreans would not have tried to take immortality from the Valar. Elendil and his sons would not have gone to Middle-earth.

And yet, if Aldarion had not become so engrossed in Gil-galad's policies, to the exclusion of his relationship with Númenor and his family, what would have become of Middle-earth? Would Númenor still have come to the aid of the Eldar when Sauron attacked? Would Númenor have been able to achieve anything were it to have tried? Aldarion's works in Middle-earth were not lasting, but he is attributed with laying the foundation of their later victories. And if he had not been so enamored of the sea, would Aldarion have paid attention to the forests? Would Númenor have been able to construct its great navy without the forestry of Tar-Aldarion, in both Middle-earth and Númenor itself?

Tolkien's two great tragic stories both had far-reaching implications. Because of Túrin's excesses, Nargothrond was destroyed, leaving Doriath isolated and without allies. Beleriand's doom may have remained uncertain even after the Nirnaeth Arnoediad, until Nargothrond was destroyed. Even more generations of Elves and Men would have been born to suffer through the long war. Or, worse, Glaurung might have been sent against a different Elven realm. If he had attacked Gondolin, would Tuor, Idril, and Ëarendil have escaped? Túrin slew the mightiest dragon of his day. With that one deed he achieved a lot of good, even though the Eldar and Edain eventually lost the war and all their realms.

Because of Aldarion's distractions, Númenor was prepared for the great role it would one day play in Middle-earth's affairs. The choices of Aldarion's descendants might have been made by other individuals, but he ensured that Númenor would be closely tied to Middle-earth. If he had remained at home, Númenor would have continued to ignore Middle-earth. Gil-galad would have found himself without powerful allies. And without the alliance, the Númenoreans might not have colonized Middle-earth. Even if Elendil and his sons still escaped the ruin of Númenor, would there have been any Númenorean colonies for them to recruit into the kingdoms-in-exile?

When Boromir tried to take the Ring from Frodo, he asked, "Is it not a strange fate that we should suffer so much fear and doubt for so small a thing?" Is love such a small thing? Not to us, no. But when people go looking for love in Tolkien, they seem to be looking in all the wrong places. *The Lord of the Rings* is not a story about passionate, sexual love. It's a story about a higher, nobler love of freedom, love of life, love of all that is good. Ultimately, it is the power of Frodo's love (for his friends, for his Shire, and for all Middle-earth) which sustains him enough to take him to the point where his actions become unnecessary. Had Sam not spurned Gollum's attempts at love and loyalty, Tolkien suggests, Gollum probably would have thrown himself into the Fire.

It is the strangeness of love which leads all of Middle-earth to the fateful choices that its heroic individuals make. Tolkien's love is tortured and tainted; it's pure and noble as well. But it is often bound up with the fates of nations, and Tolkien uses love to break down barriers his characters weren't even aware existed. Had it not been for Beren's love of Lúthien, and her reciprocation, Morwen would not have had a friend in Thingol. And had Túrin not been raised in Doriath, would he have brought down Nargothrond and slain Glaurung? Would the wars of Beleriand have been protracted because Hurin's son grew up a slave, untrained in the arts of war by the greatest warriors of the Sindar?

Every time love broke down some boundary, Middle-earth was changed. Both Elves and Men were enriched by their experiences with one another. But in the end, it was the great loves they shared which led them to their victories. Every star-crossed lover in Tolkien went on to achieve something vital: Beren and Lúthien took a Silmaril from Morgoth, Túrin killed Glaurung, Tuor and Idril saved Ëarendil, Ëarendil and Elwing reunited and found a way to Valinor; Aldarion and Erendis set into motion events which led to the Downfall of Númenor and the salvation of the Faithful Dunedain, Treebeard's loss of Fimbrethil laid the foundation for his friendship with Merry and Pippin and thus the storming of Isengard, and Aragorn's rejection of Eowyn (inspired by his love for Arwen) set Eowyn on the path to her removing a terrible evil from Middle-earth.

Maybe *The Lord of the Rings* wasn't intended to be the culmination of a long history of loves and broken (or sorely tested) relationships, but the appendices are filled with hints and glints of the mighty relationships which forged the destiny of Middle-earth. It may be that Tolkien knew what he was doing after all, and he just didn't clutter up the finale of the long tale with endless distractions. After all, it was his lifelong dream to tell the great stories that were in his heart. *The Lord of the Rings* was in a way an endless distraction for Tolkien, who really wanted to sit back and talk about lost loves, forbidden loves, and how fantastic women can be in a fantasy world.

MICHAEL MARTINEZ

Chapter 34:
The 'canon' of Middle-earth

Note: These essays make reference to an Internet project with which they were contemporary when originally written. That project inspired these essays, and though it is tempting to remove the references, the essays remain meaningful (to me) as they were originally conceived. On the other hand, I have inserted some new information which seemed necessary for the sake of completeness and relevance to currently published Tolkien works.

Is your canon on the loose?

Until now I have given only light support to a fannish effort intended to establish *a* canon for Tolkien discussions. Not *the* canon, mind you, or *the ultimate canon*, or *the final canon*, or even the *best* canon. Merely *a* canon. My light support has consisted of granting permission to people to mention the project on The Tolkien and Inklings Forum (http://www.sf-fandom.com/vb/authors/tolkien_inklings/, formerly The White Council).

The real canonical discussion was started over at a forum on The Barrowdowns web site, but it has been known to stall. And I think I can understand why it has. Part of the problem is that something like this project will take a lot of time, and it's very daunting.

But let me start at the beginning, as much as I can go back that far. The issue of "canon" has often come up in many Tolkien discussion forums. Two or more people will disagree over something in the books and start providing citations to prove their points. Hopefully the citations are full and relevant, but all too often someone objects to another person's source of information. The citation may be complete, but it may not seem relevant to all parties.

For example, is it relevant to cite *The Book of Lost Tales* when discussing *The Silmarillion*? The two works are separated by more than 50 years. Many people feel *The Book of Lost Tales* is just an early "Silmarillion" (it's not). Many people point out that Christopher Tolkien used *The Book of Lost Tales* to write portions of *The Silmarillion* (he did). So, is *The Book of Lost Tales* a relevant source of information?

Oh, the headaches that question has led to. No one can provide a definitive answer. The best answer I have ever contrived is, "It depends." Some people have (wrongly) alleged that means "it depends on whether [Michael Martinez] wants to use it". What it depends on is whether you're talking about the works of J.R.R. Tolkien or the world portrayed by *The Silmarillion. The Book of Lost Tales* is set in England. Firmly, squarely, undeniably. Tolkien even worked the geography of England into the stories. England was supposed to be that portion of Tol Eressëa which was restored to the mortal world. *The Book of Lost Tales* was a mythology Tolkien had written for England.

Somewhere in the 1920s Tolkien gave up on writing *the* mythology for England, but he didn't give up on writing *a mythology*. i.e., it was no longer intended for England. It became *the mythology for J.R.R. Tolkien*. I think he always wanted to publish it, but he realized somehow that it wasn't the sort of thing one could expect publishers to pursue. After all, false mythologies weren't exactly flooding the bookstores in those days.

The mythology was linguistically driven. That is, the stories were often bound up with Tolkien's constructed Elvish languages. He was driven by three passions: a passion for his beloved wife, Edith (whom he almost lost to another man before they were wed); a passion for language; and a passion for story-telling. It was the latter passion which eventually ensured Tolkien would be published, but it was the first passion which gave rise to Tolkien's greatest story, the tale of Beren and Lúthien. And yet he attributed the greater part of his histories to the second passion, his love of language. He wanted to know the histories behind individual words, and he tied them all together and created a fantastic imaginary history.

We can lay out the books in *The History of Middle-earth* series and say, "this one documents this period", and so forth, but these arbitrary divisions Christopher Tolkien imposed upon the history owe much to his human limitations. The reuse of stories, ideas, characters, and languages through the years blurred the distinctions for J.R.R. Tolkien, and those blurry distinctions are preserved for us. Now we find them blurry, too.

There was always, I am sure, a *world* in Tolkien's mind in which his characters lived and acted. He called it a secondary world, or a sub-creational world (his sub-creation). Christopher Tolkien has continued to call it a secondary world, set beside the primary world (our world) and consisting of imaginary times in the past, before our mundane history began.

Tolkien's secondary world at first included Gnomes and Men, and (evil) Dwarves. But with the publication of *The Hobbit* he had to confront the real burden of providing a sequel for a story he had only assigned a secondary importance to. By this time Tolkien was dropping other creatures from his secondary world which no longer suited it: pixies, fays, and other types of fairies. The Gnomes were really Elves, Elves of a special sort only glimpsed in actual northern mythologies, slightly enhanced by a twinkle in Tolkien's eye, perhaps.

To satisfy his inner need to see the mythology published, and so given a "reality" of its own, and to satisfy his publishers and readers who wanted more about Hobbits, Tolkien merged the world of *The Hobbit* with the world of "Quenta Silmarillion", which had come to replace *The Book of Lost Tales* as "the mythology". "Quenta Silmarillion" was already a very different work from the Lost Tales, but it still resembled the tales in many ways.

Hobbits, on the other hand, were a wholly new creation. They had no place in the old mythology (now more than 20 years old). They in fact had no real place in Tolkien's secondary world, so he made a place for them, and in doing so changed that world radically. The change forced Tolkien to dispense with some of the conventions he had adopted previously. Hobbits were informal creatures. And the change forced

Tolkien to look at how these creatures could share a world with the heroic, tragic, and powerful Gnomes and Men without being overwhelmed.

Tolkien produced *The Lord of the Rings*, which millions of people have now read. And he suggested some revisions for *The Hobbit* to his publisher, which were taken as de facto changes to the story. When Tolkien learned his suggestions had been made reality he had to scramble to revise the historical material he was still preparing for the yet-unpublished *Lord of the Rings*. When the book was finally published, Tolkien had to revise the historical background information yet again, compressing it and reorganizing it considerably. So, much of what he had intended for publication never saw the light of day during his lifetime.

The Hobbit and *The Lord of the Rings* were revised again years later when Ace Books took advantage of a loophole in copyright law and published an unauthorized edition of Tolkien's works. To combat the unauthorized books, he was asked to submit enough changes to both books to justify a new copyrighted edition. These changes invariably altered the evolving world in Tolkien's mind again and introduced controversies over the progression of the imaginary history.

So, many years later, people on the Internet discovered Michael Martinez and his lengthy citations from Tolkien. I have long pondered and pontificated on the worlds of *The Hobbit*, *The Lord of the Rings*, and *The Silmarillion*. And occasionally (when it suits me, some might say) I drag out some volume from *The History of Middle-earth* and include its contents in my ponderings and pontifications.

But is there a rhyme or reason to it all? Quite often my citations must seem confusing to many people. I'll quote *The Book of Lost Tales* here when discussing "The Fall of Gondolin" but I'll exclude it there when discussing the fall of Gondolin (in *The Silmarillion*). "The Silmarillion is not canonical," I'll tell people, and then I'll proceed to quote it to make whatever point I think I can.

"How do you pick and choose your texts?" I am sometimes asked.

I like to say, "Carefully."

"Why is *The Silmarillion* not canonical?"

That's the trickiest question of them all. It's not relevant to the other books because Christopher Tolkien has removed it from such relevance. In the foreword to *The Silmarillion*, Christopher warned the reader that "a complete consistency (either within the compass of *The Silmarillion* itself or between *The Silmarillion* and other published writings of my father's) is not to be looked for, and could only be achieved, if at all, at heavy and needless cost."

Christopher has since repudiated some of his editorial decisions in *The Silmarillion*, however, and of the critical changes he introduced to the story of the fall of Doriath he has gone on to say,

> ...this story was not lightly or easily conceived, but was the outcome of long contemplation among alternative conceptions....It is, and was, obvious that a step was being taken of a different order from any other 'manipulation' of my father's own writing....It seemed at that time that there were elements inherent in the story of the Ruin of Doriath as it stood that were radically incompatible with 'The Silmarillion' as projected, and that there was here an inescapable choice: either to abandon that conception, or else to alter the story. I think now that this was a mistaken view, and that the undoubted difficulties could have been, and should have been, surmounted without so far overstepping the bounds of the editorial function. (*The War of the Jewels*, p.356)

This admission all but invalidates *The Silmarillion* as a representation of J.R.R. Tolkien's hand. In fact, there is no *Silmarillion* which represents J.R.R. Tolkien's direct authorial achievement. Even the "Quenta Silmarillion" of the late 1930s is not part of a greater, more complete work which would have become *The Silmarillion*.

To be sure, most of the material in *The Silmarillion* was written by J.R.R. Tolkien...at one time or another. It was never written to be part of *this* book, however. Not by J.R.R. Tolkien. Christopher Tolkien wrote the final *Silmarillion*, and after spending nearly 20 years analyzing his father's work and comparing that to the published book, he came to the conclusion that he had not been as faithful to his father's hand as he had hoped.

So when people see *me* repudiate Christopher's *Silmarillion* they invariably ask how I would compose the book, were the task given to me to revise it. I've never been able to answer that question. I think it's inevitable that new editions of *The Silmarillion* will be published. Once the copyrights on the Tolkien materials are allowed to expire, and the stories become public domain, people will set themselves the task of writing new Silmarillions.

Such efforts will be both deplored and hailed with great praise at the same time. Self-styled Tolkien purists will argue that only one of the two Tolkiens is qualified to define the correct Silmarillion text, if such a text can be contrived. Anyone else is merely passing off a counterfeit. Perhaps, but Christopher Tolkien is retired, and he has indicated he will write no more. His achievements in documenting his father's works are unrivalled, and he has laid bare the tree which bore the odd-shaped fruit we have to share amongst ourselves.

The taste of *The Silmarillion* is both bitter and sweet, and in that end it may serve its authors' purposes better than any future edition. But it doesn't obtain the consistency with *The Hobbit* and *The Lord of the Rings* that is required of it. And to achieve such a consistency, one needs must rewrite not only *The Silmarillion* but also one of the other two books. The thought of rewriting *The Silmarillion* is barely approachable for most Tolkien fans. But none would dare rewrite either of the other two books.

And yet the deed has already been done, to both books, by publishers eager to bring the "correct" Tolkien texts to print. You see, J.R.R.T. had indicated some corrections should be made to the texts which weren't incorporated until after his death. These are the "fourth" edition of *The Hobbit* and the "third" edition of *The Lord of the Rings*, barely distinguishable from their predecessors but different enough that some readers find profound significance in their existence.

And it is a far cry from correcting texts to actually revising the story of either book. Yet, this has also been done, to both books again, and more than once. Both books have been adapted to film and television, and to radio. *The Hobbit* has been adapted to the stage as well. The stories have undergone more changes, perhaps, than any one person can ever hope to document.

So it is not much of a step, except in emotional terms, to consider a formal revision of, say, *The Hobbit*, to bring it into a more consistent state with *The Lord of the Rings*. J.R.R. Tolkien himself wrote "I think that *The Hobbit* can be seen to begin in what might be called a more 'whimsy' mode, and in places even more facetious [than *The Lord of the Rings*]....but I regret much of it all the same."

Humphrey Carpenter says in his biography that ,when Tolkien revised *The Hobbit* in rebuttal to the unauthorized Ace Books edition, "he found a good deal of it 'very poor' and had to restrain himself from rewriting the entire book."

The Vulcans have a saying, according to Mr. Spock: only Nixon can go to China. Most Tolkien fans might say, only Tolkien can rewrite Tolkien. It is true, most likely, that no one would be able to rewrite *The Hobbit* as J.R.R. Tolkien would rewrite it. Any currently published author would undoubtedly produce a thoroughly different kind of story, providing a different tone, new characters, additional "uncanonical details", foreshadowings and borrowings from *The Lord of the Rings*, and worse. That is the way of pastiches. The new writer cannot help but leave his own imprimatur on the work.

What is required is a master forger, someone who wants to produce another Rembrandt, not a painting as good as a Rembrandt. A forger would immerse himself in Tolkien's style and prose, would add nothing Tolkien himself hadn't added, would use no words Tolkien himself wouldn't have written. The peril of relying upon a forgery, however, is that the forger may nonetheless produce a stale and unentertaining work. It would look like Tolkien had written the book but it would fall flat. Only a master forger with a gift of story-telling similar to Tolkien's could have a chance of succeeding. But does such a person exist?

Invariably millions of fans would cry, *No!*

Very well. I won't try to be such a person.

But in answer to the unanswerable question, if I were to attempt to revise *The Silmarillion*, I would also try to revise *The Hobbit*. I have no idea of what I would do to the latter book, but it would require changing. A new edition of *The Hobbit* would free the author of the new *Silmarillion* from obligations to honoring inconsistencies. These obligations hampered Christopher Tolkien, who seriously abridged some historical points in order to achieve a modest level of consistency with *The Lord of the Rings*. He never took *The Hobbit* into consideration.

For my *Silmarillion* I would revise the stories of Maeglin, Beren and Lúthien, Túrin, the Fall of Gondolin, and Ëarendil. I would reassert a number of passages which were dropped from the texts. But I would also have to write new material to bring the Silmarillion stories into consistency with *The Lord of the Rings*. I would not, on the other hand, introduce Hobbits to the *Silmarillion*. They have no place in the Elvish histories. They have their own histories: lost, forgotten, buried in unfathomable traditions which have not been preserved. The lack of Hobbits in *The Silmarillion* has been regarded as a weakness of the book for Hobbit fans. Perhaps, but there is no indication that J.R.R. Tolkien ever leaned toward including Hobbits in the Elvish histories. He probably would have included the Druedain.

So a good forger cannot put Hobbits in Beleriand. How many people could resist the temptation, though, if they were given the task? The resounding thunder of former President George Bush's campaign promise comes to mind: "Read my lips: no new taxes." Two years later, he approved new taxes. To succeed, a new *Silmarillion* simply cannot include Hobbits. It would not be consistent with Tolkien's vision. We know a great deal about that vision, so we can pretend to be competent forgers if we're going to discuss the idea of "canon". Only

Tolkien could define his canon, and since he didn't bother too, if we rudely insist on doing it for him, we must become forgers.

It might be argued that, to "succeed", a new *Silmarillion* must appeal to its modern audience, especially if it's not to be written for another 50-75 years. The old book shares a vision for an audience long gone. But when forging a Rembrandt one does not paint with Picasso's style. One paints with Rembrandt's style. To approach perfection, one must use the same types of paints and brushes, canvases, and even lighting as Rembrandt. One must become Rembrandt in every way possible, and live in his world, and produce a work of art that would have come from his world. The same principle holds true for forging literature. If one would add a new book to Caesar's Gallic commentaries, one must write as Caesar did (and ignore the controversy over whether the last book was a poor forgery anyway). One must seek consistency with what is widely known and accepted by the experts as the hallmark of the artisan whose works are being forged.

And that is where I would pick and choose my texts. What is consistent with Tolkien's canon? If someone plucks a topic out of a book, I look for the relevant passages in other books (if they exist). The Middle-earth canon, as defined by J.R.R. Tolkien, already exists. He established it in *The Hobbit, 3rd edition, The Lord of the Rings, 2nd edition, The Road Goes Ever On,* and *The Adventures of Tom Bombadil.* It may be argued that the Pauline Baynes map of Middle-earth is also a part of that canon.

These books are, for the most part, consistent with each other. *The Silmarillion* deals with a lot of material not covered in those books, so the opportunities for consistency (or making errors that deviate from consistency) are not many. Tolkien himself did not say, "These books are the canon; they define the laws of my world." He merely published them. He approved them, wrote them, revised them. They are J.R.R. Tolkien's formal statement on what is and is not Middle-earth. And there are minor inconsistencies between them, but nothing like the inconsistencies which arise between these books and Christopher's *Silmarillion.*

But if one sets about revising the Silmarillion text, one must have a source for new material which is indistinguishable from J.R.R. Tolkien's material. And that, of course, is where *The History of Middle-earth* and *Unfinished Tales* become important. Christopher Tolkien has already published many of his father's previously unpublished works. He utilized some of the material in *Unfinished Tales* to write parts of *The Silmarillion*. And the direct sources for much of the book have been published in *The History of Middle-earth*.

What a modern (or future) forger can count on is having the secondary canon published by Christopher to consult. When he was composing *The Silmarillion*, Christopher did not have this extensive body of research available to him. He was only then in the first stages of undertaking the research. If he had only known then what he knows now, he would have written a different *Silmarillion*. And if Christopher Tolkien could have written a different book based on the knowledge we all now have available to us, then why not someone else? Well, that's another unanswerable question, so we'll just forge ahead and assume it's been answered satisfactorily (or this essay ends here, and I'm not ready to end it).

There are sticky questions which must be addressed. The overall length of "Quenta Silmarillion" must be considered, for example. It was never intended to convey all the details of the fuller stories. It is a summation, a layer of interpretation if you will, which stands between the reader and the "true" accounts. Hence, one cannot simply embed the entire "Narn i Chin Hurin" in the text. On the other hand, "The Wanderings of Hurin" is an important extension of the story of Túrin and his father, and it should not have been excluded, raw though it was in the form in which Christopher found it (in fact, the published version is very different from the unedited manuscripts, by Christopher's explanation). The story of Túrin must return to Doriath, and it does so quite inadequately in the published *Silmarillion* because Christopher literally chopped off the end of the story and fabricated an entirely new ending.

Another issue concerns how the older passages that Christopher used should be rewritten. And they must be rewritten, because they are so inconsistent with things J.R.R. Tolkien later introduced into the canon. Followers of the Great Balrog Debate undoubtedly know that often people plead Balrogs could not have flown because in the Dagor Bragollach Glaurung comes charging out of Angband with Balrogs in his train. Never mind the fact that his train could include flying creatures; the passage is technically inappropriate for inclusion in *The Silmarillion* because it was written before Tolkien radically altered the physical description of the Balrogs (in the 1940s, while writing "The Bridge of Khazad-dum") and their number (in the 1950s, reducing them from hundreds or thousands to no more than 7), and before Balrogs became corrupted Maiar. In fact, Tolkien rewrote that description of the battle, and he removed the Balrogs from the dragon's train. But the revised description of Glaurung's assault was not used.

There are strong emotions attached to this "train" passage. It has often been used to "prove" (unsuccessfully) that Balrogs cannot have wings and cannot fly. Well, the Balrogs for which J.R.R. Tolkien wrote those words did not have wings and did not fly, they numbered at least 1,000, and they rode on the backs of dragons and/or other creatures. They were a horrific cavalry force. They were quite unlike the Balrog of Moria. They were quite unlike the Balrogs who arrived at Lammoth as a tempest of fire.

Not to reargue the Balrog debate here, my point is that some things to which strong feelings (and loyalties) have been attached would simply have to go. Not to prove that Balrogs have wings and fly, but because they are inconsistent with Tolkien's published canon, or with Tolkien's decisions that were contemporary with the published canon.

And there arises another thorny issue. Is it fair to utilize decisions made during the years 1950 - 1966, when the published canon was established, but which were not included in it? Take the parentage of Gil-galad, for example. Christopher now readily admits that he should never have declared Gil-galad to be Fingon's son in *The Silmarillion*. He based that statement on a marginal note which he later realized had only been "an ephemeral idea". Gil-galad was a sort of genealogical hot potato, bouncing around the House of Finwë from father to father, starting out with Inglor (make that, Finrod) and moving to Fingon and back to Finrod and ultimately to Orodreth. And there he stayed as the son of Orodreth, lost in the genealogies.

It's inappropriate to use the Fingon-Gil-galad connection in *The Silmarillion*. Christopher says it would have been better had he left Gil-galad's parentage uncertain, saying nothing. I believe it would have been better to state that Gil-galad was the son of Orodreth, and to figure out some way for him to avoid the fall of Nargothrond, just as Galadriel avoided it. People want to know who Gil-galad's father and mother were. At least part of the information is established in posthumously published material.

Some folks at the Barrowdowns have asked whether the "Myths Transformed" section of *Morgoth's Ring* could or should be used in establishing a canon. They settled on the revised myth of the Sun and Moon. I would not take this step. It is completely inconsistent with what else was published. Tolkien, in his later years, became concerned, perhaps even alarmed, that the *Silmarillion* (when published) would establish the ancient myth (in terms of his life) about the creation of the Sun and Moon from the last leaves of Laurelin and Telperion in the Elvish histories. But the Elves, he reasoned, particularly the Eldar whose histories these were, had been instructed directly by the Valar and Maiar, the angelic beings who had existed since before Time. They should not be so quick to devise obviously false pseudo-religious babble about how the Sun and Moon were leaves from trees.

For a while Tolkien toyed with the idea that perhaps Men, in recording and passing on the Elvish histories, had mangled the stories. But he ultimately rejected that idea and came to the conclusion that the entire history needed to be rewritten. This is the real reason for why Tolkien never published *The Silmarillion* himself. It simply didn't exist, except in the form of odd jottings and notes to himself about what worked and what didn't. Everything was about to change again.

One simply cannot reconcile *The Hobbit*, *The Lord of the Rings*, and *The Adventures of Tom Bombadil* with actual human history, and our deductions about what came before. If one must rewrite *The Silmarillion*, then one must rewrite all these other books, too. And is that really what the forger should do? It would be like replacing all the surviving Rembrandts with new paintings to justify a less coherent forgery. In Tolkien's case he had not proceeded far enough with his extrapolations to realize the broadest implications, and perhaps it was a mercy for him that he didn't see where the revisions must end.

So inevitably one must remain faithful to the older myths, and produce a *Silmarillion* that lives in the imaginary world of the published canon. In that world, Galadriel cannot side with the Teleri at Alqualondë against the Noldor (one of the decisions Tolkien made late in his life). Nor can Celeborn be an Elda of Aman, grandson of Olwë (a relationship which would make him Galadriel's first cousin, and thereby violating a taboo against such unions he had previously established but apparently forgotten). The history of Galadriel would have to be devised for the forged *Silmarillion*. There is no real history for Galadriel. There are several attempts by Tolkien to devise one for her, but each ends all too soon, and introduces its own serious problems into the storyline.

At least, *I* would remain faithful to the older myths. Yes, the Elves should know better than to think that Ëarendil is Venus, that the Sun and Moon were only created about 11,000 years ago, and that the world was flat but made round when the Númenoreans rebelled. But, you know, I just can't get into rewriting *The Lord of the Rings*, since the whole purpose of rewriting *The Silmarillion* is supposed to be to make it consistent with the former book.

And I think that's where people who want to define a canon for discussions should go. There is a wealth of material which can be used to describe what is needed for consistency with LOTR. But if one is going to get into rewriting the myths, one is going to have to rewrite *The Lord of the Rings*, and then the point of defining a new Tolkien canon loses all value. You won't be able to discuss Tolkien according to the new canon, you'll just be able to discuss the new world you create.

Of course, some Tolkien fans might say, "Why not just create new worlds, and leave Tolkien's alone?"

That question is unanswerable, too.

A funny thing happened on the way to the canon

Well, I've been glad to see that the Barrowdowns' canon discussions haven't died down completely. Not that I think they should die down, but this was a project I felt from the start would have trouble keeping up a head of steam. Let's face it, not too many people are going to care what one small group of readers decides should comprise the "correct Silmarillion". Whatever proposal finally emerges from the discussions, I am sure to disagree with it. So are many other people. But the canon discussions represent a legitimate effort by some of Tolkien's readers to identify his intentions. This may or may not be the first such attempt, but it will undoubtedly draw some fire when something is produced.

Nonetheless, every first endeavor of this sort serves an important function in the ongoing study of literature and the past. And the canon discussions are relevant to our knowledge of the literary past. Literature doesn't make the world go round. It doesn't save lives. It doesn't put food on the table. It's just there. We read it. But it moves us, provokes us to discuss it, and to understand it. In fact, we attempt to understand things about literature which the authors never intended us to understand. A friend recently asked me, after finishing *The Lord of the Rings*, what the book is really about. I told her that not everyone agrees with Tolkien, but he said it was about death and the search for deathlessness.

No, that's not what my friend thought the book was about. In fact, until I saw a video of Tolkien explaining the story, I had never conceived of Tolkien's interpretation, either. Up until that time I had always thought it was about how heroic Hobbits can be. Some people see it as a brush stroke on the canvas of the battle between Good and Evil (I always have trouble sorting the Good guys from the Bad guys myself). Some people seem to feel *The Lord of the Rings* is a subtle allegory about expanding personal horizons through chemical processes. I suppose the 1960s weren't too good to those folks.

Inevitably, any serious discussion about Tolkien leads to the question of what is acceptable. That is, what is the "canon" we must rely upon to form a common reference? There is no answer to that question. There never has been, and I don't believe there ever will be. We have a plenitude of canons to choose from. We can fire a battery of canonical postulations at each other in debate after debate and keep our heads spinning. I often jump from one canon to another when discussing Balrogs, Elven history, geography, Tolkien's intentions, and "the mythology". If ever I tried to stick to any one canon, those days are long gone, and unlike Elrond, I don't remember them well at all.

The History of Middle-earth has undoubtedly led us to this quandary at the crossroads. We have so many choices to make that no one really knows which way to go. Every now and then someone starts off down a road and screams, "Here it is! Follow me!" And mostly the crowd just ignores them, continuing to mill about in wild confusion. Occasionally someone dumps a bucket of water on the canonists' parade, too. And we all end up sopping wet. As soon as you take up the topic of canonicity, you have put the literary equivalent of a "soak me" sign on your forehead.

The problem with defining a canon for Tolkien is that no one wants to share *your* canon. A few people have tried to be open-minded, but they inevitably get sidetracked when discussing someone else's canon. "Well, you see, in *my* canon...." Tolkien didn't make the task easy by any means. He kept starting and abandoning projects throughout his life, and because they all shared something in common (though one would be hard-pressed to identify many elements common to *all* the projects), there are people who glibly dip into one project to borrow material for discussing another project.

I am always amazed when someone brings up "The Fall of Gondolin" while discussing the Balrog of Moria, for example. There is no connection between the story from 1916 and "The Bridge of Khazad-dum". None. Tolkien uses the word "Balrog" in both, but then,

Shakespeare used the word "Elves". Are we to assume that Shakespeare's cob-webbers are somehow connected with Tolkien's Noldor?

"The Fall of Gondolin" is important to *The Silmarillion*. There is no doubt about that. But "The Fall of Gondolin" is not a part of *The Silmarillion*. "Of Tuor and the Fall of Gondolin" was literally written by Christopher Tolkien. Sure, he tried to follow his father's writings, but what he calls editorial compression is, in fact, *writing*. Christopher Tolkien had to sit down and compose his own version of the tale, which already existed in at least four different versions (as "The Fall of Gondolin" from *The Book of Lost Tales*, as sections in "Quenta Noldorinwa" and "Quenta Silmarillion" from the 1930s, and in the fragment "Of Tuor and his coming to Gondolin").

The Silmarillion is a book, composed or compiled by Christopher Tolkien. "The Silmarillion" is a story which J.R.R. Tolkien began working on about 1930. The story became the book, but the book is not the story. That is, the story was never completed, and has never been published. *The Silmarillion* is not even presented as an attempt to reconstruct the story. It's an attempt to keep J.R.R. Tolkien's fans happy. He had promised to publish *The Silmarillion* but no one really knew what that was. Tolkien himself never produced *the* Silmarillion because he would get only so far on *a* Silmarillion and then would start all over again. And there were so many associated texts which were never intended to be a part of the Silmarillion, but which inevitability became a part of *The Silmarillion*.

Confused? Now you know why I don't try to define canons. Well, okay, I define them all the time. I wear them like disposable wrist-watches. I use them until the batteries run dry and then discard them. The canons I use today may look like the ones I used yesterday, but they are really different in some subtle, obscure fashion.

The real canon, the underlying core story (which seems to have changed relatively little after Tolkien abandoned *The Book of Lost Tales*), was an evolving, growing story about an imaginary past. A historical period which never was. This historical period included the rise and fall of a great Elven civilization. The Elves have moved on, but we remember them, vaguely, and Tolkien's canon was an attempt to formalize that memory. The problem is, he never really succeeded in putting that canon down on paper.

Tolkien recorded a myriad of ideas and conflicting details and incidents. If we take them all together, we get a morass of unbelievably confused images and nits to pick. So we are forced by the differences and contradictions to pick and choose our sources. But mixing and matching sources from 1917 and 1970 is not reasonable. Galadriel doesn't even exist in 1917's stories, and *The Book of Lost Tales* had long been abandoned by the time Tolkien was winding down his musings near the end of his life. If one gets the impression that he was probably terribly depressed by the prospect of fixing up the whole thing, one might not be far from the truth. Sorting through all the traditional attempts to document the histories is a real chore. Heck, it used to put me to sleep until my body built up some immunity to the somnolent texts.

The Internet only exacerbates the situation. The Law of Mandos stipulates that, whenever Túrin or Morgoth become the focus of discussion, someone will inevitably drag in the "Second Prophecy of Mandos". This little gem has no relevance to *The Lord of the Rings*, but is frequently cited as proof that Morgoth will return at the end of Time, and that Túrin will slay him. The inconvenient fact that Tolkien abandoned the prophecy in the 1930s, and ultimately only considered restoring it in a substantially different form (due to Andreth, an Edainic woman of Beleriand, whose prophecy foretells of Túrin's temporary return at the end of the First Age), is either unknown to the faithful or disputed in some fashion.

Of course, Túrin and Morgoth have little relevance to *The Lord of the Rings*, as they are barely mentioned in it. But the Second Prophecy is not mentioned or referred to in any way in *The Silmarillion*. It's not even pointed to in *The Letters of J.R.R. Tolkien*, but there are pious souls who reverently insist it is a vital part of the canon. Woe unto he who points out that the Túrin of *The Silmarillion* cannot become a Vala, even at the end of Time. And never mind the fact that all references to a Last Battle are obscure and incomplete, making no mention of Túrin.

Other bizarre ideas have gotten thrown into the canonical soup, such as the "fact" that Elves have pointed ears. There is nothing in *The Hobbit*, *The Lord of the Rings*, *The Adventures of Tom Bombadil*, *The Road Goes Ever On*, *The Silmarillion*, or *Unfinished Tales* which suggests or hints that they might have pointed ears. From 1937 until 1987, the world of Tolkien scholarship had no reason to believe or suspect that any Tolkien Elf might have an ear which didn't look like the ear of a man. Tolkien's characters distinguished between Elves and Men by looking at their eyes, their faces, or listening to their voices. Ears never entered into the process of identifying a character's race.

But in 1987, Christopher Tolkien published *The Lost Road and Other Writings*; included in its profound revelations was "The Etymologies", an attempt by JRRT to document the Elven languages he was using in the pre-LOTR years. He updated some portions of "The Etymologies" in the first years of writing *The Lord of the Rings*, but eventually abandoned the work. And in "The Etymologies", one finds the bombshell "las-" entry where are inscribed the fateful words "Some think this is related to the next and *lasse* 'ear'. The Quendian ears were more pointed and leaf-shaped than [?human]."

That "[?human]" construction at the end of the sentence is not from J.R.R. Tolkien. It's from Christopher Tolkien. In his introduction to "The Etymologies", Christopher writes "My own contributions are always enclosed within square brackets. A question mark standing within such brackets indicates doubt as to the correctness of my reading, but in other cases is original." Well, some people insist, if JRRT didn't mean to write "human", what could he have intended? Who knows? It's not clear from the text that he intended the remark to stand. He was certainly introducing his own doubt about the allegation with the first sentence "Some think this is related to the next and *lasse* 'ear'." Little did the old boy know how seriously his philologist's sense of humor would be taken.

In 2001 and 2002, Douglas Anderson revised *The Annotated Hobbit*. While he was updating his research, I brought up the Elven ears debate with him and covered all the relevant points in my notes. Anderson consulted with Christopher Tolkien on a number of controversial points. When published, the new edition of *The Annotated Hobbit* included the following comment:

> In neither The Hobbit nor The Lord of the Rings does Tolkien give any clue to the answer to a question that has been fiercely debated among his readership: Did his Elves have pointed ears?

> The nearest thing to an answer that one can give is founded on the linguistic elements in Tolkien's invented languages. In the "Etymologies," a kind of dictionary of Elvish word relationships that Tolkien maintained for his personal use in the 1930s, which is now published in volume five of the History, The Lost Road, he notes in regard to the stem LAS(1) from lasse = "leaf" and LAS(2) "listen" (lasse = "ear") that there is a possible relationship between the two in that "Elven ears were more pointed and leaf-shaped" than human ones. All that can be said, then, is that certainly at one time (probably in the mid-1930s) Tolkien held this view.

> Tolkien's own artwork does not provide any further clues, for in the only drawing in he depicts elves, they appear as very small figures, and features such as ears are not visible. See the drawing *Taur-na-Fuin* in [*J.R.R. Tolkien: Artist & Illustrator*] (No. 54). (pp. 206-7)

However, whether Tolkien's Elves have pointed ears is not really a question of canon. One canon may have pointy-eared Elves and another might not. But whether one canon rules all, and in the darkness binds them, *is* a question of canon. Since Tolkien never bothered to refer to Elven ears again, how important was this idea (of their relative pointedness compared to something else)? Years later, while expounding upon the Elvish ancestry of Prince Imrahil (in another note intended only for himself), Tolkien made a remark, now immortalized in *Unfinished Tales*, concerning the beardlessness of Men descended from Elves. Christopher's casual mention of this note has been taken as the final authority on whether Elves should have beards. Consequently, there are numerous occasions where people ask how

Cirdan can have a beard, since Elves don't possess them. In order to preserve the canon of beardless Elves, some people jump through some intricate hoops to explain the gaffe.

The simplest explanation is that Tolkien forgot about Cirdan's beard when he was working on the Imrahil material. Had he realized he had already put a beard on an Elf in a published work, he undoubtedly would have felt bound to abide by that. So the beardlessness of Elves should be considered a moot point. Elves can have beards because that is the way Cirdan is portrayed. However, the simplest explanation seldom wins favor in a canonical debate. The more elaborate and contrived a canon seems to be, the more fervent its adherents are in propounding it to the masses. It seems to always be a case of "the most effort justifies the canon." Well, it *is* a bit disheartening to have the wind taken out of one's sails, after staying up all night working out how Cirdan alone among the Elves can have a beard.

In fact, the issue was resolved (to most people's satisfaction) in July 2000, when the linguistic journal Vinyar Tengwar published an etymological note stating that "Elves did not have beards until they entered their third cycle of life." The debate has since moved on to arguing over what constitutes a "cycle of life" for an Elf, and how many cycles an Elf should have.

The canons often become intertwined under the strangest circumstances. The pointy-ears crowd, for example, will often cite a letter Tolkien wrote in 1938 to the Houghton Mifflin Company, his American publishers. They wanted to know how to draw a Hobbit. Tolkien told them "A round, jovial face; ears only slightly pointed and 'elvish'; hair short and curling (brown)." The letter is treated with the respect accorded a Papal Bull. All well and good, I suppose, but the reference to "elvish" is certainly not to a Tolkien Elf, which no one at Houghton Mifflin had ever seen. As Anderson points out in his commentary cited above, there is nothing in the text of the book which suggests that the Elves do (or don't) have pointed ears. Tolkien's comment was intended to be taken in the context most familiar to the publishers; that is, everyone knew that Elves had pointed ears. At the time, there was no connection between *The Hobbit* and Tolkien's

Elvish legends (which the HMCo people hadn't read), except for a few borrowings Tolkien had made to liven up the story.

Nonetheless, we are still told by some with great solemnity how this letter proves that Tolkien's Elves have pointed ears. The complete and total lack of reference or relevance to any Elf in any Tolkien story aside, the letter *must* prove that Tolkien's Elves have pointed ears. Why else would he have used the word "elvish"? It couldn't possibly be that he knew a popular conception about Elves would provide a convenient reference, could it? The canon of the pointed ear has even been extended to allege that Tolkien was the first person to use "Elves" and "Elvish". I have occasionally pointed out that Shakespeare used those words, too, although Ear Debates tend not to lend themselves to Shakespearean resolutions.

Well, all this must seem like nothing more than a case of sour grapes to those whose sophisticated elocution and professional demeanor have been insulted time and again by my impish wit and disregard for the canon. Perhaps. I admit to having little reverence for any particular canon. I am a canon impurist. I obliterate canons with barrages of counter-canons. I debilitate profundities with objections. I deserve no better than to be ignored and treated with the utmost contempt, because I choose not to be swayed by a hodge-podge of unrelated citations. I laugh in the face of canon. I live on the edge of heresy. I look at when the books were published and ask, "Why does 50 years of literary canon vanish with one obscure reference in a text never intended for the light of day?"

The silliness of canonical arguments undoubtedly is responsible for more head-shaking than anything else in the world of Tolkien fandom and scholarship. We do take our Balrog debates seriously, seriously enough that more than one FAQ (Frequently Asked Questions document -- a popular question-and-answer reference aid on the Internet) has been written about the poor beasts and their wing(edness/lessness). Nothing brings out the fannish fangs and claws faster than a Balrog wings discussion. But mention canon in the midst of a Balrog discussion, and people are apt to reply, "Eh! Who cares?" There is simply very little passion about canon. Marriages have probably been arranged on the basis of who believes in Balrog wings (clap your hands if you do!), but what effect has the study of canon had upon our lives?

And the winged nature of Balrogs is very much a question of canon. The reason is that Tolkien changed his Balrogs. So if you're going to talk about Balrogs, it's important to note which Balrogs you're discussing. The Balrogs of *The Book of Lost Tales* are not the same as the Balrog of "The Bridge of Khazad-dum". A good canonist will concede this, while still arguing for or against wings. Of course, keeping the canons separate makes it difficult to argue against wings.

Nonetheless, every camp has its battery of canons which are drawn up and arrayed for battle. We're almost to the point of devising a canon numbering system. We may change them frequently, but we know our canons like we know the backs of our enemies' hands. A good canon is well-tended with loving care. It is nourished and fed with only the richest detail from the most intricately researched of debates. *The Care and Feeding of the Tolkien canon* may one day appear on bookstore shelves, and only someone who has never asked, "Were the Silvan Elves really the Avari?" will laugh.

The neatness of one's canon is all too easily disturbed by the rowdy intrusion of someone else's canon. That is most likely why there will never be a single, accepted universal Tolkien canon. Never mind the fact that there could never be such a thing. If we all agreed on one canon for anything, too many people would have to admit to being wrong about something. All the ambiguity with which we have laced Tolkien's words would vanish in a puff of reality. All the fun would be taken out of the debates, and we'd have nothing left to argue over, except whose fault it was for bringing us to such a pass.

Chapter 35:
Moving sale:
magic rings and other trinkets half off

J.R.R. Tolkien might not agree with me but I sometimes envision the rebellious Noldor traipsing down the road to Alqualondë in much the same state as Steve Martin appears in that famous promotional poster for his movie, "The Jerk". He's unshaven, bedraggled, his pants are dragging around his feet, and he's carrying a chair, a lamp, and some other stuff.

Were the Noldor jerks? One would certainly be tempted to question their wisdom. Regardless of how many Noldor you believe there would have been when Fëanor held his anti-Valar rally in Tirion upon Tuna, the sad fact is that most of those Elves who listened to him ended up dead. And they weren't very nice to the Teleri, either.

But the passage which brings the similarity to my mind is the one where Tolkien notes (in speaking of Finarfin and Finrod and the Noldor who followed them) that "more than any others of the Exiles they carried thence memories of the bliss they had forsaken, and some even of the things that they had made there they took with them: a solace and a burden on the road."

Well, I can hardly imagine why a Noldo would carry a chair along, but maybe they had some *really* good carpenters who just couldn't bear to leave their work behind. One can almost see Fëanor trying to persuade the carpenters specializing in chairs not to carry their works with them. "It may be that we can leave our chairs behind," they might have replied. "But never again shall we make their like, and if we must leave them, we shall break our hearts." Clearly, the chair guys were not numbered among the Fëanorians, although their prized possessions would have made for a good bar-fight on the quays of Alqualondë.

What sort of things would the Noldor have taken with them? Finrod and his people brought a lot of jewels out of Aman. The Noldor made gem-stones in addition to mining the mountains for precious stones and metals. Presumably they had plenty of rings, bracelets, necklaces, loose stones, stones mounted on plaques or in special frames, and ornamental brooches, etc. Would these have been magical items? Perhaps they had enchanted lustre, or radiated like the Silmarils but far less brilliantly and with less clarity.

Given the immense lengths of time the Noldor spent in Aman, and how anyone can produce many works of art over a human lifetime, one can imagine huge treasuries in nearly every house filled with all sorts of odds and ends, little trinkets which were special to their makers in the crafting but which in time were lost and forgotten. Tirion is said to have glittered with the dust of diamonds, and when Ëarendil wandered through the empty streets of the city he became covered in diamond dust.

So whatever treasures the Noldor took with them on their long journey must have been precious indeed. I'm sure the crafters would have taken such tools as they felt would be necessary for continuing their works in Middle-earth. Smiths would have to take hammers and tongs, anvils, and other tools. The Noldor had horses but they seem to have lost the majority of their herds either in the storm raised by Uinen or in crossing the Helcaraxë. Perhaps only the horses carried by ship made it to Middle-earth.

Miners would have to take their axes and hammers, their stone-cutting tools, and other implements. Hammers, saws, chisels, knives, scythes, sickles, pincers, picks, axes -- everything required to build a civilization would have to be carried by the Elves, or hauled in carts (but there is no mention of carts or wagons). They really had no idea of where they were going, or how they would get there. Fëanor had a vague plan, but he didn't share it with anyone. He just tried to get everyone to hurry up and go. And most of the Noldor wouldn't have listened to him anyway. They had decided to leave, but they wanted Fingolfin to be their leader.

More mundane treasures would have included harps, trumpets, weapons, scrolls or books, flutes, and objects for carrying food and water, and probably corn. The special corn the Valar gave the Eldar for their journey across Middle-earth. Although Araman may have been completely lifeless, I suspect that it must have supported plant and animal life of some sort. But could it really have fed all the Noldor? Fingolfin led them in the wilds for the equivalent of nearly fifty years.

My guess is the Noldor must have been baking a lot of *lembas* in those years. They would have to stop somewhere along the way, plant some corn, raise it, harvest it, and then make a batch of *lembas* before setting out again. Moses and the Hebrews at least only had to go out and scrape up manna from the ground six days a week. They pretty much had it made, although they probably got as tired of manna as the Elves must have become of *lembas*.

Lembas-corn (if I may call it that) was pretty special stuff. It would grow by starlight (since in the original conception of the world Tolkien decided that only the stars gave light to Middle-earth for many ages after Melkor destroyed the lamps of the Valar). And the corn would also, apparently, grow in a variety of climates. But it's doubtful the Noldor would always have a piece of *lembas* to chew on if they grew bored. The journey through the wilderness was a hard one. The crossing of the Helcaraxë was miserable. Fingolfin probably stopped to grow one last crop of corn before setting out across the ice.

So what became of all the stuff the Noldor took with them? For example, a lot of Noldor were slain when the Fëanorians took the ships from Alqualondë. Did Fëanor scoop up their belongings and take them aboard the ships? Were piles of duffle bags and the equivalent left on the quays or by the shore side?

And what happened when Fingolfin and his people awoke to find that Fëanor had abandoned them? Did they construct tents and huts, or perhaps even create a whole moving city? Would they have invented travois-like contraptions to haul their goods and children, or perhaps little pull-carts? Or did each Elf take only what he or she could carry on his or her back? A harp, a few extra clothes, some jewels, and a small case of precious tools?

What treasures were lost when the ships sank in Uinen's storm? And of Fingolfin's people, how many brought all their gear across the Helcaraxë? Who carried the tents and the wine? Who brought the ropes and the nets? Was there even so much as a first-aid kit among them?

In one place Tolkien suggests that all the special lamps of the Eldar were made in Aman, perhaps even by Fëanor himself (they were powered by special gems). That seems a bit limiting (how many lamps could or would Fëanor have made?), but perhaps Fingolfin's people were indeed burdened by carrying such devices (in fact, traveling by starlight without even the benefit of a moon in the wilds can be pretty rough -- I know, I've done it, and Tolkien may have, too). Fortunately the Elves had prodigious memories and they typically kept their lore in their memories. In Beleriand books were most often composed if the authors believed they might not live to pass on their knowledge. So there may have been few books among the Elves during their wanderings.

But nothing the Noldor made should have been "mundane" (by our standards). That is, the Elves were artists (according to Tolkien) and they were always practicing their "art", which was the making of new things. The Noldor, especially, were "technologists". They must have always been looking for the next best thing for the kitchen. "Honey, look at this new knife I fashioned! It slices, it dices, it Juliennes fries!"

An Elven craftsman would have enchanted the items he made, not because he could get a better price for them but because that is what he would do. Think of a carpenter putting an extra finish on a piece of furniture to protect it from buffing and scratching, or adding some ornamentation. Carefully he carves a pattern into each leg, paints something simple but beautiful into the wooden surface. Perhaps a hidden drawer is added, or a set of hinges are used to make a loose piece fold out. In Lórien the Silvan Elves told Pippin they put "the thought of all that we love into all that we make". This may have been only something the Elves of Lórien did, but I don't believe so. Tolkien's various discussions of the Elves' sub-creational (magic) abilities, and the fact that the Mithrim Sindar seem to have woven the same kind of grey cloaks used by the Lórien Elves, seem to imply that this was a fairly standard Elven concept.

In whatever way we can, we try to improve our work and imprint our wants and desires upon the things we make. Elves would be no different in that respect, but they'd be able to make the picture move, perhaps, or glow. The legs might never chip, the paint might never peel. The hinges wouldn't just open with a thought, they would do so without so much as a squeak. A Noldorin lady might possess nothing more than a pair of scissors and her jewelry box, filled with delights and gifts, baubles that floated, glowed, changed colors, fertilized gardens, caused water to cleanse itself, warmed the hands on a cold winter day, cooled the brow in summer, always rolled true, reflected the owner's mood, etc. We create such things now (even floating things). Tolkien may have felt the Elves could create them then (and by a different means).

When the Noldor arrived in Middle-earth they must have looked pretty scraggly to the Sindar. Well, Fëanor's Noldor sailed across the Sea by ship. So they might have been a little dizzy by the time they made landfall but they would not have been long without the benefits of civilization. And they also brought more horses across the water than Fingolfin's people were able to save (if they saved any). It may be that Fingolfin had a lot of horses to begin with. The Noldor might have been moving along as a group of caravans (huge caravans). So the horses would have been lost in crossing the Helcaraxë. And if they were used as beasts of burden, then there must have been carts or sledges lost aplenty along with the horses, or packs.

Araman and the Helcaraxë must have been littered with lost or forgotten artifacts. Few large items like the Palantiri could have been carried for long by the Noldor, but they must have had things beyond their enchanted swords and armor, lamps and harps. A well-equipped Tolkien Elf would probably make all but the most successful role-playing gamers drool with envy. After all, the Elves could both make magic stuff and fight (even the women). It's not for small reason that prospective players of the long-delayed online Middle-earth game feared that any player who got a Noldo should be all but unbeatable. Those guys ate Orcs for breakfast, lunched on Trolls, and finished off an occasional Balrog or two before turning in the for the night. Or so it seems.

You never see an Elf with a wand or a staff, but Galadriel shows us that they can use devices to work their magic (or, their Art, as Tolkien put it). She poured water from a pitcher into a silver basin to give Sam and Frodo a glimpse of things that might be, and things that probably were. The water came from the spring flowing through Galadriel's garden. The garden itself was "enchanted", or at least *could* be. Galadriel gave Sam a little box with some of the dirt from her garden (or orchard), "and such blessing as Galadriel has left to bestow is upon it". I'm sure the dirt was more effective than any commercial growth feed we can give our plants today. But was the spring also "enchanted"? Could be. The power of Ulmo might have been flowing through it. Or it may simply be that Galadriel and her maidens occasionally sang songs of power by the waters to invigorate them, or something.

The pitcher she used could have been a normal, everyday, Elven "only pours the water where you want it to" type of pitcher, or it could have been a special ceremonial pitcher used only for scrying purposes. I think the basin was probably very special in that respect. The pitcher and basin may have been very old but I doubt Galadriel carried them around with her on her travels through Middle-earth. Quite probably they were made after she and Celeborn settled in Lothlórien in the wake of Amroth's departure. And if Galadriel could make new stuff when she moved, then so, too, could the other Elves.

Turgon's people in Gondolin were very productive. They had to do *something* through the centuries they were refusing to have anything to do with other Elves. Imagine the enchanted lamps and light-bulbs they could have made. The old question, "How many Elves does it take to change a light-bulb" takes on new meaning, as the answer would surely be, "None. They'll just make a new one" (ba-dum-DUMP). Change a light-bulb, make a new one...oh, never mind.

One of Gondolin's names was Ondolindë, which means (more-or-less) "singing stone" (or, more appropriately, "the Rock of the Music of Water, for there were fountains upon the hill"). The city may have been constructed with acoustics in mind, so as to enlarge and scatter the sound of the waters from the fountains. But why couldn't the Elves add a little extra oomph! to their architecture and give the stone they worked an additional resonance? Think about it. There are a few domed buildings in the world where, if you stand on one side and whisper, your voice is carried clearly around to the far side of the dome. Turgon could have arranged matters so that he could address the entire city (or not) from his tower without having to interrupt their Elfevision shows.

In fact, of all the Noldorin cities in Beleriand, Gondolin was said to be most like ancient Tirion in Aman. Perhaps the Noldor of Gondolin came closer to rivaling their people's achievements in Aman of any realm in Middle-earth. They didn't produce Silmarils, but in one attempt to put a story behind Aragorn's green stone (the Elessar), Tolkien made it an artifact of Gondolin. Maeglin, of course, improved the mining and smith lore of Turgon's people, so they were probably not as good at that sort of thing as the Fëanorians. But they were nonetheless very gifted. And they had the time to focus on making things. Their seven gates show just how much time they had on their hands. Was Turgon really interested in creating a secret refuge where the Elves' last hope could be born or was he just trying to build the ultimate artists' colony?

Whatever cities the Noldor built in Hithlum were long forgotten, but Gondolin lived on in song and story, even though most Noldor never even saw it. The wonders of the city surpassed everything else achieved by the Eldar in Beleriand, and they were mostly lost. What treasures weren't buried in the ruins of Gondolin would have been looted and carried off by the Orcs for Morgoth's treasuries, and *those* were eventually buried and destroyed when Angband was ruined and sank beneath the sea. How many countless items made with all the love the Elves could muster were lost? But then, those who loved those things were also lost.

A lone warrior might have braved the perils of Dorthonion a generation later to look upon the runs of Gondolin, but none of its people ever returned there. What would such a wanderer think, seeing the crumbling ruins of the once proud city on its hill, with the bones of dead Orcs and Elves strewn about the rocks? Would anyone have defiled the ruins to dig for swords and gold, jewels and magic harps? Is that, perhaps, how the swords Glamdring and Orcrist eventually made their way to some troll-hoard in Eriador?

Nearly two thousand years later another great Noldorin city was destroyed: Ost-in-Edhil, the chief city of Eregion. There the Gwaith-i-Mirdain had labored for centuries, learning how to make the Rings of Power. But they created other treasures, and such baubles as were not carried off by the survivors or destroyed by the invading armies undoubtedly fell into the hands of Sauron. He must have sent quite a train of goods back to Mordor before pressing on with his invasion of Eriador. The Orcs must have made out pretty well, too. Perhaps a lot of them sported some genuine Elf-armor for a while (not that it seems to have done the Elves all that much good). Surely Sauron could have dined on non-tarnishing silver plate.

Thousands of years later Gandalf told Frodo that "in Eregion long ago many Elven-rings were made, magic rings as you call them, and they were, of course, of various kinds: some more potent and some less. The lesser rings were only essays in the craft before it was full-grown, and to the Elven-smiths they were but trifles -- yet still to my mind dangerous for mortals." That's a very ambiguous passage, and one which has inspired much discussion. Was Gandalf implying some of these Rings were still around, or simply stating that if any of them had survived he believed they would be dangerous artifacts for mortals to possess? He goes on to say, "But the Great Rings, the Rings of Power, they were perilous."

Perilous? Gandalf, there were a *lot* of these Great Rings. The Elves made sixteen of them before Celebrimbor went off on his own and made Three. Were the nineteen Great Rings a minority? What did the Elves do with the lesser Rings when Sauron put on the One Ring? The keepers of those "essays in the craft" must have taken off their rings, too, not just the Elves wearing the nineteen Great Rings. So by the time Sauron showed up at the border of Eregion (nearly 100 years later), where were all the lesser rings? No one would have been wearing them.

Perhaps these rings were rounded up and stored in the House of the Mirdain, which Celebrimbor defended until he was taken. And another treasury was looted. Sauron must have picked up quite a few potent items which would have been, in Gandalf's opinion, "dangerous for mortals". The Elves were interested in stopping the effects of time and preserving the beauty of their lands. They may have worked on other neat things and bestowed their virtues wherever possible. Every garden and orchard in Eregion must have been a magical place. Every tower must have held secrets of Elven sorcery. Every town and homestead must have literally gleamed with magic cutlery and pottery.

The Elves built entire civilizations and those civilizations included everything from hitching posts for their horses to crystal gems used for healing and controlling the forces of nature. They were so into doing what they would do that the very lands remembered them. Legolas said he could hear the stones of Eregion lamenting their former masters: "Deep they delved us, fair they wrought us, high they builded us. But they are gone." Did the tumbled stones actually speak to Legolas or was he merely sensing a memory of the purpose to which the stones had been devoted? Was there a resonance of the sub-creational power, the will and the song, which must have gone into building up the stoneworks, and shaping the stones.

How, indeed, did a Noldo mine or quarry? Did they use tools at all, or did they simply sing the Earth into a restive state and then extract what they required? What we call magic was second-nature to them, or at least an ability which they could develop and focus with long years of study and practice. Each Elven worker may have reached a stage in his skill where he put down his tools for the last time and sang his thought into being, shaping whatever materials he had chosen to use. Perhaps only a master craftsman, a master among masters, could achieve so much. Perhaps groups of Elves would work together to enlarge their achievements, but alone they would still need to prepare their forges and looms, and wield hammer and tongs, needle and knife.

Lúthien wove a cloak of darkness from her hair, Finrod wove illusions about himself, Beren, and their companions, and Arwen sang the White Tree into health and maturity. When Galadriel came to bid farewell to the Fellowship she sang for them: "I sang of leaves, of leaves of gold, and leaves of gold there grew; Of wind I sang, a wind there came and in the branches blew." Is she singing of the first Mallorn? Did Galadriel create the Mallorns which were carried first to Númenor and then to Lindon, and from there to Lothlórien?

Elven magic must have pervaded every aspect of their realms. Even in Lórien and Rivendell at the end of the Third Age, the Hobbits and others noticed things which made those lands feel separate from the lands of mortals. An Elven house might stand long after a mortal house had fallen. The grass and garden around the house would be imbued with the thoughts of the occupants, encouraged to grow long and healthy. Leaving their homes must have been very hard on the Elves, not just because they wouldn't be able to carry everything with them, but because they would have to leave behind labors of love. In Valinor the Elves must have sung many beautiful trees and flowers into existence, caused springs to well up and flow through gardens, dressed stones and shaped their visions in masonry and metal. They would have given their hearts to the land they left. Would it be any less so in Middle-earth, where the Elves lived for centuries in Hithlum, Gondolin, and Nargothrond?

Not all artifacts were transportable, and the most precious works may indeed have been -- for many Elves -- the very lands they worked and lived upon, year after year, century after century. Elvish country would *feel* Elvish because the power of the Elves ran through it. When Sauron swept through Eregion and Eriador, laying waste to all the lands, was he perhaps wounding the Elves who had tended the valleys and groves, the quarries and springs, in ways no mortal spirit could perceive? Why did Haldir, the march-warden of Lórien, curse the feet of the Orcs who walked across the Nimrodel river, sullying its waters? Was their presence more than just a military threat?

The Elves must have taken many of their lesser enchantments for granted. Whether it be soothing a frightened horse or merely singing up a breeze, they must have exercised their wills in countless ways that would leave mortals gaping in astonishment. And yet, if an Elf decided to leave a long-time home, a land where his or her thought and love were reflected in every bush and garden path, the decision must have been painful. Greater still, then, must have been the love for the things they took with them: gifts, perhaps, from other Elves, but surely also items made in those once-in-a-lifetime moments. An Elven house might eventually be filled with artifacts that resonated with the thought of their makers. The Elves may have lived in a sort of perpetual state of soothing music which unfeeling mortals could not hear.

And thus, when the hoards were robbed and the treasuries emptied, and the victorious soldiers of the enemies took off with their loot, the songs would continue unheard, unappreciated. The Elves most surely placed a greater value in the things they made than their enemies. Was the greater tragedy, then, that which befell the items lost in the crossing of the Helcaraxë, where they sank beneath the cold, cruel waves? Or did the Elves lament the stolen voices of their cherished treasures, trapped in cold, unfeeling walls whose masters did not even understand what the items said to them?

MICHAEL MARTINEZ

Chapter 36:
Snoopy versus the Lord of the Nazgul

It's now been awhile since Charles Schultz bid adieu to his longtime "Peanuts" fans, and sadly he passed away about the time his last comic strip was being published across America. "Peanuts" was one of the most-loved comic strips of all time, and I think it revealed a lot of our own inner fears and strengths. Charlie Brown was the lonesome stranger in his own way, an outcast, but a Good Guy striving to beat the odds. I used to love those "Peanuts" specials, and year after year I waited to find out who the Little Red-haired Girl was, and whether she liked Charlie, and whether Lucy would reform and let Charlie kick that football, and if Schroeder would change his mind about Lucy, and...

Have you ever wondered what Middle-earth would be like if Schultz had written *The Lord of the Rings*? I mean, think about it. The archetypes are all there. Charlie is Frodo. Snoopy is Sam. Sally is Arwen. Schroeder is Bombadil. And maybe Linus is Aragorn and Lucy is Saruman (go with me on this -- there's no need to explain all the Freudian family connections if we just pretend they aren't there).

So Gandalf (better known as Peppermint Patti) shows up on Charlie Brown's doorstep one day and says, "Chuck, I've got some bad news. That Ring your uncle gave you for your birthday? It's the Red Baron's secret decoder ring, the one he lost during the War, and he's coming back to get it."

"Good grief! What can I do, Patti?"

"I'm not sure, Chuck. But you might want to take it to a pal of mine who deals in lost decoder rings. His name is Pigpen. He's got all the dirt on everyone."

"Pigpen? He's got all the dirt, period!"

"Nevertheless, Chuck, you're in grave danger if you eat dinner with your folks tonight. Word has it the Baron has something special planned for you if he catches you at home. Get your funny-looking pal and a couple of other trustworthy kids together and meet me at the ballpark."

"Well, okay. But Snoopy will probably want to bring his bird scout troop, and we'll have to put up with their singing all night long."

By now you may be ready to hang me, but it gets worse, I assure you. What if, instead of meeting up with Eomer and the Rohirrim, Aragorn, Legolas, and Gimli had met up with Hagar the Horrible and his band of Viking warriors? Instead of telling them the Orcs had been destroyed, Hagar would probably report that he and his men had forgotten to bring their lunch and had to call off the battle, or, worse, their wives called them home to help with the laundry. Good-bye Merry, and Pippin. Enjoy the ride through the forest, boys.

And when it came time to rescue Minas Tirith, Hagar would look out over the Pelennor Fields and give one of his rousing speeches:

"Men, the enemy controls the Pelennor Fields! They outnumber us ten to one! They're led by nine Nazgul who instill uncontrollable fear and terror in all who oppose them. It looks like Minas Tirith is burning and we'll have no help from the city. Are you with me?"

And then he looks around and the Vikings have all slunk away to find a new comic strip. Hagar would probably have better luck if Calvin and Hobbes were in the band. At least then he'd be able to lead a savage force of super zinger-class fighters against the Nazgul...until the teacher tears up Calvin's doodling paper and leaves Hagar standing alone on the field of battle with 60,000 Orcs, Haradrim, and Nazgul facing him.

Snoopy may be no Prince Valiant but he, at least, would see the quest through to the end just like the faithful Sam. Only he'd get sidetracked and try to help Hagar out of his predicament. Just as Shelob has stung Charlie Brown and the Orcs are carrying off their bundle of despair,

Snoopy would sense the call to battle with his ancient enemy. So he'd hop on the doghouse and start cruising just under Mordor's dark cloud.

Imagine how that bright dawn would appear as Gandalf (Peppermint Patti) and the Lord of the Nazgul are facing off at the gate to Minas Tirith. The city is crumbling around the wizard, Orcs are waiting by the legion behind the Ringwraith to enter the city, and suddenly they hear...the sound of a World War I biplane as it dive bombs the gate. They look up, see a beagle setting his sights on the Lord of the Nazgul, and the old Ringwraith takes off.

So, while Hagar and Lucky Eddie are mopping up the troops on the ground, Snoopy does battle with the Lord of the Nazgul on his winged steed (whatever that thing is).

But wait, it gets worse.

Charlie wakes up in the tower of Cirith Ungol, surrounded by dead Orcs, and Lucy is there untying him. "It's gone," he says. "I've lost the secret decoder ring."

"No you haven't, you blockhead! I have the ring right here!" Lucy holds it out for him, Charlie reaches out to take it from her and...she snatches it away, Charlie tumbles down the ladder to the level below, and Lucy smiles with satisfaction as she hears a ravaged, "Aauugh!" drift up through the tower.

Fortunately for Hagar, Linus comes rowing up the river with a bunch of boy scouts in canoes. He leaps out of the lead canoe with his blanket firmly in hand and starts lashing out at the Orcs. Good thing for him the blanket is wet, and it whips out some nasty lashes. The Orcs make way for the kid and he meets Hagar in the middle of the field just as they hear an anguished cry from overhead where...

Snoopy is surrounded by Nazgul and he runs out of ammunition. He goes into evasive maneuvers, the Nazgul chase him down, shoot him out of the sky, and...

Harvey Korman rips a piece of paper out of the typewriter, wads it up, and throws it away.

And you people thought Peter Jackson was mangling the story!